Gay Rights and American Law

Gay Rights and American Law investigates how American appellate courts dealt with the struggle for lesbian and gay civil rights during the last two decades of the twentieth century. The study is grounded on an exhaustive database of both federal and state cases and of the personal attributes of the judges who decided them, as well as of the ideological, institutional, and legal environments in which the decisions were situated. The book's comprehensive quantitative examination of appellate response to an emergent minority's legal claims affords an empirically sound explication of that judicial action, as well as a pathway to more general – and telling – commentary on judicial policy making, wholly independent of the lesbian and gay context. The work both explains how diverse factors influenced the adjudication of civil rights claims during a vital era of the homosexual rights movement and formulates promising methodologies for the meaningful quantitative empirical study of law.

Daniel R. Pinello was educated at Williams College, New York University, and Yale University. His scholarship includes *The Impact of Judicial-Selection Method on State-Supreme-Court Policy: Innovation, Reaction and Atrophy* (1995) and "Linking Party to Judicial Ideology in American Courts: A Meta-Analysis," *Justice System Journal* (1999).

Gay Rights and American Law

DANIEL R. PINELLO

John Jay College of Criminal Justice of the
City University of New York

CAMBRIDGE
UNIVERSITY PRESS

PUBLISHED BY THE PRESS SYNDICATE OF THE UNIVERSITY OF CAMBRIDGE
The Pitt Building, Trumpington Street, Cambridge, United Kingdom

CAMBRIDGE UNIVERSITY PRESS
The Edinburgh Building, Cambridge CB2 2RU, UK
40 West 20th Street, New York, NY 10011-4211, USA
477 Williamstown Road, Port Melbourne, VIC 3207, Australia
Ruiz de Alarcón 13, 28014 Madrid, Spain
Dock House, The Waterfront, Cape Town 8001, South Africa

http://www.cambridge.org

First published 2003

Printed in the United States of America

Typeface Sabon 10/13 pt.   *System* LATEX 2$_\varepsilon$ [TB]

A catalog record for this book is available from the British Library.

Library of Congress Cataloging in Publication Data
Pinello, Daniel R.
  Gay rights and American law / Daniel R. Pinello.
    p.   cm.
Includes bibliographical references and index.
ISBN 0-521-81274-7 (hb.) – ISBN 0-521-01214-7 (pb.)
  1. Gays – Legal status, laws, etc. – United States.   2. Gays – Legal
status, laws, etc. – United States – Cases.   1. Title.
KF4754.5.P56   2003
342.73′087–dc21   2002041555

ISBN 0 521 81274 7 hardback
ISBN 0 521 01214 7 paperback

For

Lee Nissensohn

my domestic partner, without whose unswerving love and support
this book would not have been possible

and

Ronald Tommie Tucker

my beloved cousin, whose death from AIDS at forty-one
robbed the planet of one of its finest citizens

Contents

List of Tables

Acknowledgments

One of academe's abiding delights is collegiality. I am deeply indebted to myriad people who helped this project on its long journey and am very grateful for their unstinting support of this endeavor.

The single most important individual providing aid in the undertaking by far was Rogers M. Smith, who read the full manuscript. The book profited enormously from his generous and detailed critical commentary, particularly regarding the work's accessibility to a readership beyond judicial behaviorists and statistically sophisticated legal scholars. If the volume in fact reaches a wide audience, he deserves credit for the feat by reminding me to view a forest and not just trees.

Paul R. Brace, Evan Gerstmann, Michael Heise, Arthur S. Leonard, and Richard A. Posner also read the manuscript and offered gracious criticism. Michael Bobic, Jeff M. Gill, Herbert M. Kritzer, Keith Marcus, Kirk A. Randazzo, and Paul J. Wahlbeck provided sage advice on methodological issues.

Much of the material here premiered as papers at the annual meetings of the American and Midwest Political Science Associations. Forerunners of Chapter 3 appeared at the 1995 APSA and 1999 MPSA conferences, where Sally Kenney and Mary R. Mattingly in the former and Ellen Ann Andersen in the latter, served as discussants. Precursors of Chapters 4 and 5 were offered at the 2001 MPSA and 1999 APSA meetings, respectively, where Laura Langer and Jeff Yates were discussants. These colleagues, as well as audience members, gave valuable comments.

Numerous individuals assisted the data collection. Foremost among them were the 474 state and 5 federal judges who completed and returned the self-administered questionnaire (Appendix 3.3) soliciting personal attribute information on which the study fundamentally relies. The book would not be possible without these jurists' welcome cooperation. Similarly, the database on U.S. Court of Appeals judges amassed by Gary Zuk, Deborah J. Barrow, and Gerard S. Gryski and housed at the Inter-University Consortium for Political and Social Research was indispensable to the investigation.

In addition, Robert A. Bernstein, Richard A. Brisbin, Jr., Kyle Cheek, Michele DeMary, Craig F. Emmert, Leslie Friedman Goldstein, William K. Hall, John C. Kilwein, Douglas D. McFarland, Carla E. Molette-Ogden, Vincent K. Pollard, Holly Sellers, Kenneth S. Sherrill, Neil Snortland, James R. Soles, Kenneth D. Wald, Stephen L. Wasby, and Marvin Zalman supplemented personal attribute information about appellate judges. Charles J. Barrilleaux and Richard C. Fording provided updated citizen and government ideology scores for Berry et al. (1998). Gary Buseck of Gay and Lesbian Advocates and Defenders, Sharra E. Greer of the Servicemembers Legal Defense Network, Kate Kendell of the National Center for Lesbian Rights, Syd Peterson of Lambda Legal Defense and Education Fund, and Millie Yan of the Lesbian and Gay Rights Project of the American Civil Liberties Union reviewed the book's collection of appellate court decisions on lesbian and gay rights and facilitated a comprehensive case compilation. They also informed me in which lawsuits their organizations participated as either counsel or *amicus curiae*.

Harvard University Press and William N. Eskridge, Jr., kindly granted permission to reproduce the excerpt in Chapter 5 from *Gaylaw: Challenging the Apartheid of the Closet*. Likewise, J. Stephen Clark, Frank B. Cross, Alan Gunn, Sanford Levinson, Richard K. Neumann, Jr., James Alexander Tanford, Eugene Volokh, and Marianne Wesson charitably allowed use of the excerpts appearing in Chapter 6 from their messages posted to LAWPROF, an email discussion group moderated by Edward P. Richards III.

Along the way, Stephen D. Ansolabehere, Aaron Belkin, Frank B. Cross, Barry Friedman, Sheldon Goldman, Timothy J. Groseclose, David R. Mayhew, Joan E. McLean, Ellen D. B. Riggle, Kenneth S. Sherrill, Steven A. Shull, Susan S. Silbey, James M. Snyder, Jr., Michael E. Solimine, Isaac Unah, Kenneth D. Wald, and Stephen L. Wasby extended helpful advice and information.

At Cambridge University Press, Lewis Bateman shepherded the project. Indeed, in less than a week, he responded enthusiastically to an unsolicited proposal from an untested political scientist with few references. I pray the outcome is worthy of his largesse. Stephanie Sakson, the production editor and copy editor, adeptly helped transform my manuscript into a book. Her sure-handed guidance was indispensable.

My colleagues at John Jay College of Criminal Justice of the City University of New York – George Andreopoulos, Janice Bockmeyer, James Bowen, James N. G. Cauthen, Jack Jacobs, Barry Latzer, James P. Levine, Jill Norgren, Ruth O'Brien, Harold J. Sullivan, and Robert R. Sullivan – offered longstanding encouragement and support.

Lee Nissensohn, my domestic partner, and Patty Rae Stanley, my beloved sister, selflessly nurtured me through untold trying times – for me *and* them – while "The Book" was interminably in progress. They are suitable candidates for martyrdom and sainthood.

Wolfgang Amadeus Mozart's unique combination of genius and humility never ceased to inspire. His chamber music, especially the slow movements, reliably aided the muse to speak clearly and often.

Finally, I invite readers to visit www.danpinello.com.

I

Introduction

This is a book about how American appellate courts dealt with the struggle for lesbian and gay civil rights during the last two decades of the twentieth century. The volume also uses that conflict as a lens to scrutinize judicial behavior beyond the scope of homosexual rights.

The research is grounded on an exhaustive database of court cases about gay rights and of the personal attributes of the judges who decided them, as well as the ideological, institutional, and legal environments in which the decisions were situated. The empirical findings are striking, and I summarize some notable ones at the start.

First, a bench that is diverse with regard to age, gender, race, and religion is important to securing lesbian and gay rights. Judges who are female, African American, Latino, Jewish, or young (i.e., in their thirties or forties) are more likely than those who are male, white, Protestant, or older to recognize sexual minority rights and to treat lesbians and gay men as equal citizens whose distinctive interests and concerns merit judicial recognition. More generally, diversifying the bench to include groups that experience invidious discrimination creates sensitivity to the legal claims of other such communities. Heterogeneity among judges substantially helps to secure rights, and not just for the groups immediately represented. Moreover, this finding presumptively applies to all public officeholders.

The flip side of the coin is that other categories of jurists – for example, Roman Catholics and those with prior career experience in elective public office – have been far less hospitable to the civil rights of homosexuals.

Second, the law – both judge-made and legislatively enacted – also matters. If legal precedents supporting gay rights are won, that case law makes it significantly more likely that later tribunals, even those staffed with antigay jurists, will uphold those rights. Further, courts in jurisdictions with consensual sodomy statutes are less prone to back lesbians and gay men, while those where legislatures have adopted gay civil rights laws are more likely to embrace gay rights across the board. Thus, homosexual activists and their supporters should strive for further decriminalization of consensual sodomy in the nation, even though the offense is virtually unenforced. At the same time, successful political action for legislative passage of gay civil rights statutes will likely reverberate in the judicial arena.

Third, unlike the experience of the civil rights movement, the federal judiciary is not the most promising battle ground for the gay rights struggle. After more than three decades in which Republican presidents predominately selected federal judges, there are now numerous state courts more receptive to the legal claims of lesbians and gay men than the federal bench as a whole. Those groups pursuing litigative strategies to secure rights are best advised to work at the state level, even though participation by gay interest groups as counsel or *amicus curiae* has enhanced the likelihood of victory in federal tribunals.

Finally, the success of homosexuals in appellate courts generally has improved over time, especially with regard to gay family issues. In particular, judges have been increasingly more supportive of parental rights for gay people. Time appears to be on their side.

The Context of the Study

Lesbian and gay rights have received substantial attention in legal and political science research. For example, Koppelman (2000) reports that a "February 2000 search of articles listed under 'sexual orientation discrimination' in the *Index of Legal Periodicals* found 96 articles written on the subject from 1989 to 1994. From 1995 to the date of the search, there were 540 articles." In addition, many notable books have appeared,[1] contributing to a rich understanding of the place of lesbians and gay men in American law and politics.

---

[1] Important titles include Button, Rienzo, and Wald (1997), Strasser (1997), Keen and Goldberg (1998), Bailey (1999), Eskridge (1999), Gerstmann (1999), Halley (1999), Richards (1999), Riggle and Tadlock (1999b), Blasius (2000), Cain (2000), Rimmerman, Wald, and Wilcox (2000), Badgett (2001), Koppelman (2002), and Rimmerman (2002).

The scholarship on gays and the law, however, has been overwhelmingly normative or qualitative, with very few systematically statistical or otherwise quantitative investigations of legal issues relevant to gay people.[2] This dearth of quantitative empirical inquiry – as opposed to qualitative empirical research (Epstein and King 2002) – into the civil rights of homosexuals is in stark contrast to the wealth of statistical information on lesbian and gay politics.[3]

The comparative lack of quantitative empirical legal scholarship is not surprising, because such investigation often dismays legal academics. As Friedman (1986: 774) observes,

empirical research is hard work, and lots of it; it is also nonlibrary research, and many law teachers are afraid of it; it calls for skills that most law teachers do not have; if it is at all elaborate, it is team research, and law teachers are not used to this kind of effort; often it requires hustling grant money from foundations or government agencies, and law teachers simply do not know how to do that.... Prestige is a factor too. Law schools ... tend to exalt "theory" over applied research. Empirical research has an applied air to it, compared to "legal theory."[4]

In short, extended quantitative studies by legal academics are rare. This book is a sample of their worth.

Moreover, law professors and political scientists generally have neglected each other's contributions. Rosenberg (2000: 267) notes,

The academic disciplines of law and political science were once closely entwined under the rubric of the study of government. At the start of the twentieth century, to study government was to study law.... But as the century developed, and particularly after mid-century, the distance between the two disciplines grew. Today, legal academics and political scientists inhabit different worlds with

---

[2] The books by law professors (Cain, Eskridge, Halley, Koppelman, Richards, and Strasser) in note 1 have no consequential quantitative components; nor do most gay rights articles in law reviews and journals. Indeed, the only legal scholarship on lesbians and gay men informed by noteworthy data is Posner (1992) and Halley (1993). Examining countries tolerating homosexuality far more than the United States, Posner concludes there is no empirical evidence that elevating the social and legal status of gay people will increase their numbers. Halley reviews primary sources on the Georgia sodomy statute upheld in *Bowers v. Hardwick* (1986) and discovers that the Supreme Court's historical interpretation of the law is mistaken.

[3] Books such as Button et al. (1997), Bailey (1999), Gerstmann (1999), Riggle and Tadlock (1999b), Rimmerman et al. (2000), and Badgett (2001), as well as articles such as Sherrill (1993, 1996), Haeberle (1996), Haider-Markel and Meier (1996), Wald, Button, and Rienzo (1996), and Gamble (1997), are substantially empirical.

[4] For further explication of the paucity of empirical legal scholarship, see Schuck (1989), Nard (1995), Schlegel (1995), and Heise (1999).

little in common. If they communicate at all, they can barely hear each other; they stand on opposite sides of a great divide, and they are looking in opposite directions.[5]

Most law professors and other legal academics endorse variations of legal formalism (Cross 1997: 255–63; Gillman 2001: 466). Termed the "legal model" by political scientists, this scholarly approach to understanding judicial decision making "postulates that decisions are based on the facts of the case in light of the plain meaning of statutes and the Constitution, the intent of the framers, precedent, and a balancing of societal interests" (Segal and Spaeth 1993: 32). Case characteristics, such as whether police in search-and-seizure appeals have prior justification or intrude on the home or business (Segal 1984, 1986), have a direct impact on court decisions, and judges faithfully observe the doctrine of *stare decisis* (Segal and Spaeth 1993: 44–49).

In contrast, many political scientists recommend the "attitudinal model," which "holds that [courts] decide disputes in light of the facts of the case vis-à-vis the ideological attitudes and values of the [judges]" (Segal and Spaeth 1993: 65). Individuals' values guide judicial votes to achieve policy preferences. For example, using seven personal attributes, Tate (1981) accounted for 70 to 90 percent of the variance in Supreme Court justices' voting in nonunanimous decisions concerning civil rights and liberties as well as economics.

Advocates of these models typically brook no compromise and take no prisoners. For example, Segal and Spaeth are inflexible attitudinalists:

We believe we have sensitively analyzed the relevant internal and external non-attitudinal factors. Their impact on the decisions appears to be minimal. The eminently testable role of judicial activism and restraint effectively masks behavior; it doesn't explain it. . . . Such highly plausible external influences – such as the Solicitor General, Congress, public opinion, and interest groups – come up empty

---

[5] Graber (2002: 315) supplies some particulars:

None of the fifty most cited law reviews as of 1985 [citation omitted] engage at any length with a work written by any political scientist who studied or studies public law. Thirty of those works do not cite any work by a political scientist on courts. . . . The citation patterns in those works that cite political science scholarship on courts is best described as random. Even when articles are classified by subject matter, there does not appear to be any political scientist or work on courts that the legal community from 1947 until 1985 felt obliged to read or cite.

With [a few exceptions,] contemporary law professors are no more inclined to cite [the more than 500] members of the law and courts section of the American Political Science Association when they write books.

for the most part. . . . [W]e are simply unable to demonstrate that these forces cause the justices to behave in any *systematic* way. (1993: 363; emphasis in original)[6]

Six years later, concluding a book-length empirical investigation of legal precedent's impact on Supreme Court justices, Spaeth and Segal write:

Stare decisis is the lifeblood of the legal model, and the legal model is still the lifeblood of most legal scholars' thinking about law. Yet there has been virtually no real testing of the model, perhaps because creating falsifiable hypotheses about precedent and the legal model is not an easy task. . . . [W]e have attempted the first falsifiable, systematic test of the influence of *stare decisis* on the behavior of U.S. Supreme Court justices . . . [and find that] in the realm of *stare decisis*, minority will does not defer to majority rule. (1999: 314–15)

Critics of rigid devotion to monolithic judicial behavior models argue that scholars such as Segal and Spaeth have toppled only a straw person, because no fully articulated legal model exists to warrant meaningful fidelity (Canon 1993; Caldeira 1994; Rosenberg 1994; Smith 1994; Brisbin 1996). Caldeira (1994: 485), for example, offers a different formulation of the attitudinal model's antithesis: "[The] real foes [of Segal and Spaeth] are the many political scientists and lawyers who would belittle the analysis of [judicial] votes and say that we have to look at [court] opinions as a whole." Smith (1994: 8) proposes "legalist" targets like Ronald Dworkin and Bruce Ackerman, who – while "acknowledg[ing] the impact of judicial values on decisions" – "still try to minimize the significance of judicial values in ways that may well be vulnerable to the Segal and Spaeth critique."

This book bridges these fields of scholarly inquiry through an accessible and coherent quantitative empirical study of how state and federal appellate courts dealt with lesbian and gay rights claims over twenty years. The work identifies relevant court decisions from the 1980s and '90s and diligently investigates them using multiple factors explaining appellate court handling of the civil rights of homosexuals. Integrated models of judicial behavior harmonize the attitudinal and legal approaches. Although the volume is not a traditional doctrinal legal analysis, neither is it a quantitative enterprise wedded to just a few attitudinal variables. The survey performs statistical probes of case votes, but incorporates much more of court opinions than the scholarship of unreconstructed attitudinalists such as Segal and Spaeth. The book addresses the implications of a carefully

---

[6] Segal (1999: 238–40) provides a more nuanced view of the attitudinal model.

constructed – and unique – database, viewed through sophisticated statistical lenses, to study nascent legal doctrine.

Chapter 2's narrative overview of judicial decisions elaborates on the subject matter of the collected cases, supplies human drama behind legal battles for lesbian and gay rights in the United States, and introduces analytic concepts that permeate the research.

Chapter 3's quantitative review systematically explains why juridic struggles for homosexual rights either succeeded or failed. It examines the effects of variables from the two judicial behavior models, placed in appropriate institutional, environmental, temporal, and interest group configurations: precedent and case facts, judges' personal attributes, institutional characteristics of courts, jurisdictional environment, a period control, and interest group participation. The statistical findings are applied to specific cases to exemplify how variables had an impact on civil rights claims. The complementary qualitative and quantitative vistas furnish a comprehensive picture of the American judicial system's treatment of lesbian and gay people.

Using its gay rights models, the book next expands the quantitative investigation to far more broadly based legal concerns. Chapter 4 addresses judicial federalism, the sharing of judicial power between the fifty states and the federal government. Legal scholars have argued against trusting allegedly institutionally incompetent state courts with the vindication of individual rights. Yet despite an abundance of theory in the debate over judicial federalism and state court competence, comparatively little purposeful empirical investigation of the topic has been achieved. The volume uses its fully integrated models of judicial decision making to examine the parity dispute in a fresh way. Lesbian and gay rights are a particularly suitable vehicle for studying judicial federalism since they are an issue domain prompting strongly held positions, at both the mass and the elite levels. As noted later, judges are not indifferent to homosexual rights claims and are more disposed to vote their attitudes there than in other, less controversial areas, simply because the topic is so emotionally charged. Accordingly, federalism variables in the integrated models, as well as other methodological techniques, probe whether federal judges acted more dispassionately than state colleagues in adjudicating this minority's rights.

Introducing a highly innovative research design, Chapter 5 rigorously inspects the effect of *stare decisis* on appellate decision making, far surpassing in scope all current quantitative empirical legal scholarship on the topic. The chapter's noteworthy findings have wide import because the doctrine of precedent is central to traditional jurisprudential explanations of decision making in American courts. Moreover, *stare decisis* undergirds the Langdellian case method, dominant for more than a century in American legal education.

Concerning both judicial federalism and *stare decisis*, the book's research design conceives a "crucial case study" (Eckstein 1975: 113–23).[7] Regarding Chapter 5, for instance, if precedent holds in the arena of lesbian and gay rights, then it must work in other subject matters, given the volatile character of homosexual rights claims in American public policy making.[8] The decisive suppression by *stare decisis* of judicial preferences in the ideologically cloven terrain of gay rights would indicate it could arrest the effect of attitudes and other nonlegal forces elsewhere as well.

The same applies to Chapter 4's judicial federalism investigation. If federal judges, institutionally insulated by life tenure from public hostility to unpopular decisions, protected the constitutional rights of gay people significantly more than state colleagues, then an inference that federal courts are better equipped than state tribunals to defend minority rights is reasonable.

In sum, the book's comprehensive quantitative examination of appellate response to an emergent minority's legal claims affords an empirically sound explication of that judicial action, as well as a pathway to more general – and telling – commentary on judicial policy making, wholly independent of the lesbian and gay context. The work both explains how diverse factors influenced the adjudication of civil rights claims during a vital era of the homosexual rights movement and formulates promising methodologies for the meaningful quantitative empirical study of law, a substantially neglected field of scholarship.

The Cases

The qualitative and quantitative analyses here rest on an exhaustive collection of the published appellate court decisions in the United States adjudicating lesbian and gay rights claims during the last two decades of the twentieth century. Appendix 1.1 explains how decisions were identified,

---

[7] For a rebuttal to Eckstein, see King, Keohane, and Verba (1994: 209–12).

[8] Wald (2000: 4) ("[f]ew issues in American politics ... inspire as much passion as the struggle over civil rights for gays and lesbians. Whether it is about gays and lesbians being allowed to serve openly in the military, to marry, to adopt children, to receive partner benefits, or to gain legal protection from discrimination in housing and employment, the debate is often heated and intense").

and Appendix 1.2 lists them. The 468 cases represent a wide array of subjects. Indeed, some observers may not agree that all the decisions truly deal with legal issues that have direct impacts on the rights of homosexuals. In that regard, I have assigned cases to two broad categories: those essential to lesbian and gay rights, and those that are not. Appendix 1.2 identifies the 393 decisions in the former category by posting their names in bold.

Allocating topics between essential and nonessential categories best manifests the distinction between the two. During the 1980s and 1990s, the principal subject categories essential to homosexual rights were (in descending order of frequency): (1) lesbian and gay family matters (including same-sex marriage and its approximation; the custody, visitation, adoption, and foster care (hereafter CVAF) of children by lesbian and gay parents; and the rights of domestic partners); (2) sexual orientation discrimination in the workplace, public accommodations, and housing; (3) gays in the military; (4) the constitutionality and enforcement of consensual sodomy and solicitation laws; and (5) the free speech and free association rights of gay people. Nineteen miscellaneous cases include immigration issues, the constitutionality of hate crimes statutes covering sexual orientation, jury selection and other tangential topics in criminal prosecutions, and privacy disputes. Also, since CVAF cases represent more than three-quarters of lesbian and gay family decisions, I treat them as a separate subset.

The two principal topics not essential to lesbian and gay rights are same-sex sexual harassment and defamation involving accusations of homosexuality. Each of these legal issues arguably concerns gay people. If a man is sexually harassed on the job by another man – or a woman by another woman – that conduct may have significant homoerotic content. Likewise, determining whether statements with lesbian or gay subject matter are libelous or slanderous reflects on gay civil rights. Nonetheless, these two causes of action may principally protect heterosexuals. If judges view same-sex sexual harassment as gay men seducing straight men, or lesbians luring heterosexual women, interpreting Title VII of the Civil Rights Act or comparable state statutes to include the prohibition of same-sex harassment does not really shield gay men or lesbians. Similarly, if heterosexuals are concerned about false accusations of homosexuality, then per se defamation rules again do not principally safeguard gays. If falsely identifying someone as lesbian or gay is defamation per se, that legal rule fails to handle heterosexuals and homosexuals equally since false accusations of heterosexually are not actionable.

The book excludes AIDS law topics. Moreover, inasmuch as judicial policy making occurs principally at the appellate level (Baum 1998: 8–9), the research here is not concerned with trial court decisions.

The volume's quantitative analysis relies on the dependent variable **outcome**. I coded court decisions as 1 if decided in favor of the lesbian or gay claim asserted or defended and as 0 if against. For most cases, the coding process was forthright, in that a homosexual litigant clearly won or lost. However, when there was no such litigant, but a decision nonetheless affected the rights of gay people as a class, the coding rule became whether the court treated homosexuals as the legal equals of heterosexuals. For example, if a court determined that same-sex sexual harassment violated a jurisdiction's (theretofore only heterosexually applied) sexual harassment policy, its action was coded as favorable. In the exceptional instance where all litigants were lesbian or gay (e.g., *Thomas S. v. Robin Y.* NY 1994[9]), I determined whether the court honored the domestic relationships there in order to code the cases as 1.

Case Outcome Variation by Court System and Subject Matter

Table 1.1 reports the mean of **outcome** by court system[10] and subject matter, revealing substantial differences across both dimensions. For example, state courts decided cases essential to lesbian and gay rights more than twice as favorably, on average, as federal courts (i.e., **outcome** means of .572 vs. .256, respectively). Among essential nonmiscellaneous cases, First Amendment claims involving free speech and free association rights were decided the most favorably (.583), while cases involving gays in the military were the least successful (.241).

A nonessential subject (same-sex sexual harassment) had the highest mean (.742) of all nonmiscellaneous topics, supporting the theory that judges viewed the issue as a protection of heterosexual men from homosexual harassers. Likewise, the low mean (.308) for defamation cases tends to shield heterosexuals from false accusations of homosexuality. More on this appears in the next chapter.

---

[9] Text citations to cases listed in Appendix 1.2 use the format [case name] [jurisdiction] [year], while citations to decisions appearing in the book's References section (and not included in an appendix) use just the case name and year.

[10] The four decisions listed in Appendix 1.2 from the District of Columbia Court of Appeals are not included in Tables 1.1 and 1.2 because the district is not a state, nor are its courts comparable to federal appellate tribunals. The four cases are omitted from subsequent analysis for the same reason, as well as another indicated in Chapter 3.

TABLE 1.1 *Summary of Outcome by Court System and Subject Matter*

Case subject matter	N	Mean of outcome
All cases	456	.519
All cases essential to lesbian and gay rights	393	.503
All federal cases	108	.315
Federal cases essential to lesbian and gay rights	86	.256
All state cases	348	.582
State cases essential to lesbian and gay rights	307	.572

Cases essential to lesbian and gay rights	N	Mean of outcome
CVAF	163	.522
Sexual orientation discrimination	77	.416
Non-CVAF lesbian and gay family cases	71	.556
Gays in the military	29	.241
Constitutionality of sodomy/solicitation laws	22	.546
Free speech and free association	12	.583
Miscellaneous cases	19	.790

Cases not essential to lesbian and gay rights	N	Mean of outcome
Same-sex sexual harassment	31	.742
Defamation	13	.308
Miscellaneous cases	19	.632

Geographic Variation

Table 1.2 disaggregates cases by region.[11] Surprisingly, courts in the Midwest were the least supportive of lesbian and gay rights, with judges in the socially conservative South even voting more favorably, on average, than in the Midwest. Tribunals in the West and Northeast were the most hospitable.[12]

Table 1.3 further breaks down the cases geographically, listing jurisdictions producing at least ten decisions during the twenty-year period. Again, federal courts generally were more negative to homosexual rights claims than state tribunals. Yet substantial variation existed across states. Of the twelve with sufficient numbers of cases to make meaningful comparisons, Missouri won the dubious distinction of having appellate

---

[11] I follow Walker's (1972) assignment of states to regions.
[12] Lewis and Rogers (1999: 135) (the Northeast and West are the most supportive regions of the country for passing gay rights laws).

TABLE 1.2 *Regional Variation in* **Outcome**

| | Federal circuit and state cases combined | | | | | | | |
| | All cases | | Essential cases only | | All family cases | | CVAF cases only | |
Region	N	Mean	N	Mean	N	Mean	N	Mean
Northeast	95	.526	88	.546	64	.563	35	.600
South	126	.504	105	.519	70	.550	53	.491
Midwest	128	.484	108	.417	67	.478	56	.482
West	92	.620	79	.595	33	.546	19	.579

| | State cases only | | | | | | | |
| | All cases | | Essential cases only | | All family cases | | CVAF cases only | |
Region	N	Mean	N	Mean	N	Mean	N	Mean
Northeast	85	.565	78	.590	64	.563	35	.600
South	99	.551	89	.545	69	.544	53	.491
Midwest	97	.536	84	.500	66	.485	56	.482
West	67	.716	56	.696	31	.581	19	.579

Note: Federal circuits and states were assigned to regions in the following manner: **Northeast:** Connecticut, Delaware, Maine, Massachusetts, New Hampshire, New Jersey, New York, Pennsylvania, Rhode Island, Vermont, and First, Second, and Third Circuits. **South:** Alabama, Arkansas, Florida, Georgia, Kentucky, Louisiana, Maryland, Mississippi, North Carolina, Oklahoma, South Carolina, Tennessee, Texas, Virginia, West Virginia, and Fourth, Fifth, and Eleventh Circuits. **Midwest:** Illinois, Indiana, Iowa, Kansas, Michigan, Minnesota, Missouri, Nebraska, North Dakota, Ohio, South Dakota, Wisconsin, and Sixth, Seventh, and Eighth Circuits. **West:** Alaska, Arizona, California, Colorado, Hawaii, Idaho, Montana, Nevada, New Mexico, Oregon, Utah, Washington, Wyoming, and Ninth and Tenth Circuits.

courts that were the least validating of gay rights, followed by Virginia and Ohio. In contrast, Massachusetts courts were the most favorably disposed, with Florida, Minnesota, Colorado, and California close behind.

These state-specific findings help explain why the Midwest was the daunting region of the country for gay rights. Missouri's last-place finish tilted the Midwestern average downward, while Florida's strong support boosted the Southern mean. In fact, removing Missouri from the Midwestern data and Florida from the Southern switches those regions' relative positions in family and CVAF decisions, with the South now coming in last.[13] Indeed, further removing Maryland and West Virginia

[13] In all family cases, the new Midwestern mean is .554 and the Southern, .526. In CVAF decisions, .565 and .489, respectively.

TABLE 1.3 *Variation in **Outcome** Among Jurisdictions with Ten or More Cases*

	All cases		Essential cases only	
Jurisdiction	N	Mean	N	Mean
Fourth Circuit	10	.200	5	.200
Fifth Circuit	11	.273	6	.333
Sixth Circuit	13	.154	12	.083
Ninth Circuit	21	.381	19	.368
California	30	.667	26	.654
Colorado	10	.800	6	.667
Florida	17	.706	14	.714
Illinois	10	.600	10	.600
Massachusetts	10	.800	9	.778
Minnesota	18	.722	13	.692
Missouri	13	.154	11	.091
New York	44	.477	38	.526
Ohio	23	.435	19	.368
Pennsylvania	12	.500	12	.500
Texas	10	.500	9	.556
Virginia	10	.300	10	.300

(states with strong Northern ties) from the Southern fold and adding Missouri (with substantial Southern influence) afford an even more dramatic comparison. The appellate courts of Alabama, Arkansas, Georgia, Kentucky, Louisiana, Mississippi, Missouri, North Carolina, Oklahoma, South Carolina, Tennessee, Texas, and Virginia decided 47 lawsuits involving CVAF with gay parents. Less than a third of those decisions (15, or 31.9 percent) favored homosexual litigants. In contrast, the appellate tribunals of the other 37 states backed lesbian and gay parents 60.3 percent of the time (70 of 116 cases) – virtually twice as frequently as in the redefined South.[14]

Temporal Variation

Table 1.4 investigates trends over time. The graphic displays decennial and quintennial changes in the mean of **outcome** for all cases essential

---

[14] Ellison and Musick (1993) (four decades of research indicate that Southerners are less tolerant of unpopular groups than the rest of the country); Lewis and Rogers (1999: 135) (three decades of Gallup and CBS/*New York Times* polling data demonstrate the American South is the least supportive region of the country for passing gay rights laws).

to lesbian and gay rights, as well as within court systems, court levels, and subject matters. Further, the table separates data among all decisions in each category and then just those decided without the influence of controlling precedent.[15] The latter information focuses on how judges treated cases of first impression, that is, those for which no prior decisions existed with comparable legal issues from the same or higher courts. As Table 1.4 reveals, patterns did emerge over the investigation's twenty-year range.

First, lesbian and gay litigants in American appellate courts were generally more successful in the 1990s than before. Regardless of court or subject matter, gay people won 42.4 percent of the time in the 1980s and 53.6 percent the following decade, a rate improvement of 26.4 percent. In cases of first impression, the rate increase was 31.9 percent.

Second, state courts were responsible for the more numerous judicial victories in later years. While the success rate of lesbians and gay men in federal courts was effectively static through the twenty years (hovering between about 25 and 33 percent), state courts rendered favorable decisions just under 50 percent of the time in the 1980s and then at a rate of 60 percent the following decade. Moreover, caseloads changed. Federal courts handled 31.4 percent of homosexual rights appeals in the 1980s, but only 17.8 percent the next decade. Hence, as comparatively fewer federal courts denied rights to gay people over time, more state courts recognized them and increasingly so.

Third, courts of last resort revealed no consistent temporal pattern, although they did deliver relatively high rates of success to homosexuals through the bulk of the period of interest, except for a plummet between 1996 and 2000 caused mainly by a surge of negative Southern rulings.[16] In contrast, intermediate appellate courts significantly improved

---

[15] Chapters 3 and 5 address how binding precedents were identified, as well as other pertinent matters regarding the doctrine of *stare decisis*. The cases in the study that were subject to precedents in opposition to lesbian and gay rights were about twice the number of those in support (20.7 and 11.0 percent, respectively).

[16] *Ten* Southern court-of-last-resort losses (five CVAF cases from Alabama, Mississippi, and North Carolina; two non-CVAF family disputes from Mississippi and Virginia; a First Amendment decision from Texas; and two sodomy statute challenges in Georgia and Louisiana) occurred between 1996 and 2000, while only two Southern high court defeats (both CVAF, from Oklahoma and Virginia) took place in the first quintennial, two (a CVAF case from Mississippi and a sodomy challenge in Missouri) in the second, and four (a CVAF decision from Virginia, a non-CVAF family dispute from Oklahoma, and two sodomy cases in Oklahoma and Texas) in the third. As a result, adverse Southern court-of-last-resort rulings were substantially back-loaded in the data set.

TABLE 1.4 *Temporal Variation in* **Outcome**

All court decisions essential to lesbian and gay rights

	All essential cases		Precedent-free cases only	
Years	N	Mean of outcome	N	Mean of outcome
1981–90	118	.424	81	.432
1991–2000	275	.536	194	.570
1981–85	60	.500	48	.500
1986–90	58	.345	33	.333
1991–95	117	.560	78	.558
1996–2000	158	.519	116	.578

Federal court decisions

	All essential cases		Precedent-free cases only	
Years	N	Mean of outcome	N	Mean of outcome
1981–90	37	.270	20	.250
1991–2000	49	.245	25	.320
1981–85	19	.316	12	.333
1986–90	18	.222	8	.125
1991–95	19	.263	7	.286
1996–2000	30	.233	18	.333

State court decisions

	All essential cases		Precedent-free cases only	
Years	N	Mean of outcome	N	Mean of outcome
1981–90	81	.494	61	.492
1991–2000	226	.600	169	.607
1981–85	41	.585	36	.556
1986–90	40	.400	25	.400
1991–95	98	.617	71	.585
1996–2000	128	.586	98	.622

Court-of-last-resort decisions

	All essential cases		Precedent-free cases only	
Years	N	Mean of outcome	N	Mean of outcome
1981–90	24	.583	22	.546
1991–2000	68	.537	54	.528
1981–85	14	.571	13	.539
1986–90	10	.600	9	.556
1991–95	29	.638	22	.614
1996–2000	39	.462	32	.469

TABLE 1.4 *(continued)*

	Intermediate appellate court decisions			
	All essential cases		Precedent-free cases only	
Years	N	Mean of outcome	N	Mean of outcome
1981–90	94	.383	59	.390
1991–2000	207	.536	140	.586
1981–85	46	.478	35	.486
1986–90	48	.292	24	.250
1991–95	88	.534	56	.536
1996–2000	119	.538	84	.619

	Non-CVAF family decisions			
	All essential cases		Precedent-free cases only	
Years	N	Mean of outcome	N	Mean of outcome
1981–90	21	.476	15	.400
1991–2000	50	.590	43	.570
1981–85	11	.455	10	.400
1986–90	10	.500	5	.400
1991–95	20	.575	15	.500
1996–2000	30	.600	28	.607

	CVAF decisions			
	All essential cases		Precedent-free cases only	
Years	N	Mean of outcome	N	Mean of outcome
1981–90	45	.378	33	.394
1991–2000	118	.576	75	.600
1981–85	19	.421	17	.412
1986–90	26	.346	16	.375
1991–95	51	.588	34	.559
1996–2000	67	.567	41	.634

	Nonfamily decisions			
	All essential cases		Precedent-free cases only	
Years	N	Mean of outcome	N	Mean of outcome
1981–90	52	.442	33	.485
1991–2000	107	.467	76	.540
1981–85	30	.567	21	.619
1986–90	22	.273	12	.250
1991–95	46	.522	29	.586
1996–2000	61	.426	47	.511

their treatment of gay people between the two decades (by 50.3 percent in precedent-free cases).

Fourth, among subject matters, CVAF decisions exhibited the most notable progress between the 1980s and 1990s. All lesbian and gay care-givers seeking child custody, visitation, adoption, or foster care prevailed only 37.8 percent of the time in the first decade, but 57.6 percent in the second – a rate increase of more than 50 percent. Precedent-free cases disclose a slightly higher decennial improvement, while such decisions between 1996 and 2000 experienced the second highest win rate (63.4 per-cent) in Table 1.4. Thus, at century's end, lesbian and gay parents won almost two-thirds of the time in cases of first impression. This suggests that, over time, judges – especially those unencumbered by precedent – progressively advanced the parental rights of homosexuals.

Fifth, non-CVAF family cases were the only group in Table 1.4 with steady improvement every five years. Judges increasingly supported cou-pling claims involving the rights and responsibilities of the domestic part-ners of gay people and same-sex marriage or its approximation. These findings for CVAF and coupling decisions portend good things for gay families.

In contrast, nonfamily decisions demonstrated broad quintennial swings, with 1981 through 1985 unexpectedly showing the highest win rates. The eclectic set of legal issues constituting this category explains the temporal enigma. First Amendment claims by lesbians and gay men, for example, were the most successful in the study, and five (41.7 per-cent) of twelve free speech and association cases in the database were rendered between 1981 and 1985. By comparison, disputes involving the American military were generally futile for gays, and only four (13.8 per-cent) of twenty-nine of those contests occurred in the first quintennial. Hence, the cases with the greatest likelihood of success in this division were front-loaded, while the ones most destined to lose arose later.

Finally, in all categories except courts of last resort and non-CVAF family cases, the years 1986 through 1990 witnessed the lowest ebb for judicial recognition of lesbian and gay rights. A plausible explanation is the overt hostility to those rights manifested by the U.S. Supreme Court in *Bowers v. Hardwick*. That 1986 high court attack on gay people may have temporarily depressed judicial receptivity to their rights claims.

The next chapter enlarges on case subject matter, relates fascinating stories from legal battles for homosexual rights, and proposes analytic concepts on which the balance of the book relies.

2

Case Narratives

> Storytelling's value is in expanding legal debate and driving social transformation by illuminating legal issues from the perspectives of nomic groups frequently excluded from political and academic debate, particularly gays and lesbians. (Eskridge 1994: 607)

I offer narratives from the categories of subjects presented in the first chapter. These cases are not necessarily representative decisions. Rather, I've selected some stories simply for their human interest value. In any event, many of these narratives introduce analytic themes that continue through the book.

Child Custody, Visitation, Adoption, and Foster Care

Disputes involving the custody, visitation, adoption, or foster care (CVAF) of children by lesbian and gay parents or their domestic partners comprise the largest portion of decisions, representing 41.5 percent of essential cases (163 of 393). Thus, CVAF decisions are the most important in terms of impact on the greatest number of gay litigants. All CVAF cases are from state courts because federal tribunals have no jurisdiction over disputes involving children, except in rare instances implicating federal constitutional claims (e.g., *Michael H. v. Gerald D.* 1989).

The influence of judicial attitude may be substantial here since the universal CVAF legal standard ("the best interests of the child") is nebulous, permitting wider judicial discretion than in cases with more concrete and exacting legal criteria. In short, the law places fewer constraints on CVAF decision making than in other policy domains. Accordingly, personal biases and prejudices and other nonlegal factors may have had freer play in CVAF cases. In fact, CVAF cases as a group were decided the least favorably to lesbians and gay men compared with other major categories of state court decisions – the proper comparison, since CVAF cases came exclusively from state courts. The mean of **outcome** was .522 for CVAF cases and .575 (N = 67) for all essential state court non-CVAF family decisions, and .675 (N = 77) for essential state court nonfamily decisions.

The Homophobic Chicago Trial Judge

In re Petition of C.M.A. (IL 1999) demonstrates flagrant judicial prejudice against homosexual parents. A lesbian couple jointly sought to adopt the biological child of one of them. Pursuant to Illinois law, a guardian *ad litem* (GAL) was appointed to represent the child's interests. The Chicago Department of Supportive Services (DSS) conducted a probe of the family, and the opinion for the Appellate Court of Illinois continues the story:

The DSS investigative report was favorable and, in fact, all evidence favored the adoption. No negative matters were raised. After reviewing the file and DSS report and filing an answer, the GAL joined with the petitioners in requesting entry of judgment for adoption.

Although the adoption was uncontested, Judge [Susan J.] McDunn [the trial judge] denied the petition for adoption . . . and instead entered an order requiring that a best interests hearing be held.

[At the hearing, t]hree witnesses were called and examined by the GAL and counsel for petitioners. C.M.W. and L.A.W. [the lesbian couple] testified about their family and their care of K.D.W. [the child]. The DSS investigator, who has done studies of this type for almost 20 years, testified about the home-study investigation and the contents of her report. She testified about evidence she received supporting her decision to highly recommend the adoption and her conclusion that the parties' sexual orientation was not a concern. . . .

According to the DSS caseworker, C.M.W. and L.A.W. went through the required intake process and investigation regarding their relationship and financial matters as well as health, family, work, and educational histories. Letters from three people knowledgeable as to their parenting skills were obtained. The investigator spent several hours at the family home and determined that K.D.W. is "a beautiful baby with two people who adore him and love him and . . . seems to be just thriving in their home." The caseworker described their home environment and found [the women's] relationship to be stable. She testified further that nothing in her investigation disclosed any problems stemming from the parents' sexual orientation, nor posed any question about their suitability to adopt.

Judge McDunn asked no questions of any witness about K.D.W. or his care or welfare. Judge McDunn did, however, question each [woman] regarding her "coming out" process as a lesbian, her early sexual experiences, and whether [the women] were currently in a lesbian sexual relationship. These questions were answered completely and truthfully, over objection. The court called no witnesses of its own.

No evidence presented at the hearing indicated any indiscreet or inappropriate conduct by [the lesbian couple] or others, nor any circumstances harmful to the minor child. All evidence favored the adoption and none indicated that his best interests would be served by denying the petition to adopt. Judge McDunn took the case under advisement. (715 N.E.2d at 676)

More than two months later, Judge McDunn indicated she would not make a ruling until after a hearing in a second lesbian adoption case before her because it had "similar issues" and "similar types of circumstances." Thereafter, Judge Francis Barth, presiding judge of Cook County, granted an application to remove Judge McDunn from the proceeding based on her decision to consider evidence in the second, wholly unrelated case before ruling on the instant one. Four days later, Judge Barth entered a final judgment of adoption for the first lesbian couple.

Judge McDunn handled the second lesbian adoption case in a similar dilatory manner, despite a comparable lack of evidence against adoption. Further, almost ten months after the petition was filed, and on her own initiative, she

issued an order adding a new party to the case, the Family Research Council (FRC), of Washington, DC, and ordering that "... Gary Bauer, President of FRC, and any attorney who files an appearance on behalf of the FRC are permitted to examine the court file herein ... [and] these persons also have leave to make or receive copies of all papers and documents contained in such files," subject to maintaining identifying information as confidential. This order contained the true names of the adopting petitioners and their children [rather than their initials, as is customary in such proceedings]. The order was sent by the court to FRC by Federal Express delivery and to the parties by regular delivery through the United States Postal Service.

This order further explained that FRC was added as a "necessary" party and cited [state statutes allegedly in support]. FRC was added in the capacity of "secondary guardian" to represent the interests of the minor children before the court and of children generally. Judge McDunn indicated that FRC was a necessary party because FRC "is on public record for the position that adoptions by unmarried persons and persons living a homosexual lifestyle are not in the best interests of children" and no party to the case had advocated this position.

Judge McDunn stated further that it was necessary to add FRC because FRC has a general interest in the welfare of children and might have an interest in future cases involving similar circumstances. Judge McDunn expressed the view that no Illinois appellate decision had considered whether adoptions by lesbians and gay men were contrary to the best interests of children. (715 N.E.2d at 678)

Judge Barth immediately removed Judge McDunn from the second case and then entered a final judgment of adoption there. However, both lesbian couples later received orders entered in each case by Judge McDunn declaring

that the petitions for substitution for cause had been improperly brought, that Judge Barth did not have jurisdiction to hear or grant them, and that the substitution orders were void. In addition, Judge McDunn declared that any adoption judgments entered by Judge Barth were also void because he lacked jurisdiction to act in the cases. Judge McDunn's orders further indicated that the evidence before her was insufficient to grant or deny the adoptions and that it was necessary to hold further hearings for additional proof.

These orders again named FRC as a "necessary" party and "secondary guardian" in both of the adoption cases, and Gary Bauer was allowed immediate access to the confidential adoption files. These orders were sent to FRC by Federal Express delivery and to the parties by regular delivery through the United States Postal Service. (715 N.E.2d at 678)

The parties again went to Judge Barth, who reaffirmed his prior orders removing Judge McDunn for cause. But Judge McDunn thereafter again voided that determination.

The Illinois Appellate Court intervened between the warring lower court judges, unanimously upholding Judge Barth and condemning Judge McDunn's

extreme and patent bias against the adoptive parents based upon their sexual orientation. This bias was manifest in numerous ways, including her insensitive probing and wrongful interrogation of the adoptive parents' early sexual history. We can conceive of no legitimate motive or worthwhile purpose for questioning the petitioners on such clearly irrelevant matters. In addition, Judge McDunn joined together two totally separate adoptions, whose only common thread was the sexual orientation of the adoptive parents. As a result, she not only injected inadmissible facts into each of the cases, but also inflicted anguish on the petitioners and needlessly prolonged what should have been a simple and straightforward process. (715 N.E.2d at 679)

The Appellate Court noted that its precedents held sexual orientation to be irrelevant in adoption cases and stated:

FRC has no rights at stake in the[se] two adoption cases. It had no relationship or cognizable interest in the minor children sought to be adopted and had no legally enforceable right or claim which could properly be asserted or defended in those cases. Moreover, FRC, an organization based in Washington, DC, was not subject to the jurisdiction of the [trial] court and was not qualified under [Illinois law] to act as a guardian *ad litem*. We find Judge McDunn's actions in appointing FRC as a "secondary guardian" to be legally and logically indefensible.[1] In addition, we note that there is no indication in the record that the GAL previously appointed to represent the interests of the minor children had failed in his duty. On the contrary, the GAL appointed in the instant cases has a well-known reputation as a skilled practitioner and, based upon the evidence in the record, diligently performed his legal and ethical obligations as representative for the minor children. The appointment of FRC as a "secondary guardian," without removal of the GAL, or grounds therefore, was unwarranted. Finally, we observe that in making this appointment and permitting FRC access to the court's files, Judge McDunn improperly disseminated sensitive and confidential information to non-parties, in violation of [Illinois law]. (715 N.E.2d at 681)

The Chicago case clearly documents how a bigoted trial judge can wreak havoc on the rights of lesbian and gay litigants. Yet rarely is judicial intolerance so blatantly disclosed in the public record.[2] A more likely circumstance is for judges hostile to gay people to act more circumspectly, denying rights for ostensibly proper legal reasons.

CVAF cases offer excellent opportunities for the successful exercise of judicial bigotry. First, trial judges act alone in deciding disputes, while appellate tribunals perform in panels of at least three members. Hence, lower court judges are freer from collegial scrutiny in the discharge of their responsibilities. That is, in the immediate exercise of their power, trial judges answer to no one, while appellate judges always have to deal with at least two other colleagues of equal power. A prejudiced trial judge thus has greater leeway to discriminate invidiously than an appellate counterpart with two or more prospective censors looking over a shoulder. Further, even if the appellate bigot follows his or her preferences, he or she may be outvoted by colleagues. Thus, at least two homophobes are necessary for an appellate court to act unfairly with regard to lesbian and gay rights.

Second, the typical legal standard for appellate court review of trial court action in CVAF cases is known as "abuse of discretion," which means that appellate judges usually defer to the factual determinations of trial judges, except where the lower court acted so clearly improperly as to

---

[1] The court could have added that the Family Research Council is a notoriously homophobic interest group (Herman 1997: 15; Rimmerman 2002: 122, 142).

[2] The only other overt trial court homophobia appearing in the book's database is *Rucks v. State* (FL 1997), where, in another dispute involving a lesbian couple and child, the judge stated on the record: "I'll tell you, ma'm. This is a sick situation. I've seen a lot of sick situations since I've been in this court. I've been in this profession for 27 years and this ranks at the top. If this is the family of 1997, heaven help us." The higher court ordered his removal from the case.

demand appellate correction. The reason for high court deference to trial court factual conclusions is that trial judges observe witnesses at first hand and thereby are in a better position to evaluate how truthful their testimonies are. In comparison, appellate courts have only a printed record of testimony before them, without benefit of the "body language" of, and other sensory perceptions about, witnesses that help gauge the reliability of evidence. Thus, appellate tribunals are ill-equipped to second-guess a trial court's decision that, for example, a parent is unfit for custody, visitation, adoption, or foster care. Trial judges, accordingly, are particularly powerful in CVAF cases.

Lesbian Mother Custody and Alabama Justice

Ex parte J.M.F. (AL 1998) demonstrates the phenomenon. After a six-year marriage, a husband and wife divorced, with the mother taking custody of the parties' three-year-old daughter pursuant to prior agreement. Shortly thereafter, the mother began a lesbian relationship and moved with her daughter into an apartment with the new domestic partner. The father was aware of the relationship and believed through conversations with the mother that the two women would act discreetly, not sharing a bedroom and presenting themselves to the child merely as roommates. The father then remarried, and the child regularly visited him and his new wife in their home. Almost two years after the divorce, the father filed a petition to change custody on the ground that the mother was "now openly and notoriously cohabiting with and maintaining a sexual relationship with a member of the same sex" (*J.B.F. v. J.M.F.* AL 1997: 1187).

The trial court appointed a psychologist to evaluate the child and a guardian *ad litem* to represent the child's interests. The psychologist

sent her report to the court, stating that the child is developing normally, that the child desired to live with the mother, and that the biggest threat to the child's development was the friction between the mother and the father. She also stated as follows:

"On the basis of existing research findings, fears about children of lesbians or gay men being sexually abused by adults, ostracized by peers, or isolated in single-sex lesbian or gay communities are unfounded. All of this research suggests that custody should be determined on individual character and parenting skills, and not on the basis of sexual preference."

Following oral proceedings, the guardian *ad litem* submitted a written recommendation to the court, recommending that custody of the child should be given to the father and that the mother's visitation be exercised "with no overnight guest who is unrelated by blood or marriage." (730 So.2d at 1187)

The trial judge followed the guardian's recommendation, and the mother appealed. By a vote of five to one, the Court of Civil Appeals of Alabama reversed the trial court, stating:

It is well-established law in Alabama that once a parent has been awarded custody of a child, the noncustodial parent seeking a change in custody has a heavy burden of proving that a change of custody would materially promote the child's best interests and welfare and that the benefits of such a change would outweigh the disruptive effect caused by the change. [Citations omitted.] It is also well established that following oral proceedings, the judgment of the trial court as to child custody is presumed correct and will not be disturbed on appeal unless it is so unsupported by the evidence as to be plainly and palpably wrong or an abuse of discretion. [Citation omitted.]

The record reveals the following pertinent facts: The mother has been the child's primary caregiver since the child's birth. The child is a bright, happy, well-adjusted seven-year-old girl. She enjoys living with her mother and her mother's companion, and she enjoys visiting with her father and her stepmother.

The child sees [a private psychologist] for problems that she experiences as a result of her parents' divorce, i.e., sleep disturbances, occasional temper tantrums, and difficulty in getting to sleep before visiting the father. The child expressed to both [the court-appointed psychologist and the private psychologist] that she wants to live with her mother and [the mother's domestic partner]. She also stated that she loves the mother, [her domestic partner], the father, and [her stepmother].

The mother is an admitted lesbian. The mother and [domestic partner] have a committed relationship; they have exchanged rings, and they have lived together [for four and a half years]. The mother has not discussed her relationship with [the domestic partner] with the child, except to say that she loves [her] the way the father loves [the stepmother]. The child considers her mother, [the domestic partner], and herself to be a family. The mother and [domestic partner] both testified that they kiss, hug, and hold hands, but that they do not engage in any other activities because such acts are against the law in Alabama. Both the mother and [the domestic partner] are involved in the child's education and activities. [The domestic partner] usually takes time off from work to go on field trips with the child, and she goes to the child's school to eat lunch with the child once or twice a month. The father has not been actively involved in the child's education or activities.

The father admits that the mother is a good mother and that she has done a good job of raising the child. He has no problems with the child's development, and he feels that the child is well-cared for, is well-fed, and is doing well at school. The father also admits that he has never discussed with the mother any problems or concerns that he has regarding the child.

The father testified that he decided to file for custody after having a conversation with the child. He testified that the child told him that she had wet the bed and that she had gone to [the domestic partner's] room to ask her mother to change the sheets. The father also testified that while the child was playing with Barbie dolls, she told him that girls could marry girls and that boys could marry boys and that when he asked her who told her that, she replied her mother had.

The father testified that he took the child to the Alabama Institute of Pastoral Counseling because, he says, the child repeatedly touched herself and that twice, during play, she grabbed [the stepmother's] breast and called it tickling. He also said the child had difficulty going to sleep, which he said was unusual for the child.

[A pastoral counselor] testified that he works for the Alabama Institute of Pastoral Counseling [and] is a clinical director of the Institute. He stated that the father and [stepmother] reported their concerns that the child had been sexually abused[, and that the counselor] assessed the child. He testified that, based on watching the child play, he determined that the child was aggressive and angry and that her behavior indicated that she had been sexually abused. Thereafter, a female therapist saw the child until [the pastoral counselor] learned that the child was already being seen and treated by [a private psychologist]. On cross-examination, [the pastoral counselor] admitted that the child's aggressive play and anger could have been the result of being taken to a second therapist while she was seeing [the private psychologist].

Both [the private psychologist and the court-appointed psychologist] found that the mother's relationship with [the domestic partner] has not adversely affected the child, that the child is comfortable with her living situation, and that the child wants to live with her mother. They also stated that relevant psychological research reveals no evidence to suggest that lesbians and gay men are unfit to be parents or that psychological development among offspring of gay men or lesbians is compromised in any respect relative to that among heterosexual parents. Both stated that there is no indication that the child had been sexually abused or exposed to sexual acts. [The court-appointed psychologist] reported that the child denied being touched inappropriately and witnessing any acts between adults that were upsetting or confusing to her. A clinical psychologist at the Brewer's Porch Children's Center at the University of Alabama testified that empirical studies reveal no adverse difference between children raised by a lesbian couple and those raised by a heterosexual couple. He also stated that the problems of rejection and difficulties with peer groups occur with the same frequency and intensity with children raised by a heterosexual couple as those raised by a lesbian couple. [He] further stated that after reviewing the child's records, he concluded that there is no indication that the child was sexually abused.

"The courts of Alabama have emphasized that a change of custody from one parent to another is not a decision to be made lightly; on the contrary, it may be made only where the evidence discloses an obvious and overwhelming necessity for change" [from a 1997 Alabama Supreme Court decision]. (730 So.2d at 1188–89)

The Alabama Court of Civil Appeals then performed an exhaustive review of precedents from other states involving modifications of child custody based on allegations of parents' homosexual orientation and concluded:

We agree with [the court-appointed psychologist's] statement that "custody should be determined on individual character and parenting skills, and not on the basis of sexual preference." We conclude that it was the burden of the father to present evidence that the relationship of the mother with [her domestic partner] was so affecting the best interests and welfare of the child that a change of her custody to the father would materially promote her best interests and welfare. [Citations omitted.] We find that the father failed to carry that burden. Our review of the record reveals the opposite is true – the child is thriving, and she is happy and well-adjusted. We conclude that it cannot reasonably be said that removing a seven-year-old girl from the custody of a loving and caring mother, with whom she has lived all of her life, so promotes the best interests of the child to overcome the obviously detrimental effect of a change in custody. It is evident from the testimony that such a change of custody was entered solely because of a lesbian relationship of the mother. Therefore, we find that the trial court's change of custody is so unsupported by the evidence as to be plainly and palpably wrong. (730 So.2d at 1190)

The father then appealed to the Alabama Supreme Court, which unanimously reversed the Court of Civil Appeals, stating:

[T]he father has not sought to change the custody of the child based upon the fact that the mother is engaged in a homosexual affair; indeed, the father was aware of the mother's feelings for [the domestic partner] at the time of the divorce and was aware that they cohabited thereafter, but he did not immediately seek a change of custody. The father sought custody of the child only after he had remarried and had discovered that the mother and [her domestic partner] were not conducting a discreet affair in the guise of "roommates" but were, instead, presenting themselves openly to the child as affectionate "life partners" with a relationship similar to that of the father and the stepmother. This is, therefore, not a custody case based solely upon the mother's sexual conduct, where the "substantial detrimental effect" [standard] might be applicable. Rather, it is a custody case based upon two distinct changes in the circumstances of the parties: (1) the change in the father's life, from single parenthood to marriage and the creation of a two-parent, heterosexual home environment, and (2) the change in the mother's homosexual relationship, from a discreet affair to the creation of an openly homosexual home environment. The father was not, as the Court of Civil Appeals erroneously held, required to show that the mother's relationship with the child was having a "substantial detrimental effect" upon the child. Rather, he was required to establish that, based upon the changes in the circumstances of the parties, a change in custody would materially promote the child's best interests and that the positive good brought by this change would more than offset the inherently disruptive effect of uprooting the child. (730 So.2d at 1194; footnote and citations omitted)

The Alabama Supreme Court concluded as follows:

After carefully considering all of the evidence, we simply cannot hold that the trial court abused its discretion in determining that the positive good brought about by placing the child in the custody of her father would more than offset the inherent disruption brought about by uprooting the child from her mother's custody. While the evidence shows that the mother loves the child and has provided her with good care, it also shows that she has chosen to expose the child continuously to a lifestyle that is "neither legal in this state, nor moral in the eyes of most of its citizens." [Citation omitted.] The record contains evidence from which the trial court could have concluded that "[a] child raised by two women or two men is deprived of extremely valuable developmental experience and the opportunity for optimal individual growth and interpersonal development" and that "the degree of harm to children from the homosexual conduct of a parent is uncertain . . . and the range of potential harm is enormous." [Citation omitted.]

While much study, and even more controversy, continue to center upon the effects of homosexual parenting, the inestimable developmental benefit of a loving home environment that is anchored by a successful marriage is undisputed. The father's circumstances have changed, and he is now able to provide this benefit to the child. The mother's circumstances have also changed, in that she is unable, while choosing to conduct an open cohabitation with her lesbian life partner, to provide this benefit. The trial court's change of custody based upon the changed circumstances of the parties was not an abuse of discretion; thus, the Court of Civil Appeals erred in reversing the trial court's judgment. (730 So.2d at 1196)

The power of the trial judge here is obvious. Except for gross misconduct similar to that of Judge McDunn in the Chicago adoption case, the Alabama Supreme Court was unwilling to disrupt the trial court's choice to take custody from the lesbian mother. Yet certainly the case facts easily supported the opposite result, as five judges on the intermediate appellate court concluded. Indeed, which appellate tribunal here acted appropriately? Is it possible the Alabama Supreme Court itself was motivated by animus toward lesbians, just as Judge McDunn was?[3]

The Alabama Supreme Court unambiguously manifested its contempt for gay people. At minimum, the court applied a double standard to straight and gay parenting. The remarriage of a noncustodial parent alone

---

[3] In fairness to the Alabama Supreme Court, I note that its opinion emphasized different factual circumstances than that of the Court of Civil Appeals:

> The mother testified that she has not had any significant concern about the adverse effect her transformation from a married heterosexual to a committed homosexual could have on the child. The mother has repeatedly denied that the child will suffer any ill effects from the mother's choice of lifestyle; however, the mother has also testified that it will be up to the child to cope with any ridicule or prejudice that the child might suffer as she gets older, because, she said, "all children have to cope with prejudice anyway."
>
> The mother and [her domestic partner] have homosexual couples as guests in their home, and the evidence suggests that the child believes that "girls can marry girls." Both the mother and [domestic partner] have testified that they would not discourage the child from adopting a homosexual lifestyle. In short, the mother and [domestic partner] have established a two-parent home environment where their homosexual relationship is openly practiced and presented to the child as the social and moral equivalent of a heterosexual marriage. (730 So.2d at 1195)

clearly would be insufficient ground to change custody from a *hetero*sexual custodial parent. Moreover, consider the message that the state supreme court requires lesbian and gay people to send their children. The only way for Alabama's lesbians and gay men involved in loving, long-term relationships to maintain child custody is to be dishonest to their children. The parents have to participate in an elaborate charade that their domestic partners are mere roommates. In effect, this is the American military's "don't ask, don't tell" policy applied to lesbian and gay parenting. The children may not inquire into their parents' domestic relationships, and the parents dare not reveal them. Deception is the preferred legal value.

More from Alabama: Lesbian Mother Visitation

Further calling into question the good faith of the Alabama Supreme Court is a dissenting opinion in a case decided by that bench just four months before *J.M.F.* involving a trial judge's restricting child visitation to a lesbian mother as follows:

[The lesbian mother] shall be entitled to have visitation with the minor children every other weekend ... from Friday at 6:00 p.m. until Sunday at 6:00 p.m. and one evening of the intervening week; however, such visitation shall be exercised only at the maternal grandparents' home under their supervision and control and in no event shall the children be around [the mother's domestic partner] during *any* visitation period. [The mother] shall be entitled to liberal telephone communication with the minor children. . . .

Neither party shall have overnight adult guests (family excluded) while [the] children are in their home and under their custody unless they are married thereto. (*Ex parte D.W.W.* AL 1998: 794; emphasis in original)

The Alabama Court of Civil Appeals reversed the visitation limitation, and the state supreme court reinstated it. The high court dissenting opinion began:

Because the main opinion seems to be more interested in providing social commentary than in protecting the best interests of these parties' two children, I dissent.

In an apparent attempt to play to public opinion, the main opinion has ignored the sound reasoning of the Court of Civil Appeals and has mischaracterized much of the evidence presented in this case. In fact, one reading the main opinion may get the impression that the trial court's decision is supported by a wealth of evidence. However, I can find no evidence to support the type of severe visitation restraints placed on [the lesbian mother here]. . . . While I am not attempting to condone [her] lifestyle, I cannot ignore the fact that the trial court's decision appears to be founded primarily on prejudice. (717 So.2d at 797)

How much does this dissenting view from the visitation decision accurately reflect what happened in the change-of-custody case? Is it possible for all seven of the Alabama Supreme Court justices to be prejudiced against gay people? Why didn't the dissenting judges in the visitation case also blow the whistle on their colleagues in the custody decision?

Bias and prejudice might be inferred from judges' personal attributes. Many white officials in the United States acted with prejudice toward people of color for much of the twentieth century, with Jim Crow laws being ample evidence of official racial animus in the South. Perhaps similar patterns of the personal attributes of the people holding public office influencing official conduct emerge with regard to the adjudication of the civil rights of lesbians and gay men. At age forty-six, for instance, the judge who wrote the dissenting opinion in the visitation case was the youngest member of the Alabama Supreme Court. In fact, the average age of the two dissenting jurists in the visitation dispute was fifty, while that of the five-member majority was sixty-three. The thirteen-year age differential possibly had an impact on how the justices voted on the lesbian mother's rights because research in other contexts has found young people to be more gay-supportive than older citizens (Gibson 1987; Haeberle 1999; Klawitter and Hammer 1999; Lewis and Rogers 1999).

Moreover, the other dissenting judge in the visitation appeal was the only African American on the Alabama Supreme Court. Maybe his experience as a member of a historically oppressed group caused him to look with more sympathy on the legal plight of another persecuted minority. In public-opinion polling data, Haeberle (1999) found African Americans more supportive of lesbian and gay rights than whites.

Judges' religious beliefs may also play a part. In a concurring opinion in another Alabama Supreme Court case[4] addressing lesbian mother custody rights, the state's Chief Justice declared that homosexuality is an "inherent evil against which children must be protected." He elaborated that "homosexual conduct is, and has been, considered abhorrent, immoral, detestable, a crime against nature, and a violation of the laws of nature and of nature's God upon which this Nation and our laws are predicated."[5] Age, minority-group status, and religion are examples of *attitudinal* forces that can sway judicial behavior.

Furthermore, as the visitation-case dissent suggests, public opinion may be an important factor in answering questions about what molds judicial

---

[4] *Ex parte H.H.* (2002), rendered after the time frame of the book's database.
[5] On a lower state bench, the same judge gained wide public attention by hanging the Ten Commandments on his courtroom wall, and Alabama voters rewarded him with promotion to the state's top judicial post.

action. Alabama appellate judges are popularly elected to six-year terms of office, the shortest in the nation. Perhaps the motivating issue for the state high court was not its members' personal animus toward lesbians and gay men, as was certainly the circumstance for Judge McDunn in the Chicago adoption case. Maybe appellate judges otherwise tolerant of gay people were concerned about facing conservative Alabama voters at the next election more hostile to gay rights than, say, the Illinois electorate. Deciding a custody case in favor of a mother living openly with her lesbian lover and against a heterosexually married father might provide potent ammunition for a political opponent in a contested judicial race. Indeed, the history of state supreme court elections has at least one notorious example of incumbent justices losing bids to stay in office because of voter reaction to unpopular high court decisions ("After California, What's Next for Judicial Elections?" 1987; Grodin 1989). Yet if worry over remaining in office prompted the seven Alabama Supreme Court justices to deny the lesbian mother continued custody of her daughter, why didn't the five Alabama Court of Civil Appeals judges – who also face the same conservative voters every six years – vote against that mother, too? Judicial selection method and term length are instances of *institutional* factors possibly affecting how judges discharge their duties.

Additional hypotheses are available to explain the Alabama Supreme Court's actions. The visitation case was decided about four months before the custody appeal. In the former, the majority opinion noted that

the conduct inherent in lesbianism is illegal in Alabama [citing the state's consensual sodomy statute]. [The mother], therefore, is continually engaging in conduct that violates the criminal law of this state. Exposing her children to such a lifestyle, one that is illegal under the laws of this state and immoral in the eyes of most of its citizens, could greatly traumatize them. (717 So.2d at 796)

The court apparently viewed the restriction on the lesbian mother's visitation with her children merely as a mechanism of criminal code enforcement. Thus, the high court justices, regardless of both their personal attitudes toward homosexuality and their strategies for reelection to the bench, may have felt bound by the Alabama legislature's policy choices expressed in the state's criminal code. Restricting visitation, then, was nothing more than a simple act of judicial deference to majoritarian democracy by enforcing state laws enacted by the people's representatives. Sodomy statutes exemplify *environmental* determinants that may have an impact on judges' conduct.

Further, once the visitation case was rendered, it became binding precedent for the custody case that followed a few months later. That is, once the Alabama Supreme Court determined the state's sodomy law required limiting child visitation with homosexual parents, the next logical step would be denying child custody to those same parents. Accordingly, the Alabama Supreme Court justices who dissented so vigorously in the visitation decision may have felt legally bound by that precedent and therefore acquiesced to the custody denial.

Indeed, *stare decisis* is a fundamental notion in the American legal system, with adjudged cases furnishing authority for analogous future fact patterns or similar questions of law. The doctrine of precedent provides security and certainty, mandating established legal principles under which rights may accrue, be recognized, and be followed. *Stare decisis* facilitates a predictable system of laws and is a *legal* force potentially shaping court decisions.

As should be clear, divining the reasons for judicial behavior is not a simple task. Few instances are as unambiguous on their face as Judge McDunn in the Chicago adoption case. Thus, one can ask: How does a distant observer of judicial behavior ascertain whether judges are demonstrating bias for or prejudice against litigants, are motivated by other non-legal concerns such as winning an election, or indeed are acting as they perceive the law requires? I suggest the only meaningful way to make such distinctions is to investigate a wide array of court decisions systematically and to discern patterns of judicial behavior among them. This can be accomplished only through the kinds of sophisticated statistical analyses offered later in the book. For the moment, however, I return to storytelling.

Mississippi Outdoes Alabama: The Monstrous Stepfather
A sharper example of appellate court prejudice against gay parents comes from the Mississippi Supreme Court, where the opening paragraphs of a dissenting opinion place the case in bold relief:

The [trial judge] and majority believe a minor is best served by living in an explosive environment in which the unemployed stepfather is a convicted felon, drinker, drug-taker, adulterer, wife-beater, and child-threatener, and in which the mother has been transitory, works two jobs, and has limited time with the child. The [trial judge] makes such a decision despite the fact that the [biological] father has a good job, a stable home, and does all within his power to care for his son. The [trial judge] and majority are blinded by the fact that the father is gay. Such should not be the issue. The issue is that [the son] is living in a psychologically and physically dangerous environment from which he should be saved not blindly forced to remain. I dissent.

From the facts of this case, it is disturbingly clear that the majority, like the [trial judge,] has based its opinion neither on what is in the best interest of the child nor the law of child custody but on its own moral perceptions of human sexuality. The morality of homosexuality, however, should not be at issue before this Court or the lower court. Rather, the polestar consideration to which we are bound by the law to follow is whether a custody decision is in the best interests of the child. (*Weigand v. Houghton* MS 1999: 588)

Once more, the sole African American on the court dissented (in favor of a gay parent), while the Mississippi court's precedents against homosexual parents' rights and the state's consensual sodomy statute may have predisposed the majority. In addition, four majority justices had prior career experience in elective public office, two as state legislators for many years and another two as district attorneys. Perhaps, once on the bench, former legislators and executive officials defer to the nonjudicial branches for innovative government action. Thus, service in prior nonjudicial public office – another attitudinal force – may spawn ideologically conservative judicial practice.

The Child with Three Lesbian and Gay Parents

LaChapelle v. Mitten (MN 2000), the last CVAF case discussed here, exposes how complicated lesbian and gay parenting can be:

Mitten and Ohanian were lesbian partners [in Minnesota]. LaChapelle was in a gay partnership with another man. The four met in 1990 to discuss the possibility of conceiving and raising a child. They agreed in writing that LaChapelle would donate sperm for the artificial insemination of Mitten, that LaChapelle would have no parental rights, and that Mitten would not hold him responsible for the child. Mitten became pregnant in April 1992.

In May 1992, the four signed another agreement stating that Mitten and Ohanian would have physical and legal custody of the child and LaChapelle and his partner would be entitled to a "significant relationship" with the child. The child, L.M.K.O., was born January 4, 1993.

After L.M.K.O.'s birth, Mitten and Ohanian petitioned for adoption. On the petition they identified the father as "artificial insemination" and did not inform the court of the donor's identity or of the parties' various agreements. The court granted the adoption in September 1993.

LaChapelle visited L.M.K.O. regularly until August 1994, when Mitten and Ohanian terminated visitation. LaChapelle then moved the court to vacate the adoption, alleging fraud on the court for failure to disclose the parties' agreements. The court vacated the adoption. In August 1995, LaChapelle filed an affidavit with the court stating his intention to retain parental rights. He then filed a petition to adjudicate paternity. The court granted Mitten temporary custody of L.M.K.O.

Mitten and Ohanian ended their relationship in the spring of 1996. Later, Mitten requested the court's permission to move with L.M.K.O. to Michigan for employment reasons. At the same time, Ohanian petitioned for custody. The court granted Mitten's request pending further proceedings, ordered blood tests in the paternity action, and granted Ohanian's motion to consolidate her custody petition with LaChapelle's paternity petition.

Mitten moved to Michigan with L.M.K.O. in October 1996. The court granted visitation rights to Ohanian and LaChapelle while L.M.K.O. was in Michigan. One month they would fly to Michigan for three or four days. The next month L.M.K.O. would fly to Minnesota to visit them.

The court adjudicated LaChapelle to be L.M.K.O.'s biological father in June 1997, but allowed Mitten to retain interim custody. The court then ordered a custody and visitation evaluation, joined L.M.K.O. in the action, and appointed a guardian *ad litem* for her. In November 1997, the court ordered LaChapelle to pay past and future child support.

After a trial in February 1999, the court awarded sole physical custody of L.M.K.O. to Mitten on the condition that Mitten provide a permanent residence for L.M.K.O. in Minnesota. The court found that the parties had agreed before trial that Mitten and Ohanian would have joint legal custody of L.M.K.O., and the court ruled that such custody was in L.M.K.O.'s best interests. The court made awards of visitation [to LaChapelle and Ohanian], child support, and expenses for the daycare, medical, and dental needs of L.M.K.O.... (607 N.W.2d at 157–58)

The Minnesota Court of Appeals affirmed the trial court, thereby acknowledging the child had *three legally recognized **and honored** lesbian and gay parents*! What would the Alabama and Mississippi judges think about *that*?

As Table 1.3 indicates, Minnesota courts were far more receptive to lesbian and gay rights claims than tribunals in many other states during the twenty years of this study. A potential environmental explanation for comparative judicial hospitality in the Land of 10,000 Lakes occurred in 1993, when the Minnesota legislature adopted a gay civil rights law, banning discrimination based on sexual orientation in credit services, education, employment, public accommodations, public services, and real property transactions. Among seven decisions in the book's data set rendered before that legislation, four (57.1 percent) favored gay rights. Yet five (83.3 percent) of six cases decided after the statutory protection was in place were positive. In other words, the legislative cue may have prompted Minnesota judges to act ever more favorably toward the Gopher State's lesbian and gay citizens.

Indeed, environmental ideology may be a key concept for understanding why courts act as they do. The political ideology alone of states such as Alabama and Mississippi – regardless of the presence of sodomy statutes or how frequently judges are elected – may determine how courts adjudge civil rights, and differently than in Minnesota or Illinois. Likewise, the political climate prompting the Minnesota legislature to enact a gay civil rights statute may not exist (or at least not to the same degree) in Alabama or Mississippi.

Yet how does one capture empirically this notion of environmental ideology? The introductory chapter intimates that region itself may not be an adequate yardstick for measuring receptivity to civil rights claims. Recall that the exclusion of Missouri from the Midwest substantially boosted that area's average support for gay rights, while removing Florida from the South deflated that region's mean. Consequently, a state-by-state approach is likely to be more reliable than a regional formulation.

In fact, four political scientists (Berry et al. 1998) devised dynamic scales for citizen and government ideology in each of the fifty states. The Berry et al. evaluations are based on year-by-year combinations of the roll-call voting scores of state congressional delegations, the outcomes of congressional elections, the partisan division of state legislatures, and the political party of the governor. The Berry et al. citizen ideology measure is "the mean position on a liberal-conservative continuum of the 'active electorate' in a state," while their government ideology scale quantifies "the mean position on the same continuum of the elected officials in a state, weighted according to the power they have over public policy decisions" (ibid.: 327–28). Thus, when judges are popularly elected, the former number – capturing the relative ideological position of the voters who select and retain judges – is the appropriate dimension. In contrast, when judges are selected by state elites (typically through appointment and legislative confirmation) *and* not subject to retention elections, Berry et al. state government ideology scores are apt.

The Berry et al. measures range from 0 to 100. The lower the score, the more conservative the ideology, while the higher the number, the more liberal. For example, when the Alabama Supreme Court decided the lesbian mother visitation and custody cases, the Heart of Dixie's citizen ideology score was 41.51. When the Mississippi Supreme Court forced the boy to live with his monstrous stepfather, the Magnolia State's citizen ideology rating was 35.77. When the Minnesota Court of Appeals approved of three lesbian and gay parents for one child, the Gopher State's citizen ideology was 52.37.[6] Factoring such environmental ideology controls into

---

[6] Again, since Alabama, Minnesota, and Mississippi elect state judges, Berry et al. *citizen*, not *government*, ideology is the relevant measure.

the equation for what stimulates judicial behavior may substantially improve the probe. That, in fact, is what the next chapter's vote analysis (as opposed to the present case investigation) does.

Lesbian and Gay Family Issues Not Involving CVAF

Appendix 2.1 contains seventy-seven non-CVAF lesbian and gay family cases covering a broad range of issues, often affecting the rights and responsibilities of the domestic partners of gay people.

The Jilted – but Prudent – Domestic Partner

Nancy Layton was a doctor practicing at the Halifax Hospital in Volusia County [, Florida,] and Emma Posik was a nurse working at the same facility when Dr. Layton decided to remove her practice to Brevard County. In order to induce Ms. Posik to give up her job and sell her home in Volusia County, to accompany her to Brevard County, and to reside with her "for the remainder of Emma Posik's life to maintain and care for the home," Dr. Layton agreed that she would provide essentially all of the support for the two, would make a will leaving her entire estate to Ms. Posik, and would "maintain bank accounts and other investments which constitute non-probatable assets in Emma Posik's name to the extent of 100% of her entire non-probatable assets." Also, as a part of the agreement, Ms. Posik agree to loan Dr. Layton $20,000 which was evidenced by a note. The agreement provided that Ms. Posik could cease residing with Dr. Layton if Layton failed to provide adequate support, if she requested in writing that Ms. Posik leave for any reason, if she brought a third person into the home for a period greater than four weeks without Ms. Posik's consent, or if her abuse, harassment or abnormal behavior made Ms. Posik's continued residence intolerable. In any such event, Dr. Layton agreed to pay as liquidated damages the sum of $2,500 per month for the remainder of Ms. Posik's life.

It is apparent that Ms. Posik required this agreement as a condition of accompanying Dr. Layton to Brevard. The agreement was drawn by a lawyer and properly witnessed. Ms. Posik, fifty-five years old at the time of the agreement, testified that she required the agreement because she feared that Dr. Layton might become interested in a younger companion. Her fears were well founded. Some four years after the parties moved to Brevard County and without Ms. Posik's consent, Dr. Layton announced that she wished to move another woman into the house. When Ms. Posik expressed strong displeasure with this idea, Dr. Layton moved out and took up residence with the other woman.

Dr. Layton served a three-day eviction notice on Ms. Posik. Ms. Posik later moved from the home and sued to enforce the terms of the agreement and to collect on the note evidencing the loan made in conjunction with the agreement. Dr. Layton defended on the basis that Ms. Posik first breached the agreement. Dr. Layton counterclaimed for a declaratory judgment as to whether the liquidated damages portion of the agreement was enforceable.

The trial judge found that because Ms. Posik's economic losses were reasonably ascertainable as to her employment and relocation costs, the $2,500 a month payment upon breach amounted to a penalty and was therefore unenforceable. The court further found that although Dr. Layton had materially breached the contract within a year or so of its creation, Ms. Posik waived the breach by acquiescence. Finally, the court found that Ms. Posik breached the agreement by refusing to continue to perform the house work, yard work and cooking for the parties and by her hostile attitude which required Dr. Layton to move from the house. Although the trial court determined that Ms. Posik was entitled to quantum meruit [i.e., the reasonable value of services rendered], it also determined that those damages were off-set by the benefits Ms. Posik received by being permitted to live with Dr. Layton. The court did award Ms. Posik a judgment on the note executed by Dr. Layton. (*Posik v. Layton* FL 1997: 760–61)

Thus, despite the written agreement between the parties, the Florida trial court allowed Posik only to get back her $20,000 loan from Layton after their breakup. Posik appealed, and the District Court of Appeal reversed the trial court:

The obligations imposed on Ms. Posik by the agreement include the obligation "to immediately commence residing with Nancy L. R. Layton at her said residence for the remainder of Emma Posik's life. . . ." This is very similar to a "until death do us part" commitment. And although the parties undoubtedly expected a sexual relationship, this record shows that they contemplated much more. They contracted for a permanent sharing of, and participating in, one another's lives. We find the contract enforceable.

We disagree with the trial court that waiver was proved in this case. Ms. Posik consistently urged Dr. Layton to make the will as required by the agreement and her failure to do so was sufficient grounds to declare default. And even more important to Ms. Posik was the implied agreement that her lifetime commitment would be reciprocated by a lifetime commitment by Dr. Layton – and that this mutual commitment would be monogamous. When Dr. Layton introduced a third person into the relationship, although it was not an express breach of the written agreement, it explains why Ms. Posik took that opportunity to hold Dr. Layton to her express obligations and to consider the agreement in default.

We also disagree with the trial court that Ms. Posik breached the agreement by refusing to perform house work, yard work, provisioning the house, and cooking for the parties. This conduct did not occur until after Dr. Layton had first breached the agreement. One need not continue to perform a contract when the other party has first breached. [Citation omitted.] Therefore, this conduct did not authorize Dr. Layton to send the three-day notice of eviction, which constituted a separate default under the agreement.

We also disagree that the commitment to pay $2,500 per month upon termination of the agreement is unenforceable as a penalty. We agree with Ms. Posik that her damages, which would include more than lost wages and moving expenses, were not readily ascertainable at the time the contract was created. Further, the agreed sum is reasonable under the circumstances of this case. It is less than

Ms. Posik was earning some four years earlier when she entered into this arrangement. It is also less than Ms. Posik would have received had the long-term provisions of the contract been performed. She is now in her sixties and her working opportunities are greatly reduced.

We recognize that this contract, insisted on by Ms. Posik before she would relocate with Dr. Layton, is extremely favorable to her. But there is no allegation of fraud or overreaching on Ms. Posik's part. . . . "The freedom to contract includes the right to make a bad bargain.". . .

Contracts can be dangerous to one's well-being. That is why they are kept away from children. Perhaps warning labels should be attached. In any event, contracts should be taken seriously. Dr. Layton's comment that she considered the agreement a sham and never intended to be bound by it shows that she did not take it seriously. That is regrettable. (695 So.2d at 762–63)

Emma Posik acted wisely to protect her interests legally before rushing off to live happily ever after with Nancy Layton. Equally noteworthy is that the Florida appellate court treated the parties' relationship as something substantially more than a sexual one. The judges honored the women's involvement as a personal, loving commitment. In effect, the contract converted the bond into a marriage, and the philandering spouse paid alimony to the aggrieved one.

The Bereft – and Unprotected – Domestic Partner

Unlike heterosexuals, however, lesbians and gay men in domestic relationships that are not as well planned as the one in *Posik* are not otherwise defended by the state:

William Thomas Cooper died on February 19, 1988. The decedent died testate [i.e., with a last will and testament], leaving everything to [Ernest Chin] as a specific and residuary legatee, with the exception of certain real estate, allegedly constituting over 80 percent of the value of the estate, which was left to a former homosexual lover of the decedent.

In support of this proceeding to determine that he is entitled to exercise a right of election against the decedent's will [i.e., New York law permits surviving spouses to take up to 50 percent of deceased spouses' estates, regardless of will provisions to the contrary], [Chin] alleged, *inter alia*, as follows:

"I met William Cooper in 1984. From approximately the middle of 1984 until his sudden death from a congenital heart condition in February 1988, I lived with him . . . in a spousal-type situation. Except for the fact that we were of the same sex, our lives were identical to that of a husband and wife. We kept a common home; we shared expenses; our friends recognized us as spouses; we had a physical relationship. Of course, we could not obtain a marriage license because no marriage license clerk in New York will issue such a document to two people of the same sex."

"The only reason Mr. Cooper and I were not legally married is because marriage license clerks in New York State will not issue licenses to persons of the same sex."

"However unconstitutional the denial of the right to a marriage license to Mr. Cooper and myself may have been, the Court cannot undo that now that Mr. Cooper is deceased. Since the Court, however, also is an instrument of the State ... it cannot compound this unconstitutionality by saying that because we could not obtain a State-issued marriage license, I cannot be recognized as a spouse by [the] State Court for the purpose of claiming spousal rights."

"I ask this Court simply to declare that *if* I can establish that Mr. Cooper and I, at the time of his death, were living in a spousal-type relationship, I am entitled to spousal rights, and the State-imposed unconstitutional impediment of making it impossible for two people of the same sex to obtain a marriage license does not alter this."

... [The trial court] held that a survivor of a homosexual relationship, alleged to be a "spousal relationship," was not entitled to a right of election against the decedent's will pursuant to [New York law].... (*Matter of Cooper* NY 1993: 797–98; emphasis in the original)

The appellate court affirmed the trial court, and Chin ended up with less than 20 percent of Cooper's estate, instead of the 50 percent he sought. Indeed, without Cooper's will, Chin would have gotten nothing – although married spouses in New York receive up to 50 percent of estates by law even when their partners die without wills. Hence, gay people have a special burden to plan their relationships legally that straight counterparts do not have.

Was the fact that Emma Posik documented her relationship with Nancy Layton by means of a written contract – and Ernest Chin did not do the same regarding his with William Cooper – the dispositive issue causing Posik to win and Chin to lose? Indeed, heeding state environmental factors, an informed observer might easily have guessed the opposite result: a win for lesbian and gay rights in New York and a loss in Florida. The Berry et al. citizen ideology score for the Empire State in 1993 was 70.73, while the Sunshine State's citizen ideology in 1997 measured 44.60.[7] In addition, Florida had an enforceable sodomy statute, while New York did not. Thus, the combination of two ostensibly important components of environmental ideology created a strong expectation for a different outcome. What happened?

Attitudinal forces most likely overcame the environmental context. The four New York appellate judges denying Chin's claim were Roman

---

[7] The judges of the New York appellate court deciding *Matter of Cooper* are popularly elected, while Florida uses merit selection with retention elections.

Catholic, while the Florida jurists acknowledging the worth of Posik's relationship with Layton were Episcopalian and Presbyterian. Catholic Church dogma is less tolerant of gays than the policies of liberal Protestant denominations such as the Episcopal and Presbyterian churches. In short, the attitudinal force of religion apparently played a decisive role in determining these domestic partners' legal rights.

What is more, three of the four New York judges served in prior non-judicial elective office, while none of the Florida jurists did.

A Sheltering State

Fortunately, the law does shield gay couples on rare occasion:

[The Oregon Health Sciences University (OHSU)] provided group health insurance benefits to its employees. It provided each employee a certain amount of money and authorized each employee to select insurance benefits within the limits of the money provided. In accordance with [State Employees' Benefits Board (SEBB)] eligibility criteria, OHSU permitted employees to purchase insurance coverage for "family members." Under the SEBB criteria, unmarried domestic partners of employees were not "family members" who were entitled to insurance coverage.

Plaintiffs are three lesbian nursing professionals employed by OHSU and their unmarried domestic partners. Each of the couples has enjoyed a long-term and committed relationship, which each wishes to continue for life. Each of the couples would be married if Oregon law permitted homosexual couples to marry.

All three OHSU employees applied for medical and dental insurance benefits for their domestic partners. The OHSU benefits manager refused to process the applications on the ground that the domestic partners of the employees did not meet the SEBB eligibility criteria. . . .

At trial, the parties stipulated that OHSU paid the same amount of money for a fringe benefit package to all employees in a given category, without regard to marital status or sexual orientation. The parties further stipulated that, in administering its employee benefits program, OHSU treated heterosexual unmarried couples and homosexual unmarried couples the same. . . . OHSU elicited testimony from the State Administrator of the Human Resource Management Division of the Department of Administrative Services that the sex or sexual orientation of employees was not taken into account in any way in the administration of state benefits programs. Plaintiffs offered no contrary testimony. . . .

[The trial court] enjoined the State of Oregon, OHSU, SEBB, and the State Board of Higher Education from continuing the practice of denying group life, health, and dental insurance coverage to domestic partners of homosexual employees when those benefits are offered to spouses of heterosexual employees. The judgment defined "domestic partners" as homosexual persons not related by blood closer than first cousins who are not legally married, who have continuously lived together in an exclusive and loving relationship that they intend to maintain for the rest of their lives, who have joint financial accounts and joint financial responsibilities, who would be married to each other if Oregon law permitted it, who have no other domestic partners, and who are 18 years of age or older....

Defendants appealed....

Plaintiffs acknowledge that, at least on the surface, OHSU denied benefits to unmarried domestic partners of its employees without regard to their sexual orientation. They argue that OHSU's denial of benefits to domestic partners nevertheless violates [Oregon law] because, although OHSU's denials did not facially discriminate against homosexual couples, the denials had the effect of discriminating against homosexual couples. That is so, plaintiffs argue, because homosexual couples cannot marry. Heterosexual couples can marry and thus at least have the option of doing so to avail themselves of the employee benefits; homosexual couples cannot marry and have no such option. Because of the disparate impact on homosexual couples of denying benefits on the otherwise facially neutral basis of marital status, plaintiffs argue, OHSU has discriminated on the basis of the sex of persons with whom employees associate, in violation of [Oregon law]....

[T]he Oregon Constitution ... provides:

"No law shall be passed granting to any citizen or class of citizens privileges or immunities, which, upon the same terms, shall not equally belong to all citizens."

... [T]here is no question but that plaintiffs are members of a ... class – unmarried homosexual couples – ... [that] clearly is defined in terms of ad hominem, personal and social characteristics.... Sexual orientation, like gender, race, alienage, and religious affiliation is widely regarded as defining a distinct, socially recognized group of citizens, and certainly it is beyond dispute that homosexuals in our society have been and continue to be the subject of adverse social and political stereotyping and prejudice....

OHSU's defense is that it determined eligibility for insurance benefits on the basis of marital status, not sexual orientation. According to OHSU, the fact that such a facially neutral classification has the unintended side effect of discriminating against homosexual couples who cannot marry is not actionable under [the Oregon Constitution]. We are not persuaded by the asserted defense.... OHSU has taken action with no apparent intention to treat disparately members of any true class of citizens. Nevertheless, its actions have the undeniable effect of doing just that.... OHSU's intentions in this case are not relevant. What is relevant is the extent to which privileges or immunities are not made available to all citizens on equal terms.

OHSU insists that in this case privileges and immunities are available to all on equal terms: All married employees – heterosexual and homosexual alike – are permitted to acquire insurance benefits for their spouses. That reasoning misses the point, however. Homosexual couples may not marry. Accordingly, the benefits are not made available on equal terms. They are made available on terms that, for gay and lesbian couples, are a legal impossibility.

We conclude that OHSU's denial of insurance benefits to the unmarried domestic partners of its homosexual employees violated [the Oregon Constitution]. (*Tanner v. Oregon Health Services University* OR 1998: 437–48)

Lamentably, the decision of the Oregon Court of Appeals is an exceptional judicial response to the denial of health insurance and other benefits to the domestic partners of lesbian and gay state employees. The courts in *Hinman v. Department of Personnel Administration* (CA 1985), *Ross v. Denver Department of Health and Hospitals* (CO 1994), *Rutgers Council of AAUP Chapters v. Rutgers, the State University* (NJ 1997), and *Phillips v. Wisconsin Personnel Commission* (WI 1992) refused to recognize gay domestic partners as family members entitled to such coverage.

Prospective attitudinal explanations for the Oregon Court of Appeal's progressive approach are that two judges on the panel were Jewish and the third was a woman. Whereas eight of ten judges in the book's data set voting against domestic partner benefits in the California, Colorado, New Jersey, and Wisconsin cases were not Jewish, and all were men. Jews are significantly more permissive than other Americans with regard to social codes, particularly issues relating to sex (Cohen and Liebman 1997). Women have more favorable attitudes toward gays and lesbians than do men (Herek 1993: 123; Kite and Whitley 1996) and are more supportive of homosexual rights (Haeberle 1999; Schroedel 1999: 110). Accordingly, judges' gender and religious affiliations may have been of crucial importance in Oregon.

Moreover, as in the Alabama lesbian mother visitation case, age may have played a role, too. The Oregon judges' average age was fifty, while the mean age in the four other domestic partner benefits decisions was sixty-two.

The Triumphant Peeping Tom

The last non-CVAF family story comes from Mississippi, with its evidently inexhaustible supply of captivating case facts:

Glenn Michael and his wife were divorced. They had one female child who was about six years old at the time of trial. The [trial court] gave custody of the child to Michael's wife[, who lived with the child] in a cabin that had been rented by Michael as the family home prior to their divorce. [Rita] Plaxico moved into the cabin with Michael's former wife and his child sometime after the divorce.

Michael was later informed that his ex-wife was having a relationship with ... Plaxico. Michael wanted to modify the child custody based on the fact that his former wife and Plaxico were romantically involved with each other.

[One night,] Michael slipped up to a window in the cabin through which [he] witnessed Plaxico and his former wife having sexual relations. He left to retrieve a camera from his [truck]. After doing so, he returned and took three photographs of Plaxico, who was sitting in bed naked. However, the bed covers covered her from the waist down.

Michael had the photographs developed and delivered the pictures to his attorney. He then ... filed for modification of child custody. Michael testified that he did not show the photographs to anyone other than his lawyer. His lawyer produced the photographs to Michael's former wife's attorney in response to discovery requests in the child custody matter pending between Michael and his former wife in which the [trial judge] granted Michael the custody of the child. Plaxico became aware of the photographs through Michael's former wife's attorney, who represented both Plaxico and Mrs. Michael.

Plaxico subsequently filed suit [against Michael] for invasion of privacy. She claimed that Michael intentionally intruded upon her seclusion and solitude, and she suffered damages as a result of this tort. She further testified and acknowledged that she and Michael's former wife were lovers and had engaged in sexual relations. Plaxico's complaint and action were dismissed by the [trial court], and appealed to this Court....

Plaxico did not prove each element of intentional intrusion upon solitude or seclusion of another. Plaxico was in a state of solitude or seclusion in the privacy of her bedroom where she had an expectation of privacy. However, we conclude that a reasonable person would not feel Michael's interference with Plaxico's seclusion was a substantial one that would rise to the level of gross offensiveness as required to prove the sub-tort of intentional intrusion upon seclusion or solitude....

... Michael [wanted] to file for modification of child custody. However, he had no proof that there actually was [a] lesbian sexual relationship which could be adversely affecting his minor child. In order to obtain such proof, he went to the cabin, peered through the window and took pictures of the two women engaged in sexual conduct. Three pictures were actually developed which were of Plaxico in a naked state from her waist up in her bed. Michael believed that he took these pictures for the sole purpose to protect his minor child. Although these actions were done without Plaxico's consent, this conduct is not highly offensive to the ordinary person which would cause the reasonable person to object. In fact, most reasonable persons would feel Michael's actions were justified in order to protect the welfare of his minor child. Therefore, the elements necessary to establish the tort of intentional intrusion upon solitude or seclusion are not present. (*Plaxico v. Michael* MS 1999: 1038–40)

The Mississippi Supreme Court's remarkable majority opinion provoked dissent:

Upon the apparent theory that no reasonable person could believe that the ends do not justify the means in this case[,] the majority opinion improperly concludes that Michael's unreasonably intrusive conduct would not be highly offensive to a reasonable person. I disagree with both the premise and the conclusion. Accordingly, I respectfully dissent.

In my view, peeping into the bedroom window of another is a gross invasion of privacy which may subject one to liability for intentional intrusion upon the solitude or seclusion of that other. [Citations omitted.]

The trial court found refuge in what it found to be a qualified privilege to see to the best interest of a child. Neither rumors concerning an ex-wife's lifestyle nor a parent's justifiable concern over the best of interests of his child, however, gave Michael license to spy on a person's bedroom, take photographs of her in a semi-nude state and have those photographs developed by third parties and de-livered to his attorney thereby exposing them to others. . . .

In another context, we have observed that "the end does not justify the means. . . . Our society is one of law, not expediency. This message must be re-peated at every opportunity. . . ." [Citation omitted.] I regret that today's majority here does not follow these worthy ideals. (735 So.2d at 1040–41)

Again, personal attributes seemingly help explain case outcome. The Mississippi Supreme Court's only minority justice and its only woman both voted in dissent (favoring the lesbian litigant), while four members of the majority had prior career experience in nonjudicial elective office. Further, a majority of judges voting against the rights claim were Republi-cans, when a majority favoring it were Democrats. This partisan difference may be important because Democratic judges generally are more liberal than Republican counterparts (Pinello 1999).

Cases Adjudicating Sexual Orientation Discrimination Claims Not Related to Lesbian and Gay Family Issues

Appendix 2.2 lists eighty nonfamily cases involving invidious discrimina-tion against gay people.

The Drunk and the Fabricated Lesbian

Perhaps the most astounding case facts in the book's database come from *Stemler v. City of Florence* (6th Cir. 1997):

On February 18, 1994, at about 10:45 p.m., Conni Black and her boyfriend, Steve Kritis, arrived at Willie's Saloon in the Ramada Inn in Florence, Kentucky. Both Black and Kritis had been drinking heavily. While line dancing, Black met Susan Stemler. Around 2:00 a.m., the two went to the women's restroom and discussed problems that each had with their respective boyfriends. During this conversation, Black told Stemler that she wanted to leave Kritis. According to one witness, Christine Stillwell:

"Steve Kritis then burst into the restroom and slung the door to the restroom hard. He came into the restroom yelling. He stated in part, 'If you don't get your fucking sister out of here, I'll kill the bitch.' He yelled this at Laura Stemler."

"He grabbed Conni . . . as he screamed at her. He slammed her against a toilet stall. He then yanked her out of the restroom. After he left . . . I could still hear him screaming. . . ."

"At this point, I wondered why nobody had called the police. When I went out . . . into the lobby of the Ramada, I observed Kritis pushing Conni around. . . ."

According to Stemler, after Kritis removed Black from the restroom, Kritis slammed Black against a concrete wall in the hotel lobby; Black's head hit the wall and she briefly passed out. Black asked Stemler to drive her home, and Stemler agreed. As they were leaving, Kritis struck Stemler in the back of the head with a blunt object. Stemler and Black got into Stemler's car and drove away at about 2:15 a.m. Kritis pursued them in his truck. Kritis did not have his headlights on. At one point during the chase, Kritis rear-ended Stemler's car with his truck in an attempt to make her car stop. A witness, Terry Barker, was driving east on U.S. 42 in Florence at the time; he saw that Kritis was chasing the women and that the women were in obvious distress, and decided to follow the vehicles.

According to Barker, at one point the truck got ahead of the car and forced it down Woodland Avenue, which ends in a cul-de-sac. Stemler pulled her car into a driveway, and Kritis stopped his car behind her to block her access to the street. Fortunately, the driveway belonged to William Minnick, a retired Florence police officer. His wife, Nancy Minnick, heard a horn blowing at about 2:30 a.m. When she opened her door, she saw Kritis standing in her driveway on the passenger side of the car. Kritis was hitting the car window and yelling. The car backed out around the truck and drove up the street. Kritis jumped in [his truck] and again gave chase; according to Barker, he was driving at about sixty miles per hour on the sidewalk of the residential street. By this point, Mr. Minnick was awake and dressed; he called 911, and then got in his car and followed Kritis and Stemler. Barker also continued to follow them.

After the vehicles pulled back on to U.S. 42 ... Barker flashed his lights to alert ... Lieutenant Thomas Dusing, an officer of the Florence Police Department, who was responding to the 911 call. When Dusing pulled up to Barker, Barker informed him that there was a "serious problem" with the two vehicles ahead of him, and that Kritis appeared to be a threat to the safety of the two women. After speaking with Barker, Dusing pulled his cruiser in front of Stemler's car and Kritis's truck at the intersection. As he left the cruiser, Stemler jumped out of her car and ran to him. Stemler told Dusing that Kritis was drunk, that he had assaulted both her and Black, that he had threatened to kill her, and that he had placed both of them in danger by chasing after them at high speed. She was obviously emotionally distraught, and cried while she related the evening's events to Dusing. While Dusing spoke with Stemler, four other officers arrived at the scene in separate cars: officers Bobby Joe Wince and John Dolan of the Florence Police Department, and officers Rob Reuthe and Chris Alsip of the Boone County Sheriff's Office. . . .

During Stemler's conversation with Dusing, Reuthe approached Kritis, who was seated in his truck. Acording to Reuthe's testimony, Kritis told him that Stemler was a lesbian [a footnote here in the court's opinion states: Stemler denies that she is a lesbian.], and that she was kidnapping his girlfriend. After speaking with Stemler, Dusing approached Reuthe; Dusing would later testify that Reuthe told him at that time that Stemler was a lesbian. Reuthe also told Dusing that Kritis smelled of alcohol, but that he had not tested Kritis for intoxication. Dusing then approached Kritis, who repeated his assertion that Stemler was a lesbian. Kritis also asked Dusing to bring Black to his truck; Dusing told him that he would see what he could do. Dusing asked Kritis whether he had seen Stemler driving the car, and whether he would be willing to testify against Stemler.

Dusing would later submit a police report claiming that he did not smell alcohol on Kritis's breath at that time. This claim is contrary to his contemporaneous statements to Wince and to Mr. Minnick that Kritis smelled of alcohol. A blood test taken over two hours later would reveal that Kritis had a blood alcohol level of .115, which indicates that at the time of the police stop, his blood alcohol level was probably between .155 and .175, at least one-and-a-half times the legal limit in Kentucky of .10. Subsequent observers would also testify that, over an hour after the police stop, it was immediately apparent that Kritis was very drunk. Nevertheless, neither Dusing nor any other officer ever tested Kritis for intoxication, or even asked him to step out of the truck.

At some point, Dusing asked Wince to test Stemler for intoxication. By that time, Wince had already heard Kritis's allegation that Stemler was a lesbian. Wince did not find any of the standard DUI indicators in examining Stemler; she did not have affected speech, impaired balance, impaired walking, or impaired coordination, and she did not seem disoriented. According to Wince, Stemler failed the horizontal nystagmus gaze field test, a test in which uncontrolled movement in a suspect's eyes may indicate drunkenness. However, Stemler alleges that Wince did not know how to perform that test properly, and had to ask for assistance with the test from Dolan. Stemler alleges further that Dolan also did not know how to perform the nystagmus test. Wince testified that the breathalyzer revealed a blood alcohol level of .105. Stemler alleges that the breathalyzer was not properly calibrated.

After performing the field tests, Wince conferred with Dusing and Dolan. By this time, all three officers had heard Kritis's claim that Stemler was a lesbian. Dusing decided that they should arrest Stemler for driving under the influence, and the other officers agreed. Dusing would later concede that, in deciding to arrest Stemler and not Kritis, he relied on Kritis's version of events more than he did Stemler's. Wince approached Stemler, informed her that she was under arrest, and asked her who she would like to tow her car. Stemler broke into tears, pointed at Kritis, and asked Wince, "Aren't you going to check him? Why don't you check him?" As she was pointing, Wince grabbed her arm, pulled it behind her, and placed her in handcuffs.

At approximately the same time, two unknown officers, one each from Florence and from Boone County, approached Barker, who was parked across the street. Barker related the complete story of the chase to both officers. Barker overheard one of the officers relating his story to a third officer. The officers asked him whether he saw Stemler driving the car, and whether he would be willing to testify against Stemler in court. Upon learning that Stemler was being placed under arrest, Barker told the officers that they were arresting the wrong person and that Kritis was obviously "crazy"; the officers didn't appreciate that, became "arrogant," and told him that he didn't "know what's going on" and that he could "go on about your business." Barker was dumbfounded and angered by the officers' actions. Barker confirms that the police never asked Kritis to leave the truck, despite the fact that, as during the chase, Kritis still had not turned his headlights on. Although the officers told Barker that they would contact him to be a witness against Stemler, they never did so. Furthermore, Wince failed to list Barker as a witness at the scene in his field notes, and the card on which the officers supposedly were writing down Barker's name and telephone number were lost.

While Wince was testing Stemler for intoxication, Mr. Minnick arrived at the scene. He spoke first with ... Boone County Officer Chris Alsip. Alsip immediately "informed" him that Stemler was a lesbian. Minnick thought that it was odd that Alsip could state that fact with such certainty, given that Stemler had out-of-state license plates. Wince also made a point of informing Minnick that Stemler was a lesbian. Although the officers at the police stop were aware that Minnick had observed Kritis chasing Stemler, they asked him only whether [he] observed Stemler driving her car.

Dusing ordered Dolan to approach Black, who was still in the passenger seat of Stemler's car, and to inform her that she would be arrested for public intoxication "if she didn't want to leave with the male." At that time, Black was very intoxicated; her eyes were glassy and she slurred her words. Alsip and Dolan lifted her out of the car and assisted her to Kritis's truck. Black stumbled as she walked to the truck. Alsip physically placed her into the passenger seat in the truck. Alsip would later admit that he never heard Black say that she wanted to leave with Kritis. Dusing told Alsip only that Stemler was a lesbian and that Kritis did not want his girlfriend with her; Alsip would later concede that, if he had known of all the preceding events that evening, he would not have placed Black in the truck but instead would have arrested Kritis.

As soon as Black was in the truck, at about 3:00 a.m., Kritis drove away. Kritis drove two blocks from the police stop and then turned onto the northbound lanes of I-75. Black had passed out in the truck. According to Kritis, when she woke up, she "went haywire" and began hitting him; he hit her back and lost control of the truck. The truck swerved to the right and collided side-to-side with a guardrail. The impact threw Black partially out of the passenger side window. Black's arm was completely severed from her body and her head was severed into two parts. The truck was damaged and the front tire was blown. Kritis continued to drive slowly on I-75 and then east on I-275 until the truck could proceed no further.

A passing motorist, Kristopher Waldespuhl, was waved down by Kritis around 3:45 a.m. Kritis said, "my girlfriend is kind of hurt," and asked for help. According to Waldespuhl, Kritis spoke "very nonchalantly," and "had no emotions at all, wasn't upset." It was immediately obvious to Waldespuhl that Kritis was drunk; Kritis had alcohol on his breath, his eyes were glazed and bloodshot, and he was not acting sober. Kritis admitted to Waldespuhl that he was drunk. He also told Waldespuhl that "they were fighting at Willie's and some dyke bitch took her from me." Waldespuhl walked over to the other side of the truck. It was immediately apparent to Waldespuhl that Black was dead, although Kritis was unaware of this fact. Waldespuhl left to place a 911 call.

Officer Stephen Johnson of the Lakeside Park-Crestview Police Department arrived at the scene. It was obvious to Johnson that Kritis was drunk; he did not even need to conduct a field sobriety test to determine that he had probable cause to arrest Kritis. Another officer at the scene, Mike Mann, also immediately determined that Kritis was drunk. According to Mann, "Steve Kritis told me that he and his girlfriend were fighting and exchanging blows. He stated that he felt a large 'thud' but continued driving the truck. His truck started to quit and he pulled over." Johnson placed Kritis under arrest for driving under the influence at 4:30 a.m.

An accident reconstruction specialist, Detective Jack Prindle, determined that, at the time of the impact with the guardrail, the truck was traveling at sixty-six miles per hour. The truck had traveled from the scene of the police stop to the scene of the accident in about five minutes. The accident occurred when the steering wheel turned abruptly to the right; there is no way to know what caused the wheel to turn. As the vehicle struck the guardrail, Black was partially ejected, causing her head and right arm to be severed on the guardrail. Kritis continued on for 2.5 miles before stopping.

After arresting Stemler, Wince took her for a blood test. Stemler claims that she had had only a half-glass of beer and two Irish coffees over the course of the night. She suspects that the officers tampered with her blood sample, which allegedly revealed a .17 blood alcohol level an hour after the breathalyzer allegedly revealed a .105 blood alcohol level. Wince handled her blood sample after he learned that Black had died. Larry Dehus, a "forensic scientist," reviewed the specimens and the timing of the tests and concluded that the sample's integrity had been destroyed, given that Wince waited five days to deliver the sample and that there were no procedures to guard against tampering. When a blood sample is submitted to the detective's office of the Florence Police Department, the clerk of that office, Mary Hayes, is supposed to receive a property card and an evidence tag; Hayes never received either with respect to Stemler's blood sample. This was a violation of department policy. Stemler's sample was the only sample that Wince had ever kept in the Florence Police Department refrigerator for five days in his career, and was also the only sample that he had ever personally driven to the lab. According to Officer Chester Snow, who supervised the property room, it would be "highly irregular" to keep a sample in the refrigerator for five days.

Stemler was prosecuted in the Boone County District Court for driving under the influence of alcohol. She defended the charge on the ground that the evidence against her had been fabricated. Dr. Gordon James testified at her trial that the handling of the blood sample was "arbitrary" and that the chain of custody had not been established. Her first trial resulted in a hung jury. She was retried. Although Wince claimed at Stemler's first DUI trial that he had not completed an evidence card, at the retrial he produced a completed card which neither Hayes nor Snow had ever seen. He claimed that he completed the card on February 19, at the time of the arrest. Hayes testified that if that were true, she should have seen the card. The second jury acquitted Stemler. (126 F.3d at 860–64; footnotes omitted)

Steve Kritis plead guilty in state court to manslaughter in the second degree for Conni Black's death and to wanton endangerment in the first degree. Astonishingly, he was sentenced only to probation, although a probation violation brought a five-year prison term.

Susan Stemler sued the City of Florence and Police Officers Dolan, Dusing, and Wince for false arrest, malicious prosecution, and violation of equal protection, alleging the officers arrested her solely because they believed her to be lesbian. The federal trial court found in favor of the defendants and against Stemler. On appeal, the U.S. Court of Appeals reversed:

We believe that this is the rare case in which a plaintiff has successfully stated a claim of selective prosecution.... [T]he defendant officers chose to arrest and prosecute her for driving under the influence because they perceived her to be a lesbian, and out of a desire to effectuate an animus against homosexuals. Each of the defendants was aware of Kritis's assertion that Stemler was a lesbian, and Dusing admitted that he relied on Kritis's version of the facts in deciding to arrest Stemler. Furthermore, the record supports a finding that Kritis was similarly situated to Stemler (or, indeed, far drunker than she), that the defendant officers perceived Kritis to be heterosexual, and that consequently they chose not to arrest him at the same time that they arrested Stemler.

The defendants concede that Stemler's complaint alleges, and the record evidence could support a finding, that they decided to arrest and prosecute her because they perceived her to be a lesbian. They do not attempt to assert any justification whatsoever for this decision; instead they argue that as a blanket matter it is always constitutional to discriminate on the basis of sexual orientation, citing *Bowers v. Hardwick* [U.S. Sup. Ct 1986]. However, *Bowers* held only that there is no substantive due process right to engage in homosexual sodomy, and expressly declined to consider an equal protection claim.... It is inconceivable that *Bowers* stands for the proposition that the state may discriminate against individuals on the basis of their sexual orientation solely out of animus to that orientation: " 'If the constitutional conception of equal protection of the laws means anything, it must at the very least mean that a bare desire to harm a politically unpopular group cannot constitute a legitimate governmental interest.' " *Romer v. Evans* [U.S. Sup. Ct. 1996] ... Stated differently, since governmental action "must bear a rational relationship to a legitimate governmental purpose," *Romer*..., and the desire to effectuate one's animus against homosexuals can never be a legitimate governmental purpose, a state action based on that animus alone violates the Equal Protection Clause....

It is beyond cavil that Stemler has adequately alleged a selective-enforcement claim here. The record supports a finding that she was perceived to be a member of "an identifiable group," and that defendants sought to implement their animus against that group by arresting and seeking to prosecute her. The defendants officers are unable, and indeed have not even attempted, to demonstrate that there is any conceivable rational basis for a decision to enforce the drunk-driving laws against homosexuals but not against heterosexuals. The defendants can rely only on their assertion that discrimination on the basis of sexual orientation should be accorded no scrutiny whatsoever. We emphatically reject this assertion; the proposition that the state may constitutionally discriminate by enforcing laws only against homosexuals ... is not now, and never has been, the law. Under the facts [of this case], the defendants violated the core principle of the Equal Protection Clause by choosing to exercise the power of the state against Stemler solely for the reason that they disapproved of her perceived sexual orientation. (126 F.3d at 873–74)

The *Stemler* case is remarkable not only for its extraordinary facts – a drunkard's *mere allegation* of lesbianism prompted five police officers to deviate dramatically from standard law enforcement procedure, culminating in the loss of a life – but also because a federal appellate court upheld a claim of invidious discrimination based on sexual orientation, though by a vote of just two to one. The mean of **outcome** for the federal court decisions in Appendix 2.2 is .135 – only five of thirty-seven federal cases involving sexual orientation discrimination resulted in rulings favorable to lesbians and gay men.

Indeed, an argument can be made that *Stemler* is not a bona fide gay rights victory. Recall that Steve Kritis *falsely* accused Susan Stemler of lesbianism, and the police officers believed him. Moreover, it's clear from the court's opinion that the judges accepted her heterosexuality as fact. Thus, the nature of the sexual orientation discrimination in the lawsuit was that state officials seriously mistreated a straight person they mistakenly thought was gay. Would the decision have been as favorable to Stemler if she in fact were a lesbian?

The following case, and others like it, reasonably lead to an answer of "No."

The Brutally Harassed Gay Postal Worker

Much more typical of federal court treatment of prejudice against gay people is *Simonton v. Runyon* (2nd Cir. 2000):

[Dwayne] Simonton was employed as a postal worker in Farmingdale, New York, for approximately twelve years. He repeatedly received satisfactory to excellent performance evaluations. He was, however, subjected to an abusive and hostile work environment by reason of his sexual orientation. The abuse he allegedly endured was so severe that he ultimately suffered a heart attack.

For the sake of decency and judicial propriety, we hesitate before reciting in detail the incidents of Simonton's abuse. Nevertheless, we think it is important both to acknowledge the appalling persecution Simonton allegedly endured and to identify the precise nature of the abuse so as to distinguish this case from future cases as they arise. We therefore relate some, but not all, of the alleged harassment that forms the basis for this suit.

Simonton's sexual orientation was known to his co-workers who repeatedly assaulted him with such comments as "go fuck yourself, fag," "suck my dick," and "so you like it up the ass?" Notes were placed on the wall in the employees' bathroom with Simonton's name and the name of celebrities who had died of AIDS. Pornographic photographs were taped to his work area, male dolls were placed in his vehicle, and copies of *Playgirl* magazine were sent to his home. Pictures of an erect penis were posted in his work place, as were posters stating that Simonton suffered from mental illness as a result of "bung hole disorder." There were repeated statements that Simonton was a "fucking faggot." (232 F.3d at 34–35)

Despite this shameful history, the federal Court of Appeals affirmed the trial court's dismissal of Simonton's claim against the Postal Service, holding there was no federal remedy for sexual orientation discrimination. Likewise, *Dillon v. Frank* (6th Cir. 1992), another lawsuit against the Postal Service itemizing equally outrageous treatment of a postal employee perceived by his fellow workers to be gay, was thrown out.

The question arises, then, as to why Susan Stemler won her case, while Dwayne Simonton, Ernest Dillon, and other gay people lost theirs.[8] A prospective reason for the different results is that, decided just a year before *Stemler*, the U.S. Supreme Court's positive disposition in *Romer v. Evans* (1996) was a controlling precedent. But if that were true, then *Romer* would have been an equally compelling precedent for *Simonton* and other post-1996 federal decisions listed in Appendix 2.2 in which gay people lost.

Another plausible explanation for *Stemler*'s outcome is that the court's opinion was written by a Jewish judge and concurred in by a Democrat. However, the attitudinal account founders because two Jews and two Democrats denied a remedy for the discrimination in *Simonton* and a Jew and a Democrat voted down the claim in *Dillon*.

Patently, the only meaningful distinction separating the victorious result in *Stemler* from losses in numerous other sexual orientation discrimination lawsuits is that two federal judges believed she was a badly treated heterosexual, while jurists in the remaining disputes accepted as fact the homosexuality of the grievously abused plaintiffs there. As the introductory chapter suggests, winning in federal fora was a nearly insurmountable task for lesbians and gay men. Chapter 4 explores the reasons why.

The Cruelly Harassed Gay Student

A rare federal court triumph, offering hope to beleaguered lesbian and gay youth, is *Nabozny v. Podlesny* (7th Cir. 1996):

From his birth in 1975, [Jamie] Nabozny lived in Ashland, Wisconsin. Throughout his childhood, adolescence, and teenaged years he attended schools owned and operated by the Ashland Public School District. In elementary school, Nabozny proved to be a good student and enjoyed a positive educational experience.

---

[8] In point of fact, *Dillon* was a negative precedent for *Stemler*, since both cases were decided by the U.S. Court of Appeals for the Sixth Circuit.

When Nabozny graduated to the Ashland Middle School in 1988, his life changed. Around the time that Nabozny entered the seventh grade, Nabozny realized that he is gay. Many of Nabozny's fellow classmates soon realized it too. Nabozny decided not to "closet" his sexuality, and considerable harassment from his fellow students ensued. Nabozny's classmates regularly referred to him as "faggot," and subjected him to various forms of physical abuse, including striking and spitting on him. Nabozny spoke to the school's guidance counselor, Ms. Peterson, about the abuse, informing Peterson that he is gay. Peterson took action, ordering the offending students to stop the harassment and placing two of them in detention. However, the students' abusive behavior toward Nabozny stopped only briefly. Meanwhile, Peterson was replaced as guidance counselor by Mr. Nowakowski. Nabozny similarly informed Nowakowski that he is gay, and asked for protection from the student harassment. Nowakowski, in turn, referred the matter to school Principal Mary Podlesny; Podlesny was responsible for school discipline.

Just before the 1988 Winter holiday, Nabozny met with Nowakowski and Podlesny to discuss the harassment. During the meeting, Nabozny explained the nature of the harassment and again revealed his homosexuality. Podlesny promised to protect Nabozny, but took no action. Following the holiday season, student harassment of Nabozny worsened, especially at the hands of students Jason Welty and Roy Grande. Nabozny complained to Nowakowski, and school administrators spoke to the students. The harassment, however, only intensified. A short time later, in a science classroom, Welty grabbed Nabozny and pushed him to the floor. Welty and Grande held Nabozny down and performed a mock rape on Nabozny, exclaiming that Nabozny should enjoy it. The boys carried out the mock rape as twenty other students looked on and laughed. Nabozny escaped and fled to Podlesny's office. Podlesny's alleged response is somewhat astonishing; she said that "boys will be boys" and told Nabozny that if he was "going to be so openly gay," he should "expect" such behavior from his fellow students. In the wake of Podlesny's comments, Nabozny ran home. The next day Nabozny was forced to speak with a counselor, not because he was subjected to a mock rape in a classroom, but because he left the school without obtaining the proper permission. No action was taken against the students involved. Nabozny was forced to return to his regular schedule. Understandably, Nabozny was "petrified" to attend school; he was subjected to abuse throughout the duration of the school year.

The situation hardly improved when Nabozny entered the eighth grade. Shortly after the school year began, several boys attacked Nabozny in a school bathroom, hitting him and pushing his books from his hands. This time Nabozny's parents met with Podlesny and the alleged perpetrators. The offending boys denied that the incident occurred, and no action was taken. Podlesny told both Nabozny and his parents that Nabozny should expect such incidents because his is "openly" gay. Several similar meetings between Nabozny's parents and Podlesny followed subsequent incidents involving Nabozny. Each time perpetrators were identified to Podlesny. Each time Podlesny pledged to take action. And, each time nothing was done. Toward the end of the school year, the harassment against Nabozny intensified to the point that a district attorney purportedly advised Nabozny to take time off from school. Nabozny took one and a half weeks off from school.

When he returned, the harassment resumed, driving Nabozny to attempt suicide. After a stint in a hospital, Nabozny finished his eighth grade year in a Catholic school.

The Catholic school attended by Nabozny did not offer classes beyond the eighth grade. Therefore, to attend the ninth grade, Nabozny enrolled in Ashland High School. Almost immediately Nabozny's fellow students sang an all too familiar tune. Early in the year, while Nabozny was using a urinal in the restroom, Nabozny was assaulted. Student Stephen Huntley struck Nabozny in the back of the knee, forcing him to fall into the urinal. Roy Grande then urinated on Nabozny. Nabozny immediately reported the incident to the principal's office. Nabozny recounted the incident to the office secretary, who in turn relayed the story to Principal William Davis. Davis ordered Nabozny to go home and change clothes. Nabozny's parents scheduled a meeting with Davis and Assistant Principal Thomas Blauert. At the meeting, the parties discussed numerous instances of harassment against Nabozny, including the restroom incident.

Rather than taking action against the perpetrators, Davis and Blauert referred Nabozny to Mr. Reeder, a school guidance counselor. Reeder was supposed to change Nabozny's schedule so as to minimize Nabozny's exposure to the offending students. Eventually the school placed Nabozny in a special education class; Stephen Huntley and Roy Grande were special education students. Nabozny's parents continued to insist that the school take action, repeatedly meeting with Davis and Blauert among others. Nabozny's parents' efforts were futile; no action was taken. In the middle of his ninth grade year, Nabozny again attempted suicide. Following another hospital stay and a period living with relatives, Nabozny ran away to Minneapolis. His parents convinced him to return to Ashland by promising that Nabozny would not have to attend Ashland High. Because Nabozny's parents were unable to afford private schooling, however, the Department of Social Services ordered Nabozny to return to Ashland High.

In tenth grade, Nabozny fared no better. Nabozny's parents moved, forcing Nabozny to rely on the school bus to take him to school. Students on the school bus regularly used epithets, such as "fag" and "queer," to refer to Nabozny. Some students even pelted Nabozny with dangerous objects such as steel nuts and bolts. When Nabozny's parents complained to the school, school officials changed Nabozny's assigned seat and moved him to the front of the bus. The harassment continued. Ms. Hanson, a school guidance counselor, lobbied the school's administration to take more aggressive action to no avail. The worst was yet to come, however. One morning when Nabozny arrived early to school, he went to the library to study. The library was not yet open, so Nabozny sat down in the hallway. Minutes later he was met by a group of eight boys led by Stephen Huntley. Huntley began kicking Nabozny in the stomach, and continued to do so for five to ten minutes while the other students looked on laughing. Nabozny reported the incident to Hanson, who referred him to the school's "police liaison" Dan Crawford. Nabozny told Crawford that he wanted to press charges, but Crawford dissuaded him. Crawford promised to speak to the offending boys instead. Meanwhile, at Crawford's behest, Nabozny reported the incident to Blauert. Blauert, the school official supposedly in charge of disciplining, laughed and told Nabozny that Nabozny deserved such treatment because he is gay. Weeks later

Nabozny collapsed from internal bleeding that resulted from Huntley's beating. Nabozny's parents and counselor Hanson repeatedly urged Davis and Blauert to take action to protect Nabozny. Each time aggressive action was promised. And, each time nothing was done.

Finally, in his eleventh grade year, Nabozny withdrew from Ashland High School. Hanson told Nabozny and his parents that school administrators were unwilling to help him and that he should seek educational opportunities elsewhere. Nabozny left Ashland and moved to Minneapolis where he was diagnosed with Post Traumatic Stress Disorder. (92 F.3d at 451–52)

Nabozny sued the school district and it officials for violation of his Fourteenth Amendment rights and lost in the trial court. The U.S. Court of Appeals reversed:

[T]he Constitution prohibits intentional invidious discrimination between otherwise similarly situated persons based on one's membership in a definable minority, absent at least a rational basis for the discrimination. There can be little doubt that homosexuals are an identifiable minority subjected to discrimination in our society.... [The state of Wisconsin] expressly prohibits discrimination on the basis of sexual orientation. Obviously that language was included because the Wisconsin legislature both recognized that homosexuals are discriminated against, and sought to prohibit such discrimination in Wisconsin schools.... We are unable to garner any rational basis for permitting one student to assault another based on the victim's sexual orientation, and the defendants do not offer us one. (92 F.3d at 457–58)

Despite the harrowing abuse from bullies, Jamie Nabozny was fortunate. First, his parents fully supported him, which is not always true for gay youth. Indeed, where would he have turned had both his school and home ostracized him? Second, he lived in a state with a gay civil rights law. The federal appellate court specifically relied on that statute to hold school officials liable for their failure to protect Nabozny from physical and verbal injury. The court might easily have reached a different result if Nabozny had resided in one of the forty-one states then without such legal protection. Hence, the Wisconsin statute was an environmental element essential to the success of his federal legal claim.

Third, the defendants contended that *Bowers v. Hardwick* (U.S. Sup. Ct. 1986) gave states license to discriminate against gays across the board. If states are free to criminalize same-sex sexual activity, the argument goes, then they are equally at liberty to treat homosexuals as second-class citizens in every facet of government activity. Luckily for Jamie Nabozny, the Supreme Court's *Romer* decision (rendered just two months before his) – which some scholars believe effectively overruled *Hardwick*

(Estin 1997: 366; Schacter 1997: 388; McDonnell 1998: 300) – nipped that logic in the bud. Thus, both timing and location were crucial to Nabozny's victory.

A fourth component potentially critical to his good legal fortune was interest group participation. Lambda Legal Defense and Education Fund, a national lesbian and gay rights legal organization patterned after celebrated civil rights advocacy groups such as the NAACP Legal Defense and Education Fund, represented Nabozny. In addition, P-FLAG (Parents, Family, and Friends of Lesbians and Gays), another national gay interest group, appeared as *amicus curiae* ("friend of the court") in the appeal, with its attorney also arguing in favor of the rights claim. In brief, Nabozny's legal team was absolutely top-drawer, and that fact might have made a difference.

Gays in the Military

The United States is the only major Western power to discharge military personnel because of their sexual orientation. Despite the "don't ask, don't tell" law adopted by Congress and the Clinton administration in 1993, the ban is the most blatant form of sexual orientation apartheid in America, responsible for the annual separation of about 1,000 lesbians and gay men from the armed forces (Eskridge 1999: 381–82; Marquis 2001, 2002). Diverse arguments against the taboo have been made to the federal courts for over twenty years, and every constitutional claim has failed (Rimmerman 2002: 64–72).

Eskridge (1994) provides a compelling narrative on *Watkins v. United States Army* (9th Cir. 1983, 1988, 1989), the most fascinating epic of gay people in the military. Accordingly, I refer readers to the Eskridge story and do not repeat the tale here, except to note Perry Watkins was one of only three gay service members ultimately prevailing in the federal appellate courts.[9] As revealed in Appendix 2.3, at least seventeen other military personnel cases lost in those tribunals during the last two decades of the twentieth century. One of those is *Steffan v. Aspin* (DC Cir. 1993) and *Steffan v. Perry* (DC Cir. 1994), where a U.S. Naval Academy midshipman who consistently ranked near the top of his class was discharged in his senior year for being gay. Again, since other scholars (Wolinsky and Sherrill 1993) admirably recount this saga, I decline to do so. Suffice it that, but

---

[9] *Pruitt v. Cheney* (9th Cir. 1992) and *Meinhold v. U.S. Department of Defense* (9th Cir. 1994) are the other victories.

for the three successes, most stories about gays in the military involve ineffable personal tragedy.

Cases Adjudicating the Constitutionality of Consensual Sodomy and Related Solicitation Statutes and Their Enforcement Against Gay People

Gay rights and American law are understood well through the prism of the penal regulation of same-sex sexual activity. Although usually applying on their face to all people regardless of sexual orientation, proscriptions of consensual sodomy historically have been selectively enforced against homosexuals.

As suggested earlier, more important to the late twentieth century than their criminal sting is that sodomy laws have been used to justify denying civil rights and liberties to lesbians and gay men. Thus, sodomy statutes affect the home, cited, for instance, as good reason to refuse lesbian and gay parents custody of, and visitation with, their children (e.g, *Bottoms v. Bottoms* VA 1995, *Ex Parte D. W. W.* AL 1998, and *Thigpen v. Carpenter* AR 1987). These laws also encroach on the workplace, with the federal ban on lesbian and gay military servicemembers the most conspicuous example (*Dronenburg v. Zech* DC Cir. 1984). At the state level, an attorney general's denial of employment to an otherwise qualified lesbian attorney was upheld in part because of a sodomy law (*Shahar v. Bowers* 11th Cir. 1997).

States have taken other antigay actions in deference to sodomy statutes. In 1995, Alabama passed a law forbidding the use of public funds by colleges and universities to support activities of groups fostering lifestyles proscribed by the state's sodomy law (*Gay Lesbian Bisexual Alliance v. Pryor* 11th Cir. 1997). Oklahoma adopted a law dismissing or suspending teachers engaged in the advocacy of homosexual conduct that might come to the attention of school children or employees (*National Gay Task Force v. Board of Education of the City of Oklahoma City* 10th Cir. 1984). State universities withheld formal recognition of lesbian and gay student organizations because school officials thought their approval would lead to sodomy law violations (e.g., *Gay Lib v. University of Missouri* 1977).

Bowers v. Hardwick (U.S. Sup. Ct. 1986) upheld the constitutionality of states' criminalizing same-sex consensual sodomy. Appendix 2.4 contains other rulings addressing the constitutionality or other legal propriety of government regulation of gay sexuality. Although obviously of vital concern to the civil rights of lesbians and gay men, these cases often lack factual backgrounds with appreciable human interest value.

The Overzealous Cops
Baluyut v. Superior Court (CA 1995) is an exception to that general rule:

Mountain View[, California,] police officers arrested petitioners [several gay men] on separate occasions for soliciting a lewd act, some form of homosexual conduct, from a male police decoy. The criminal component of the act is that it is alleged that petitioners intended to perform the act in a place exposed to public view, the decoy officer's car, parked near [an] adult bookstore. . . .

[At a discovery hearing,] the Mountain View Police Department produced copies of ten arrest reports [regarding allegedly similar conduct]. All of the arrests involved male solicitation of another male. . . . The supervisor of this decoy operation testified that he could not recall, with the exception of prostitution cases, any time during his twenty-five years as a police officer that he had made or heard of an arrest of a man soliciting a woman for a sexual act in a public place.

The evidence presented at the motion to dismiss included testimony that petitioners and others were contacted by decoy undercover police officers in the vicinity of the Video Cassette Outlet adult bookstore in Mountain View. Typically, a young, attractive, casually dressed male police officer would "hang around" the bookstore either watching homosexual films from a peep show booth with the door ajar, or wander around the parking lot making eye contact with male customers and engaging them in small talk. If the customer hinted that he might be interested in an encounter with the officer, the decoy would ask him for specifics until the customer made his sexual intentions clear. If the customer suggested that they go to his place, the decoy would decline to accompany the customer. If the customer suggested that they go to the decoy's home, the decoy would explain that he wasn't comfortable bringing people there. At some point there would be a suggestion that the customer accompany the decoy to the decoy's car nearby. When the decoy and customer would arrive at the car, the customer would be arrested for soliciting a lewd act to be performed in a public place, the car.

An expert testified that the modus operandi used by the decoy officer amounted to the typical "cruising" patterns of homosexuals and invited strangers who were homosexual to make contact with the decoy officers.

The bookstore contains about eighty percent heterosexual materials and twenty percent homosexual materials. Ninety percent of the customers are men. Some customers did complain to the store owner about being solicited for lewd acts, but the owner didn't notify the police and simply told the offenders to leave. [In a footnote here, the Court said: Of course, one reason not to report this activity to the police would be because it is not criminal. We take no position on whether citizen reports to police about conduct which, though lawful, is distasteful to the complaining citizen would justify selective enforcement activity.] In 1990, the police received complaints about sexual acts in the parking lot behind the bookstore, persons masturbating there, someone backing his car into a fence, and public urination. None of these complaints identified the offenders as homosexuals. [The arrests here occurred in 1993.] . . .

The [trial] court noted "that the citizen complaint lodged in April of 1990 had nothing to do with homosexuals. It was a complaint that 'people' were out in the back lot doing this, not that homosexuals as a group were habitually inclined to be in violation of [the law]. . . . [E]very once in a while the police would go back and respond . . . and do undercover operations. . . . The undercover operations they did were clearly focused solely upon those persons with a proclivity to engage in homosexual conduct."

The [trial] court distinguished this situation from claims of discriminatory prosecution raised in other situations in which the police focused on uncovering homosexual activity because "in those cases it was because it was the homosexuals who were creating the problem in the particular location. . . . In those circumstances, the fact of the defendant's homosexuality is not indicative, in my mind, of discrimination because it was the homosexuals and only the homosexuals that were the problem. This case is totally different. There is no showing that the homosexuals were ever the problem in the parking lot or anyplace else. So, if and when the police decide to undertake undercover enforcement action, in my mind they must do so in a rational and even-handed manner. Here, instead of doing surveillance, drive-bys or other types of investigation that is neutral in terms of sexual orientation, they specifically sought out homosexual suspects in the various different modalities they used."

The [trial] court described how its review of the police reports of all the other [public lewdness] arrests by the Mountain View Police Department supported petitioners' claim of discriminatory enforcement. One case in particular the court found "highly suggestive of the police attitude. [In this case], [the officer] was hanging out by the back door [of the bookstore], the suspect approached, did a little chitchat, the suspect invited [the officer] to go to his house without specifically saying what for – nothing different than what happens in bars and restaurants all over the land between heterosexuals – and at that point the officer arrests the person on the spot for suggesting they go to his house to engage in some mutual masturbation. That, to me, shows homophobia on the part of the officers. The officers later said we didn't know that that wasn't illegal."

The [trial] court reviewed other cases, including one in which "an undercover officer observes the defendant urinate in the parking lot, which allegedly was part of the problem, people urinating in the parking lot, he watches the guy urinate, doesn't do anything, doesn't cite him for a Municipal Code violation or a Penal Code violation. . . .

"[T]he Court does come inevitably to the conclusion that there was discrimination, quote unquote, evidenced by the officers' method of operation; that their method of operation was designed to ferret out homosexuals or those who were likely to engage in homosexual acts, and that it did so without any relationship to the alleged problems at that location for which the citizen complaint had been initially lodged. . . . But for the discrimination practiced by the Mountain View Police Department, there would have been no detection and prosecution of these people. As a matter of fact, but for their manipulation of the situation to get people to agree to public sex acts rather than going home with them, there wouldn't have been any violation either."

The [trial] court [said] "there was a subconscious homophobia at work in the Mountain View Police Department during the time frame in question, which accounted for this course of conduct on their part, and I think that that subconscious or unconscious homophobia did subtly guide the police officers' thought processes as they went about their business in deciding how to respond to this problem." (37 Cal.Rptr.2d at 743–45; footnotes omitted)

Despite his firm belief that the police acted selectively against gay men, the trial judge interpreted California case law to require a subjective specific intent by the police to punish the gay men for engaging in homosexual conduct before the court could find a constitutional violation.

The California Court of Appeal reversed:

These findings by the municipal court establish that the Mountain View Policy Department ... engaged in discriminatory enforcement in violation of the equal protection clause. Petitioners were deliberately selected for arrest on an invidious basis for acts which would not have been detected, prosecuted or even criminal had it not been for the police conduct. (37 Cal.Rptr.2d at 746)

Here, unlike Judge McDunn in the Chicago adoption case, an alert and fair-minded trial judge discovered and exposed discriminatory enforcement of state law against gay people that another, less impartial jurist easily might have overlooked or buried. Moreover, as in Minnesota and Wisconsin, California's gay civil rights law may have triggered favorable judicial treatment of homosexuals.

Cases Adjudicating the Free Speech and Free Association Rights of Lesbians and Gay Men

Table 1.1 reveals that First Amendment claims by lesbians and gay men experienced the highest rate of judicial success among essential nonmiscellaneous gay rights topics.

Homophobes in the Ivory Tower

Gay Student Services v. Texas A & M University (5th Cir. 1984) presents a free speech and association controversy typical of many cases in Appendix 2.5:

In April of 1976, a group of students on the Texas A & M University (TAMU) campus met with Dr. John Koldus, the University's Vice President for Student Affairs, to discuss with him the possibility of using University facilities to conduct the business of a group they had formed, Gay Student Services (GSS). The students informed Koldus that they did not at that time seek official recognition, but merely wished to post notices on school bulletin boards, meet on campus, and have access to the student newspaper and radio. [In a footnote here, the Court observed: The advantages of official recognition include the following: use of campus facilities; advertising on campus; availability of student activities' funds; use of office area within the Student Programs Office; assistance in preparing an organization budget; secretarial services; authorization to hold meetings and functions on campus; primarily free use of university meeting rooms and facilities; free use of banking facilities at the Student Finance Center; use of an organization mailbox in the Student Finance Center; access to free publicity for the organization in publications such as the "All-University Calendar," the "Student Organization Guide," and others; use of campus bulletin boards to publicize activities; use of kiosks; use of a locator service maintained at the student activities office; facilities scheduling; use of university vehicles; office, work and storage space; and use of graphics arts operations for posters, duplicating and other printing services.] Their reasons for not seeking official recognition included their wish to maintain the anonymity of some of their members as well as their understanding that the group's existence might pose an "uncomfortable" problem in the conservative TAMU community.

Koldus advised the students that no form of limited recognition was available and referred them to Dr. Carolyn Adair, Director of Student Affairs, to receive information regarding the requirements for official recognition. Dr. Adair advised the students to apply for recognition as a service group rather than a political or social group because there would be fewer problems. Accordingly, the goals and purposes reflected on GSS's application were service-related. The application, dated April 5, 1976, stated the following goals and purposes: to provide a referral service for students desiring professional counseling including psychological, religious, medical, and legal fields; to provide to the TAMU community information concerning the structures and realities of gay life; to provide speakers to classes and organizations who wish to know more about gay lifestyles; and to provide a forum for the interchange of ideas and constructive solutions to gay people's problems.

Dr. Koldus directed Dr. Adair to forward GSS's application directly to him rather than to the Student Organization Board, which is ordinarily the first step in attaining recognition. Koldus, who is responsible for the final decision regarding recognition, stated that this was his usual procedure when dealing with applications presenting special problems. Sherri Skinner, one of the group's founding members, testified that Koldus had informed the students at the initial meeting that the University would deny their application.

On May 4, 1976, the student representatives of GSS again met with Koldus, who told them that he had written a response to their application. Koldus stated that University officials had asked him to delay release of the response until Jack Williams, President of the University, and the University legal staff had had an opportunity to study the request. A memorandum dated May 28, 1976, from Williams to Koldus indicated that Koldus had provided information regarding other Texas universities' treatment of similar situations. Furthermore, Williams' memo stated that TAMU would not recognize GSS "until and unless we are ordered by higher authority to do so." The students met with Koldus in June and September of 1976, again requesting action on their application. Finally, Dr. Koldus issued a letter denying recognition on November 29, 1976.

Dr. Koldus' denial was premised on two points. First, Koldus asserted that because homosexual conduct was illegal in Texas at that time, it would be inappropriate for TAMU officially to support an organization likely to "incite, promote and result" in homosexual activity. Second, Koldus stated that the TAMU staff and faculty, not TAMU student organizations, were responsible for providing referral services, educational information, and speakers to students and the larger public. Thus, Koldus concluded that the stated purposes and goals of [GSS] were not "consistent with the philosophy and goals" of TAMU. Nowhere in the letter did Koldus assert that denial of recognition was premised on the fraternal nature of GSS. (737 F.2d at 1319–21; footnotes omitted)

GSS sued TAMU in February 1977. The federal trial court dismissed the case without stating reasons for doing so. GSS appealed, and the U.S. Court of Appeals vacated the trial court dismissal and remanded the case for trial. After a bench trial in November 1981, the trial court again found for TAMU, and the appellate court again reversed:

In its findings of fact, the [trial court] found that TAMU "did not and has not to the time of trial in this case, recognized fraternal organizations, i.e. student groups whose principal if not sole purpose is to hold social gatherings to encourage friendships and personal affinity." The record shows that in October 1977, Dr. Koldus denied recognition to Sigma Phi Epsilon, a national social fraternity, by stating the following policy:

"For over one hundred years, Texas A & M University has chosen not to include the national social fraternity and sorority system as an official part of its educational program. The University has supported the premise that its social character was developed in the concept of togetherness in that all students were Aggies and that a social caste system would detract from this most important concept which welded together the students that attended Texas A & M...."

"As an administrator, it is my responsibility to attempt to perpetuate these traditions which have added not only to the character of the institution but to its strength. It is upon this premise that I deny official university recognition of Sigma Phi Epsilon."

At the heart of the findings and conclusions of the [trial court] was its decision that GSS was merely a "fraternal or social" group "whose message is mere friendship and personal affinity." This led the Court to conclude that GSS was not denied recognition "based upon the content of [its] ideas about homosexuality, since the group is not trying to convey any message about homosexuality," but rather because GSS was a "fraternal" organization subject to TAMU's traditional ban. We think this factual finding was clearly erroneous, for several reasons.

Such a finding is utterly at odds with the asserted purposes of GSS, which sought recognition to provide services and information regarding gay issues to gay persons and to the general public.... Moreover, Dr. Koldus' asserted reasons for denying recognition were clearly based on his perception that the organization *would* attempt to convey ideas about homosexuality. Nowhere in his letter of November 29 does Koldus state that the University's refusal to recognize GSS was based on anything other than reasons tied to the homosexual nature of the group.... Further evidence of TAMU's opposition to recognizing a gay student group is found in a resolution passed by the TAMU Board of Regents following the filing of this lawsuit in 1977. The minutes of the Board's meeting of March 22, 1977, state that the following "policy position" was approved:

"So-called 'gay' activities run diabolically [*sic* – diametrically?] counter to the traditions and standards of Texas A & M University, and the Board of Regents is determined to defend the suit filed against it by three students seeking 'gay' recognition and, if necessary, to proceed in every legal way to prohibit any group with such goals from organizing or operating on this or any other campus for which this Board is responsible."

Moreover, TAMU presented no evidence at trial regarding the "fraternal" nature of GSS. Such a theory for denying recognition was never advanced in the case until TAMU filed its post-trial brief. Indeed, the sole evidence alleged to support the theory was advanced by GSS itself, in its attempt to show that GSS was a "normal" student group rather than a hotbed of deviant homosexuals anxious to influence the morals of impressionable TAMU students at on-campus meetings. TAMU relies, for example, on the testimony of Dr. Kenneth Nyberg, who agreed to become GSS' faculty advisor and attended some of its early meetings. Dr. Nyberg stated:

"Theirs was a quintessential typical student group.... What you are talking about are students so their interests are those of students.... How do you, you know, how do you get registered? What person to take for a class, what person not to take for a class. What did you do last week? It was mostly concerning ... student issues...."

"They reflected most of the same goals and aspirations and concerns almost all my students did. They subsequently looked into most of the same issues. The singular exception was, of course, the homosexual aspect."

It later became clear that GSS elicited such testimony from Dr. Nyberg in order to contravene a later opinion by defense witness Dr. Cameron, who opined that in light of statistical evidence regarding homosexual behavior, "it would be a shock really, if there were not homosexual acts engaged in at or immediately after" a meeting of a homosexual student organization.

Apparently relying upon the testimony of Dr. Sherri Skinner, the [trial court] also found that GSS was a fraternal group that was "not trying to convey any message about homosexuality" because it was "not organized for political advocacy" and had "no official position regarding repeal of [the Texas sodomy statute], which makes homosexual conduct a misdemeanor." Dr. Skinner's testimony, like that of Dr. Nyberg, was elicited by GSS for the express purpose of showing that GSS was a typical student service group deserving recognition rather than a substitute for a gay singles bar. Moreover, Dr. Skinner emphasized that any political or social goals GSS may have had were intentionally eliminated from the application for recognition because Dr. Adair had advised the students to seek recognition as a service-type group. What Dr. Skinner actually said, in the context of emphasizing the service-related purposes of GSS, was that while the individual members of GSS would probably support repeal of the anti-homosexuality laws, "the organization itself has been very careful to keep clear of political action or activism, per se." In light of the fact that TAMU recognizes more service-related student organizations than it does political ones, we simply cannot agree that GSS's failure to organize as a political group renders it a social or fraternal group subject to the TAMU ban.

Finally, we point out that recognition was denied before GSS ever had the opportunity to function as the service-type group it sought to become. The Court's determination regarding the nature of the group was based on how it functioned as an off campus group that had been denied the benefits and privileges of official recognition. The minutes of GSS's meetings reveal that much of the group's meeting time was consumed by discussion of the pending lawsuit. We think evidence concerning how GSS functioned as an off campus group is irrelevant to the determination whether GSS, as it sought to exist, was entitled to official recognition.

For all the foregoing reasons, we conclude that the [trial court's] factual findings with regard to the nature of GSS were clearly erroneous. We think it clear from the facts that TAMU refused officially to recognize GSS based upon the homosexual content of the group's ideas – which it sought to convey through implementing its stated goals and purposes....

In his letter denying GSS official recognition, Dr. Koldus stated that GSS's goals and purposes were not consistent with the philosophy and goals of TAMU. This alone as a reason for denying recognition is clearly forbidden by [U.S. Supreme Court precedent], where the Court specifically rejected for constitutional purposes the college president's statement that [Students for a Democratic Society's] philosophies of destruction, violence and disruption were "counter to the official policy of the college." ... The [Supreme] Court held that:

"The mere disagreement of the [College's] President with the group's philosophy affords no reason to deny it recognition. As repugnant as these views may have been ..., the mere expression of them would not justify the denial of First Amendment rights. Whether [SDS] did in fact advocate a philosophy of 'destruction' thus becomes immaterial. The College, acting here as the instrumentality of the State, may not restrict speech or association simply because it finds the views expressed by any group to be abhorrent."...

Dr. Koldus proffered two additional, more specific reasons for denying recognition to GSS. First, he stated that because homosexual conduct was illegal in Texas, it would be inappropriate for TAMU to recognize a group likely to "incite, promote, and result" in homosexual acts. Second, he stated that student organizations did not have the "educational experience, the responsibility or the authority to educate the larger public."...

As to TAMU's asserted interest in preventing expression likely to "incite, promote, and result" in then-illegal homosexual activity, we emphasize that while Texas law may prohibit certain homosexual practices, no Texas law makes it a crime to *be* a homosexual. Furthermore, there is no evidence that any illegal activity has taken place as a result of GSS's existence in the past, nor is there any evidence that GSS is an organization devoted to advocacy and incitement of imminent illegal, specifically proscribed homosexual activity....

With regard to Koldus' assertion that GSS lacked the experience to educate the public or provide referral services, we point out that even if Koldus was correct in arguing that the University faculty and staff are better equipped to perform these functions, "the state and its agents are forbidden from usurping the students' right to choose." [Citation omitted.] At the heart of the freedom guaranteed by our Constitution is the freedom to choose – even if that choice does not accord with the state's view as to which choice is superior.... TAMU presented no evidence, nor did the [trial court] find, that such a goal would "infringe reasonable campus rules, interrupt classes, or substantially interfere with the opportunity of other students to obtain an education." [Citation omitted.]

We therefore conclude that none of the reasons for nonrecognition proferred by Dr. Koldus are sufficient to justify the infringement on [GSS's] First Amendment rights. At trial, however, TAMU asserted yet another alleged justification. It claimed that recognition of GSS would encourage more homosexual conduct, resulting in an increase in the number of persons with the psychological and physiological problems TAMU's experts claimed were more prevalent among homosexuals than among heterosexuals. Thus, TAMU argued that denial of recognition was justifiable as an appropriate means of protecting public health....

This asserted justification must fail for the same reasons the others did: TAMU has simply not proven that recognition will indeed imminently result in such dire consequences. The speculative evidence offered by the defendants' experts "for which no historical or empirical basis is disclosed," cannot justify TAMU's content-based refusal to recognize GSS. [Citation omitted.] We think that on this record TAMU's public health argument is precisely the kind of "undifferentiated fear or apprehension" that the Supreme Court has repeatedly held "is not enough to overcome the right to freedom of expression." [Citations omitted.]...

[D]enying recognition to a gay group "smacks of penalizing persons for their status [as homosexuals] rather than their conduct, which is constitutionally impermissible." [Citations omitted.] (737 F.2d at 1321–24 and 1327–30; footnotes omitted; emphasis in the original)

Thus, eight years after applying for official acknowledgment – when all the individuals seeking the group's recognition most likely were no longer students – and after overcoming every legal gimmick the university and its governing board could muster, GSS finally prevailed in court. The TAMU case manifests the lengths that homophobes – here with Ph.D.s and governing a public research university – will go to deny lesbian and gay rights, even when virtually every appellate court First Amendment precedent in 1976 unequivocally indicated that GSS would triumph. The dispute also manifests how state officials capitalized on the Texas sodomy statute to deny basic civil rights to gay people.

In addition, the TAMU appeal is important attitudinally because the case is one of relatively few federal court decisions in the book's database with Democratic appointees comprising a majority of the judicial panel. That resulted from timing.

With Democrats in control of both Congress and the White House, the Omnibus Judgeship Act of 1978 enlarged the number of lower federal court judgeships by 152, an increase of about 30 percent (Goldman 1997: 241–42). President Jimmy Carter staffed the new positions, and although serving just one term, he selected almost 40 percent of the federal bench (ibid.: 238). Thus, Democratic nominees dominated the lower federal courts in the early 1980s.

Recall that Chapter 1 discloses that the book's First Amendment appeals were front-loaded. Four (57.1 percent) of seven federal court, free speech and association decisions were rendered before 1986, while only one occurred in the 1990s. In contrast, only 19.0 percent of all other federal court cases were litigated before 1986.

As a result, almost two-thirds of votes in federal court First Amendment cases in the book's data set were cast by Democratic judges, whereas only about one-third in the remaining federal decisions were. This temporal happenstance of positioning of Democrats on the federal bench is the principal reason why free speech and association claims by gay people were decided the most favorably of any subject matter category. Chapter 4 confirms the fact.

Miscellaneous Cases Essential to Lesbian and Gay Rights

The cases in Appendix 2.6 are a motley collection. Four (*Nemetz v. Immigration and Naturalization Service* 4th Cir. 1981, *Matter of Longstaff* 5th Cir. 1983, *Hill v. U.S. Immigration and Naturalization Service* 9th Cir. 1983, and *Hernandez-Montiel v. Immigration and Naturalization Service* 9th Cir. 2000) concern immigration issues involving lesbian and gay aliens. Three (*In re Joshua H.* CA 1993, *People v. M.S.* CA 1993, and *Reeves v. State* FL 1994) deal with hate crimes statutes. Four (*Beam v. Paskett* 9th Cir. 1992, *People v. Garcia* CA 2000, *State v. Lovely* ME 1982, and *State v. Pattno* NE 1998) address jury selection and other tangential topics in criminal prosecutions. Three (*Sterling v. Borough of Minersville* 3rd Cir. 2000, *Walls v. City of Petersburg* 4th Cir. 1990, and *Schowengerdt v. General Dynamics Corp.* 9th Cir. 1987) touch on privacy issues.

The Preacher in Police Clothing
A particularly distressing story underpins *Sterling v. Borough of Minersville* (3rd Cir. 2000):

On April 17, 1997, 18-year-old Marcus Wayman and a 17-year-old male friend were parked in a lot adjacent to a beer distributor. The car and its occupants were observed by ... police officer F. Scott Wilinsky. Wilinsky was concerned about previous burglaries of the beer distributor and was suspicious of the fact that the headlights on the car were out. Wilinsky called for backup and, shortly thereafter, Officer Thomas Hoban ... arrived at the scene.

The officers' investigation did not show any sign of a break-in at the business, but it was apparent to the officers that the young men had been drinking alcohol. The boys were also evasive when asked what they were doing in the parking lot. When an eventual search uncovered two condoms, Wilinsky questioned whether the boys were in the parking lot for a sexual assignation. Wilinsky testified that both Wayman and his companion eventually acknowledged that they were homosexuals and were in the parking lot to engage in consensual sex, but we note that the 17-year old denied making such admissions.

The two boys were arrested for underage drinking and were taken to the Minersville police station. At the station, Wilinsky lectured them that the Bible counseled against homosexual activity. Wilinsky then warned Wayman that if Wayman did not inform his grandfather about his homosexuality that Wilinsky would take it upon himself to disclose this information. After hearing this statement, Wayman confided to his friend that he was going to kill himself. Upon his release from custody, Wayman committed suicide in his home.

Wayman's mother ... filed suit ... against the Borough of Minersville, Wilinsky and Hoban, as individuals and in their capacity as police officers, and the Chief of Police of Minersville. The complaint alleged that the officers and the borough violated Wayman's ... Fourteenth Amendment rights to privacy and equal protection and the laws and the Constitution of the Commonwealth of Pennsylvania....

[The trial court] ruled that the officers ... violated Wayman's clearly established right to privacy as protected by the Constitution....

[U.S. Supreme Court and U.S. Court of Appeals precedents indicate that w]e thus guard one's right to privacy against unwarranted government intrusion. It is difficult to imagine a more private matter than one's sexuality and a less likely probability that the government would have a legitimate interest in disclosure of sexual identity.

We can, therefore, readily conclude that Wayman's sexual orientation was an intimate aspect of his personality entitled to privacy protection under [these precedents]. The Supreme Court, despite the *Bowers* [*v. Hardwick*] decision, and our court have clearly spoken that matters of personal intimacy are safeguarded against unwarranted disclosure....

[Moreover, t]he threat to breach some confidential aspect of one's life ... is tantamount to a violation of the privacy right because the security of one's privacy has been compromised by the threat of disclosure. Thus, Wilinsky's threat to disclose Wayman's suspected homosexuality suffices as a violation of Wayman's constitutionally protected privacy interest. (232 F.3d at 192–93 and 196–97; footnotes omitted)

Thus, a bigot masquerading as a secular officer of a state constitutionally separated from the church was held accountable for the tragic consequence of his misplaced religious zealotry. Indeed, if people want to preach or be busybodies of putative salvation, they should become missionaries and not police officers.

Of particular irony here is that the young gay men's use of prophylactics evidently contributed to the detection of their sexual orientation and hence to the youth's suicide. If the couple had been less scrupulous about protecting their health, Wayman might have lived.

Sex Education and Faith in South Dakota

A second interesting story from the miscellaneous case collection is *Collins v. Faith School District* (SD 1998):

Richard Collins was employed by the Faith School District for twenty-nine years.... During most of those years he was a fifth-grade teacher. Although he was being reassigned to teach the fourth-grade class during the 1995–96 school year, Collins had a valid contract and was entitled to the protections of South Dakota's continuing contract law....

The Faith School Board (Board) had not established any formal sex education curriculum for its elementary school students. However, Board had made it a practice to contract with the community health nurse to provide sex education for elementary students for approximately fifteen years prior to 1995. The makeup of this program was basically set by the community health nurse without any prescreening by Board or administration.

A video chosen by the community health nurse covering the topics of puberty, maturation, and reproduction was shown to fourth, fifth, and sixth grade boys on April 24, 1995. This was the first time this particular video had been used by the nurse and this was the first time fourth grade students were included in the program. At the end of the video, the nurse went through a worksheet with the boys, addressing such topics as circumcision, nocturnal emissions, and semen. An opportunity for the boys to ask the nurse questions was then provided, but none were asked. The school nurse attributed this to the fact she was a woman and the boys were not comfortable discussing the subject with her.

As in past years, following the sex education presentation, the boys then went to Collins' classroom for a question and answer session. Before starting the session, Collins excused one student from the room because the student's parents did not wish to have the child involved in the sex education program. Collins then proceeded to ask if the boys had any questions. Collins undertook this duty because he had been asked by a previous health nurse to solicit questions after sex education programs from the boys because the female nurse realized that the boys would be uncomfortable asking her questions. Collins was instructed to answer the boys' questions as honestly as possible and he continued to carry out what had been an established practice for fifteen years. Questions were raised by the boys about circumcision, masturbation, nocturnal emissions and other topics from the film and worksheet. During the session, one of the boys also related that he had heard that two men could have sex and asked how this was possible. Collins preceded his explanation with the disclaimers that this type of conduct is frowned upon, most people do not believe in it, and the boys would find it gross. Collins then described oral and anal sexual intercourse in explicit language.

On April 25, 1995, complaints from parents were received by the superintendent which were critical of what the grade school boys had heard from Collins during school the previous day.

In essence, the complaining parents were concerned about the effect Collins' answer to the question about homosexual intercourse would have on the boys. An informal meeting was conducted, involving one boy's parents, the superintendent, the principal, and Collins. At the conclusion of the meeting, Collins was advised by the superintendent that the matter was not resolved. Later that day, the superintendent took the matter to Board. Board directed the superintendent to send notice to Collins that a termination hearing would be scheduled before Board to consider his dismissal.

A notice of hearing and charges was provided to Collins on April 28, 1995, which referenced the parental complaint as well as warnings by Collins' evaluators in regard to lesson plans, instruction, maintenance of records and personal hygiene since 1985 that could be relevant as to his competence. On May 17, 1995, the hearing was held before Board, at which time witnesses and evidence were presented.

Although the notice of hearing had made vague references to issues other than the parental complaints, the only evidence Board heard pertained to the question and answer session and Collins' inappropriate response. [In a footnote here, the court noted: Collins admitted that his description of homosexual intercourse was ill-advised and that he regretted making the statement.] Debbie and Newton Brown were the only complaining parents to testify at the hearing. Debbie Brown testified that she felt that homosexuality was "very immoral" and both parents were bothered by the reference to homosexual activity by Collins. Although the parents felt that they should be the ones presenting the information on these subjects to their kids, neither had seen the video or worksheet before they were shown to the boys, nor had they opted to remove their son from the presentation.

The high school principal testified that it was inappropriate and immoral for a teacher to discuss homosexual activities with fourth and fifth grade boys. However, she indicated she did not have any evidence that the children had been harmed in any way by the activity. She also testified that there had been no increased absenteeism or discipline problems of any kind. Nor were there any complaints from the children about feeling uncomfortable around Collins.

The superintendent testified without elaboration that the incident adversely affected Collins' ability to perform his teaching duties. However, the superintendent also testified that there was no evidence of any adverse impact on the students. In fact, the superintendent had not even been in Collins' classroom since the question and answer session to monitor for problems that may have developed because of the incident. Furthermore, he acknowledged that he had no evidence whatsoever that the children had lost confidence in Collins as a teacher and agreed that they evidently had some level of trust in Collins or they would not have been comfortable in asking the questions of him in the first place. The superintendent also indicated that he had no reason to question Collins' character.

At the conclusion of the hearing, Board voted to terminate Collins' contract on the basis of incompetency. The [trial court] upheld this action. Appeal was brought....

Ignoring twenty-nine years of faithful service, the Board terminated Collins' teaching contract on the basis that he was incompetent. This determination rested purely on his indiscreet answer with regard to homosexual activity – a subject which invariably invokes intense debate and undoubtedly stirred emotions in this case.

It is undisputed that there is no evidence that the conduct of Collins complained of by Board violated any directive, regulation, rule, or order given to him by any administrator or Board. In fact, the evidence showed that the administration had abdicated total control over the sex education program to the health nurse. Neither the superintendent nor the Board took any steps to personally plan the program or place any limits on it. It is also undisputed that Collins had been asked by the previous health nurse to answer questions after sex education videos in the past, and had done so for the past fifteen years without incident. Even so, the Board terminated Collins' employment on the basis of incompetence for one moment of poor judgment....

[T]he Faith School Board's decision to terminate its contract with Collins on the basis of one ill-advised answer, honestly given, was not the type of habitual and ongoing action that would support Board's conclusion that Collins was incompetent.... There has been no showing that Collins' teaching ability has been or will be impaired, or that any children have been detrimentally affected.... Nor has there been a showing that Collins is likely to exercise poor judgment in a similar situation in the future, since he has acknowledged that he used poor judgment in this case and regretted making the statement....

Where is the relationship between Collins' ill-advised answer to the boys and the impairment of his capacity as a teacher? ... Collins' teaching ability is judged incompetent without more proof than the mere assertions that it is so. While the superintendent makes the bare claim that the incident adversely affected Collins' ability to perform his teaching duties, he admits that he has not bothered to sit in on any of Collins' classes to actually note any problems. There have been no allegations that the students' education has suffered in any way. Absences have not increased. Discipline problems have not increased. Moreover, Board had the ability, pursuant to school policies, to suspend Collins prior to his termination. Instead, they chose to allow him to continue teaching from the April 24th incident to the May 17th board hearing, impliedly admitting they were not worried about Collins' ability to effectively teach his students after the incident. Furthermore, Board voted to extend Collins' contract for another year on the very same night that they discussed Brown's complaint that lead to the hearing to determine if Collins should be dismissed.... The record contains no credible evidence that Collins' teaching ability has been impaired or even that the incident in question has any connection with his continued effectiveness as a teacher.

Accordingly, the decision of the [trial court] is reversed and the case is remanded for reinstatement of Collins' teaching position and for a determination of the amount of back pay that Collins is entitled.... (574 N.W.2d at 890–95; footnotes omitted)

The South Dakota Supreme Court's gloss suggests that in *Collins*, a proverbial mountain was made out of a molehill. Yet clearly the mere mention of homosexual acts – even in a routine, school-sponsored, sex education context – sparked a public furor costing a dedicated teacher his job after three decades of service.

Is it any surprise, then, only two years after Richard Collins's firing in rural South Dakota – and just three years after Susan Stemler, in small-town Kentucky, was arrested simply because of an abusive drunk's false accusation of lesbianism – that in small-town Pennsylvania a local cop's threat to expose Marcus Wayman's homosexuality triggered the youth's suicide? And these are just the very rare stories coming to the attention of appellate courts and thereby to us here. Can there be any doubt that the United States at the end of the twentieth century was riddled with homophobia?[10]

Same-Sex Sexual Harassment

An analysis of the thirty-one decisions in Appendix 2.7 reveals that same-sex sexual harassment cases aren't essential to lesbian and gay rights. As hypothesized in Chapter 1, this area of the law evolved in large measure to protect heterosexual males from being solicited by gay men. In fact, there is no case among the thirty-one here alleging the sexual harassment of one gay person by another. Rather, virtually all targets of the alleged harassment are either explicitly described as heterosexual or presumptively so. None is unequivocally identified as gay or lesbian. Moreover, before the Supreme Court's preemption of the field with *Oncale v. Sundowner Offshore Services, Inc.* (U.S. Sup. Ct. 1998), one federal circuit (*Wrightson v. Pizza Hut of America, Inc.* 4th Cir. 1996) held that legally cognizable same-sex sexual harassment occurred *only* when the perpetrator was homosexual. It couldn't happen, as a legal matter, when the harasser was heterosexual.

The mean of **outcome** for the fourteen pre-*Oncale* decisions in Appendix 2.7 not involving perpetrators identified as gay is .500. That for the five pre-*Oncale* cases with harassers determined to be gay is .800. In other words, before *Oncale* in 1998, the odds for judicial recognition of same-sex sexual harassment without explicitly gay perpetrators were one in two. That ratio increased to four of five when alleged harassers

---

[10] See Thomas (1992: 1463–64), Reed (1999: 903), and Garland (2001: 2–4) for further evidence of American homophobia.

were known to be gay. Clearly, judges viewed the law of same-sex sexual harassment as a sanction for gay men hitting on straight men[11] and not as an extension of Title VII or comparable state statutes to embrace gay victims of sexual harassment. This prism makes the high mean of **outcome** for same-sex sexual harassment in Table 1.1 understandable.

Defamation Involving Homosexuality

Similarly, an analysis of the thirteen decisions in Appendix 2.8 discloses that defamation cases involving allegations of homosexuality aren't essential to lesbian and gay rights. *Logan v. Sears, Roebuck & Co.* (AL 1985) presents one judicial view of the issue:

Robert Logan operates a beauty salon in Birmingham. On May 11, 1982, an employee of Sears, Roebuck and Company phoned Logan at his place of business to inquire whether he had made his monthly charge account payment. While looking for his checkbook, Logan heard the Sears employee tell someone on her end of the line, "This guy is as queer as a three-dollar bill. He owns a beauty salon, and he just told me that if you'll hold the line I will check my checkbook." No one on Logan's end of the conversation, other than Logan, heard the statement.

Logan brought suit against Sears, seeking damages based on the torts of outrage and invasion of privacy....

It is undisputed that the Sears employee indeed made the statement complained of by Logan. It is further undisputed that Logan is, in fact, a homosexual....

Since Logan is admittedly a homosexual, can it be said realistically that being described as "queer" should cause him shame or humiliation? We think not. In order to create a cause of action, the conduct must be such that would cause mental suffering, shame, or humiliation to a person of ordinary sensibilities, not conduct which would be considered unacceptable merely by homosexuals. (466 So.2d at 122 and 124)

Thus, calling a gay man "queer" – undeniably an affront in the Alabama of 1982 – doesn't defame him because "a person of ordinary sensibilities" wouldn't be offended by the usage, regardless of what gay men think about it. In other words, since gay people are insulted all the time, what's the problem? Indeed, the Alabama Supreme Court's analysis is remarkable. Taken to its logical extension, the court's opinion sanctions majority use of slurs for any minority.

Boehm v. American Bankers Insurance Group, Inc. (FL 1990) is the only other case in Appendix 2.8 with a gay plaintiff or one presumptively so.

---

[11] A rare case – *Police Officers Federation of Minneapolis v. City of Minneapolis* (MN 2000) – disclosed a presumptive lesbian making a pass at a heterosexual woman in the workplace.

His defamation claim also was denied. In contrast, seven (64 percent) of the eleven cases with presumptively heterosexual plaintiffs upheld their per se defamation claims. Thus, the bulk of decisions here involve heterosexuals concerned about false accusations of homosexuality. Again, this isn't a lesbian and gay rights category.

Miscellaneous Cases Not Essential to Lesbian and Gay Rights

The decisions in Appendix 2.9 are a potpourri of legal issues tangentially involving lesbians and gay men. Six involve the legal authority of political subdivisions of the state to adopt ordinances or executive orders touching lesbian and gay issues. Two deal with evidentiary issues in criminal trials. The rest concern other legal subjects not immediately important to gay rights.

Conclusion

This chapter's narrative case overview enlarges on the major subject matter categories involving lesbian and gay litigants in the United States during the last two decades of the twentieth century, exposes some of the human drama behind their legal battles for civil rights,[12] and introduces analytic concepts on which the balance of the book relies. The quantitative approaches of Chapters 3, 4, and 5 seek to answer fundamental questions about why the lesbian and gay rights judicial struggles detailed here either succeeded or failed.

For example, is the judicial bigotry against gay people evidenced by Judge McDunn in the Chicago lesbian adoption case widespread? In that regard, what influence do attitudes – evidenced by personal attributes such as age, gender, political party affiliation, prior career experience, race, and religion – have on how the civil rights of homosexuals are adjudicated?

Do the institutional features of courts matter? For instance, did the Alabama method of selection and tenure of judges – popular election every six years – make a difference in the lesbian mother visitation and custody decisions?

What about the ideological and political environment? Do consensual sodomy laws like the ones in Alabama, Florida, Mississippi, and Texas diminish how frequently judges vote in favor of lesbian and gay rights? Do the gay civil rights statutes of states such as California, Minnesota, and

---

[12] Murdoch and Price (2001) offer fascinating stories behind U.S. Supreme Court cases involving lesbian and gay rights from the last half of the twentieth century.

Wisconsin enhance judicial receptiveness to rights claims? How accurately do the Berry et al. ideology measures track court action regarding lesbians and gay litigants?

Finally, what about legal factors? Most importantly, do precedents significantly influence judicial behavior? Do jurists in fact abide by the doctrine of *stare decisis*?

Systematically investigating the book's wide array of court decisions, the rest of the study provides statistical analyses to discern patterns of judicial behavior among those cases in order to answer these and other questions.

3

The Lesbian and Gay Rights Claims Models

The narratives chapter offers sets of cases exhibiting contradictory judicial treatment of lesbian and gay rights claims. Alabama and Mississippi courts denied child custody to gay parents and severely limited their visitation, while Minnesota judges enforced the custody and visitation rights of lesbians and gay men. Florida jurists recognized responsibilities inherent in domestic partnerships, while New York judges forbade privileges arising from them. Chapter 2 focuses on stories with abundant human interest value. Yet the policy choices that courts make, regardless of factual setting, determine the civil rights of lesbians and gay men in the long run.

From the policy perspective, American homosexuals indeed have experienced widely disparate results in legal struggles to secure rights.[1] The United States Supreme Court's treatment of gay people is a case in point. In *Bowers v. Hardwick* (U.S. Sup. Ct. 1986), the Court rejected an extension of privacy rights granted heterosexuals in *Griswold v. Connecticut* (1965) and its progeny. Indeed, the *Hardwick* Court derided the privacy claim, characterizing the issue as "whether the Federal Constitution confers a fundamental right upon homosexuals to engage in sodomy" and then labeling that assertion as, "at best, facetious" (478 U.S. at 190 and 194). Ten years later, however, the Court upheld an equal-protection attack on Colorado's Amendment 2, a popularly mandated state constitutional revision forbidding localities from enacting ordinances outlawing discrimination against lesbians and gay men:

---

[1] Others noting dissimilar judicial treatment of lesbians and gay men are Starr (1998) and Rivera (1999: 1187–90).

Amendment 2 classifies homosexuals not to further a proper legislative end but to make them unequal to everyone else. This Colorado cannot do. A State cannot so deem a class of persons a stranger to its laws. (*Romer v. Evans*, U.S. Sup. Ct. 1996: 635)[2]

Appellate court handling of state lesbian and gay rights claims has been equally mixed. A dozen years after the *Hardwick* decision, for example, the Georgia Supreme Court struck down the consensual sodomy law upheld in *Hardwick*, but on state, not federal, privacy grounds (*Powell v. State* GA 1998). Four years earlier, in another Southern state, the Texas Supreme Court passed up an opportunity to invalidate a sodomy statute on privacy grounds (*State v. Morales* TX 1994). In 1993, the Vermont Supreme Court, by unanimous vote, permitted the domestic partner of a lesbian mother to adopt the latter's children without terminating the birth mother's parental rights (*Adoptions of B.L.V.B. and E.L.V.B.* VT 1993). Two years later in neighboring New York, its intermediate appellate court, also by unanimous vote, refused to allow the domestic partner of a lesbian mother to adopt the latter's child without the biological mother's giving up her parental rights (*Matter of Dana* NY 1995). The domestic partner appealed, and New York's court of last resort reversed by a vote of 4 to 3 (*Matter of Jacob*[3] NY 1995).

Inconsistencies even appear almost simultaneously in the same court. In 1988, the Appellate Division of the New York Supreme Court, First Department, held that surviving domestic partners of deceased, gay tenants of record of rent-controlled apartments were not entitled to continued occupancy of those dwellings as surviving spouses or family members – although heterosexual spouses would be afforded that right under New York City's rent-control law (*Braschi v. Stahl Associates Company* NY 1988). Eighteen months later, the Appellate Division, First Department, ruled that surviving domestic partners of deceased, gay tenants of record deserved legal protections equal to traditional family members regarding rent-stabilized apartments (*East 10th Street Associates v. Estate of Goldstein* NY 1990).

What accounts for the contradictory judicial action? This chapter offers an answer, investigating factors explaining appellate court treatment of lesbians and gay men by means of integrated models of judicial behavior.

---

[2] Interestingly, the majority opinion never referenced *Hardwick*.
[3] The court-of-last-resort case name is different from the one in the intermediate appellate court decision because the former was a consolidated appeal and the *Jacob* case came first in the caption.

Research by legal scholars has incorporated empirical models developed by political scientists[4] to explain judicial decision making in sundry areas of the law.[5] Yet these endeavors often suffer from methodological limitations (such as small data sets, underspecified models with too few independent variables, and temporal snapshots rather than extended landscapes of judicial action), hindering the generalizability of findings to account for how judges decide cases.[6] This study, in contrast, investigates the impacts of 39 variables and interaction terms on 1,439 votes by 849 appellate judges in 393 decisions[7] essential to lesbian and gay rights from 87 courts in all federal appellate jurisdictions and 47 states over a two-decade-long period.[8]

---

[4] Judicial behavior has a long pedigree in political science, dating at least to C. Hermann Pritchett's classic *The Roosevelt Court* (1948) more than half a century ago. Grossman (1966) marked the first presentation in a leading law review of empirical research on courts and judges by a political scientist. Yet see Cross (1997) and Epstein and King (2002). Baum (1997) provides an excellent overview of the study of judicial behavior in political science.

[5] Examples of this scholarship include Eisenberg and Johnson (1991), Cohen (1992), Schultz and Petterson (1992), Ashenfelter, Eisenberg, and Schwab (1995), Swanson and Melone (1995), Quinn (1996), Revesz (1997), Cross and Tiller (1998), George (1998), Sisk, Heise, and Morriss (1998), and Lim (2000).

[6] Of the articles in the last note, Ashenfelter et al. examine the greatest number of judicial votes (2,258), but observe merely forty-seven judges during only one year. Cohen scrutinizes the largest group of jurists (the actual number is unspecified, but appears to be about 300 federal district judges), yet analyzes just three personal attributes (age, political party affiliation, and prior experience as a prosecutor). Cross and Tiller address the impact of party on a dozen or so judges on the D.C. Circuit for a five-year period. Eisenberg and Johnson consider 176 judicial votes. George discusses decisions from a single federal circuit. Lim evaluates how a handful of variables influence just thirteen justices. Quinn inspects 108 judicial votes. Revesz looks at eighteen judges and one personal attribute (party). Schultz and Petterson survey the effect of party on 245 judicial votes. Sisk et al. weigh 291 decisions from one year. Swanson and Melone review fifty-four cases by one state supreme court. See Epstein and King (2002) for elaboration of further limitations in empirical legal research.

[7] In addition to the 393 decisions where courts reached homosexual rights claims, seven concurring and dissenting opinions in cases (*Cox v. Florida Department of Health and Rehabilitative Services* FL 1995, *State v. Baxley* LA 1994 and 1995, *Neville v. State* MD 1981, *People v. Lino* MI 1994, *Johnson v. Schlotman* ND 1993, and *Minshall v. Health Care & Retirement Corp.* WV 2000) where court majorities did not get to such claims are included in the data set. Moreover, Appendix 1.2's four decisions of the Court of Appeals of the District of Columbia are excluded here because the Berry et al. environmental ideology measures are unavailable for the district.

[8] Giles and Zorn (2000: 13) ("estimates of judge-level effects are improved by increasing our sample of judges, and those for case-level effects by including more cases in our analyses").

Introduced in Chapter 1, the legal and attitudinal models seek to account for court policy outcomes by explaining the stimuli shaping judicial action, and they inform this research. Supplementing the two models are four sets of forces mediating judicial outcomes. *Institutional* attributes are structural characteristics of courts (such as method of judicial selection, length of term of office, and rules for opinion assignment) affecting decision making (Hall and Brace 1989, 1992; Brace and Hall 1995). *Environmental* determinates center on jurisdiction-specific characteristics (such as citizen or government ideology and extent of partisan competition) moderating court action (Brace and Hall 1990, 1993, 1995). *Temporal* forces gauge the power of time on judicial enterprise (Brace and Hall 1997). Participation by *amici curiae* reveals *interest group* influence in judicial decision making (Caldeira and Wright 1988, 1990; Songer and Kuersten 1995; Hausegger 1998; Tauber 1998).

Political science scholarship demonstrates the advantage of combining models of judicial behavior with institutional, environmental, and temporal components (Emmert 1992; Hall and Brace 1992; Brace and Hall 1995, 1997; Songer 1995; Traut and Emmert 1998). Accordingly, this chapter examines variables from the two judicial behavior models, placed in appropriate institutional, environmental, temporal, and interest group configurations, to investigate success and failure of lesbian and gay rights claims in federal and state appellate decisions.

As the introductory chapters reveal, the book's database covers a wide variety of subjects, ranging from free speech and association to child custody and visitation. Readers may wonder about the propriety of aggregating such diverse topics in the quantitative examinations that follow. Perhaps the legal issues are not sufficiently consistent and uniform to combine cases and their votes for empirical investigation.

As Chapter 2's narratives suggest, however, common concerns do unite these court decisions. Judicial awareness of the political, religious, and social imperatives surrounding rights claims by lesbians and gay men in late-twentieth-century America transcended the discrete subject matters of the volume's case collection. In like manner, sensitivity to race unified court decisions addressing the rights of African Americans across disparate legal causes in midcentury, just as cognizance of gender did in women's rights litigation thereafter.[9]

---

[9] For evidence beyond the last chapter's narratives, see Justice Scalia's acknowledgment of a "Kulturkampf" in *Romer*, as well as Bork (1990: 123–24) and Aden (2000).

The Statistical Analysis

Appendices 3.1 to 3.4 identify and explain the independent variables, coding rules, further data collection, and statistical technique used to analyze the gay rights cases that the first two chapters introduce. Reference to these appendices provides specifications for variables (with their names in bold in the main text) and methods.

Several data subsets canvass independent-variable impact on **outcome**. Although the most obvious maneuver for data examination (lumping all votes together without regard to court or topic) provides the largest number of observations for statistical manipulation – a considerable virtue – more nuanced approaches are available.

One layer of data dissection arises between intermediate appellate courts and courts of last resort. Intermediate appellate courts' mandatory jurisdiction buffers courts of last resort from trial-court error correction and facilitates greater focus by courts of last resort on policy formulation (Groot 1971: 548; Carrington, Meador, and Rosenberg 1976: 150; Wenzel, Bowler, and Lanoue 1997: 376; Songer, Sheehan, and Haire 2000: 133–34). Accordingly, the two sets of judges may have acted differently.

Another analytic tier concerns subject matter, with the division emerging from the observation that there is

> increased emphasis on issues related to children and the family in gay rights litigation. The prototypical gay litigant is not a lone individual asserting rights to employment or military service but rather a gay couple or family seeking recognition and the rights that go with it. (Brown 2000: 365)

Some 846 (58.8 percent) of 1,439 judicial votes in the study involved lesbian and gay family issues. A majority of Americans believes the law should protect lesbians and gay men from job discrimination and that homosexual relations between consenting adults in private should be legal, but two-thirds think lesbians and gay men should be allowed neither to adopt children nor to marry (Yang 1998: 162). Hence, judges may have behaved differently when the subject before them touched family matters than when it was an employment discrimination case or consensual sodomy statute challenge.

A third level of analysis compares federal and state courts and is addressed separately in Chapter 4.

Finally, a judicial behavior investigative tradition counsels that, in inspecting personal attributes, scholars should pay more attention to opinion writers than to their concurring colleagues (Sickels 1965; Atkins and Green 1976; Dubois 1988). According to the theory, crowded court dockets simply do not permit each person on a multimember bench the time to scrutinize every appeal carefully. Specialists in particular fields thus emerge, the argument goes, and are assigned every such appeal, with associates deferring to their judgment.[10] Thus, I examine opinion writers separately from their concurring colleagues.[11]

Findings

For ease of reference, interpretive statements about statistical findings are italicized in this section and subsequent ones that announce findings. Readers not interested in statistical details buttressing such data may focus on these italicized summaries.

The logistic regression statistics are arrayed in seven appendices, with their integrated models reasonably accounting for variation in judicial outcome. All models are significant at the .0001 level and correctly classify between 69.26 and 76.39 percent of cases, with proportional reductions in error ranging from 37.71 to 50.18 percent.[12] These measures strongly

---

[10] This scholarly wisdom certainly holds true for appeals in routine or noncontroversial matters of criminal justice, commercial law, and the like. Yet it may not be pertinent to this study because I have good reason to believe that most judges here were actively involved in the adjudication process. For example, only 63 (16.0 percent) of 393 essential decisions were resolved by per curiam opinions and memorandum decisions, while 82 cases (20.9 percent) had two signed opinions each; 33 (8.4 percent), three signed opinions; eleven, four signed opinions; four, five signed opinions; and one extraordinary case (*Shahar v. Bowers* 11th Cir. 1997 (114 F.3d 1097)) had six signed opinions. Indeed, the mean number of signed opinions for the 330 non–per curiam decisions was 1.61, a remarkably high average.

[11] Although Sickels (1965), Atkins and Green (1976), and Dubois (1988) were concerned about an "illusion of consensus" in unanimous decisions, I am unable to compare the votes of opinion writers with concurring colleagues not separately writing because the number of votes of judges authoring opinions for courts (as opposed to those concurring separately or dissenting) in the data set is too small (N = 282) to avoid Type II errors in a model with 39 degrees of freedom (Hart and Clark 1999). Accordingly, my opinion writer model combines the votes of judges authoring opinions for courts with those concurring separately or dissenting.

[12] Proportional reductions in error quantify models' predictive capacities. The higher the reduction, the greater the prediction. The measures are calculated by first subtracting a model's modal classification (i.e., the percent of cases of the dependent variable correctly classified by a null model – an intercept with no independent variables) from the percent of cases correctly classified by the full model itself. The resultant difference then is divided by 100 percent minus the modal (Brenner, Hagle, and Spaeth 1990; George and Epstein 1992). For example, if a model correctly classified 69.89 percent of cases and its modal were 52.04 percent, then 69.89 minus 52.04 is 17.85. That amount divided by 47.96 (100 − 52.04) is 37.22 percent, the model's proportional reduction in error.

TABLE 3.1 *Summary of Significant Variables for All Essential Votes[a]*

Category and variable	Sign	p value	Impact
Legal			
Negative precedent	Negative	.026	−.096
Positive precedent	Positive	.000	+.340
Gay family issue	Negative	.000	−.390
Gays in the military	Negative	.000	−.367
Sexual orientation discrimination	Negative	.000	−.395
Sodomy constitutionality	Negative	.018	−.250
Attitudinal			
Age	Negative	.052	−.045
Catholic	Negative	.006	−.104
Jewish	Positive	.003	+.154
Female	Positive	.006	+.123
Minority	Positive	.001	+.201
Prior nonjudicial office	Negative	.024	−.086
Institutional			
Merit★term	Negative	.002	
Term	Positive	.001	
Environmental			
Environmental ideology	Positive	.008	
Consensual sodomy law	Negative	.035	−.085
Gay civil rights law	Positive	.011	+.134
Interest group			
Gay interest group	Positive	.019	+.078
Mixed			
Merit★environmental ideology★term	Positive	.023	
Environmental ideology★term	Negative	.000	
Control			
Federal court	Negative	.000	−.341

[a] Taken from Appendix 3.5.

suggest that the models and their predictions are not merely products of chance but substantially help to explain the phenomena of interest far beyond what an intercept alone would do. The null hypothesis that the independent variables together have no effect may be rejected.

The Overview

Appendix 3.5 displays the results from all 1,439 votes in both court systems and on all essential policy issues.[13] Table 3.1 summarizes important

[13] Significance tests in all appendices are single tailed.

findings from Appendix 3.5.[14] Five categories of independent variable (legal, attitudinal, institutional, environmental, and interest group) are important. Indeed, both judicial behavior models find support here. Six of eight legal variables and six of seven attitudinal variables are statistically significant with consequential impact statistics.[15] *Both precedent and case facts substantially affected judicial decision making, as did judges' personal attributes.*

Appendices 3.6 and 3.7 disaggregate votes by court level.[16] Tables 3.2 and 3.3 summarize those noteworthy results. Both court-level models have noticeably higher proportional error reductions (48.4 and 49.8 percent, respectively) than when all votes are combined (41.7 percent), indicating that court-level disaggregation makes statistical sense.

Since courts of last resort more actively and consistently make policy than intermediate appellate tribunals, intermediate appellate court judges revealed their precedent-adhering role by responding far more faithfully to stare decisis *than high court justices.* In Table 3.3, **positive precedent** is significant at the .001 level and has a consequential, positively signed impact statistic. Although not listed in the table, **negative precedent** has a p value near the threshold of significance (.080) and an impact statistic of −.105. On average, then, the presence of binding precedent substantially increased the probability that an intermediate appellate court judge would follow the precedent's lead. In contrast, court-of-last-resort justices honored only **positive precedent** consistently. Most notably, **negative precedent**, although significant, is *positively* signed in Table 3.2, a truly anomalous

[14] Although not below the customarily accepted maximum p value of .05 for a finding of statistical significance, **age** is close enough to that threshold to be included in Table 3.1. Of course, as p values get smaller, evidence of correlation increases. See, generally, Barnes (2001: 198–99) and Peterson and Conley (2001: 218–19).

[15] Known as first differences among statisticians, impact statistics are reported only for statistically significant variables and measure the change in probability of a dependent variable when an independent variable at issue is increased in value while all other independent variables are held constant at their means (Segal and Spaeth 1993: 370–72). The statistics are not reported for interacted variables because the calculations involving second-order interactions are so complex as not to convey practically useful information (Gill 2001: 25–26). For a discussion of the impact of interactive effects on probability, see Huang and Shields (2000: 81–82).

[16] Legis★term and legis★environmental ideology★term were removed from the model in Appendix 3.6 because the former was perfectly collinear with **legis**, and the latter with **legis★environmental ideology**. Likewise, **appointed★term** was collinear with **appointed**, and **appointed★environmental ideology★term** with **appointed★environmental ideology** in Appendix 3.7. Other interaction terms in subsequent appendices are omitted for the same reasons.

TABLE 3.2 *Summary of Significant Variables for Courts of Last Resort*[a]

Category and variable	Sign	p value	Impact
Legal			
Negative precedent	Positive	.029	+.182
Positive precedent	Positive	.005	+.338
Gay male litigant	Positive	.000	+.268
Attitudinal			
Jewish	Positive	.030	+.216
Female	Positive	.003	+.217
Minority	Positive	.028	+.215
Institutional			
Appointed	Negative	.001	
Appointed*term	Positive	.001	
Legis	Positive	.001	
Merit*term	Positive	.027	
Environmental			
Consensual sodomy law	Negative	.045	−.172
Gay civil rights law	Positive	.028	+.191
Interest group			
Gay interest group	Positive	.046	+.155
Mixed			
Appointed*environmental ideology	Positive	.016	
Appointed*environmental ideology*term	Negative	.013	
Legis*environmental ideology	Negative	.000	
Merit*environmental ideology	Positive	.004	
Merit*environmental ideology*term	Negative	.002	
Control			
Federal court	Negative	.013	−.371

[a] Taken from Appendix 3.6.

finding. Chapter 5 addresses judges' allegiance to *stare decisis* more systematically.

The proportion of attitudinal, institutional, and environmental forces (including the "mixed" interaction terms) in Table 3.2 (14, or 74 percent, of 19 variables) is higher than in Table 3.3 (11, or 65 percent, of 17 variables), whereas the share of legal variables in the latter is 29 percent compared with 16 percent in the former.

An alternative approach for capturing these relative court-level effects is to compare marginal reductions in error. These measures help gauge the proportionate impacts of the legal and attitudinal models, as well as those of institutional and environmental forces. Table 3.4 displays this information. The first row of data comes from all 1,439 essential judicial

TABLE 3.3 *Summary of Significant Variables for Intermediate Appellate Courts*[a]

Category and variable	Sign	p value	Impact
Legal			
Positive precedent	Positive	.000	+.374
Gay family issue	Negative	.000	−.499
Free speech and association	Positive	.019	+.341
Gays in the military	Negative	.002	−.344
Sexual orientation discrimination	Negative	.000	−.449
Attitudinal			
Age	Negative	.002	−.101
Catholic	Negative	.035	−.109
Jewish	Positive	.004	+.189
Minority	Positive	.001	+.272
Institutional			
Appointed	Negative	.000	
Merit⋆term	Negative	.002	
Term	Positive	.003	
Environmental			
Gay civil rights law	Positive	.002	+.236
Temporal			
Post-1990	Positive	.004	+.142
Mixed			
Appointed⋆environmental ideology	Positive	.000	
Merit⋆environmental ideology⋆term	Positive	.013	
Environmental ideology⋆term	Negative	.008	

[a] Taken from Appendix 3.7.

TABLE 3.4 *Comparative Predictive Capacity Statistics (%)*

	Marginal reduction in error achieved from all:			
Model	Legal variables	Attitudinal variables and interaction terms	Institutional variables and interaction terms	Environmental variables and interaction terms
All votes	25.41	23.09	17.95	19.32
Courts of last resort	12.19	26.00	20.32	32.51
Intermediate appellate courts	29.54	20.45	16.84	18.16
Family cases	23.57	27.48	26.16	21.58
Nonfamily cases	14.17	22.72	16.32	14.17
CVAF cases	3.56	25.49	12.33	21.98
Opinion writers	17.42	42.99	13.92	17.42

votes and reveals the marginal reductions in model error for the legal, attitudinal, institutional, and environmental variables and their respective interaction terms. In other words, these figures demonstrate how the addition of one of those variable groups to all of the others increased a model's proportional error reduction, thereby creating a meaningful comparative measure for how much each group separately improved predicative capacity. For example, eliminating the eight legal variables of Appendix 3.5 trimmed the proportional reduction in error for the fully specified model there from 41.67 to 31.08 percent. Hence, those eight variables collectively accounted for a margin of 10.59 points of the reduced error, or 25.41 percent thereof (see the cell of the first row and first column of Table 3.4). Likewise, cutting the seven attitudinal variables (together with the three interaction terms involving **Democrat**) from Appendix 3.5's full model resulted in a proportional reduction in model error of 32.05 percent, so that the attitudinal variables and their interaction terms jointly represented a margin of 9.62 points, or 23.09 percent (see the cell of the first row and second column of Table 3.4). Similar calculations were done for the institutional and environmental components.

Accordingly, the variable-group ranking in order of predictive capacity among all essential votes was legal (25.41 percent), attitudinal (23.09 percent), environmental (19.32 percent), and institutional (17.95 percent). However, the approximate equivalence in impact between the two judicial behavior models vanished when votes were disaggregated by court level. Among votes of courts of last resort, the marginal error reductions produced this rank order: environmental (32.51 percent), attitudinal (26.00 percent), institutional (20.32 percent), and legal (12.19 percent). Among votes of intermediate appellate courts, the order was: legal (29.54 percent), attitudinal (20.45 percent), environmental (18.16 percent), and institutional (16.84 percent). In short, *environmental variables were the most important influences in courts of last resort, with attitudinal forces in a respectable second place, institutional determinants a more distant third, and legal elements almost inconsequential.* In contrast, *legal variables assumed the lead in intermediate appellate courts, while attitudinal, environmental, and institutional effects had important supporting roles. Thus, "the law" was more prominent in intermediate appellate courts – and constrained judges there to a greater extent – than in courts of last resort, which depended far less on "the law" than on the environmental, attitudinal, and institutional forces that went into creating it.*

Appendices 3.8 and 3.9 separate votes by subject matter, with Tables 3.5 and 3.6 summarizing significant findings. As noted, issues

TABLE 3.5 *Summary of Significant Variables for Gay Family Issues*[a]

Category and variable	Sign	p value	Impact
Legal			
Positive precedent	Positive	.000	+.358
Attitudinal			
Age	Negative	.011	−.079
Jewish	Positive	.000	+.235
Female	Positive	.006	+.163
Minority	Positive	.003	+.223
Institutional			
Merit★term	Negative	.001	
Term	Positive	.030	
Environmental			
Consensual sodomy law	Negative	.010	−.145
Temporal			
Post-1990	Positive	.027	+.111
Mixed			
Merit★environmental ideology★term	Positve	.005	
Environmental ideology★term	Negative	.008	

[a] Taken from Appendix 3.8.

TABLE 3.6 *Summary of Significant Variables for Nonfamily Issues*[a]

Category and variable	Sign	p value	Impact
Legal			
Positive precedent	Positive	.011	+.311
Gays in the military	Negative	.000	−.442
Sexual orientation discrimination	Negative	.000	−.469
Attitudinal			
Catholic	Negative	.028	−.141
Minority	Positive	.040	+.210
Prior nonjudicial office	Negative	.036	−.156
Environmental			
Gay civil rights law	Positive	.003	+.294
Interest group			
Gay interest group	Positive	.006	+.176
Mixed			
Merit★environmental ideology	Positive	.018	
Merit★environmental ideology★term	Negative	.020	
Control			
Federal court	Negative	.004	−.468

[a] Taken from Appendix 3.9.

arising from lesbian and gay family creation and maintenance dominated appellate decision making in the 1980s and 1990s, representing 59.5 percent of essential cases. Thus, comparing votes in family and nonfamily decisions is appropriate.

The proportional reduction in model error among votes in nonfamily cases generated by legal, institutional, environmental, temporal, and interest group variables was 38.78 percent, while the corresponding figure among family cases was 28.03 percent. Stated differently, all forces exogenous to judges themselves improved error reduction by almost 40 percent more when jurists addressed nonfamily topics (e.g., the constitutionality of consensual sodomy laws, sexual orientation discrimination in public accommodations, housing, and the workplace, gays in the military, and free speech and association rights) than when they considered family issues (child custody, visitation, adoption, and foster care, domestic partner rights, and same-sex marriage). Moreover, attitudinal forces' marginal error reduction in family cases was more than 20 percent higher than in nonfamily cases (Table 3.4). Thus, *judges' attitudes, as measured by their age, gender, political party affiliation, prior career experience, race, and religion, were vitally important in fashioning appellate court response to the issues most intimate to lesbians and gay men.*

Appendix 3.10 displays the statistics from the 595 (70.3 percent) of 846 family votes involving child custody, visitation, adoption, and foster care, and Table 3.7 summarizes significant findings. That hefty percentage helps explain the influence of judicial attitude in lesbian and gay family decisions because, as Chapter 2 mentions, the universal CVAF legal standard ("the best interests of the child") is nebulous, permitting greater judicial discretion than in cases invoking more concrete and exacting legal criteria. Indeed, Table 3.4 discloses that, in CVAF case votes, attitudinal variables had a marginal error reduction 16 percent greater than environmental forces and more than twice that of institutional factors. In contrast, legal determinants, with a marginal error reduction of only 3.56 percent, had virtually no impact in CVAF cases. Thus, *with the law placing far fewer constraints on CVAF decision making than in other policy domains, judges' personal biases and prejudices had free play there.*

Appendix 3.11 and Table 3.8 address opinion writers, the judges most engaged in the decision-making process. Often faced with daunting caseloads, opinion writers nonetheless take the time and expend the energy to craft opinions for courts or themselves alone. Since the subset includes concurring and dissenting voices as well as authors of majority and unanimous opinions, the overwhelming dominance of attitudinal forces

TABLE 3.7 *Summary of Significant Variables for Child Custody, Visitation, Adoption, and Foster Care[a]*

Category and variable	Sign	p value	Impact
Legal			
Positive precedent	Positive	.002	+.236
Attitudinal			
Age	Negative	.005	−.105
Catholic	Negative	.027	−.133
Jewish	Positive	.038	+.187
Female	Positive	.000	+.268
Minority	Positive	.027	+.222
Institutional			
Merit	Positive	.016	
Merit⋆term	Negative	.002	
Environmental			
Consensual sodomy law	Negative	.000	−.246
Temporal			
Post-1990	Positive	.026	+.145
Mixed			
Legis⋆environmental ideology⋆term	Negative	.045	
Merit⋆environmental ideology⋆term	Positive	.005	

[a] Taken from Appendix 3.10.

TABLE 3.8 *Summary of Significant Variables for Opinion Writers[a]*

Category and variable	Sign	p value	Impact
Legal			
Gays in the military	Negative	.045	−.322
Sexual orientation discrimination	Negative	.043	−.305
Attitudinal			
Catholic	Negative	.040	−.140
Jewish	Positive	.007	+.241
Minority	Positive	.011	+.404
Prior nonjudicial office	Negative	.009	−.181
Temporal			
Post-1990	Positive	.025	+.148

[a] Taken from Appendix 3.11.

(Table 3.4) is unsurprising. Indeed, opinion writers' personal attributes have the highest marginal error reduction of any data set, two and a half times the predictive capacity of either legal or environmental forces, the second-ranking variable categories.

Individual Variables

Among legal factors, **positive precedent** is the most consistently consequential variable, with statistically significant measures in six of seven
layers of analysis, three at the .001 level. Only the smallest data subset
(votes of opinion writers) – the one most dominated by attitudes – provides
the exception. Moreover, the estimates of **positive precedent** are consistently positive and its impact statistics substantial. As Table 3.1 indicates,
favorable precedents increased the probability of dispositions supportive
of lesbian and gay rights claims by .34.[17]

Probabilities are measured on a scale of zero to one, where the former
value represents absolute certainty that an event of interest will not occur,
and the latter absolute certainty that it will. The proverbial 50-50 chance is
signified by .50. The probability baseline of **outcome** for the all-decisions
model of Appendix 3.5 is .509. That is, if all independent variables and
interaction terms in the model are set at their means, the model predicts a
mean for the dependent variable of .509 (compared with its actual mean
of .508). The probability baseline of **positive precedent** in the same model
is .467. That is, the predicted mean of **outcome** with **positive precedent** set
at zero (instead of its mean) in the equation is reduced to .467. Then, with
positive precedent set at one, the prediction becomes .807 (i.e., .467 plus
the impact statistic of +.340), virtually assuring victory in most instances.
A less technical way to understand **positive precedent**'s impact statistic is
this: *The presence of positive precedents in lesbian and gay rights decisions favorably determined 34.0 percent of the probability "space" between complete
success and utter failure for those claims.*

Likewise, although not signed as expected among court-of-last-resort
votes, **negative precedent** is significant in two levels of analysis (r =
−.18, p = .000). Accordingly, *stare decisis was a powerful force among lesbian and gay rights decisions.* Chapter 5 expands the analysis.

Fact-based variables, the other major component of the legal model,
are significant in five tiers of analysis (with family and CVAF models

---

[17] The Pearson product-moment correlation coefficient (r) for **positive precedent** and
outcome is .17 (p = .000). The closer r is to zero, the less indication the measure gives
of correlation between variables. The closer to (an absolute value of) one, the greater the
connection. Negative signs signal inverse relationships between variables. Correlation
coefficients are bivariate measures and do not necessarily capture the nuance of estimates
from multivariate regression, where the effects of numerous potentially important independent variables can be tested at the same time. All r's reported in the book address
independent-variable correlations with **outcome** and arise from the all-votes model unless
otherwise indicated.

the exceptions). **Gays in the military** ($r = -.13$, $p = .000$) and **sexual orientation discrimination** ($r = -.11$, $p = .000$) are each significant in four, at or near the .001 level three of the times. **Gay family issue** ($r = .06$, $p = .03$) is important in two, and **free speech and association** ($r = .07$, $p = .006$) and **sodomy constitutionality** ($r = .04$, $p = .13$) in one each. As Table 1.1 foreshadowed, the variable signs for all votes but those in free speech and association cases are negative because miscellaneous essential cases (the comparison group for the fact-based variables) were decided more favorably to lesbian and gay litigants than any other category. Thus, instead of absolute measures, the impact statistics of the fact-based variables in Table 3.1 and elsewhere are more meaningfully understood to rank order how legal facts affected judicial voting. Consequently, in the vote-based analysis, *sexual orientation discrimination claims were the least well received, with family and military issues close behind.*

Contrary to the expectation in Appendix 3.1, **gay male litigant** enhanced the probability of positive judicial action, by .27 in courts of last resort ($r = .12$, $p = .005$). Judicial sexism is a plausible explanation. Among courts of last resort, the mean of **outcome** for 199 nonfamily votes was .56, for 344 family votes, .51, and for 257 CVAF votes, .47. In other words, CVAF decisions experienced the least success in courts of last resort. Moreover, lesbians were litigants in CVAF cases almost four times as frequently as gay men, while the latter participated in nonfamily cases 82 percent of the time. Thus, *lesbians lost more CVAF cases, while gay men won more nonfamily disputes – all while 84 percent of votes cast in courts of last resort were by male judges.*

Attitudinal variables provide a wealth of information. **Minority** (African Americans, Latinos, and Latinas) is the only variable attaining statistical significance in all seven analytic tiers. *Minority judges were more likely to vote in favor of lesbian and gay rights than majority-race counterparts by a probability factor of about .20* (Table 3.1; $r = .09$, $p = .001$).

Religion also was a powerful force. Significant in six of seven models, **Jewish** is the next most important attitudinal variable ($r = .13$, $p = .000$). *Jewish judges had a probability of voting in favor of gay rights by .15 more than Protestants, and by .26 more than Catholics.*[18] This finding is consistent with Cohen and Liebman's (1997) conclusion that "[American] Jews are firmly committed to permissive social codes, sexual codes in particular."

[18] The difference between Catholics and Jews is greatest (.31) in CVAF cases.

Similarly, **Catholic** is significant in five tiers of analysis ($r = -.07$, $p = .01$). *Roman Catholic judges, compared with Protestant colleagues, were more likely to vote against lesbian and gay rights* by a factor of .10.[19]

Gender was consequential, too. Women judges were more sympathetic than male jurists in four levels of analysis, ranging from .12 among all essential votes ($r = .12$, $p = .000$) to a staggering .27 in decisions involving child custody, visitation, adoption, and foster care ($r = .20$, $p = .000$).

*These robust positive estimates for **minority**, **Jewish**, and **female** fortify historically powerless group empathy as a dimension for analyzing judicial behavior toward lesbians and gay men. The findings bolster the notion that judicial officials from traditionally powerless communities empathize with the plight of other disfranchised groups.*

In contrast, though, American Catholics' nineteenth-century and early-twentieth-century experiences of invidious discrimination and political powerlessness had long faded from memory by late century. Instead, antihomosexual church dogma filtered into Catholic judges' official action. The findings here are particularly telling because five of six prior judicial behavior studies identifying

---

[19] The means of **outcome** in precedent-free decisions appear below. The numbers of votes from which averages were calculated are in parentheses.

	All cases	CLR	IAC
All votes	.520 (1,005)	.528 (428)	.515 (577)
Catholic	.448 (268)	.459 (109)	.440 (159)
Protestant	.506 (557)	.490 (243)	.519 (314)
Jewish	.685 (130)	.764 (55)	.627 (75)
Other	.600 (15)	.600 (5)	.600 (10)
No religion	.657 (35)	.750 (16)	.579 (19)

	Family	Nonfamily	Opinion writers
All votes	.530 (577)	.507 (428)	.532 (331)
Catholic	.431 (153)	.470 (115)	.386 (83)
Protestant	.532 (316)	.473 (241)	.530 (183)
Jewish	.714 (77)	.642 (53)	.756 (45)
Other	.546 (11)	.750 (4)	.800 (5)
No religion	.550 (20)	.800 (15)	.600 (15)

One reason the subject matter means for the votes of Catholic judges are lower in family decisions ($r = -.08$, $p = .02$) and higher in nonfamily ($r = -.05$, $p = .21$) is that Catholic judges may not have been as hostile to claims of invidious discrimination based on sexual orientation as they were to disputes evincing homosexual behavior (Button et al. 1997: 182–84). Notably, the lowest mean of any in the table arises from Catholic opinion writers ($r = -.13$, $p = .004$), in the model most dominated by attitudinal forces.

conspicuous differences based on religion concluded that Catholic judges were more liberal than Protestant jurists (Vines 1964; Bowen 1965; Nagel 1974; Wold 1974; Goldman 1975; cf. Songer and Tabrizi 1999).[20]

Equally noteworthy, Protestant fundamentalists have been among the most prominent opponents of advances in lesbian and gay rights.[21] Some 803 votes in the study were by Protestant judges. Of the 665 I was able to identify with specific denominations, 147 were fundamentalist (classified pursuant to Smith 1987). Fifty-two (55.3 percent) of 94 votes by fundamentalist Protestants in cases without the influence of controlling precedent went against gay rights, while 164 (45.2 percent) of 363 votes by moderate and liberal Protestants were negative. This comparison suggests fundamentalists were roughly 20 percent more likely to deny lesbian and gay rights claims than other Protestants (cf. Songer and Tabrizi 1999). Hence, although more than 20 percent (i.e., 147 of 665) of Protestant votes in the study (the comparison group for **Catholic** and **Jewish**) were potentially very opposed to lesbian and gay rights, **Catholic** still produced statistically significant measures with consequential negative impact statistics.

---

[20] Although the data supporting most of these investigations date from the 1950s, '60s, and '70s, the comparative ideological positions of American Catholics and Protestants appear to have remained constant over time. For example, a 1996 National Election Study sample of 1,500 respondents found that 269 Roman Catholics were more liberal, on average, than 95 percent of 607 Protestants (Busch 1999). Likewise, Schroedel (1999), using survey data from 1994, found Catholic political elites more politically tolerant of homosexuality than Protestants, while Lewis and Rogers (1999), relying on three decades of Gallup and CBS/*New York Times* polling data, discovered the same result at the mass level.

[21] Rand National Defense Research Institute (1993: 200) ("Southern Baptists . . . have come out strongly against measures that would 'secure legal, social or religious acceptance for homosexuality,' or legitimate homosexuality as a normal behavior"); Haider-Markel and Meier (1996) (in a multiple regression analysis of the 1992 antigay ballot initiatives in Oregon and Colorado, Protestant fundamentalism was statistically significant and inversely related to votes in favor of gay rights); Wald et al. (1996) (in a study of 126 cities and counties with gay rights ordinances or policies and of 125 localities chosen at random, the number of conservative Protestants in a community was significant and inversely related to the success of ordinance adoption); Button et al. (1997: 177–82 and 197) ("the [most] common pattern [of opposition to campaigns for gay rights] was for public leadership to be vested in religious groups in the evangelical, or fundamentalist, wing of American Protestantism"); Fisher and Farhi (1997); Haeberle (1999: 157) ("[e]vangelicals [among all categories of NES respondents] were the most firmly opposed to sanctioning the rights of gay men and lesbians"); Green (2000: 122) ("[e]vangelical Protestantism . . . is especially prone to stigmatize homosexuality. . . . In recent times, Evangelicals have been the mainspring of opposition to gay rights, often joined by other theologically conservative churches, such as the Mormons"); and Kohut et al. (2000: 40, 106).

Thus, *these data provide striking evidence of Catholic judges' hostility to lesbian and gay rights.*[22]

Commonwealth v. Wasson (KY 1992) illustrates religion's impact. Voting four to three, the Kentucky Supreme Court held that a statute criminalizing consensual same-sex sodomy violated the Kentucky Constitution's privacy and equal protection guarantees. Kentucky's Berry et al. environmental ideology score, a moderate 49.22 in 1992, presaged a close vote. The progay majority consisted of one Jew, one moderate Protestant (a Disciple of Christ), and two liberal Protestants (an Episcopalian and a Presbyterian), while the dissent was made up of one fundamentalist

---

[22] Arguably the most overtly homophobic opinion in the data set came from a Catholic judge. In *Chicoine v. Chicoine* (SD 1992), the South Dakota Supreme Court reviewed a trial court order awarding a lesbian mother overnight visitation with her five- and six-year-old sons, but only when no unrelated lesbians or gay men were present. The father objected that the visitation was unsupervised. The high court reversed the trial judge, remanding the case for a home study and the provision of adequate enforcement mechanisms for the lesbian and gay visitor prohibition. The facts recited in the appellate opinion reveal that the mother often acted immaturely, perhaps without her children's best interests at heart. Nonetheless, much of the conduct of which the judges disapproved would have been unobjectionable between the mother and a boyfriend (e.g., being "affectionate toward each other in front of the children, caressing, kissing, and saying 'I love you.' "). Most important, though, a concurring opinion stated:

Lesbian mother has harmed these children forever. To give her rights of reasonable visitation so that she can teach them to be homosexuals would be the zenith of poor judgment for the judiciary of this state. Until such time that she can establish, after years of therapy and demonstrated conduct, that she is no longer a lesbian living a life of abomination (*see* Leviticus 18:22), she should be totally estopped from contaminating these children. ... It appears that homosexuals, such as Lisa Chicoine, are committing felonies by their acts against nature and God. [South Dakota decriminalized consensual sodomy in 1977.] ...
There appears to be a transitory phenomenon on the American scene that homosexuality is okay. Not so. The Bible decries it. Even the pagan "Egyptian Book of the Dead" bespoke against it. ... Kings could not become heavenly beings if they had lain with men. In other words, even the pagans, centuries ago, before the birth of Jesus Christ, looked upon it as total defilement. 479 N.W.2d at 896–97.

In a footnote, the concurring justice added:

Article VI of the United States Constitution provides that, inter alia, "no religious test shall ever be required as a qualification to any office or public trust of the United States." Notice the word "ever." Too many constitutional scholars engage in careless theory concerning church-state conflict; this thought process, often, is an effort to impose a religious gag upon judges of our country. 479 N.W.2d at 897.

Here is the clearest example of a Catholic judge manifestly prepared to map his religious beliefs onto secular law, despite the nation's constitutional tradition of separation of church and state.

Protestant (a Baptist) and two Catholics. No other distinction among the popularly elected judges is noteworthy. All seven were white men, none of whom held prior nonjudicial elective office. Even party affiliation split evenly. The majority had three Democrats and one Republican; the dissent, two Democrats and one Republican. Religion offers the only interpretive prism to understand *Wasson*'s split result.

All but one of the remaining attitudinal variables are moderately important. *Prior service in nonjudicial elective government produced more conservative action on gay rights*, by .09 among all votes ($r = -.08$, $p = .004$) and .16 in nonfamily cases ($r = -.09$, $p = .03$). *Once on the bench, former legislators and executives deferred to other branches for innovative government action. Prior career experience in nonjudicial public office spawned ideologically conservative judicial practice.* This reinforces Tate's (1981) findings regarding U.S. Supreme Court justices' votes in civil liberties and economics decisions. There, former prosecutors were consistently conservative (although justices appointed from elective office were liberal in economics cases).

Age *is negative, with the largest impact in cases involving child custody, visitation, adoption, and foster care* ($r = -.11$, $p = .008$). *Judges sixty years of age or older had a probability of voting against lesbian or gay parents by a factor of .20 more than jurists under fifty years of age.*[23] Yet the ideological impact of age across subject matters is less clear. Goldman (1975) found older federal court of appeals judges more conservative than younger colleagues, just as here. But Brace and Hall (1997) discovered that older state supreme court judges were more opposed to the death penalty – a liberal posture – than younger ones.

Despite the general importance of political party to judicial ideology in American courts (Pinello 1999), neither **Democrat** ($r = .20$, $p = .000$) nor its interactions ever reach statistical significance in the models. However, Chapter 4 reveals additional information about party effects in federal courts.

Institutional variables are important to the calculus of gay rights. Contrary to the expectation from Pinello (1995), *appointed judges were not necessarily more liberal than elected jurists on lesbian and gay rights.* Indeed, **appointed** is negatively signed throughout all seven models and significant in two ($r = -.10$, $p = .000$). But **appointed**'s interactions with **environmental ideology** and **term**, when significant, are positive, indicating *the*

---

[23] Estimates obtained for **age** apply to *each* of the two variations in cohort specified in Appendix 3.4.

selection method's otherwise unfavorable impact was moderated as environmental ideology and term length increased.[24]

In contrast, **merit**, when significant, is positively signed (r = .06, p = .02), but negatively mediated by **term**.[25] The fact that *merit selected judges with shorter terms of office were more permissive regarding lesbian and gay rights than merit selected judges with longer terms* is puzzling. A partial explanation comes from Missouri, which, as Chapter 1 notes, had appellate courts that were the least supportive of gay rights. The Show Me State contributed 29 negative CVAF votes (28.2 percent of 103) by merit selected judges against lesbians and gay men in family cases – and has twelve-year terms of office, the longest for this selection method.

As suggested, *the length of judicial term was a consequential institutional force in the adjudication of lesbian and gay rights claims.* Positively signed and significant at the .001 level among all votes (r = −.11, p = .000), and mediating **appointed, merit,** or **environmental ideology** in six models, **term** is a very important variable. *Except among merit selected judges, longer terms of office helped insulate politically vulnerable jurists from disapproving public opinion and resultant electoral and other reprisal when making potentially unpopular decisions. Thus, as hypothesized in the last chapter, institutional factors did constrain the adjudication of gay rights claims.*

All environmental variables were consequential to gay rights, especially in courts of last resort (Table 3.4). As in other political contexts (Berry et al. 1998), **environmental ideology**, significant at the .01 level and positively signed among all votes, *was highly predictive of securing lesbian and gay rights* (r = .05, p = .05). *The more liberal the jurisdiction, the more likely its courts protect gay people.*

Likewise, *the presence of state consensual sodomy and gay civil rights laws helped foretell judicial outcome. Gay activists prophetically knew that*

---

[24] Presumptively, appointed judges in conservative jurisdictions with short terms voted against lesbian and gay rights. However, that premise held infrequently because the mean of **environmental ideology** for votes by appointed judges was 57.11; merit selected, 46.55; popularly elected, 50.22; and legislatively selected, 29.63. Similarly, the mean of **term** for votes by appointed judges was 4.63; merit selected, 2.52; popularly elected, 2.23; and legislatively selected, 2.80. **Outcome**'s mean for votes by appointed judges was .44; merit-selected, .57; popularly elected, .54; and legislatively selected, .40.

[25] Some 180 (56.8 percent) of 317 votes by merit-selected judges in Appendix 3.5 were in favor of lesbian and gay rights claims. Yet 55 (30.6 percent) of those 180 favorable votes were by judges serving six-year terms, as opposed to 32 (17.8 percent) on twelve-year terms. Of the 137 merit-selected votes against rights claims, 38 (27.7 percent) were by judges on six-year terms and 57 (41.6 percent) by those serving twelve years.

the presence of sodomy laws would not bode well for favorable judicial action in non-sodomy-related rights claims. Indeed, the criminalization of same-sex sexual activity had the most evident effect civilly in CVAF cases ($r = -.19$, $p = .000$), boosting adverse action by a remarkable .25. In contrast, gay civil rights statutes augured favorable rulings, by an equally prominent .29 in nonfamily decisions ($r = .11$, $p = .006$).

Time was a consequential independent force, enhancing lesbian and gay litigants' chances in intermediate appellate courts (by .14; $r = .08$, $p = .03$) and among family (.11; $r = .09$, $p = .009$) and CVAF (.15; $r = .10$, $p = .02$) cases. Like public opinion, judges looked more favorably on homosexual rights in the 1990s than in the preceding decade.

The last notable finding concerns **gay interest group**, which had an impressive positive impact in nonfamily decisions (.18; $r = .05$, $p = .28$) and courts of last resort (.16; $r = .14$, $p = .001$). *Judges responded favorably to gay interest group participation in high courts, or generally when considering sexual orientation discrimination, the constitutionality of sodomy laws, free speech and association rights, and the like.*

Applying the Models

The findings here help explain the disparate judicial treatment of lesbians and gay men noted near the beginning of the chapter. Table 3.9 displays the results of model application to those cases.

I first discuss the state court decisions. The second part of Table 3.9 exhibits the probability estimates for the state supreme court treatment of consensual sodomy laws in Georgia, Kentucky, and Texas. The mean estimate (derived from the court-of-last-resort model, Appendix 3.6) for the six Georgia justices invalidating their state's statute is .88, while that of the five jurists upholding the Texas law is .37. Table 3.2 suggests how these results occurred. Although both courts have six-year terms of office, Georgia chooses justices by merit selection, while Texas employs popular election. Environmental ideology varied between the two states: 40.27 for Georgia in 1998 and 29.57 for Texas in 1994. Thus, the strong interaction between selection method and environmental ideology indicated in Table 3.2 favored more positive action in Georgia. Moreover, two of the six Georgia justices in the *Powell* majority were African Americans and two were women, while one in the Texas majority was Catholic. Collectively, these attitudinal, environmental, and institutional characteristics predisposed the Texas sodomy statute challenge to defeat while facilitating a victory in Georgia. Similar results arise from the nonfamily case

TABLE 3.9 *Probability Estimates for Selected Cases*

	Court-of-last-resort (CLR) model				Nonfamily cases model			
	Votes favoring gay rights		Votes opposing gay rights		Votes favoring gay rights		Votes opposing gay rights	
U.S. Supreme Court cases	N	Mean	N	Mean	N	Mean	N	Mean
Bowers v. Hardwick	4	.51	4	.45	4	.42	4	.33
Hurley v. Irish-American	9		9	.37			9	.21
Romer v. Evans	6	.44	3	.24	6	.24	3	.14
Boy Scouts v. Dale	4	.53	5	.26	4	.32	5	.12

	CLR model				Nonfamily cases model			
	Votes favoring gay rights		Votes opposing gay rights		Votes favoring gay rights		Votes opposing gay rights	
State supreme court cases addressing constitutionality of sodomy statues	N	Mean	N	Mean	N	Mean	N	Mean
Powell v. State (GA)	6	.88	1	.78	6	.68	1	.43
Com. v. Wasson (KY)	4	.74	3	.59	4	.80	3	.69
State v. Morales (TX)	4	.46	5	.37	4	.34	5	.28

Cases involving adoptions by lesbian mothers' domestic partners	CLR model				Intermediate appellate court (IAC) model				CVAF model			
	Favoring		Opposing		Favoring		Opposing		Favoring		Opposing	
	N	Mean	N	Mean	N	Mean	N	Mean	N	Mean	N	Mean
Adoptions of B.L.V.B. (VT)	5	.61							5	.58		
Matter of Dana (NY)	4	.51	3	.16			4	.35	4	.62	4	.30
Matter of Jacob (NY)									4	.62	3	.20

Cases involving rights of surviving domestic partners to New York City apartments	IAC model				Family cases model			
	Votes favoring gay rights		Votes opposing gay rights		Votes favoring gay rights		Votes opposing gay rights	
	N	Mean	N	Mean	N	Mean	N	Mean
Braschi v. Stahl Associates Co.	4	.63	4	.21	4	.73	4	.27
East 10th St. Assoc. v. Goldstein								

model (Appendix 3.9), displayed on the right side of Table 3.9's second part. As Table 3.6 indicates, an additionally important variable in the nonfamily cases here was the participation of gay interest groups. Lambda Legal Defense and Education Fund was *amicus* in the Georgia case, while no such group appeared in the Texas appeal.

The difference in probability means of Table 3.9's second part is greater between the Georgia and Texas cases than between the majority and dissenting opinions within each case. Yet finding larger inter-court gaps than intracourt ones should not be surprising because the only variables accounting for the latter are attitudinal. All other variables are invariate within individual cases. Moreover, the combination of environmental, institutional, legal, temporal, and interest group forces always had substantially greater impact than attitudinal factors alone (Table 3.4). That is, attitudinal variables approach parity with the combined strength of other forces affecting judicial policy only when the former's marginal error reduction nears 50 percent – which only the opinion writer model comes close to doing. Thus, differences between courts were consistently likely to be much greater than within them. Accordingly, although the lone Georgia dissenter's probability estimate of .78 (under the court-of-last-resort model) and the Texas dissenters' mean of .34 (under the nonfamily model) appear anomalous, the respective majority estimates of .88 and .28 provide the meaningful bases for understanding the dissenters' scores. *Commonwealth v. Wasson*, the Kentucky sodomy decision best understood through the lens of religion, also failed to produce probability means dramatically different from each other.

In similar fashion, the models for courts of last resort (Appendix 3.6), intermediate appellate courts (Appendix 3.7), and CVAF cases (Appendix 3.10) facilitate comprehension of the different outcomes in Vermont and New York regarding adoption by lesbian couples, displayed in the third part of Table 3.9. Personal attributes were vitally important in this subset of family cases. The four *Dana* judges were Catholic males with a mean age of sixty-five (Tables 3.3 and 3.7), while none of the Vermont justices was Catholic, one was a woman, and their mean age was fifty-six (Tables 3.2 and 3.7). Similarly, the four *Jacob* judges overturning *Dana* had a mean age of fifty-eight, two were Jewish, two were women, one was African American, and one was Latina (Tables 3.2 and 3.7).[26] The three

---

[26] The votes of four Catholic minority women are in the book's data set, one of whom served on a court of last resort. In *Jacob*, her probability estimates are .62 (under the

Jacob dissenters were white males with a mean age of sixty-four, two of whom were Catholic.[27] A final distinction differentiating New York's split result from Vermont's unanimous action is the Green Mountain State's gay civil rights law (Tables 3.1 and 3.2).

The explanation for the eighteen-month difference in domestic partner rights to continued possession of rent-controlled and rent-stabilized New York apartments is binding positive precedent. The Court of Appeals, the state's highest tribunal, reversed the adverse result in the *Braschi* decision; hence, the members of the second intermediate appellate court panel deferred to that positive controlling authority (Tables 3.3 and 3.5). The probability means are displayed in the bottom part of Table 3.9.

Finally, the top part of Table 3.9 reveals that the models do not work quite as well for the U.S. Supreme Court. The *Hardwick* estimates under the court-of-last-resort model indicate a closely divided court,[28] while the nonfamily model estimates disclose a bench leaning against gay rights. Likewise, the *Hurley* and *Dale* estimates presage losses there. *Romer* is the only decision not accurately predicted, especially by the nonfamily cases model. Yet Table 3.6 discloses the largest impact statistic ($-.468$) for federal courts of any model, with that ($-.371$) of Table 3.2 close behind. In other words, *any federal court decision was likely to be predisposed against gay rights*, a topic catalogued in greater detail in the next chapter. Thus,

---

court-of-last-resort model) and .77 (under the CVAF one). The mean estimate (under the model for all essential votes, Appendix 3.5) for the six votes of the four Catholic minority women is .67. Two of the votes were negative, one in an intermediate appellate court case with a controlling negative court-of-last-resort precedent. Accordingly, *the two personal attributes (gender and minority status) of these judges that tended to enhance favorable treatment of lesbian and gay rights usually outweighed their one characteristic (religion) working against those rights.*

[27] Despite the tendency toward modest intracourt probability differences noted in the text's preceding paragraph, other dramatic examples of personal attribute impact are available. In *Constant A. v. Paul C.A.* (PA 1985), the antigay majority was two Catholic men (probability mean of .35 under the family case model), the dissenter a Jewish woman (.73). The progay majority in *Doe v. Casey* (DC Cir. 1986) consisted of Jewish and African American Protestant males with mean age of 43 (.39), the dissent of a 63-year-old Catholic man (.05) (Table 3.1). The progay majority in *Adult Anonymous II* (NY 1982) were three Jewish men and a Latino (mean of .64), the dissenter a white Catholic male (.43). There, the positive impact of the majority's religion and minority status even offset the negative effect of their mean age (66), while the negative force of the dissenter's religion overwhelmed the positive influence of his youth (51) (Tables 3.3 and 3.5).

[28] I was unable to include the *Hardwick* vote of Justice Byron R. White in my data set because of incomplete personal attribute information about him.

the models' inability to predict the rare Supreme Court outcome favorable to lesbian and gay rights comes as no surprise.[29]

Answers to Questions Posed in Chapter 2

The findings from this chapter's statistical models provide answers to questions posed in the narratives chapter. For example, when the Alabama Supreme Court severely limited child visitation by the lesbian mother in *Ex Parte D.W.W.*, the thirteen-year mean age differential between the majority and dissenting justices indeed helps explain the disposition. **Age** is significant and negatively signed in the CVAF model (Table 3.7). Further, Tables 3.2 and 3.7 indicate that the African American judge's support for the gay mother was no coincidence. That personal attribute alone positively determined more than 20 percent of the probability space for his vote.

With **appointed** negatively signed in Table 3.2, Alabama's judicial selection method of popular election – used in 157 (39.9 percent) of 393 cases, and the most frequently employed system in the book's data set – was not necessarily an unfavorable institutional factor compared with appointment (at 30.9 percent, the second most utilized method). However, the positive interaction between **appointed** and **term** means that, as their term length increased, appointed court-of-last-resort judges supported gay rights more than elected counterparts. Thus, compared with court-of-last-resort judges in Massachusetts, New Hampshire, and New York (appointed for fourteen-year terms or longer), Alabama Supreme Court justices, elected every six years, were not as institutionally disposed to favor civil rights claims by lesbians and gay men.

The large negative impact statistic for **consensual sodomy law** in Table 3.7 clearly indicates that the sodomy statutes in Alabama and Mississippi substantially reduced the likelihood that gay people would prevail there in CVAF cases. Sodomy laws negatively shaped almost one-quarter of the probability space for gay litigants in those disputes.

Interestingly, the negative precedent that the Alabama lesbian mother visitation case provided for the custody suit did not incline the latter case to lose. In fact, the peculiar positive finding for **negative precedent** in Table 3.2 signals that the visitation decision conceivably might have borne

---

[29] As discussed below, Table 3.11 confirms this observation. The all-votes model dispositively predicts 80.0 percent of federal cases opposing gay rights, but only 25.0 percent of those favoring them.

favorably on the custodial disposition. However, the failure of **negative precedent** to be significant in Table 3.7 discounts the probability the Alabama precedent had any effect. Again, Chapter 5 tests *stare decisis* in detail.

The prior career experience in nonjudicial elective office of the Mississippi Supreme Court justices who awarded custody of the boy to his mother and monstrous stepfather apparently had no pivotal impact on their votes. Although **prior nonjudicial office** is significant in Table 3.1, the variable doesn't appear in either Table 3.2 or Table 3.7.

Minnesota's gay civil rights law may have been important for the intermediate appellate court grant of custody and visitation to the two lesbians and gay man in the LaChapelle case (Table 3.3). Yet the presence of **gay civil rights law** in Table 3.6, and not in Table 3.7, denotes that such legislative action was more consequential in nonfamily scenarios than otherwise.

The Berry et al. environmental ideology measures were significant by themselves only in Table 3.1. Their singular value diminished when data were disaggregated, either by court level or by subject matter. Instead, **environmental ideology** remained consequential by means of its interactions with institutional variables. Thus, enhanced Berry et al. scores increased the likelihood that appointed court-of-last-resort judges would favor gay rights (Table 3.2). For instance, the appointed justices of the New Hampshire Supreme Court, with **environmental ideology** measures below 20, were not as receptive to the rights claims in *Opinion of the Justices* and *Stuart v. State* as the appointed justices of the Vermont Supreme Court, with scores above 80, in *Baker v. State, Adoptions of B.L.V.B. and E.L.V.B.*, and *Nickerson v. Nickerson*. Hence, lesbians and gay men lost in the Granite State, but won in the Green Mountain State.

With regard to the disparate dispositions between jilted and unprotected domestic partners in Florida and New York, religion may have been eventful for those intermediate appellate court decisions because **Catholic** is negatively signed in Table 3.3. But the variable's appearance in Table 3.6, and not in Table 3.5, indicates that the participation of Roman Catholic judges was more fateful in the nonfamily arena than elsewhere. Likewise, prior career experience in nonjudicial elective office had the most negative impact in nonfamily disputes.

Attitudinal forces were vital to the cases involving health insurance benefits to domestic partners. The age, gender, and religion of the Oregon judges, compared with that of the jurists in California, Colorado, New Jersey, and Wisconsin (Table 3.5), were crucial to success in the Sheltering State.

The dissents by the only African American and only woman on the Mississippi Supreme Court in the triumphant peeping Tom decision are no surprise (Tables 3.2 and 3.5), although the majority justices' prior career experience appears not to have significantly influenced their votes. Also, the partisan differences in composition between the majority and dissent was not a substantial catalyst there.

Finally, as hypothesized in Chapter 2, Wisconsin's gay civil rights law was key to Jamie Nabozny's win in federal court (Table 3.6). In addition, the participation by two gay interest groups as counsel and *amicus curiae* helped secure victory. The two variables combined positively determined 44.8 percent of the probability space in the case.[30]

Model Performance

Of course, the models are not perfect. Some Catholic judges such as William Brennan, Jr., supported gay rights, and some African Americans such as Clarence Thomas did not.[31] In fact, U.S. Supreme Court justices provide numerous prominent exceptions to the chapter's findings. As septuagenarians and octogenarians, Brennan, Thurgood Marshall, and John Paul Stevens were among the justices most supportive of gay rights, while much younger colleagues (e.g., Antonin Scalia and Thomas) were not. Harry Blackmun became an ardent gay rights advocate as he aged. These examples fly in the face of the book's general proposition that older judges were less receptive to lesbian and gay rights claims than younger ones. Also, the Court's first female justice was among the majority in *Hardwick*, despite the chapter's finding that women jurists usually voted more favorably on gay rights issues than men. Last, the next chapter demonstrates that presidential party was the most reliable attribute for predicting federal judicial action, with Republican appointees far less responsive to lesbian and gay litigants than judges selected by Democrats. Nonetheless, Blackmun, Brennan, and Stevens were appointed by Republicans.

---

[30] Since logistic regression is not a linear function, combined variable effects may not be calculated through the addition of impact statistics. Thus, the pooled result of **gay civil rights law** and **gay interest group** in Table 3.6 is not +.470 but +.448.

[31] Some 120 (44.8 percent) of 268 votes of Catholic judges in cases without the influence of controlling precedent were in favor of lesbian and gay rights, while 24 (31.6 percent) of 76 votes of minority judges opposed those rights. Some 51 (33.6 percent) of 152 votes of women judges, 41 (31.5 percent) of 130 votes of Jewish judges, and 57 (39.0 percent) of 146 votes of judges under the age of 50 were negative. Eighty-seven (40.8 percent) of 213 votes of judges with prior service in nonjudicial public office and 240 (47.3 percent) of 507 votes of judges 60 or older were positive.

The book's statistical findings about personal attribute impacts are statements of probabilities. That exceptions exist does not disprove the findings but merely reinforces the reality that probabilities never predict behavior absolutely. Moreover, if indeed U.S. Supreme Court justices frequently behaved differently than other appellate jurists (a topic not systematically addressed here), that fortifies the Court's exceptionalism.

Indeed, readers may leave this volume with an appreciation of the importance to lesbians and gay men of tribunals other than the high federal bench. Only 86 (21.9 percent) of the study's 393 cases essential to gay rights were from federal courts, and merely 53 of the 307 state court decisions raised federal questions. Thus, potential U.S. Supreme Court involvement was limited to 139 cases, just slightly more than one-third (35.4 percent) of the decisions forming the nation's judicial response to lesbian and gay rights claims in the last two decades of the twentieth century.

As mentioned earlier, the chapter's models correctly classify between 69.26 and 76.39 percent of cases, with proportional error reductions between 37.71 and 50.18 percent. In the universe of judicial model performance, these predictive measures are acceptable.[32]

Dividing the probability scale into thirds provides a useful categorization of estimates and further elaborates models' predictive capacity. Scores below .333 predict negative votes regarding lesbian and gay rights, and those above .667, favorable ones. The middle third represents an indeterminate range, where votes may go either way. Under this analysis, then, only four (10.5 percent) of 38 estimates in Table 3.9 are inconsistent – those for the *Romer* majority under the nonfamily case model, the *Dale* dissent with the same model, the lone Georgia dissenter via the court-of-last-resort model, and the *Wasson* dissent through the nonfamily model. All other estimates are consistent – either .667 or below for votes against gay rights or .333 or above for those in favor. At the same time, 16 (42.1 percent) estimates are dispositive – either below .333 for votes against gay rights or above .667 for favorable ones.

As further illustration, Table 3.10 arrays probability estimates for the case narratives of Chapter 2. There, only 2 (8.7 percent) of 23 estimates are

---

[32] For example, George and Epstein (1992) achieved correctly predicted cases and reductions in error of 81 and 58 percent, respectively; Unah (1997), 80 and 58 percent; Wahlbeck (1998), 75 and 55 percent; Maltzman, Spriggs, and Wahlbeck (2000), 79 and 43 percent; and Richards and Kritzer (2002), 77 and 39 percent.

TABLE 3.10 *Probability Estimates for Votes in Cases Essential to Lesbian and Gay Rights Discussed in Chapter 2*[a]

Category and case[b]	Votes favoring gay rights		Votes opposing gay rights	
	N	Mean	N	Mean
CVAF				
Petition of C.M.A.	I	.77		
J.B.F. v. J.M.F.	4	.31	I	.29
Ex Parte J.M.F.			7	.28
Ex Parte D.W.W.	2	.47	5	.29
Weigand v. Houghton	2	.52	6	.43
LaChapelle v. Mitten	3	.68		
Lesbian and gay family issues not involving CVAF				
Posik v. Layton	2	.53		
Matter of Cooper			4	.19
Tanner v. O.H.S.U.	I	.76		
Plaxico v. Michael	3	.50	5	.35
Sexual orientation discrimination				
Stemler v. City of Florence	2	.58	I	.43
Simonton v. Runyon			2	.31
Nabozny v. Podlesny	3	.25		
Sodomy enforcement				
Baluyut v. Superior Court	I	.64		
First Amendment				
Gay Student Services v. TAMU	3	.68		
Miscellaneous				
Sterling v. Minersville	2	.79	I	.61
Collins v. Faith School District	5	.81		

[a] Derived from the model in Appendix 3.5.
[b] Case names in bold indicate complete information for all votes cast in the decision.

inconsistent – the favorable votes in *J.B.F.* and *Nabozny*. Eleven (47.8 percent) estimates are dispositive.[33]

---

[33] The opinion (*Matter of Cooper* NY 1993) with the lowest mean (.19) is notable regarding the impact of judges' personal attributes. The four *Cooper* jurists were Catholic men, with a mean age of 65, three of whom served in prior nonjudicial public office – all characteristics generally having negative effects on lesbian and gay rights (Table 3.1). Thus, the combination of those four attributes gave the gay litigant before that bench very little chance.

TABLE 3.11 *Distribution of Probability Estimates of Opinions*[a]

| Court system | Opposing lesbian and gay rights | | | | | | |
| | Prob < .33 | | .33 ≤ Prob ≤ .67 | | Prob > .67 | | |
	N	Percent	N	Percent	N	Percent	Total
Federal	56	80.0	12	17.1	2	2.9	70
State	39	22.9	103	60.6	28	16.5	170
Both	95	39.6	115	47.9	30	12.5	240

| Court system | Favoring lesbian and gay rights | | | | | | |
| | Prob < .33 | | .33 ≤ Prob ≤ .67 | | Prob > .67 | | |
	N	Percent	N	Percent	N	Percent	Total
Federal	6	16.7	21	58.3	9	25.0	36
State	15	6.9	102	47.0	100	46.1	217
Both	21	8.3	123	48.6	109	43.1	253

| Court system | Combined | | | | | | |
| | Inconsistent | | .33 ≤ Prob ≤ .67 | | Dispositive | | |
	N	Percent	N	Percent	N	Percent	Total
Federal	8	7.5	33	31.1	65	61.3	106
State	43	11.1	205	53.0	139	35.9	387
Both	51	10.3	238	48.3	204	41.4	493

[a] Derived from the model in Appendix 3.5.

Table 3.11 displays estimates for all opinions in the data set.[34] Clearly, the model for votes in all essential decisions (Appendix 3.5) works most effectively for federal court opinions opposing gay rights. Estimates there are dispositive 80.0 percent of the time and inconsistent at a rate of only

[34] Estimates for votes of concurring opinions were consolidated with those for majority-opinion votes. Likewise, all dissenting votes were treated jointly. Thus, the 493 estimates of Table 3.11 represent votes either in opposition to or in favor of gay rights claims, regardless of the number of discrete authored opinions. Further, I lack complete information for any votes in six decisions (*Kovatch v. California Casualty Management Company* CA 1998; *Murray v. Oceanside Unified School District* CA 2000; *V.C. v. M.J.B.* NJ 1999; *Adoption of Pavlik* NY 1983; *Ireland v. Flanagan* OR 1981; and *Marriage of Wicklund* WA 1996) of the data set. Also, I do not include in Table 3.11 decisions in three litigations where judges' votes were duplicated because of en banc review or other reconsideration (*Watkins v. U.S. Army* 9th Cir. 1988; *Shahar v. Bowers* 11th Cir. (120 F.3d 211); *Republican Party of Texas v. Dietz* TX 1996).

2.9 percent. However, the same model is also the least efficient in estimating federal opinions favoring rights claims, dispositive only 25.0 percent of the time, and substantially more inconsistent (16.7 percent). Yet overall the model is wholly off the mark only 10 percent of the time and right on target in about 45 percent of the remaining instances.

A final predictive strategy estimates the probability of all votes in each case, regardless of direction, and finds how well these all-vote means predict case outcome. The estimates (via Appendix 3.5's model) for 80 (42.1 percent) of 190 cases decided against lesbian and gay rights are dispositive, while 22 (11.6 percent) are inconsistent. For cases supporting rights, 81 (42.6 percent) estimates of 190 are dispositive, 17 (8.9 percent) inconsistent.[35] Overall, dispositive estimates represent 42.4 percent of the case population, and inconsistent ones, 10.3 percent – virtually identical to the results from opinions.[36]

Accordingly, the lesbian and gay rights claims models developed here predict case outcomes with reasonable degrees of accuracy.

Conclusion

Integrated models of judicial behavior provide a good understanding of federal and state appellate court treatment of lesbian and gay rights claims in the last two decades of the twentieth century. Logistic regression of 1,439 votes by 849 appellate judges in 400 decisions and opinions from 87 courts in all federal appellate jurisdictions and 47 states reveals that legal variables (precedent and case facts), attitudinal variables (judges' age, gender, minority group status, religion, and service in prior nonjudicial elective office), environmental factors (jurisdictional ideology, consensual sodomy laws, and gay civil rights laws), institutional determinants (judicial selection method and term length), time, and interest group participation are statistically significant with consequential impact statistics.

---

[35] *City of Atlanta v. McKinney* (GA 1995) is not included here because the decision involved three separate rights claims, two of which prevailed. Thus, **outcome** for the case was coded as .5 rather than as either a clear loss or win.

[36] The model for courts of last resort (Appendix 3.6) substantially improves prediction. There, estimates for 20 (50.0 percent) of 40 decisions against gay rights are dispositive, while three (7.5 percent) are inconsistent. For cases supporting rights, 30 (60.0 percent) of 50 estimates are dispositive, and none is inconsistent. In all, dispositive estimates account for 55.6 percent of the population, and inconsistent ones, just 3.3 percent. Appendix 3.6's enhanced proportional reduction in error explains the model's better performance.

4

Judicial Federalism and the "Myth of Parity"

For at least a generation, scholars have debated the value of judicial federalism – the sharing of judicial power between the fifty states and the federal government. The U.S. Supreme Court itself helped provoke the debate by quoting Bator (1963: 509), in *Stone v. Powell* (1976: 494, n. 35), that "there is 'no intrinsic reason why the fact that a man is a federal judge should make him more competent, or conscientious, or learned with respect to [federal law] than his neighbor in the state courthouse.'" The controversy over judicial federalism remains timely because the second iteration of Bator's assertion by a Supreme Court justice occurred in Ruth Bader Ginsburg's dissent in *Bush v. Gore* (2000). Moreover, the debate apparently transcends ideology since the conservative majority in *Stone* endorsed judicial federalism, while the liberal dissenters did so in *Bush*.

Prompted by *Stone*, Neuborne's "The Myth of Parity" (1977) argued against trusting allegedly institutionally incompetent state courts with the adjudication and possible vindication of federal constitutional rights. Neuborne's thesis is that federal courts are superior because they enjoy several institutional advantages. First, the federal bench, perceived to be far more prestigious than state posts, attracts more competent and diligent judges. Second, federal judges are more familiar with federal law than state jurists since that is the former's specialty. Third, since all federal judges enjoy life tenure, they are more insulated from majoritarian pressures than state judges, many of whom are elected to fixed terms. Finally, federal judges have a psychological predisposition in favor of protecting federal constitutional rights because they are more likely than state judges to see enforcing the federal Constitution as their responsibility, while state judges are prone to be jealous of state authority. Other scholars reinforce Neuborne's position (Amar 1985, 1991; Yackle 1994: 44 and 50; Jackson 1998).

Arguing that federal courts are not inherently preferable to safeguard federal constitutional rights, Chemerinsky (1988, 1991) posed a significant challenge to Neuborne. Chemerinsky thinks a historical anomaly explains the scholarly preference for federal court enforcement of federal constitutional rights. The 1950s and '60s witnessed an unprecedented federal court expansion of civil rights and civil liberties at the expense of state power. The federal courts, dominated by Democrats and liberal Republicans, were thought to be "more likely to enforce desegregation, apply constitutional criminal procedure protections, and follow Warren Court decisions than were their state counterparts" (Chemerinsky 1991: 597). In this historical context, "[t]he assumption of a lack of parity between federal and state courts is not surprising" (ibid.). Yet in different circumstances (such as the 1980s, with conservative Reagan and Bush appointees dominating the federal bench), Chemerinsky maintains that there is no reason to expect federal judges to protect federal constitutional rights more than state judges.[1]

Despite an abundance of theory regarding judicial federalism and state court competence, little purposeful empirical investigation of the topic has been achieved. Indeed, only three published empirical studies (Solimine and Walker 1983; Solimine 1991; Gerry 1999) compare federal and state court action.[2]

Solimine and Walker (1983) analyze approximately 1,000 federal district court and state appellate cases between 1974 and 1980 adjudicating claims based on the First Amendment, the Fourth Amendment, and the Equal Protection Clause of the Fourteenth Amendment. Although outcomes in criminal cases were virtually identical (33.9 percent of claims were upheld in federal courts and 30.5 percent in state courts), federal courts sustained one-third more civil claims than state courts (44.6 vs. 33.2 percent). The authors conclude, nonetheless,

> that these data show no clear, across-the-board hostility on the part of state courts to claims of federal constitutional rights, and that they therefore support the existence of relative parity between the state and federal systems. (Solimine and Walker 1999: 50)[3]

---

[1] For elaboration of the judicial federalism debate, and an expansion of the rebuttal to Neuborne, see Bator (1981), and Solimine and Walker (1999).

[2] Solimine and Walker (1983) and Solimine (1991) are updated and rewritten in Solimine and Walker (1999).

[3] Questioning *inter alia* whether the proper comparison is between state appellate courts and federal district courts, Herman (1991: 660) nonetheless believes Solimine and Walker's

Solimine's (1991) data are more modest, comparing 20 federal appellate opinions and 114 state trial and appellate decisions from 1987, all interpreting 42 U.S.C. §1983. Summarizing the findings, Solimine and Walker (1999: 79) observe that "[i]n both systems plaintiffs find it difficult but not impossible to prevail at the trial level, though they meet with more success on appeal.... [S]tate courts are competent to adjudicate federal causes of action."

Gerry (1999) investigates state and lower federal court interpretations of *Nollan v. California Coastal Commission* (1987), a landmark Supreme Court takings-clause precedent. Comparing 112 reported state cases and 47 reported lower federal decisions between 1987 and 1997, the author notes that

[t]he aggregate findings are startling in their similarity. A roughly equal percentage of federal and state court opinions offered deferential (39.5 percent and 31 percent) and nondeferential (26.5 percent and 26 percent) readings of *Nollan*'s heightened scrutiny. If the more ambiguous cases ... are dropped from the study, the ratio of deferential to nondeferential opinions under *Nollan* in the state and federal courts is closer still. With respect to *Nollan*'s breadth, the similarities are even more striking. A similar percentage of state and federal courts (36 percent and 40 percent) apply a narrow reading to *Nollan*, and the percentage of federal and state courts offering an explicitly broad interpretation of *Nollan* is almost identical (24 percent and 23 percent). (Gerry 1999: 285)

Gerry concludes that his study "offers strong empirical evidence of parity between state and federal courts in the takings area" (290).

Despite this assertion, these studies do not supply compelling evidence proving or disproving Neuborne's thesis. Several limitations hinder the inference of broad conclusions from the three articles.[4] First, their statistical methods are rudimentary. Unadorned frequency distributions lack the nuance of regression analysis, where the effects of numerous potentially consequential independent variables can be tested simultaneously. Second, although Neuborne's thesis centers on the ability of judges to implement individual rights, each of these empirical studies uses the case as its unit of analysis. Although not problematic for trial court observation, examining cases at the appellate level is risky because it involves the

data in fact support disparity between the systems because their finding demonstrates that federal courts were moderately more likely to uphold federal constitutional claims than state counterparts.

[4] Since others (Marvell 1984: 1338–39; Chemerinsky 1988: 267–68; Herman 1991: 658–59) have critiqued the analytical approach of Solimine and Walker (1983) and Solimine (1991), I mention here only those issues not yet adequately addressed. For a response to their critics, see Solimine and Walker (1999: 51–55).

observation of group action. Drawing conclusions about judges from that scrutiny invites ecological fallacy (discussed more fully in the next chapter). At any rate, research can more profitably disaggregate appellate court action to the level of individual judges,[5] which none of these studies does. Finally, although Gerry's results are highly suggestive, interpretations of one takings-law precedent are not a good surrogate for other legal topics. His findings cannot be generalized convincingly.

This chapter helps ameliorate the observational and analytical gap regarding the myth of parity through the prism of lesbian and gay rights litigation in American appellate courts during the last two decades of the twentieth century. Indeed, gay rights cases offer an excellent opportunity for the empirical study of judicial federalism. A comprehensive quantitative examination of appellate court response to an emergent minority's legal claims affords the occasion for fresh insights into the relative advantages of federal and state courts in the resolution of individual rights. In particular, lesbian and gay rights issues are an especially suitable vehicle for studying judicial federalism since they are a comparatively new issue domain in the law that prompts strongly held positions, at both the mass and the elite levels (Haeberle 1999; Schroedel 1999). As the introductory chapter urges, the research design conceives a crucial case study, that is, if federal courts protect the rights of this especially despised minority better than state tribunals, then the myth of parity must apply across the board.

In contrast to the dominant view on judicial federalism among law professors, Rubenstein (1999: 599–600) argues that "gay litigants seeking to establish and vindicate rights have generally fared better in state courts than they have in federal courts" and that there are "institutional advantages of state courts in protecting individual rights that are missing from Neuborne's depiction of these competing fora." First, Rubenstein points out that state judges have greater technical competence over the subject matters most important to lesbians and gay men because those issues (frequently involving domestic relations) typically are ones of state, not federal, law. Second,

the three primary ways gay people interact with the legal system in which their sexual orientation might be put at issue [are] in family law cases, criminal cases, and as jurors. Because of this fact, state judges in their judicial capacity are far

---

[5] "[F]or [much] if not most analysis of judicial behavior the case, or more precisely the judge-case (i.e., the vote), is the appropriate unit [of analysis]." Giles and Zorn (2000: 10)

more likely to have dealt, in a professional environment and in a professional manner, with lesbians and gay men [. . ., leading directly to] gay people be[ing] treated fairly in the courtroom. (ibid.: 616–17)

Finally, Rubenstein notes that state judges' greater involvement in local politics may make them more institutionally responsive to minority claims than more politically insulated federal jurists.

Judicial federalism variables added to the fully integrated judicial behavior models of Chapter 3 will probe whether the federal court/state court dichotomy is statistically significant, thereby determining whether federal courts protected lesbian and gay rights more vigorously than state tribunals.

Judicial Federalism Variables

Four measures test parity between federal and state courts.[6] First, significant and positive estimates for **federal court** will support the Neuborne hypothesis that federal tribunals are preferable to state courts for the protection of individual rights. Second, comparing the effects of judicial interpretation of the federal Constitution (**federal constitutional issue**), on the one hand, and of state constitutions (**state constitutional issue**), on the other, will add nuance to the analysis.[7] Significant and positive estimates for the latter will support the Rubenstein (1999) hypothesis that state courts are superior to federal courts for the protection of lesbian and gay rights because all instances of state constitutional construction in my data set were by state courts.[8] Accordingly, this variable examines the "new" judicial federalism – "state judges' increased reliance on state declarations of rights to secure rights unavailable under the U.S. Constitution" (Tarr 1994: 63; Cauthen 2000a, 2000b). Appendix 4.2 identifies decisions in both subject matter categories. Finally, **privacy clause** tests whether explicit privacy guarantees contained in the constitutions of ten states enhanced state court protection of lesbians and gay men (Flemming, Holian, and Mezey 1998).

---

[6] The coding rules of the last three of these variables appear in Appendix 4.1, while the first is in Appendix 3.4.

[7] In the event both federal and state constitutional claims appeared in a case, it and its votes were coded as a **federal constitutional issue**. Hence, **state constitutional issue** addresses decisions interpreting only state constitutions and not the federal charter.

[8] Although federal courts in diversity actions might have occasion to interpret state constitutions, there were no such opportunities here.

Findings

Table 4.1 displays frequency distributions – the rudimentary statistics of earlier judicial federalism studies – for the 393 decisions and 1,665 votes in my data set.[9] *No support for the Neuborne hypothesis is found* there. Concerning all decisions, regardless of subject matter, *state courts decided cases in favor of lesbian and gay rights more than twice as frequently as federal fora* (i.e., at rates of 57.2 vs. 25.6 percent, respectively). The same is true both for state supreme courts compared with the U.S. Supreme Court (56.3 vs. 25.0 percent) and for state intermediate appellate courts and their federal counterparts (57.6 vs. 25.6 percent).

With regard to those decisions adjudicating federal constitutional issues – the heart of Neuborne's concern – state tribunals resolved lesbian and gay rights claims 56.3 percent more positively than federal courts (47.2 vs. 30.2 percent). State courts of last resort interpreted the federal charter more than twice as favorably for lesbians and gay men as the U.S. Supreme Court (55.0 vs. 25.0 percent). State intermediate appellate courts did so 39.0 percent more often than federal courts of appeals (42.4 vs. 30.5 percent).

In contrast, *state courts interpreting state constitutions were far more receptive to lesbian and gay rights claims than either court system was in applying the federal Constitution.* In particular, *state supreme courts construed state constitutions at a rate greater than two and a half times more favorable to gays than the U.S. Supreme Court did when reading the federal charter* (67.9 vs. 25.0 percent) – a remarkable discovery because "[o]verall, twenty-five years of the new judicial federalism have not led to state supreme courts becoming leaders in civil liberties policymaking" (Cauthen 2000a: 1202).[10]

These frequency distributions provide absolutely no evidence in support of Neuborne's thesis because *federal courts never acted more hospitably*

---

[9] Table 4.1 has more judicial votes than appear in the N of subsequent charts because logistic regression requires complete data for each entry. I lack comprehensive personal attribute information for 226 (13.6 percent) of the 1,665 votes. For example, I was unable to identify the religious affiliation of Justice Byron R. White and, therefore, could not include his vote in *Hardwick* from Table 4.1 in the logistic regressions of Tables 4.2 through 4.5.

[10] Cauthen's conclusion differs with Baum's (1993: 149) remark that "perhaps the most important trend in state supreme courts has been a movement toward ideologically liberal policies." Further, in a four-state study of overruling of precedent by courts of last resort between 1965 and 1996, Alabama, Florida, and Pennsylvania were "remarkably consistent in the percentage of liberal overrulings – approximately 66 percent," while the rate in New Jersey was 75 percent liberal (Lindquist and Pybas 1998: 31).

TABLE 4.1 *Frequency Distributions*

	All decisions, regardless of subject matter					
	Federal courts			State courts		
		In favor of lesbian and gay rights			In favor of lesbian and gay rights	
	Total	N	%	Total	N	%
Both court levels						
Cases	86	22	25.6	307	17.5[a]	57.2
Votes	353	122	34.6	1,312	740	56.4
Courts of last resort						
Cases	4	1	25.0	88	49.5[a]	56.3
Votes	36	14	38.9	562	303	53.9
Intermediate appellate courts						
Cases	82	21	25.6	219	126	57.5
Votes	317	110	34.1	750	437	58.3

	Only decisions adjudicating federal constitutional issues					
	Federal courts			State courts		
		In favor of lesbian and gay rights			In favor of lesbian and gay rights	
	Total	N	%	Total	N	%
Both court levels						
Cases	63	19	30.2	53	25	47.2
Votes	269	106	39.4	239	119	49.8
Courts of last resort						
Cases	4	1	25.0	20	11	55.0
Votes	36	14	38.9	128	77	60.2
Intermediate appellate courts						
Cases	59	18	30.5	33	14	42.4
Votes	233	92	39.5	111	42	37.8

	Only decisions adjudicating state constitutional issues (and not interpreting the federal constitution)		
	State courts		
		In favor of lesbian and gay rights	
	Total	N	%
Both court levels			
Cases	28	18.5[a]	66.1
Votes	137	88	64.2
Courts of last resort			
Cases	14	9.5[a]	67.9
Votes	92	58	63.0
Intermediate appellate courts			
Cases	14	9	64.3
Votes	45	30	66.7

[a] *City of Atlanta v. McKinney* (GA 1995) involved three separate lesbian and gay rights claims, two of which prevailed. Thus, outcome here was coded as .5 rather than either 0 or 1.

toward this dispossessed minority than their state counterparts.[11] Indeed, these percentages amply bolster Rubenstein's (1999) assertion that state courts have been considerably more responsive to lesbian and gay litigants than federal tribunals.

Logistic regression confirms these findings and supplies other consequential quantitative empirical information further discrediting the hypothesis that federal judges are in institutionally superior positions to protect minority interests from majority discrimination.

Appendix 4.3, combining Chapter 3's model for all essential decisions with the judicial federalism variables, discloses that the estimate for **federal court** is statistically significant (p = .0007) and negatively signed (r = −.18, p = .000). Litigating in federal courts, compared with state fora, increased the probability of dispositions *against* lesbian and gay rights claims by the staggering factor of .31. Although the Neuborne hypothesis concentrates on federal court protection of federal constitutional rights, this statistical datum reveals that federal judges were much less favorably disposed to lesbian and gay rights claims, regardless of subject matter, than state jurists.

Moreover, **federal constitutional issue** in Appendix 4.3 has a significant (p = .000), *negatively* signed estimate (r = −.10, p = .000). In other words, compared with all nonconstitutionally founded lesbian and gay rights claims in either court system, the presence of causes of action based on the federal Constitution increased the probability of gay people's *losing* by .19. Indeed, lesbian and gay litigants lost both federal and state lawsuits based on the federal Constitution 35.6 percent more often than nonconstitutional cases in the data set (i.e., loss rates of 62.1 percent and 45.8 percent, respectively).

An essential ingredient of the Neuborne thesis is that appointed, lifetenured federal judges are in an institutionally superior position, compared with state judges (selected by sundry methods and usually sitting for fixed terms, ranging from six to fourteen years), to resist majoritarian forces opposing minority rights. Accordingly, one would anticipate that executive appointment of judges and term length would be significant positive forces in judicial action on lesbian and gay rights claims, notwithstanding court system or subject matter. Nonetheless, **appointed**'s estimate in Appendix 4.3, as in every model of Chapter 3, is *negatively*

---

[11] There is parity in vote outcomes between federal and state intermediate appellate courts interpreting the federal Constitution (39.5 vs. 37.8 percent), although that equivalence disappears at the case level.

signed (although not significant; p = .07). This suggests that judges appointed by presidents or governors favored minority rights *less* frequently than their *elected* counterparts.

Further, the significant (p = .04) and positively signed estimate for **merit** in Appendix 4.3 means that Missouri Plan judges were more sympathetic to rights claims than either appointed or elected analogues, despite the fact that 93 (29.3 percent) of the merit selected votes were by public officials facing retention elections every six years, and another 55 (17.4 percent) every eight years. Indeed, **term**'s significant (p = .001) and negatively signed interaction with **merit** indicates that the *shorter* the term length of Missouri Plan judges (casting 22.0 percent of votes in the data set), the *greater* the probability of positive treatment of lesbian and gay litigants.

The crucial point for judicial federalism among these findings is that *neither presidential appointment nor life tenure of federal judges necessarily improves the probability that their policy making will be more favorable to disfranchised minorities than that of state counterparts selected by other methods or for shorter terms of office.*

Appendix 4.4 examines the 454 votes adjudicating federal constitutional claims. This array analyzes the data set most directly pertinent to the Neuborne thesis. Again, **federal court** (representing just over half of the votes) is negatively signed, although not significant (p = .56; r = −.09, p = .06). Hence, there is no support here for Neuborne.

Appendix 4.5 exhibits the regression analysis of the 576 votes adjudicating either federal or state constitutional claims. Once again, **federal court** is negative, although not significant (p = .37; r = −.14, p = .001). **State constitutional issue** is positively signed and approaches the threshold of significance (p = .09; r = .16, p = .000). This suggests that, compared with federal and state decisions construing the federal Constitution, state courts interpreting their own state constitutions did so more favorably for the rights and liberties of lesbians and gay men – supporting the notion that a new judicial federalism has been at work in the nation.

Appendix 4.6 looks at courts of last resort, and once more, **federal court** is negative and now marginally significant (p = .057; r = −.07, p = .11). Moreover, both **appointed** and **term** are negatively signed and significant (.000, r = .07, p = .09, and .014, r = −.01, p = .91, respectively). Thus, *in the courts most responsible for policy making, both executive appointment and long term of office alone were inversely related to positive results for lesbian and gay litigants.* Yet **appointed** was moderated through its positive and significant (.005 and .000, respectively) interactions with environmental ideology and term. Differently stated, *appointed judges in ideologically liberal jurisdictions were far more likely to rule in favor of lesbians and gay men than appointed judges in conservative jurisdictions.* Further, *appointed judges were more disposed to positive dispositions as their term of office increased.* Although the latter finding offers evidence of Neuborne's institutional structure hypothesis, the former one, together with those on the separate effects of **appointed, federal court**, and **term**, most definitely contradict the theory.

Additionally, **privacy clause** is positive and significant (p = .017; r = .09, p = .05) in Appendix 4.6, signifying that *the presence of state constitutional privacy provisions facilitated greater rights recognition by state courts of last resort.*

Appendix 4.7 investigates intermediate appellate courts, again with **federal court** negative and not significant (p = .15; r = −.21, p = .000). In addition, **federal constitutional issue** is negative and significant (p = .003; r = −.15, p = .000) for the second time. **Privacy clause** is as well (.014; r = .07, p = .04), indicating that among lower state appellate courts, constitutional privacy provisions hindered rights recognition, unlike state high courts – a puzzling incongruity.

As in the court-of-last-resort model, **appointed** is negative and significant (p = .000; r = −.21, p = .000) and positively interacts (p = .000) with **environmental ideology**. Contrary to that model, though, **term** here is positive and significant (p = .000; r = −.17, p = .000), the second finding of support for the institutional structure thesis.

Appendix 4.8 analyzes federal court votes separately. The model's most noteworthy attribute is the significant (p = .000; r = .39, p = .000) and positive estimate for **Democrat**.[12] *Votes by federal judges appointed by Democratic presidents, compared with those by Republican appointees, had a greater probability of favoring lesbian and gay rights claims* by the colossal factor of .41. Indeed, **Democrat**'s impact statistic here is larger than that of *any* attitudinal variable in Chapter 3. The mean of **outcome** for the 83 votes by Democratic appointees in federal court decisions without the influence of binding precedent was .60. In contrast, **outcome**'s mean for the 116 votes by Republican appointees in precedent-free cases

---

[12] To conserve degrees of freedom, no interaction terms were included in this model with the smallest N in the book (Hart and Clark 1999). Moreover, the addition of **Democrat∗environmental ideology** to Appendix 4.8 did not improve proportional reduction in error, as it did in other models with larger N's.

was .27. Thus, *Democratic appointees voted 122 percent more favorably for gay rights than Republican counterparts.*[13] These findings strongly bolster Chemerinsky's (1991) assertion that the historical aberration of Democrats and liberal Republicans dominating the federal judiciary in the 1950s and '60s best explains the surge in federal court civil rights successes of the period, and not the institutional features of the courts themselves.[14]

State court votes appear separately in Appendix 4.9, with little new information for this chapter, except that the alleged strategy of lesbian, gay, bisexual, and transgender interest groups to establish a "state-based judicial declaration of human rights" (Salokar 2001: 266) did not materialize, at least with regard to the effect of those groups' participation as counsel and *amicus.* **Gay interest group**'s estimate in state court cases (Appendix 4.9) is effectively zero, while its impact in federal court decisions (Appendix 4.8) is a very impressive .32.[15]

Disaggregating case subject matter between the two court systems discloses a final point. Table 4.2 displays the distribution between federal and state systems of the subjects that were statistically significant in Appendix 4.3. Clearly, federal courts dominated the adjudication of cases involving gays in the military and shared sexual orientation disputes with state tribunals, while the latter reigned in gay family issues and sodomy constitutionality challenges. To quantify how these relationships affected judicial behavior, I use Appendix 4.3's impact figures to calculate a comparison of what effect subject matter distribution had on the two court

[13] These findings for **Democrat** are not artifacts of coding the variable by means of the appointing president's party (cf. Epstein and King 2002: 74–75, 88–90, and 95, with Cross, Heise, and Sisk 2002: 136, and Revesz 2002: 181). Adopting an alternative coding rule for the variable of using federal judges' own personal party affiliations instead of the appointing president's party still results in significance at the .001 level and an impressive impact statistic (+.370, compared with +.405 for presidential party). In contrast to the federal court findings here, $r = .10$ ($p = .001$) for **Democrat** and **outcome** in state court votes.

[14] Pinello's (1999) meta-analytic finding that judges' party affiliation alone explains 48 percent of the ideological variance in federal courts also supports Chemerinsky's position. In 1996, moreover, the U.S. Senate voted on the Employment Nondiscrimination Act largely along party lines, with Democrats supporting the legislation and Republicans opposing it.

[15] Appendices 3.8 and 3.9 help explain the anomaly. **Gay interest group** has a significant positive effect in nonfamily case votes, 52.8 percent of which came from federal courts, while the variable's estimate in CVAF votes, all of which came from state courts, is negative (although not significant). In short, state judges hearing appeals involving children apparently did not respond favorably to the participation of groups such as Lambda and the ACLU, while federal judges in nonfamily disputes did.

TABLE 4.2 *Distribution of Case Subject Matters Between Federal and State Courts*

	Federal courts				State courts			
	Cases		Votes		Cases		Votes	
	N	%	N	%	N	%	N	%
Gay family issue	4	1.7	11	1.3	230	98.3	835	98.7
Gays in the military	26	89.7	87	85.3	3	10.3	15	14.7
Sexual orientation discrimination	37	48.1	137	52.5	40	51.9	124	47.5
Sodomy constitutionality	4	18.2	28	25.2	18	81.8	83	74.8

systems.[16] Specifically, I multiply each impact statistic by the percentage that each system's caseload represents as a portion of the subject matter (pursuant to Table 4.2). For instance, state courts cast 98.7 percent of the votes in gay family issues, and federal tribunals, 1.3 percent. The impact statistic for **gay family issue** in Appendix 4.3 is −.442. Thus, family votes contribute −.436 (−.442 × .987) to the state court product and −.006 (−.442 × .013) to the federal. Treating all four significant subject matters this way, I estimate the cumulative federal court product is −.598, and the state court, −.863.[17] In other words, *state courts adjudicated appreciably more cases with topics predisposed to lose than federal courts did. Nonetheless, the former still substantially outperformed the latter in securing minority rights.*

Conclusion

Multiple data slices from twenty years of lesbian and gay rights litigation in American appellate courts never once demonstrate that federal courts were more hospitable to this disfranchised minority than state tribunals. On the contrary, these empirical vistas manifest that state courts were by far the more responsive arena for protecting sexual minorities.

The book's introductory chapter notes that its research design conceives a crucial case study: If federal courts protect the rights of this especially

---

[16] Admittedly not an orthodox use of the impact statistic (addressing a nonlinear concept), my improvisation illustrates a point that might be gleaned elsewhere in the book.

[17] The four significant subject matters represent 94.8 percent of all state court votes, but only 81.2 percent of the federal ones. **Free speech and association** and miscellaneous cases comprise the remaining votes. Both categories are more positively associated with **outcome** than the other four. Hence, the former's inclusion would make the federal product proportionally more positive and thus further widen the gap between the court systems.

despised minority more than state tribunals, then the myth of parity must apply across the board. Since the data here disprove Neuborne's thesis as applied to lesbian and gay rights claims, what about the broader proposition? Does a failure of proof for a crucial case study hypothesis confirm its obverse (i.e., if federal courts do not protect the rights of this minority better than state tribunals, then they never will with regard to any disfranchised group)? Obviously not. Yet in light of these lesbian and gay rights findings, no one can make a credible argument that appointed, life-tenured federal judges necessarily are institutionally preferable, compared with their colleagues on the state bench, to resist majoritarian forces opposing minority rights. Instead, the far more meaningful inquiry into securing rights in federal courts focuses on the partisanship of presidents selecting appellate judges.

Perversely, the myth of parity still endures because federal and state courts have not treated minority litigants comparably. This time, though, state tribunals – rather than their once vaunted federal counterparts – are the superior forum for rights vindication.

5

A Test of *Stare Decisis*

The doctrine of *stare decisis* is central to traditional jurisprudential explanations of decision making in American courts. In theory, adjudged cases furnish examples or authority for analogous future fact patterns or similar questions of law. *Stare decisis* provides security and certainty, mandating established legal principles under which rights may accrue, be recognized, and be followed. The doctrine facilitates a predictable legal system.[1] Moreover, precedent undergirds the Langdellian case method, dominant for more than a century in American legal education (Stevens 1983; LaPiana 1994).

Despite an abundance of theory, however, comparatively little purposeful empirical investigation of *stare decisis* has been achieved. Early studies by law professors and economists used judicial citation analysis to scrutinize precedential effect (Merryman 1954, 1977; Landes and Posner 1976),[2] but the technique inadequately captured the phenomenon (Klein 1976; Landes, Lessig, and Solimine 1998: 271–76). Early quantitative research in political science was chiefly descriptive (Ulmer 1959; Schmidhauser 1962; Danelski 1986; Banks 1992).[3] Not until the 1990s did law professors and economists (Cohen 1991; Schuck and Elliott 1991; Merrill 1992; Cohen and Spitzer 1994; Cross and Tiller 1998; Kerr 1998; Sisk, Heise, and Morriss 1998; Lim 2000) and political scientists (Pacelle and Baum 1992; Songer, Segal, and Cameron 1994; Brenner and Spaeth

---

[1] See, e.g., Schauer (1987), Eisenhower (1988), Maltz (1988), Alexander (1989), Caminker (1994), and Carp and Stidham (2001: 286).

[2] For later examples of citation analysis, see Kosma (1998) and Landes, Lessig, and Solimine (1998).

[3] See Johnson (1987) for a more analytic approach.

1995; Brenner and Stier 1996; Knight and Epstein 1996; Segal and Spaeth 1996; Songer and Lindquist 1996; Gerber and Park 1997; Lindquist and Pybas 1998; Banks 1999; Brent 1999; Spaeth and Segal 1999; Spriggs and Hansford 2001) systematically address precedential impact.

This research produced conflicting results, regarding both hierarchical (or "vertical") *stare decisis* – where higher court decisions bind lower courts – and the collegial (or "horizontal") variety[4] – where courts are obliged to follow their own prior decisions (Caminker 1994; Bergman 1996: 982–983; Camp 1997: 1662).

The Legal Literature

Four empirical articles by law professors and economists published in legal periodicals focused on vertical *stare decisis* (Schuck and Elliott 1991; Cohen and Spitzer 1994; Cross and Tiller 1998; Kerr 1998), two on horizontal (Merrill 1992; Lim 2000), and two on federal district judges' deference to other, nonbinding district court decisions (Cohen 1991; Sisk et al. 1998). The hierarchical studies investigated lower court submission to *Chevron U.S.A., Inc. v. Natural Resources Defense Council, Inc.* (1984), which required federal courts to defer to permissible agency interpretations of ambiguous statutes. One of the collegial articles explored the high court's adherence to the same precedent (Merrill 1992). Indeed, *Chevron* was a treasure trove for law professors, begetting an academic cottage industry without which the legal literature evidently would be bereft of empirical fodder for precedential-impact research.[5]

The four articles scrutinizing vertical *stare decisis* exhibit the contradictory findings of the literature. Schuck and Elliott (1991) performed the first consequential hierarchical study and identified a short-term *stare decisis* effect. They analyzed lower court review of agency statutory interpretations during six-month periods before and after *Chevron* and found a substantial increase in the rate of affirmances of agency action and significant decreases in the frequencies of remands and reversals after the 1984 precedent, although the effects had weakened somewhat by 1988.

---

[4] I follow the usage of "collegial" *stare decisis* by Kornhauser and Sage (1993: 6), rather than "intertemporal," proposed by Stearns (1995: 1315).

[5] Electronic databases such as *Lexis* and *Westlaw* greatly facilitate the observation of appellate courts' affirming, reversing, or remanding cases, and the calculation of frequency distributions is mathematically straightforward. Yet, as the introductory chapter notes, more challenging quantitative investigation often dismays legal scholars.

The authors concluded that *Chevron* did indeed cause lower courts to defer more to agencies, as the Supreme Court mandated. Cohen and Spitzer (1994) documented that the appellate court affirmance rate of agency interpretations decreased from the mid–70 percent range in 1983–87 to the mid–60 percent range in 1988–90, discrediting *Chevron*'s long-term impact. Cross and Tiller's (1998) investigation of 170 agency reviews by the District of Columbia Circuit between 1991 and 1995 led to the conclusion that judges' partisanship far better explained case outcome than obedience to precedent. In contrast, Kerr (1998), examining 223 published circuit court decisions applying *Chevron* in 1995 and 1996, found that 38 percent of courts engaging in two-step analyses resolved the interpretive issue at step one, and 62 percent at step two, while 58 percent of the step one cases reversed the agency, but only 11 percent of the step two cases did – suggesting that *Chevron* had its intended effect through the mid-1990s.

Merrill (1992), a horizontal *stare decisis* study, found that before *Chevron*, the Supreme Court deferred to agencies 75 percent of the time, while afterward the overall high court deference rate was 70 percent, and that for the cases in which the Court cited the *Chevron* two-step procedure, it deferred only 59 percent of the time – hardly frequencies manifesting the Court's unswerving fidelity to its own policy.

The confusion of outcome among these appellate court studies may be attributable in part to a serious methodological flaw: ecological fallacy, or drawing conclusions about individuals based solely on the observation of groups (Robinson 1950).[6] Schuck and Elliott, for example, introduced their conclusions about *Chevron*'s precedential impact as follows:

> In recent years, scholars associated with the Critical Legal Studies movement have emphasized that legal doctrine is "indeterminate" in the sense that it does not constrain *judges* in *their* resolution of disputes. These "law skeptics" argue that because legal rules are "sufficiently ambiguous or internally contradictory to justify any result we can imagine," *judges* can use it to rationalize decisions reached on other, usually undisclosed grounds.
>
> This claim, law skeptics acknowledge, is at bottom an empirical one, and it has implications that can be tested. At least in its strong form, the claim implies that doctrinal changes such as *Chevron* should not affect the pattern of results

---

[6] King (1997) proposes methods for dealing with such issues, but the book is not a panacea (Rivers 1998). More important, ecological fallacies are avoidable in judicial behavior research because judges are not so more numerous than cases that individual-level observation is unfeasible. Even more accessible is the "judge-case" – the vote by each judge in each case (Giles and Zorn 2000).

reached in subsequent cases by lower courts, provided that the *judges'* personal and political predilections remain essentially unchanged during the period under study. (1991: 1029; footnotes omitted; emphasis added)

Clearly, the authors were concerned here with how attributes of judges affected outcomes in cases, but their unit of analysis was the case, not the judge. Had their empirical investigation focused on judges, the findings may have varied significantly. Likewise, the units of analysis in Merrill (1992) and Cohen and Spitzer (1994) were cases, not judges.

The other horizontal *stare decisis* study, by an economist, is the most statistically sophisticated. Lim (2000) used logit regression and linear probability models constructed from factor analysis to demonstrate that Supreme Court justices' votes in precedent-setting cases very much influenced their actions in later decisions. Yet Lim's article suffers from methodological limitations, too. For example, his data set is confined to just thirteen judges over an eight-year span, and as Supreme Court case studies, his models do not incorporate important institutional or environmental variables. Moreover, the paper fails to report proportional reductions in error for the logit models, while the adjusted R^2 values for the linear probability analysis are often modest at best. These shortcomings hinder the generalizability of, and confidence in, Lim's findings and conclusions.

With regard to the empirical examination of federal district judges' deference to other district court decisions, Cohen (1991) conducted a study of 196 judges adjudicating the constitutionality of the federal Sentencing Guidelines and found none of his precedent variables was statistically significant, while Sisk et al. (1998: 1497), investigating 291 district court votes on the same issue, did conclude that "judges appear to find the written opinions of other judges valuable as persuasive precedent when they confront difficult issues and there is no binding higher authority" – again, contradictory results.

The Political Science Literature

Five published studies by political scientists examined vertical *stare decisis*. Gruhl (1980) found that 93 percent of libel decisions by U.S. Courts of Appeals between 1964 and 1974 fully complied with Supreme Court mandates. Using lower federal court reactions to fourteen randomly selected Supreme Court decisions between 1950 and 1975, Johnson (1987) found inferior courts did heed high court precedent. Pacelle and Baum

(1992) studied cases remanded by the Supreme Court during its 1965 through 1974 terms and documented that the high court's authority significantly shaped the behavior of lower court judges. However, Songer et al. (1994), tracking how Supreme Court search-and-seizure precedents fared in federal circuit courts, reached mixed conclusions about the impact of *stare decisis*. Although Songer and Sheehan (1990) confirmed *New York Times v. Sullivan*'s (1964) very substantial impact in federal libel law, those authors discovered no impact at all of *Miranda v. Arizona* (1966) in the federal criminal procedure context. A sixth article, examining Supreme Court cases in which justices were faced with overturning their own precedent from lower courts on which they served, determined that the most important information for anticipating justices' behavior was their policy preferences (Gerber and Park 1997).

Most of the published precedential-impact research in political science focused on horizontal *stare decisis*. Segal and Spaeth surveyed a 40 percent random sample of landmark, nonunanimous U.S. Supreme Court decisions between 1953 and 1995 and checked the frequency with which dissenting justices in precedent-setting cases followed, in progeny, the majority opinions with which they disagreed. The researchers found justices voted their preferences, and against precedent, 90.8 percent of the time, concluding:

> While we have no argument with Cardozo's claim that *stare decisis* should be the rule and not the exception, the empirical results are to the contrary. Potter Stewart and Lewis Powell are the sole exceptions among modern Supreme Court justices who virtually never subjugate their preferences to the norms of *stare decisis*. (1996: 987)

In contrast, Knight and Epstein believe that precedent acts as a meaningful constraint on judicial decision making, just as a norm of consensus impeded the filing of separate opinions during the Marshall Court era. Counting attorneys' use of authorities in case briefs, justices' appeals to precedent during conference, their invocation of precedent in opinions, and the Court's infrequent alterations of *stare decisis*, the authors concluded that justices strategically modify their positions in deference to the *stare decisis* norm in order to produce outcomes close to policy preferences. Knight and Epstein view the Segal and Spaeth research design as myopic:

> [J]ust as one would be unable to make claims about the operation of the no-dissent norm by looking only at the content of Marshall Court votes, one would be unable to demonstrate the importance of precedent by merely considering dissents cast by justices in the progeny of important cases. (1996: 1019)

Brenner and Stier (1996) tracked how the four center justices of the Warren Court conformed to the precedent of thirty-six major decisions from which they dissented, used selection rules for progeny cases different from Segal and Spaeth, and also included memorandum and per curiam decisions as progeny. The research discovered the four center justices complied with precedent 47 percent of the time.

Songer and Lindquist (1996) criticize Segal and Spaeth as misunderstanding the nature of the choices justices face when addressing precedent, oversimplifying the process of *stare decisis*, and using an unrepresentative sample of Supreme Court decisions. The authors recoded some of the Segal and Spaeth data and included summary decisions associated with their landmark cases, determining that support for preferences dropped to 68.8 percent, compared with the earlier finding of 89.4 percent (Segal and Spaeth 1994).

In their "first falsifiable, systematic test of the influence of *stare decisis* on the behavior of U.S. Supreme Court justices," Spaeth and Segal (1999: 315), in the book-length sequel to their 1996 journal article and the most ambitious empirical examination of *stare decisis* to date, argue that precedent is key when compelling justices to vote for case outcomes they otherwise would not support. Indeed, scholars testing *stare decisis* should not be concerned primarily with precedent's preaching to the choir – or to congregants generally. Judges already adhering or indifferent to policies that precedents promote are not the attentive audience for gauging *stare decisis*'s coercive power. Rather, precedent is consequential when it converts atheists (to strain the metaphor). Judge Jerome Frank recognized this long ago, writing that "[s]*tare decisis* has no bite when it means merely that a court adheres to a precedent that it considers correct. It is significant only when a court feels constrained to stick to a former ruling although the Court has come to regard it as unwise or unjust" (*United States ex rel. Fong Foo v. Shaughnessy* 1955: 719).

Thus, researchers' methodological challenge is specifying the jurists constituting the relevant yardstick for measuring the full import of *stare decisis*: the precedential atheists. In fact, much of the precedential impact literature is irreparably flawed because it fails to disaggregate judges into precedential congregants and indifferents, on the one hand, and atheists, on the other. Without the distinction, scholars cannot make meaningful estimates of *stare decisis*'s constraining effect.

Spaeth and Segal met the challenge again by investigating, now throughout the Court's history, how dissenting justices in both major and minor precedent-setting decisions voted in progeny cases. Their inquiry continued an insistence that justices vote *twice*, once in dissent and again in progeny cases. The book indubitably is a pathbreaking achievement whose primary – and substantial – methodological virtue is its caution: Justices' issue positions are clear once they have voted publicly, and there is no need for conjecture about how they would vote with or without precedent. Indeed, *any other vote-based research design testing precedential impact necessarily will be less scrupulous than Spaeth and Segal's approach.* Certainly, the least attractive surrogates involve speculating about how judges would vote under the sway of precedent. That option is untenable, begetting too much uncertainty. Rather, alternative empirical strategies minimally must require votes subjected to the influence of *stare decisis* and then ascertain precedential atheists by other means.

Spaeth and Segal's admirable methodological clarity and circumspection come with a considerable price. For example, their analysis disregards the clout of unanimously decided precedents, the ones most likely to command respect in progeny cases. Chief Justice William Rehnquist, writing for the Court in *Payne v. Tennessee* (1991), argued that *stare decisis* carries less force for decisions rendered by close margins. Moreover, scholars' use of only nonunanimous opinions has been identified as a research-design moderator distorting findings of variable strength for the broad range of judicial action.[7]

The title of the book by Spaeth and Segal, *Majority Rule or Minority Will*, should more properly be *Institutional Precedent versus Personal Precedent*. The psychological dynamic of justices' adherence to personal precedent prevents the generalizability of the results.[8] Publicly switching policy positions requires political actors with abundant humility, a character trait typically in short supply on the high bench. The Spaeth and

---

[7] Pinello (1999: 243) (meta-analysis of 84 judicial behavior studies conducted between 1959 and 1998 revealed that "scholars' use of only nonunanimous appellate opinions overestimates [political] party's effect" on judicial performance).

[8] Lim (2000: 723) ("differentiating between two kinds of stare decisis [is crucial in judicial behavior research]: institutional stare decisis and individual stare decisis. The former pays attention to whether a justice [generally] follows precedent, while the latter focuses on whether a justice follows her own prior voting in the earlier case ... she participated in") and Woodward and Armstrong (1979: 479–80) ("[m]oreover, [Justice Potter] Stewart felt trapped by a phrase that [Justice William] Rehnquist had convinced him to add to a 1972 opinion (*Bd. of Regents v. Roth*). Though it had seemed harmless to Stewart at the time, the phrase said that due process should be invoked only for those property interests specifically created by governments. The Court should not be in the business of creating new interests. *Stewart was bound by his own precedent*") (emphasis added).

Segal research blueprint in fact focuses on the least psychologically prepared group of jurists likely to bend to precedent's bidding. The authors
require that justices not only acquiesce to policies they oppose but also to
contradict themselves *conspicuously*.

The research design conceived a crucial case study, that is, if precedent
works here, then it must work everywhere. Spaeth and Segal discovered
that justices later deferred to majority positions from which they dissented
only 11.9 percent of the time and concluded that "the justices are rarely
influenced by *stare decisis*" (1999: 287–88). But as noted at the end of the
last chapter, a failure of proof for a crucial case study hypothesis does
not confirm its obverse, that is, if precedent does not work here, then
it does not work anywhere. Hence, Spaeth and Segal's finding does not
warrant an inference that precedent is impotent under less exacting – and
more frequently occurring – conditions. The book mistakenly conflates
the imperatives of its ingenious research technique with the universe of
latent judicial obedience to *stare decisis*.

Spaeth and Segal in fact test the resolve of justices only under singular
conditions. Clearly, for example, a group of jurists more pliable to precedent's siren call are those opposed to precedential policies but joining the
bench after they were rendered. There, judges do not have to humble
themselves publicly by abandoning vanquished positions, and thus, submission to *stare decisis* may be more pervasive than Spaeth and Segal's
divining rod detects.

Inconspicuous compliance with *stare decisis*, furthermore, promises a
vastly larger usable-vote pool than Spaeth and Segal's circumscribing
methodology permits. Approximately 214,000 votes by justices in signed
opinions of the Court have been cast since its creation.[9] Unaware of
the actual number decided under the authority of *stare decisis*, I adopt,
for argument's sake, the same proportion of precedent-controlled cases
for the Supreme Court found among court-of-last-resort decisions in the
present study: 17.4 percent. Relying on this premise, I estimate a total of
37,236 precedent-bound high court votes, which indicates that the 2,425
qualifying for Spaeth and Segal's inspection (1999: 287) represent roughly

[9] The figure is a rough estimate. Using the data from Table 9 ("Supreme Court Opinions:
Count per Court Term") of Blaustein and Mersky (1978) and from Table 2-7 ("Number of
Signed Opinions and Number of Cases Disposed of by Signed Opinion and by Per Curiam
Opinion, 1926–1992 Terms") of Epstein et al. (1994), I multiplied the number of signed
opinions of the Court per term by the number of justices on the Court and cumulated the
results.

6.5 percent of the Court's *stare decisis*–constrained output.[10] Surely, even the most hostile adversaries of the legal model (Segal and Spaeth 1993) cannot believe *stare decisis* is *potentially* decisive *at best* less than 7 percent of the time. If that were true, their 300-plus-page book would be the quintessential quixotic quest.

The Spaeth and Segal analysis, dependent on dissenting justices' remaining on the bench, also inflicts a severely limiting temporal constraint on the progeny votes collected. The mean judicial tenure for all justices (through Lewis Powell) completing their service is sixteen years, four months.[11] The Spaeth and Segal approach, then, allows about sixteen years, on average, for progeny cases to appear – presuming, of course, that justices dissent in precedent-setting cases at the beginning of high court careers, a sizable postulate itself. As a result, Spaeth and Segal miss progeny cases decided, on average, more than sixteen years after precedent-setting decisions. This is important, considering how long precedents last. The mean number of years between overruled and overruling cases for the more than 200 overruled decisions in Table 2-14 ("Supreme Court Decisions Overruled by Subsequent Decisions, 1789–1990") of Epstein, Segal, Spaeth, and Walker (1994) is 28.7 years. Similarly, Brenner and Spaeth (1995) calculated the mean age of overruled decisions between 1946 and 1992 to be 29.4 years. Thus, from the perspective of overruled cases, the Spaeth and Segal research design overlooks, on average, about thirteen years' worth of progeny (i.e., more than 40 percent). However, overruling delineates the *minimum* span of precedential life. Since the overwhelming majority of precedents are never overruled (Ulmer 1959; Knight and Epstein 1996), the prospect for multigenerational progeny is patent. Accordingly, Spaeth and Segal tap only a peripheral portion of progenial potential.

Of course, the authors reasonably might retort to these methodological criticisms: "Yes, that's all true, but how otherwise do we pinpoint

---

[10] For precedent-setting cases, Spaeth and Segal investigated all major decisions of the Court and random samples of (1) 1 percent of all minor cases with dissent from 1937 to the present and (2) 100 minor cases with dissent from each of the periods 1793 to 1867 and 1868 to 1936. Their database could be expanded to include all minor cases, and the usable vote pool might be substantially larger. Nonetheless, judicial behavior scholars rarely examine court action motivated primarily by concern about how judges decide expendable cases. Segal and Spaeth's 1996 journal article, the precursor of their book, investigated only landmark decisions, manifesting the genuine catalyst for the research. Hence, all votes truly mattering to the authors are already among the 2,425 at issue.

[11] Derived from Table 5-1 ("Length of Service") of Epstein et al. (1994).

precedential converts never publicly coming out of the atheist closet?" This chapter answers the question, and avoids the pitfalls detailed above, by offering a different empirical strategy to test *stare decisis*.

I note again the challenge in analyzing precedential potency: identifying objective indicators demonstrating that judges, faced with controlling precedent compelling a particular policy outcome, indeed follow that authority, especially when personal attitudes, or environmental or institutional forces, militate against the result. To do so, researchers must measure how judges would vote in the absence of precedent in order to match that assessment with how they actually vote under its putative authority. No meaningful empirical appraisal of *stare decisis* is possible without reliable yardsticks for gauging judicial votes in precedent-free environments.

Scanning adjudicated cases alone, nonetheless, usually provides only one side of a comparison. A control is necessary to measure impact, and excessive speculation about counterfactuals is not a sufficient proxy. Yet opportunities to observe, in the same policy domain, adequate numbers of both court decisions resolved within the presumed constraint of precedent and those without it are rare.

This book is such an occasion.

Lesbian and Gay Rights Claims and Precedent

Lesbian and gay rights cases offer an excellent opportunity for empirical study of precedential leverage. Through the 1960s, American society – and particularly its courts – treated homosexuals as pariahs. In January 1966, for example, *Time* magazine published an unsigned essay, "The Homosexual in America," that concluded:

[Homosexuality] is a pathetic little second-rate substitute for reality, a pitiable flight from life. As such it deserves fairness, compassion, understanding and when possible, treatment. But it deserves no encouragement, no glamorization, no rationalization, no fake status as minority martyrdom, no sophistry about simple differences in taste – and above all, no pretense that it is anything but a pernicious sickness. (1966, January 21, p. 41)

A 1965 Harris public opinion survey rated homosexuals the third most dangerous group (after communists and atheists) in the United States; a 1966 CBS poll found that only one in five respondents would support legalizing homosexual behavior between consenting adults; and a 1969 Harris poll found that 63 percent of respondents considered homosexuals to be harmful to American life (Weinberg and Williams 1974: 19–20). The federal government prohibited employment of gays in the civil service until 1975 (Lewis 1997). Symptomatic of society's fearful attitude toward lesbians and gay men, the American Psychiatric Association classified homosexuality as a mental disorder until 1973 (Marcus 1993: 172–73). Homophobia also was the legal norm in the 1960s:

The homosexual in 1961 was smothered by law. She or he risked arrest and possible police brutalization for dancing with someone of the same sex, cross-dressing, propositioning another adult homosexual, possessing a homophile publication, writing about homosexuality without disapproval, displaying pictures of two people of the same sex in intimate positions, operating a lesbian or gay bar, or actually having oral or anal sex with another adult homosexual. The last was a serious felony in all states but one, and in most jurisdictions also carried with it possible indefinite incarceration as a sexual psychopath. Misdemeanor arrests for sex-related vagrancy or disorderly conduct offenses meant that the homosexual might have her or his name published in the local newspaper, would probably lose her or his job, and in several states would have to register as a sex offender. If the homosexual were not a citizen, she or he would likely be deported. If the homosexual were a professional – teacher, lawyer, doctor, mortician, beautician – she or he could lose the certification needed to practice that profession. If the charged homosexual were a member of the armed forces, she or he might be court-martialed and would likely be dishonorably discharged and lose all veterans' benefits. (Eskridge 1999: 98)[12]

As a result of gays' outcast status, a federal judge at the end of the 1960s could assert prosaically, without fear of appellate or political censure, that "[a]ny schoolboy knows that a homosexual act is immoral, indecent, lewd, and obscene" (*Schlegel v. United States* 1969: 1378).

Very few court decisions before 1970 addressed legal claims by self-identified and self-affirming lesbians and gay men (Cain 1993: 1564–79). For example, a *Westlaw* database search of state court cases between 1960 and 1969 for the keywords "homosexual," "lesbian," and their cognates retrieved relevant decisions almost exclusively in four categories: revocation and suspension of liquor licenses of bars and restaurants catering to homosexuals; revocation of homosexuals' teaching licenses; determinations of whether homosexual solicitation or other activity constituted gross indecency, disorderly or lewd conduct, or comparable offenses; and prosecutions for possession and distribution of obscene materials with

---

[12] Reprinted by permission of the publisher from *Gaylaw: Challenging the Apartheid of the Closet*, by William N. Eskridge, Jr., Cambridge, Mass.: Harvard University Press, Copyright © by the President and Fellows of Harvard College.

lesbian and gay content – in other words, disputes typically with closeted lesbians and gay men in defensive posture. All but three[13] appellate decisions were resolved against the interests of the gay people involved. State appellate court treatment of homosexuals during the 1960s is best illustrated by the disposition in a rare child visitation case: A Los Angeles trial court granted a gay father visitation rights with his children on the condition that he

"immediately quit his present residence [with another man] and take up residence in the home of his parents"; [and] obtain psychiatric treatment and continue with such "care until further order of the Court." The order also required that the paternal grandmother accompany the children "at all times" during [the father's] custody of them. (*Evans v. Evans* 1960: 568)

When the mother remarried and moved to Salt Lake City with the children, the California Court of Appeal ordered the gay father to continue making child support payments, even though the children's relocation to Utah effectively terminated his visitation with them.

In essence, American law in the 1960s concerning what today would be considered lesbian and gay rights claims – for example, child custody, visitation, adoption, and foster care by lesbian or gay parents or their domestic partners; health insurance and other benefits for domestic partners; same-sex marriage or its approximation; the constitutionality of consensual sodomy laws; and discrimination in public accommodations, housing, and the workplace – was a *tabula rasa*. Doubtless, legal precedents existed regarding child custody and visitation, marriage, invidious discrimination in public accommodations and the workplace, and so forth. And, doubtless, homosexuals were parties to lawsuits (albeit reluctantly in the kinds of cases outlined above). But courts in the 1960s and before did not apply precedents created with heterosexual litigants to lesbians and gay men because they were perceived as deviants unworthy of equal legal treatment (Pacelle 1996: 200; Wald 2000: 9). Moreover, although homosexuals and their advocates argued that civil rights precedents from the African American and other minority contexts should be applied to homosexuals, that thesis required courts' acknowledging lesbians and gay men as a legitimate minority, which was

---

[13] *Nadler v. Superior Court* (1967), *One Eleven Wines & Liquors, Inc., v. Division of Alcoholic Beverage Control* (1967), and *Morrison v. State Board of Education* (1969). A notable federal court victory is *Norton v. Macy* (1969).

universally denied in the 1960s.[14] Indeed, even through much of the 1970s and early '80s, appellate cases on lesbian and gay rights claims virtually ignored civil rights jurisprudence since judges apparently were unwilling to sully those precedents with even the suggestion that homosexuals were in any way comparably circumstanced to African Americans and other minorities.

Further, even in the rare instances that legal standards such as "best interests of the child" were invoked in cases with lesbian and gay litigants, courts' next sentences would be variants of "and the best interests of the child require as close to total separation from these immoral, sexual-predator monsters as possible." Again, *Evans* and *Schlegel* epitomized contemporary judicial attitudes toward homosexuals. Accordingly, the 1960s and before were to lesbians and gay men what much of the nineteenth century was to people of color in this country. Homosexual rights was an oxymoron in American law.[15]

---

[14] Murdoch and Price (2001: 39) observe:

> In 1957, the ACLU's board of directors defended the constitutionality of laws that made homosexual behavior criminal. Homosexuals simply were not viewed as a mistreated minority group. Thinking of homosexuals in that way would have seemed as inappropriate to most Americans as considering purse snatchers or Communists an oppressed group.

> Lewis and Rogers (1999: 123) point out a similar phenomenon regarding public-opinion polling:

> In separate polls conducted in the 1990s a full 60 percent supported "laws to protect homosexuals against job discrimination," but only 44 percent to 48 percent agreed that "the laws which protect the civil rights of racial or religious minorities should be used to protect the rights of homosexuals," only 39 percent to 46 percent favored "extending . . . civil rights laws to include homosexuals," and only 26 percent to 43 percent believed that "homosexuals should get protection under civil rights laws in the way racial minorities and women have been protected." Questions that ask about extending civil rights laws may raise . . . doubts that gays are as "legitimate" a minority as blacks or women . . . in ways that a question about "laws to protect homosexuals against job discrimination" does not.

[15] As Dorris (1999: 39) observes:

> With controversial issues policy makers can use their power of definition to keep a policy aimed at redressing these issues from coming into being. With policies that are incompatible with the morals or beliefs of the policy makers, a specific policy can be defined as nonessential and rarely appears on the agenda (Bachrach and Baratz 1962). This process of nondecision is what Crenson calls "un-politics" (Crenson 1971). Those with grievances are at a disadvantage if their issue is considered illegitimate. Consequently, their voice in the process may be muffled or even silenced (Bachrach and Baratz 1970).

> See D'Emilio (1983), Cain (1993), and Rimmerman (2002: 47–55) for histories of this era.

The lesbian and gay rights social movement changed that. New York's Stonewall Rebellion in the summer of 1969 touched off mass protests by newly self-identified, out-of-the-closet lesbians and gay men (Marotta 1981; Duberman 1993; Button, Rienzo, and Wald 1997: 25; Keen and Goldberg 1998: 91–94). As a result, beginning in the 1970s, American courts started resolving disputes with self-proclaimed and self-confident lesbians and gay men as parties to lawsuits, and a pool of gay civil rights precedent slowly took form.[16] That process continues today, with the mean of the annual number of appellate court lesbian and gay rights decisions increasing from 11.8 for the ten years beginning 1981 to 27.3 for the following decade (with 36 in 2000). Hence, because of homosexuals' thirty-year metamorphosis from pariahs to ordinary litigants, lesbian and gay rights cases offer a policy area inviting comparison of judicial decision making in precedent-free and precedent-bound environments.

In addition, lesbian and gay rights, like abortion, is an issue domain prompting strongly held positions, at both the mass and the elite levels (Haeberle 1999; Schroedel 1999). Judges thus are not apt to be indifferent to lesbian and gay rights claims and are more disposed to vote their attitudes there than in other, less controversial areas, simply because the topic is so emotionally charged (Rand National Defense Research Institute 1993; Sherrill 1993, 1996; Gamble 1997).

Yet, as lesbian and gay rights precedents accumulated, nonlegal factors such as attitudinal attributes should not have had the free rein to influence decisions in the late 1980s and '90s as they did in the 1970s and early '80s, if *stare decisis* in fact plays a decisive role in adjudication.

I test precedential power in lesbian and gay rights jurisprudence in two ways. First, I reconsider the *stare decisis* components of Chapter 3's models. The book's database permits a level of comparative analysis, incorporating environmental and institutional dynamics, not possible in a U.S. Supreme Court case study such as that of Spaeth and Segal (1999).[17]

---

[16] Clearly, judicial attitudes did not change quickly. Rivera (1979) painted a fairly bleak portrait even a decade after Stonewall.

[17] Hall and Brace (1999: 281–82) ("case studies necessarily generate a body of findings and theories that are highly circumscribed by time and place. Moreover, except with longitudinal designs capable of addressing a limited range of contextual and institutional hypotheses, case studies reduce discussions concerning the likely effects of institutional arrangements largely to speculation, a serious deficiency given the critical role played by these forces in the politics of the judiciary. To achieve the primary scientific goal of developing general theory that takes into account the complete range of forces affecting the politics of courts, comparative analysis is essential"); Pinello (1996: 135) ("[w]ith a pool of 50 jurisdictions, state [judicial] politics, like state and

Second, since more than two-thirds (69.8 percent) of the votes in the lesbian and gay rights data here were cast without the influence of binding precedent, I identify precedential atheists in the 30.2 percent decided under the authority of *stare decisis* by estimating the probabilities of how precedent-bound votes would be cast in precedent-free environments and then inspect how the probability-delineated atheists actually voted. In other words, the precedent-free votes serve as benchmarks for how judicial attitudes, case characteristics, environmental factors, institutional forces, time, and *amicus* participation affected judicial dispositions of lesbian and gay rights claims, independent of *stare decisis*. My methodology relaxes the Spaeth and Segal two-judicial-vote requirement to one – that done in the ambit of binding precedent – and consequently expands the parameters of the usable-vote pool.

Test One

Chapter 3's models demonstrate that *stare decisis* was a powerful force in the adjudication of lesbian and gay rights claims. **Positive precedent** was statistically significant in six of seven layers of analysis, three at the .001 level. Its estimates were uniformly positive, and its impact statistics ranged from .236 to .374.[18] Among 38 other variables and interaction terms, just one (**minority**) was more consistently significant than **positive precedent**, and only in the singular subpopulation of opinion writers (where attitudinal factors understandably held greatest sway) was **minority**'s impact ever larger than that of **positive precedent**. At the same time, **negative precedent** was significant in two levels of analysis. Hence, *stare decisis* undeniably is a powerful force in judicial decision making. The only issue is whether its influence can be further explicated.

The intermediate appellate court model permits more nuanced *stare decisis* specification because precedents there come from the same courts or higher ones. Also, intermediate appellate court judges sometimes cite decisions from other districts in their states as authority (although, as observed in Appendix 3.1, sister-district cases usually are not controlling).

---

local politics generally, beckons scholars to meaningful comparative inquiry.... Public-law students should mine this rich ore more. Untold research hovers around single data points while so little yearns for comparative gold"). See, generally, King et al. (1994).

[18] Appendix 4.4 reports the variable's greatest impact: .458.

Accordingly, six *stare decisis* variables in the intermediate appellate court model here substitute for Chapter 3's two. Descriptions of the new variables and their coding rules appear in Appendix 5.1. All cases in the study decided under the influence of *stare decisis* are listed in Appendix 5.2, together with relevant controlling precedents.[19]

Appendix 5.3 exhibits the intermediate appellate court regression analysis with the expanded *stare decisis* variables. Four of the six are statistically significant there: **negative precedent, same court; negative precedent, higher court; positive precedent, higher court;** and **negative precedent, other district.** In addition, **positive precedent, same court** is on the verge of significance (p = .051; impact = +.166). That five of six precedent variables are consequential (with four signed as predicted) is not surprising because Table 3.4 demonstrated intermediate courts to be the most responsive to the legal model. In addition, the positive signs of both higher court estimates intimate that hierarchical *stare decisis* constrained prospectively conservative intermediate appellate court votes, while the estimate for **negative precedent, other district** implies that liberal votes were responsive even to nonbinding sister-district decisions.

Equally important, the dominant impact statistics of the positive-precedent variables throughout Chapter 3 and here, coupled with the comparative inability of negative precedents to defeat lesbian and gay rights claims, suggest that *stare decisis* encumbered conservative votes more reliably than liberal ones. Further, same-court negative precedents having dependably negative weight, while higher court negative precedents do not, hints that liberal court-of-last-resort justices responded differently to *stare decisis* than did liberal intermediate appellate court judges. These

---

[19] Brenner and Stier (1996: 1039), quoting Segal and Spaeth (1996: 979), warned that "'the determination of progeny is not a bright-line enterprise' and that there is inevitable 'subjectivity' involved in such an analysis." My methodology facilitates identification of both precedent-setting and progeny cases much more straightforwardly than in Supreme Court precedential-impact research. First, 76.5 percent of the decisions in the book's database come from intermediate appellate courts. Unlike courts of last resort, intermediate tribunals have mandatory jurisdiction, and distinctive or novel legal issues thus are less likely to appear in progeny cases. Second, my data search guarantees that all progeny cases are identified, since Appendix 1.2 is a comprehensive list of a single, highly focused issue domain in which factual and legal similarities across cases are usually conspicuous. Third, I performed an analogous database search for lesbian and gay rights decisions between 1960 and 1980 to identify precedents relevant to the 1981–2000 cases in the study.

clues to differential precedential impact are explored more conclusively in the next section.

Test Two

I use the beta coefficients from the precedent-free versions of Chapter 3's five principal models to estimate vote probabilities for both precedent-free and precedent-bound votes in each model, thereby predicting how all votes would be cast in precedent-free environments. I identify precedential atheists among the precedent-bound votes from those probability estimates by comparing judges' probabilities with how they actually voted in the ambit of *stare decisis*. Following earlier precedential-impact research (Brenner and Stier 1996: 1037) and Chapter 3's practice, I divide the probability scale into thirds.

Table 5.1 displays frequency distributions for the six actual-vote subpopulations of each model determined by **outcome** and either the absence of precedent or the presence of negative or positive precedent: (1) actual votes *against* lesbian and gay rights claims *without* the influence of precedent; (2) votes *against* claims with *negative* precedent; (3) votes *against* claims controlled by *positive* precedent; (4) votes *in favor of* claims *without* precedent; (5) votes *favoring* claims with *negative* precedent; and (6) votes *favoring* claims with *positive* precedent. Further, actual votes are classified according to their probability estimates into four categories: suppressed, not suppressed, inconsistent, and consistent. For example, the first row of Table 5.1 presents the 482 votes cast in all 400 decisions and opinions *against* lesbian and gay rights claims *without* controlling precedent. Some 204 votes have probability estimates under .333, qualifying them as *conservative* and therefore *consistent* votes, since conservative votes by definition opposed lesbian and gay rights claims. Likewise, 216 votes have probability estimates between, or equal to, .333 and .667, designating them as *center* and also as *consistent* since center votes by definition were not predisposed to particular outcomes. However, the 62 *liberal* votes, with probability estimates above .667, are *inconsistent*, since, *ceteris paribus*, they should have favored the claims, not opposed them. The second row of Table 5.1 arrays the 188 votes *against* lesbian and gay claims with controlling *negative* precedent. Again, the *conservative* and *center* votes are *consistent*, but now *stare decisis suppressed* the 20 *liberal* votes of precedential atheists not abiding by predispositions to support the lesbian and gay claims. In the third row, displaying votes *against* claims with controlling *positive* precedent, *stare decisis* did *not suppress* the 16 *conservative* votes of

TABLE 5.1 *Frequency Distributions of Precedent-Free Vote Probabilities*

Outcome and precedent	Conservative		Center		Liberal		Total
	N	%	N	%	N	%	
All							
Lose; none	204	42.3	216	44.8	62[a]	12.9[a]	482
Lose; negative only	87	46.3	81	43.1	20[b]	10.6[b]	188
Lose; positive only	16[c]	42.1[c]	17[a]	44.7[a]	5[a]	13.2[a]	38
Win; none	46[a]	8.8[a]	239	45.7	238	45.5	523
Win; negative only	24[a]	26.1[a]	50[a]	54.3[a]	18[c]	19.6[c]	92
Win; positive only	32[b]	27.6[b]	65	56.0	19	16.4	116
Total	409	28.4	668	46.4	362	25.2	1,439
Courts of last resort							
Lose; none	112	55.4	65	32.2	25[a]	12.4[a]	202
Lose; negative only	31	72.1	9	20.9	3[b]	7.0[b]	43
Lose; positive only	7[c]	77.8[c]	2[a]	22.2[a]	0[a]	0.0[a]	9
Win; none	24[a]	10.6[a]	68	30.1	134	59.3	226
Win; negative only	16[a]	44.4[a]	12[a]	33.3[a]	8[c]	22.2[c]	36
Win; positive only	4[b]	14.8[b]	13	48.1	10	37.0	27
Total	194	35.7	169	31.1	180	33.1	543
Intermediate appellate courts							
Lose; none	161	57.5	97	34.6	22[a]	7.9[a]	280
Lose; negative only	79	54.5	34	23.4	32[b]	22.1[b]	145
Lose; positive only	12[c]	41.4[c]	9[a]	31.0[a]	8[a]	27.6[a]	29
Win; none	33[a]	11.1[a]	77	25.9	187	63.0	297
Win; negative only	18[a]	32.1[a]	16[a]	28.6[a]	22[c]	39.3[c]	56
Win; positive only	44[b]	49.4[b]	28	31.5	17	19.1	89
Total	347	38.7	261	29.1	288	32.1	896
Family decisions							
Lose; none	103	38.0	129	47.6	39[a]	14.4[a]	271
Lose; negative only	33	34.7	38	40.0	24[b]	25.3[b]	95
Lose; positive only	14[c]	46.7[c]	9[a]	30.0[a]	7[a]	23.3[a]	30
Win; none	24[a]	7.8[a]	134	43.8	148	48.4	306
Win; negative only	11[a]	22.0[a]	21[a]	42.0[a]	18[c]	36.0[c]	50
Win; positive only	41[b]	43.6[b]	40	42.6	13	13.8	94
Total	226	26.7	371	43.9	249	29.4	846
Nonfamily decisions							
Lose; none	121	57.3	69	32.7	21[a]	10.0[a]	211
Lose; negative only	60	64.5	20	21.5	13[b]	14.0[b]	93
Lose; positive only	4[c]	50.0[c]	2[a]	25.0[a]	2[a]	25.0[a]	8
Win; none	27[a]	12.4[a]	52	24.0	138	63.6	217
Win; negative only	14[a]	33.3[a]	12[a]	28.6[a]	16[c]	38.1[c]	42
Win; positive only	9[b]	40.9[b]	2	9.1	11	50.0	22
Total	235	39.6	157	26.5	201	33.9	593

Note: Unless otherwise indicated, votes are consistent.
[a] Inconsistent votes.
[b] Suppressed votes.
[c] Votes not suppressed.

precedential atheists there, since they were cast according to predilections to oppose the claims and against the positive precedent. The *center* and *liberal* votes are *inconsistent* since the former was indifferent to outcome and thus should have followed the positive precedent, while the latter favored claims regardless of positive precedent. The other rows and model subpopulations in Table 5.1 follow similar analyses.

Table 5.2 summarizes Table 5.1's probability-distribution data[20] and reveals several noteworthy phenomena. First, as intimated in test one, *stare decisis, unsurprisingly, was more influential in intermediate appellate courts than courts of last resort. Controlling precedent governed almost 70 percent of precedential atheists' votes in the intermediate appellate court pool, whereas only about 30 percent of pertinent court-of-last-resort votes deferred to it.* The latter finding comports with Brenner and Stier (1996) and Songer and Lindquist (1996), who concluded that *stare decisis* constrained Supreme Court justices between about 30 and 45 percent of the time. The discovery also challenges the 12 percent compliance rate of Spaeth and Segal (1999), the most comprehensive study in both the legal and political science literatures separating precedential atheists from judges sympathetic or indifferent to the policies precedents promote. As explained in this chapter's introduction, their book's abridged vision of the full gamut of latent precedential impact is the price paid for a supremely scrupulous yet circumscribing methodology.

Table 5.2's second prominent feature is that *stare decisis subdued conservative votes at a noticeably higher rate than liberal ones.* The smallest proportional difference occurred in the all-decisions model, where the votes of conservative atheists were suppressed at a rate 26.8 percent higher than those of liberal atheists (66.7 vs. 52.6 percent). Courts of last resort had a 33.3 percent proportional difference (36.4 vs. 27.3 percent), while the largest was 54.5 percent in the nonfamily model (69.2 vs. 44.8 percent). Not surprisingly, opinion writers (not displayed in Tables 5.1 and 5.2) were the only conservative precedential atheists not suppressed more frequently than liberal counterparts. The respective suppression rates in that subpopulation were 37.5 and 45.5 percent. Yet only eight relevant conservative votes were in play, compared with 22 liberal ones, thus limiting the comparison's reliability.

[20] Both the suppressed and unsuppressed votes in Table 5.1 are included in Table 5.2's consistent-vote tallies because the former were cast compatibly with controlling precedent and the latter congruently with propensities determined by the judicial attitudes, case characteristic, environmental factors, institutional forces, temporal control, and *amicus* participation specified in Chapter 3's models.

TABLE 5.2 *Summaries of Precedent-Free Vote Probability Distributions from Table 5.1*

	Conservative (probability <.33)		Center (.33 ≤ prob ≤ .67)		Liberal (.67 < probability)		Total	
	N	%	N	%	N	%	N	%
All decisions[a]								
Suppressed	32	66.7			20	52.6	52	60.5
Not suppressed	16	33.3			18	47.4	34	39.5
Inconsistent	70	17.1	67	10.0	67	18.5	204	14.2
Consistent	339	82.9	601	90.0	295	81.5	1,235	85.8
Court-of-last-resort decisions[b]								
Suppressed	4	36.4			3	27.3	7	31.8
Not suppressed	7	63.6			8	72.7	15	68.2
Inconsistent	40	20.6	14	8.3	25	13.9	79	14.5
Consistent	154	79.4	155	91.7	155	86.1	464	85.5
Intermediate appellate court decisions[c]								
Suppressed	44	78.6			32	59.3	76	69.1
Not suppressed	12	21.4			22	40.7	34	30.9
Inconsistent	51	14.7	25	9.6	30	10.4	106	11.8
Consistent	296	85.3	236	90.4	258	89.6	790	88.2
Family decisions[d]								
Suppressed	41	74.5			24	57.1	65	67.0
Not suppressed	14	25.5			18	42.9	32	33.0
Inconsistent	35	15.5	30	8.1	46	18.5	111	13.1
Consistent	191	84.5	341	91.9	203	81.5	735	86.9
Nonfamily decisions[e]								
Suppressed	9	69.2			13	44.8	22	52.4
Not suppressed	4	30.8			16	55.2	20	47.6
Inconsistent	41	17.4	14	8.9	23	11.4	78	13.2
Consistent	194	82.6	143	91.1	178	88.6	515	86.8

[a] Of 1,439 votes, 1,005 (69.8%) derive from precedent-free environments.
[b] Of 543 votes, 428 (78.8%) derive from precedent-free environments.
[c] Of 896 votes, 577 (64.4%) derive from precedent-free environments.
[d] Of 846 votes, 577 (68.2%) derive from precedent-free environments.
[e] Of 593 votes, 428 (72.2%) derive from precedent-free environments.

The substantially higher precedential suppression rates for conservative votes, compared with liberal ones, are not easily explained. Theorists might proffer that *stare decisis* is innately conservative and therefore bridled even the sympathetic, ideologically conservative forces opposing the lesbian and gay rights claims studied here. But empirical evidence exogenous to this study supporting the theory is hard to find. For example, matching justices' civil liberties voting scores from Table 6–1

("Aggregate Liberal Voting of Justices, 1953–1991 Terms") of Epstein
et al. (1994) with their participation rates in precedential alteration from
Table 6-8 ("Votes in Support of and Opposition to Decisions Formally
Altering Precedent, 1953–1991 Terms") of the same volume uncovers no
significant correlation.[21] Cross-tabulating the civil liberties scores with
corresponding percentages of preferential versus precedential votes from
Table 9.1 ("Justices' Precedential Behavior by Case Type") of Spaeth and
Segal (1999) discloses a modest relationship.[22] Instead, the relative liberal atheist defiance of *stare decisis* in my study may be an artifact of
improved public opinion on lesbian and gay issues (Yang 1998; Blendon
et al. 2000: 26–29; Wilcox and Wolpert 2000). Yet **post-1990**, Chapter
3's temporal control, was not consistently significant across models and
thus provides little support for this interpretation.[23] In any event, further
quantitative precedential impact research on other legal subjects is necessary for conclusive documentation of a conservative-liberal *stare decisis*
fidelity gap.

Tables 5.3 and 5.4 display the votes of precedential atheists in Tables
5.1 and 5.2 disaggregated by vertical and horizontal *stare decisis* effects.[24]
Although the total-vote suppression rates in the all-decisions model are
nearly identical in the two tables, the gap between conservative and

---

[21] The Pearson product-moment correlation coefficient (r) for the nineteen justices (Black,
Blackmun, Brennan, Burger, Clark, Douglas, Fortas, Goldberg, Harlan, Kennedy,
Marshall, O'Connor, Powell, Rehnquist, Scalia, Stevens, Stewart, Warren, and White)
participating in sufficient cases for meaningful comparison is .26 (p = .28).

[22] For the sixteen justices (Black, Blackmun, Brennan, Burger, Burton, Clark, Douglas,
Frankfurter, Harlan, Marshall, O'Connor, Rehnquist, Stevens, Stewart, Warren, and
White) with sufficient cases in the Spaeth and Segal table for meaningful comparison, r =
.42 (p = .11).

[23] Also weighing against disproportionately large conservative vote allegiance to *stare decisis*
is Gerhardt (1991: 74):

> The [Supreme] Court's conservative majority is split between two views on the appropri-
> ate standard for overruling decisions. One view (followed in large part by Chief Justice
> Rehnquist and Justice Scalia) urges the overruling of virtually any precedent that they con-
> sider erroneously reasoned, while the other view (advanced at various times by Justices
> White, O'Connor, Kennedy, and Souter) bases the overruling of a precedent on its erro-
> neous reasoning and some other substantial consideration.

[24] Votes between models delineated by either subject matter or court level may sum to
more than in the all-decisions model in Tables 5.3 and 5.4 because some intermediate
appellate court cases in the study were affected by both vertical and horizontal precedents.
Moreover, the number of votes across models in Tables 5.3 and 5.4 vary due to the models'
differences in proportional error reduction. Suppressed votes in Table 5.4 come only from
cases not subject to higher court precedent.

TABLE 5.3 *Votes of Precedential Atheists Subject to Vertical* Stare Decisis

	Conservative		Liberal		Total	
	N	%	N	%	N	%
All decisions						
Suppressed	15	71.4	7	38.9	22	56.4
Not suppressed	6	28.6	11	61.1	17	43.6
Intermediate appellate courts						
Suppressed	32	76.2	16	48.5	48	64.0
Not suppressed	10	23.8	17	51.5	27	36.0
Family decisions						
Suppressed	18	81.8	4	33.3	22	64.7
Not suppressed	4	18.2	8	66.7	12	35.3
Nonfamily decisions						
Suppressed	6	66.7	10	43.5	16	50.0
Not suppressed	3	33.3	13	56.5	16	50.0

TABLE 5.4 *Votes of Precedential Atheists Subject to Horizontal* Stare Decisis

	Conservative		Liberal		Total	
	N	%	N	%	N	%
All decisions						
Suppressed	17	63.0	14	56.0	31	59.6
Not suppressed	10	37.0	11	44.0	21	40.4
Courts of last resort						
Suppressed	4	36.4	3	27.3	7	31.8
Not suppressed	7	63.6	8	72.7	15	68.2
Intermediate appellate courts						
Suppressed	13	86.7	17	70.8	30	76.9
Not suppressed	2	13.3	7	29.2	9	23.1
Family decisions						
Suppressed	23	69.7	20	66.7	43	68.3
Not suppressed	10	30.3	10	33.3	20	31.7
Nonfamily decisions						
Suppressed	3	75.0	3	42.9	6	54.5
Not suppressed	1	25.0	4	57.1	5	45.5

liberal suppression rates is substantially higher for hierarchical *stare decisis* (71.4 vs. 38.9 percent) than collegial (63.0 vs. 56.0 percent). In other words, *conservative precedential atheists honored higher court precedents more faithfully than same-court precedents, while liberal atheists gave less*

TABLE 5.5 *Votes of State Court Precedential Atheists Only*

| | Subject to vertical *Stare Decisis* | | | | | |
| | Conservative | | Liberal | | Total | |
	N	%	N	%	N	%
All decisions						
Suppressed	16	80.0	1	50.0	17	77.3
Not suppressed	4	20.0	1	50.0	5	22.7
Intermediate appellate courts						
Suppressed	29	80.6	2	40.0	31	75.6
Not suppressed	7	19.4	3	60.0	10	24.4
	Subject to horizontal *Stare Decisis*					
All decisions						
Suppressed	18	66.7	7	46.7	25	59.5
Not suppressed	9	33.3	8	53.3	17	40.5
Courts of last resort						
Suppressed	4	36.4	3	30.0	7	33.3
Not suppressed	7	63.6	7	70.0	14	66.7
Intermediate appellate courts						
Suppressed	15	78.9	13	72.2	28	75.7
Not suppressed	4	21.1	5	27.8	9	24.3

deference to higher authority than to colleagues. The latter finding is counterintuitive and flies in the face of *stare decisis* theory. Yet some consolation is available comparing Table 5.4's court-of-last-resort data with those for intermediate appellate courts. Liberal high court atheists honored collegial precedent about a quarter of the time, while those on lower courts did so two and a half times more frequently (27.3 vs. 70.8 percent). Indeed, the liberal court-of-last-resort suppression rate is the lowest in Tables 5.2–5.4.

Table 5.5 segregates the vertical and horizontal effects of state court precedential atheists.[25] Both the conservative and total-vote suppression rates in the all-decisions model demonstrate greater deference to higher court precedents than to same-court (80.0 vs. 66.7 percent, and 77.3 vs. 59.5 percent, respectively). In contrast, the liberal rates of the intermediate appellate court model are reversed (40.0 vs. 72.2 percent), while too few votes-in-play in the all-decisions model prevent meaningful comparison

---

[25] Too few federal court votes without the influence of *stare decisis* (N = 199) prevent a separate analysis for federal atheists.

between liberal-vote levels there. Thus, although the combined federal and state court votes of Tables 5.3 and 5.4 do not manifest a consistently greater potency of hierarchical *stare decisis* compared with collegial, the dominant state court votes of Table 5.5 do. Accordingly, judicial federalism may be in play here, too.

Indeed, variation in vertical and horizontal *stare decisis* effects should be the norm. Subject to both varieties of precedential influence, intermediate appellate courts responded to each at relatively similar rates, between approximately 65 and 75 percent of the time, in Tables 5.3–5.5. Remarkably, conservative and liberal suppression rates are both high in the intermediate appellate court and family models of Table 5.4 and the horizontal intermediate appellate court data of Table 5.5 – aberrations from the general trend of greater liberal defiance. Hence, liberal votes in nonfamily court-of-last-resort decisions were the least pliable to *stare decisis*.

Subject only to collegial precedential effects, courts of last resort are the fly in the ointment of *stare decisis*. Court-of-last-resort suppression rates are by far the lowest of any in Tables 5.3–5.5, again reflecting the high courts' greater policy-making role and their resultant propensity to follow attitudinal, environmental, and institutional forces more than legal ones.

Caveats

The chapter's introduction catalogs pitfalls in Spaeth and Segal's landmark precedential impact testing scheme. Let me be equally candid about problems with my alternative methodology. To repeat: Any vote-based approach to gauge the potency of *stare decisis* different from Spaeth and Segal necessarily will be less cautious in ascertaining precedential atheists. Nothing predicts a vote as well as, or better than, the vote itself. By relaxing Spaeth and Segal's two-judicial-vote requirement to a single precedent-influenced one and relying on precedent-free votes to identify suitable reference points, I inject error into the analysis since my models do not perfectly predict votes, either precedent-free or precedent-bound. In the precedent-free versions, on which the probability estimates of test two rely, votes correctly classified range from 69.50 percent for family cases to 79.72 percent for intermediate appellate court rulings, with proportional reductions in error from 35.06 to 58.21 percent. The inconsistent votes in Tables 5.1 and 5.2 result from this model imperfection and thus measure error in the analysis. Table 5.2's inconsistent-vote percentages are relatively stable across subpopulations, disclosing fairly uniform and modest error rates.

Moreover, the research method here is not subject to the kinds of criticism lodged by Baum (1994: 4)[26] because I use fully integrated models of judicial behavior, investigating much more than judicial attitude. Indeed, mine is not a test of the attitudinal model versus the legal model, but rather of all measurable nonprecedential stimuli shaping judicial behavior versus the power of precedent.

Another problem arises from test two's focus only on ideologues: No center-vote analysis analogous to Brenner and Stier (1996) is possible because I postulate center votes are fully acquiescent to *stare decisis*.

A worry apparently endemic to precedential-impact research is small usable-vote pools. Brisbin (1996: 1006) noted the issue for Segal and Spaeth (1996). My data provide a maximum of 86 votes of precedential atheists for test two (Table 5.2, "All Decisions," total of "Suppressed" and "Not Suppressed"), 6.0 percent of the total in the study. Yet my usable votes are 19.8 percent of the precedent-bound ones – *three times* Spaeth and Segal's estimated 6.5 percent. Their confining research design, then, may have missed up to two-thirds of the evidence relevant to a comprehensive evaluation of justices' deference to *stare decisis*.

Although the results here are highly suggestive, one issue domain alone is not a surrogate for all. I cannot necessarily generalize my findings to every legal topic. However, in light of the highly emotionally charged character of lesbian and gay rights claims in American public policy making, *stare decisis*'s decisive suppression of conservative votes in this ideologically cloven terrain certainly resembles a crucial case study for precedential impact, much like Spaeth and Segal's strategy of investigating how frequently dissenting justices later conformed to majority opinions with which they disagreed. That is, if *stare decisis* arrested attitudinal and other important effects in the lesbian and gay rights policy domain, then it should everywhere else as well.

Conclusion

In 1980, a legal scholar announced the demise of collegial precedent in constitutional law (Maltz 1980). Almost twenty years later, two eminent political scientists published a similar obituary (Spaeth and Segal 1999).

---

[26] Segal and Spaeth (1993) "make an intuitive leap, resting on the unstated premise that the structure they find in justices' votes could have no basis other than the attitudes of justices about public policy. It is a highly reasonable leap, one that other students of the Court have made, but it is not compelled by the evidence presented in the book."

Yet rumors of *stare decisis*'s death have been greatly exaggerated. Fully integrated models of appellate court treatment of lesbian and gay rights claims reveal that *stare decisis* is statistically significant with consequential impact statistics. In particular, precedent is alive and well in intermediate appellate courts, was pivotal in courts of last resort over a quarter of the time, and suppressed potentially conservative votes at a much higher rate than liberal ones. Further, vertical *stare decisis* swayed judicial decision making in state courts more consistently than horizontal *stare decisis*.

6

Conclusion

This investigation of twenty years of appellate litigation over lesbian and gay rights in the United States uncovered important findings. I repeat central ones and offer lessons they suggest.

Location, Location, Location

Southern judges (as specified in Chapter 1) were the most hostile to gay people. In particular, the appellate courts of Alabama, Arkansas, Georgia, Kentucky, Louisiana, Mississippi, Missouri, North Carolina, Oklahoma, South Carolina, Tennessee, Texas, and Virginia decided lawsuits involving child custody, visitation, adoption, and foster care (CVAF) at rates about 50 percent less favorable to homosexual parents than the rest of the nation.

Children's best interests ought not vary by place. If lesbians and gay men are good parents in California, Illinois, and Massachusetts, then presumptively they have the same caring skills in Alabama, Mississippi, and Missouri. Nonetheless, by the beginning of the twenty-first century, Southern judges had not thoroughly grasped that simple truth. At minimum, gay people planning to raise families and living in the thirteen states named above should consider the wisdom of relocating to more favorable legal environs.

Indeed, all self-affirming lesbians and gay men should realize that where they live has an impact on their civil rights. Of the twelve states in the study producing at least ten appellate court decisions during the last two decades of the twentieth century, Missouri had tribunals the least supportive of gay rights, followed by Virginia and Ohio (Table 1.3).

Alternatively, Massachusetts courts were the most favorably disposed, with Florida, Minnesota, Colorado, and California close behind.[1] Generally, the West and Northeast were hospitable regions for rights claims.

A key factor beyond region is whether states have consensual sodomy statutes. Even though such criminal prohibitions typically are unenforced, they nonetheless helped predict 8.5 percent more negative judicial action on homosexual civil rights claims than in states without the laws (Table 3.1).[2] In contrast, legislatively enacted gay civil rights laws boded well (by 13.4 percent) for court outcomes positive to gay people.[3] Hence, awareness of the legal consequences arising from location should be of paramount importance to self-respecting lesbians and gay men.

The Promise of the States

The combination of presidential appointment and life tenure of federal judges does not necessarily improve the probability that their policy making will be more favorable to disfranchised minorities than that of state counterparts selected by other methods or for shorter terms of office (Chapter 4). In fact, lesbian and gay litigants experienced substantially greater success in state courts than in federal fora, with the former deciding sexual minority rights cases more than twice as favorably, on average, as the latter. In particular, state appellate courts interpreting their own state constitutions enhanced the rights and liberties of lesbians and gay men far more than federal and state decisions construing the federal Constitution, with a state supreme court rate two and a half times more favorable than that of the U.S. Supreme Court (Table 4.1). The results provide empirical support for the notion that a new judicial federalism has been at work in the nation. Accordingly, those interest groups pursuing litigative campaigns to secure rights – for either homosexuals or other beleaguered minorities – are best advised to work at the state level, in great contrast to the best strategies during the civil rights era of the 1960s and '70s.

Doubtless, a state-centered scheme is likely to be far more time-consuming, costly, and inefficient than one focused primarily on the

---

[1] Of course, Colorado voters adopted the homophobic Amendment 2 struck down in *Romer v. Evans*, and Florida is the only state with a statutory prohibition of adoptions by homosexuals.

[2] The website at www.aclu.org lists states with enforceable sodomy statutes.

[3] The website at www.aclu.org lists jurisdictions with laws prohibiting sexual orientation discrimination.

federal system, and doubtless, the results in the states will be uneven. Nonetheless, the findings here unveil virtually no empirically based reason to anticipate success for lesbian and gay litigants in federal fora as they are constituted currently or in the foreseeable future. This reality dramatizes how far the nation has changed from the 1960s.

In 1940, the U.S. Supreme Court majestically proclaimed that "[u]nder our constitutional system, courts stand against any winds that blow as havens of refuge for those who might otherwise suffer because they are helpless, weak, outnumbered, or because they are non-conforming victims of prejudice and public excitement" (*Chambers v. Florida* 1940: 241). Regrettably, with regard to the rights of homosexuals in late-twentieth-century America, only state courts evidenced any fidelity to that lofty judicial mission.

The parity debate, involving the comparative competence of federal and state courts, embraces a plethora of subjects beyond gay rights. Racial equality in education, voting, and other political activities and federal review of state criminal convictions and sentences are classic parity issues (e.g., Latzer 1996; Hasen 1997; Lee 2000). Yet judicial federalism is relevant to sundry other topics, ranging from the provision of tort remedies for mass disasters and widely distributed product injuries (Weber 1994) and the adjudication of Fifth Amendment takings claims (Kovacs 1999) to the state initiative process (Vitiello and Glendon 1998) and the vitality of the judicial prohibition of tort claims against religious institutions and clergy (Idleman 2000). Minimally, reliable quantitative empirical proof of the capacity of state courts to vindicate rights on a par with – let alone better than – federal courts could alter the distribution of judicial power through the mechanism of litigant forum shopping.

The Value of Diversity on the Bench

Legal scholars have advocated diversifying the bench in terms of race and gender (e.g., Beiner 1999; Ifill 2000). Arguments in favor of judicial heterogeneity cover numerous claims: (1) women and minority judges enhance colleagues' understanding of complex issues, such as abortion and discrimination; (2) female and minority jurists reduce gender and racial bias in the courts; (3) selection of such judges signifies commitment to improved conditions for women and minorities in the legal profession and justice system; and (4) the public has greater confidence in a bench more closely reflecting society's composition. Objections to diversity include that (1) it unnecessarily politicizes the legal system and that (2)

TABLE 6.1 *Summary of Voting Statistics of Selected Groups of Judges in All Cases Essential to Lesbian and Gay Rights*

Category of judges	Votes in precedent-free decisions		Opinion writers in precedent-free decisions		Opinion writers in all decisions	
	N	Percent favoring gay rights	N	Percent favoring gay rights	N	Percent favoring gay rights
Race/ethnicity						
Minority	76	68.4	13	92.3	19	89.5
Nonminority	929	50.7	318	51.6	443	49.0
Gender						
Female	152	66.4	46	71.7	66	69.7
Male	853	49.5	285	50.2	396	47.5
Religion						
Jewish	130	68.5	45	75.6	73	69.9
Protestant	557	50.6	183	53.0	249	49.0
Roman Catholic	268	44.8	83	38.6	117	39.3
Other or none	50	64.0	20	65.0	23	65.2
Age						
33–49	146	61.0	48	60.4	62	53.2
50–59	352	55.1	123	56.1	174	54.0
60–90	507	47.3	160	48.8	226	47.3
Career experience						
Prior nonjudicial office	213	40.8	69	37.7	99	38.4
No prior nonjudicial office	792	55.1	262	57.3	363	54.0
Political party affiliation						
Democrat	592	59.1	196	61.2	265	61.1
Republican	413	41.9	135	41.5	197	36.5

"as the ideological solidarity of the judiciary breaks down, so too does the predictability of legal decision making, and hence, the stability of the law" (Hasnas 1995: 216).

Table 6.1 displays selected voting data from all cases essential to lesbian and gay rights and arrays the information by the personal attributes of judges.[4] The graphic clearly demonstrates the benefit of diversity on the bench to the civil rights of homosexuals.

---

[4] The tables in this chapter display frequency distributions, which, although conveying useful and important knowledge, remain rudimentary statistical measures without the nuance of Chapter 3's multivariate regression analysis.

The initial row supplies statistics on minority judges by first listing the votes of African American, Latino, and Latina judges in precedent-free decisions – when the jurists were not under the influence of controlling precedent and therefore free to follow their attitudes. Of 76 such votes, 68.4 percent went for lesbian and gay litigants. Next in the row, and by far the table's most striking datum, 92.3 percent of 13 opinions written by minority judges in precedent-free cases favored gay people. Finally in the row, even with the inclusion of decisions rendered subject to *stare decisis*, 89.5 percent of 19 opinions penned by African Americans, Latinos, and Latinas were positive. Comparing these support rates with those of nonminority judges (in the second row) manifests the pivotal importance to lesbians and gay men of racial and ethnic diversity on the bench.

The data regarding opinion writers are especially noteworthy because, compared with concurring colleagues not separately writing, they are the jurists most actively involved in the adjudication process. Thus, when these judges from social groups with an extensive history of invidious discrimination and powerlessness in the United States authored signed opinions in gay rights appeals, they spoke resoundingly in favor of the civil rights of another downtrodden minority.

Likewise, consequential voting differences based on gender and religion also appear in Table 6.1. Women and Jews – other historically disempowered groups – voted and wrote opinions in favor of gay rights considerably more frequently than either men or Protestants and Roman Catholics. Some of the variation is truly startling. For example, when not subject to *stare decisis*, Jews on the bench authored signed opinions in favor of gay people virtually twice as frequently as their Catholic colleagues (75.6 vs. 38.6 percent).

Age diversity serves the interests of homosexual litigants, too. In both precedent-free columns of Table 6.1, the younger the judge, the more likely she would vote for gay rights. Sadly, as the number in each age cohort suggests, American courts are top-heavy with older jurists.

Unfortunately, Table 6.1's bivariate statistics do not control for the simultaneous influence of multiple attributes. The illustration does not reveal, for example, the percentage of votes by Roman Catholic Republican women under the age of fifty and without prior nonjudicial career experience favoring gay rights in precedent-free cases. Indeed, the display of a comprehensive tabulation of all frequency distributions arising from Table 6.1's six sets of independent variables would be entirely unmanageable. Nonetheless, the findings here and in Chapters 3 and 4 offer a reasonably thorough picture of personal attributes' relative impacts.

TABLE 6.2 *Summary of Voting Statistics of Selected Groups of Judges in Child Custody, Visitation, Adoption, and Foster Care Cases*

Category of judges	Votes in precedent-free decisions		Opinion writers in precedent-free decisions		Opinion writers in all decisions	
	N	Percent favoring gay rights	N	Percent favoring gay rights	N	Percent favoring gay rights
Race/ethnicity						
Minority	24	75.0	5	100.0	7	100.0
Nonminority	358	51.7	123	52.0	181	49.2
Gender						
Female	58	77.6	22	72.7	31	74.2
Male	324	48.8	106	50.0	157	46.5
Religion						
Jewish	45	77.8	20	75.0	28	71.4
Protestant	218	50.9	69	55.1	103	48.5
Roman Catholic	104	44.2	34	35.3	51	41.2
Other or none	15	73.3	5	80.0	6	83.3
Age						
33–49	64	68.8	22	63.6	29	51.7
50–59	136	55.9	51	60.8	74	59.5
60–90	182	45.6	55	43.6	85	43.5
Career experience						
Prior nonjudicial office	103	41.7	29	37.9	44	40.9
No prior nonjudicial office	279	57.3	99	58.6	144	54.2
Political party affiliation						
Democrat	232	58.2	79	64.6	111	61.3
Republican	150	45.3	49	36.7	77	36.4

Because cases adjudicating the CVAF of children represented 41.5 percent of all decisions essential to lesbian and gay rights during the period of interest, Table 6.2 displays these CVAF data separately. This table divulges even more pronounced differences in voting than Table 6.1. Most of the gaps based on race, gender, religion, and age – especially in precedent-free environments – are wider, with age and gender disparities remarkably about 70 percent greater than in Table 6.1. As a result, diversity on the bench is particularly crucial to the legal success of gay caregivers.

Time Is on Our Side, Yes It Is!

Homosexual litigants in American appellate courts were approximately 25 percent more successful in the 1990s than the decade before (and state courts were responsible for the later more numerous judicial victories). In particular, judges unencumbered by precedent advanced the parental rights of lesbians and gay men over time, with their winning almost two-thirds of CVAF cases of first impression between 1996 and 2000 (Table 1.4). Courts also increasingly supported coupling claims involving the rights and responsibilities of the domestic partners of gay people and same-sex marriage or its approximation. Thus, more and more, judges view gay families as legitimate and worthy of legal recognition.

The Vital Role of Interest Groups

Participation by legal interest groups (i.e., Gay and Lesbian Advocates and Defenders, Lambda Legal Defense and Education Fund, the Lesbian and Gay Rights Project of the American Civil Liberties Union, the National Center for Lesbian Rights, and the Servicemembers Legal Defense Network) as counsel or *amicus curiae* enhanced success by 7.8 percent generally (Table 3.1). In nonfamily cases – for example, the constitutionality of consensual sodomy laws; sexual orientation discrimination in public accommodations, housing, and the workplace; gays in the military; and free speech and association rights – the figure jumped to 17.6 percent (Table 3.6), and in federal court decisions to 32.2 percent (Appendix 4.8). Hence, lesbians, gay men, and their friends are wise to support the worthy efforts of these diligent organizations.

The Power of Precedent

About 70 percent of intermediate appellate court votes predisposed to results contrary to those fostered by binding precedent nonetheless yielded to *stare decisis*, while roughly 30 percent of pertinent court-of-last-resort votes did (Table 5.2). Precedent constrained conservative votes at a much higher rate than liberal ones (Table 5.2), and vertical *stare decisis* influenced state appellate decision making more consistently than horizontal *stare decisis* (Table 5.5).

As a practical matter, if legal precedents are won supporting gay rights, *stare decisis* makes it significantly more likely that later tribunals, even those staffed with antigay jurists, will uphold those rights. For example, as amply demonstrated in Chapter 3, Roman Catholic judges were some of the most hostile to the civil rights of homosexuals. Yet among 39 votes by Catholics participating in cases under the influence of controlling precedents favoring gay rights, 69.2 percent followed that case law and supported the lesbian and gay rights claims – a rate more than 50 percent higher than Table 6.1 discloses for Catholic jurists unconstrained by *stare decisis*.

Similarly, Chapters 3 and 4 and the tables here clearly establish that older judges, those affiliated with the Republican party, and those with prior career experience in nonjudicial elective office also tended to vote against gay rights when free to follow their attitudes. However, among 98 votes by jurists 60 years of age or older taking part in decisions subject to positive precedents, 74.5 percent were cast in favor of the rights claims – 57.5 percent greater than in Table 6.1. Of 49 votes by Republicans confined by *stare decisis* favorable to homosexual litigants, 71.4 percent followed the precedents' lead – an increase of 70.4 percent. Finally, among 40 votes by judges with prior service in nonjudicial office and acting in decisions controlled by positive precedents, 82.5 percent went for gay rights – more than twice as frequently as in Table 6.1.

Thus, although the book offers abundant evidence of a history of homophobic court rulings in the United States, lesbian and gay reformers reasonably can invest hope in a litigative struggle, especially in light of the temporal trends noted above.

More broadly, the storied Langdellian case method of American legal education is not mistaken after all. Notwithstanding importunate naysaying such as that of Spaeth and Segal (1999), Chapter 5's data demonstrate that *stare decisis* is in fact important – modestly in courts of last resort and decisively in intermediate appellate tribunals. Moreover, despite the former's glamour, the latter are the appellate workhorses of the American judiciary, handling 76.5 percent of the caseload here.

Democrats, Republicans, and Gay Rights

Federal judges selected by Democratic presidents, compared with Republican appointees, positively determined an astonishing 40.5 percent of the probability "space" between complete success and utter failure of lesbian and gay rights claims in federal appellate courts (Appendix 4.8). Among

45 federal cases in the study not influenced by controlling precedent, only 26.7 percent of 116 votes by judges nominated by Republican presidents were favorable to sexual minorities, while 60.2 percent of 83 votes by Democratic appointees supported homosexuals – a difference of 125 percent! Indeed, presidential party predicted case outcome far better than any other personal attribute of federal judges in the investigation.[5] The frequency distributions of Tables 6.1 and 6.2 also confirm significant partisan differences, especially among opinion writers.

Moreover, the Republican party's antigay policy positions and actions are well documented (Keen and Goldberg 1998: 105–6; Haeberle 1999: 152–53; D'Emilio 2000: 37, 40; Donovan, Wenzel, and Bowler 2000: 182–83; Haider-Markel 2000: 300; Lewis and Edelson 2000: 203). Thus, gay people who vote for, or otherwise support, Republican candidates engage in acts of self-immolation.

Nonetheless, in November 2000, an estimated 1.05 million lesbian and gay votes went for the Republican ticket nationwide.[6] Approximately 59,000 homosexual voters cast ballots for George W. Bush in Florida alone, where he won by fewer than 600 votes – and of course, the Florida outcome decided the race. Lamentably, this book's findings unequivocally establish that Bush's choices for the federal bench will serve principally to deny the civil rights of that political constituency so critical to his elevation to the presidency.

As a result, in addition to litigating in state fora, seeking the total decriminalization of consensual sodomy,[7] and lobbying for legislative passage of gay civil rights statutes, a comprehensive reform agenda necessarily includes educating lesbians, gay men, and their friends not to champion presidents who appoint socially conservative federal judges or members of Congress who pass repressive legislation such as "don't ask, don't tell" and the Defense of Marriage Act.

---

[5] Party identification was less decisive in 228 precedent-free state appellate decisions, where 58.9 and 47.8 percent of 509 Democratic and 297 Republican votes, respectively, backed gays.

[6] According to exit polls conducted by various organizations, including Voter News Service, CNN, and ABC, the total lesbian and gay portion of all votes cast in the 2000 General Election was 4 percent, and Bush–Cheney received 25 percent of that total gay vote (Rimmerman 2002: 161–62).

[7] When this book was in production, the U.S. Supreme Court granted certiorari in *Lawrence v. Texas* (No. 02–102) and agreed to reconsider whether state consensual sodomy statutes violate the Constitution. The Court's decision in *Lawrence* may unilaterally decriminalize same-sex sexual activity.

Reprise

A question remains. *Why* were state courts more responsive to rights vindication than federal tribunals?

Since this inquiry documents that diversity among judges fosters a more favorable attitudinal climate for gay rights, perhaps the multiplicity of state recruitment methods makes that bench more heterogeneous than the federal. However, the population of jurists here (which is not a random sample of either federal or state judges) doesn't provide evidence for that hypothesis. For instance, 15.0 percent of the federal votes in the study were by women judges, while 15.6 percent of state votes were. With regard to race and ethnicity, 7.1 percent of federal votes came from minority judges, and 7.0 percent of state votes did. Roman Catholic judges provided 25.6 percent of federal votes and 26.2 percent of state votes. Jewish judges supplied 14.2 percent and 13.8 percent, respectively. The only potentially consequential difference among personal attributes involved age, where the mean was 61.9 for federal votes and 58.9 for state. Yet that's not enough to account for the variance in outcome observed between court systems.

Removing Southern states (Alabama, Arkansas, Georgia, Kentucky, Louisiana, Mississippi, Missouri, North Carolina, Oklahoma, South Carolina, Tennessee, Texas, and Virginia) from the analysis produces slightly different results. The percentage of state votes by women judges increases to 16.2 and by Jewish judges to 18.0 – both indicating enhanced receptivity to gay rights claims. At the same time, however, state votes by Catholic judges rise (to 32.9 percent), and those by minority judges diminish (to 6.6 percent) – predicting less sensitivity to those claims. The mean age is 59.9. Thus, even accounting for prospective regional differences in attitude doesn't provide much traction.

Institutional forces weren't dispositive either. Appointment as a selection method was negatively signed (compared with popular election), but was positively moderated as state environmental ideology and term length increased (Chapter 3). Indeed, except for merit selected judges, longer terms of office appeared to insulate jurists from disapproving public opinion on gay rights issues (Chapter 3 and Appendix 4.9) – a finding that fails to distinguish state courts from federal.

In short, there is no empirical reason here to believe that state courts are inherently more receptive to rights claims than their federal counterparts. Instead, the meaningful conclusion rests on the flip side of the coin. Presidents possess virtually unilateral power over federal judicial selection. Even when controlled by the opposing party, the U.S. Senate engages only in symbolic politics, voting down at most a handful of judicial nominees to appease relevant interest groups. The overwhelming number of presidential designees are confirmed. Even the few defeats are followed by replacements from the same mold. Thus, federal courts are far more susceptible to ideological manipulation by a single source than the state bench.[8]

Republican dominance of the federal judiciary during the last three decades of the twentieth century is key. Only 38.9 percent of federal votes in the book's database were by Democratic appointees. Hence, state courts did not necessarily become substantially more progressive. Rather, the point of reference migrated far right.

The Forces Motivating Judicial Decision Making

Environmental and attitudinal effects were dominant in courts of last resort, while legal variables prevailed in intermediate appellate tribunals (Table 3.4). Of thirty-six independent variables and interaction terms in Chapter 3's analysis, three environmental forces and their interactions accounted for a marginal reduction in model error of nearly 33 percent among court-of-last-resort votes, with seven attitudinal factors and their interactions in second place at 26 percent. Four institutional variables and their interactions were in third place at 20 percent, and eight legal variables trailed at 12 percent.

In contrast, among intermediate appellate court votes, the legal vector's marginal error reduction led at almost 30 percent, while those for attitudinal, environmental, and institutional forces were clustered at 20, 18, and 17 percent, respectively. These comparative court-level findings are the

---

[8] The different findings in Appendices 4.8 and 4.9 for **environmental ideology** bolster this point. The Berry et al. measures are positive and significant at the .01 level in the state court model, but their population-weighted analogs (Appendix 3.3) are irrelevant to the federal bench. In other words, state judges were responsive to their environment; federal jurists were not.

In a study of U.S. Court of Appeals decisions from 1960 to 1993, Songer and Ginn (2002: 321) reach a similar conclusion:

[J]udicial voting behavior does reflect the political preferences of appointing Presidents. The preferences of appointing Presidents remain strongly related to judges' voting behavior even when one controls for the preferences of senators involved in the selection process, the preferences of other home state elites, and current opinions in judges' home states. Thus, the association between presidential preferences and judicial behavior does not appear to be simply an artifact of a common partisan background.

first from a comprehensive database offering equal numbers of empirical measures for both the legal and attitudinal models of judicial behavior. Although this information partially bolsters the findings of Segal and Spaeth (1993), their coronation of the attitudinal model may be ill-advised because environmental effects exceeded those from judges' personal attributes in courts of last resort. Granted, Segal and Spaeth are concerned only with the U.S. Supreme Court, and as Chapter 3 notes, the justices of that tribunal may be exceptional in terms of judicial behavior. Nonetheless, the debate between legal scholars and political scientists over the attitudinal and legal models of judicial behavior referenced in Chapter 1 does not have to be a zero-sum game. The book's findings demonstrate that the models are complementary, not mutually exclusive.

The Quantitative Study of Rights and of Law

In collecting judges' personal attribute data, I blundered into normative objections to my investigation from legal academics. I share the experience here because it's instructive about the propriety of my survey and the interpretation of its findings. More important, however, the debate highlights the diversity of opinion over the place of quantitative empirical legal study in academe and beyond.

As noted in Appendix 3.1, I posted research queries to LAWCOURTS and LAWPROF, two internet discussion groups.[9] The first list, composed principally of political scientists, had well over 500 subscribers, none of whom questioned whether my data-collection inquiry was appropriate. The message to the second group, made up mainly of law professors, elicited a different response, reported by Wiehl (2000: 292):

A recent exchange of e-mails between law and [political science] professors nationwide illustrates that the issue of judges and religion is a volatile one. A Professor Dan Pinello, Government Department, John Jay College CUNY, sent out a national e-mail dated November 2, 2000, in which he said he was conducting

---

[9] The subject line of the message to LAWPROF was "Federal-Judge Query" and the text read:

I'm conducting research involving the religious affiliations of federal judges. Using the Zuk-Barrow-Gryski courts-of-appeals database, I've identified affiliations for most appellate judges. However, a few aren't revealed in that ICPSR source. Also, judicial biographies like *The American Bench* have incomplete information.... So I turn to LAWPROF subscribers to tap their vast personal knowledge. If you know the religious affiliations of any of these judges, please let me know privately.... [A list of the names of 25 federal judges followed.]

research involving the religious affiliations of federal judges. He asked the law professors on this national e-mail server list to help provide him with information [on] the religious affiliation of federal judges. The response to his e-mail was heated. For example, Professor Marianne Wesson, University of Colorado Law School, responded to Professor Pinello on November 2, 2000: "Why don't you write to the identified judges and ask them? And (please excuse me if this sounds rude) if you do and they do not reply or decline to reveal their 'religious affiliation,' why don't you conclude that it's none of your business?"

With the permission of the participants in the LAWPROF debate, I reproduce further excerpts from it here. Professor Wesson's initial email message (of November 2, 2000) continued as follows:

I know it's de rigeur to make a great show of one's "religious affiliation" these days, but does that mean everyone in public life is required to disclose his or hers? Do you really think it's proper to ask other subscribers to this list to give you such information if the judges have decided (as seems to be the case) that they do not wish to reveal it? I assume you have a proper scholarly purpose, but doesn't a judge's decision to keep this information private tell you enough for your purposes?

Professor Richard K. Neumann, Jr., of Hofstra Law School, added (November 3):

Not only is religious affiliation a private matter, if the person involved views it that way, but inferences you attempt to draw from religious affiliation alone do not have much scholarly validity. Because of family history, some people consider themselves affiliated with religions they barely understand and whose places of worship they haven't frequented since childhood. Other people consider themselves affiliated with religions but dissent 100 percent from certain positions those religions have taken in public controversies (for example, abortion) which judges sometimes rule on. And still others do not consider themselves affiliated with any religion but have very thoughtful and carefully worked out beliefs on religious matters. In fact, these three groups, added together, probably represent a large proportion of Americans.

Judges yield privacy on questions like conflicts of interest. But they are not customarily asked their religions in confirmation hearings, perhaps because (setting aside the issue of whether religious tests were being interposed) much of the public would see that kind of questioning as inappropriate.

Lincoln carefully avoided making definitive statements about his religious views, and it would be hard to argue that he had no right to do that, even though he exercised power far in excess of what any federal judge ever might.

Responding to Professor Neumann, Professor Alan Gunn, of Notre Dame Law School, wrote (on November 3):

Questions about membership may be somewhat different, though; these are questions about what someone has done (joined a particular church), not about the details of belief, to which "none of your business" is often an appropriate response. Indeed, even in the setting of religious practices, questions about belief may be out of bounds. My church (United Methodist) has no creed; indeed, if there is one defining attribute of Methodism it is its insistence (biblically based, to be sure) that, within very broad limits, variations in beliefs about theological matters are not important.

Professor James A. Tanford, of Indiana University School of Law, noted (on November 3):

I am a bit surprised by the tone of moral criticism being leveled against Dr. Pinello's innocuous request to see if anyone knows the religious affiliation of several judges for whom he was having trouble finding the data. Religious affiliation is a fairly standard variable in social science research concerning human behavior. Before any such questions can be probed, federal law requires that they must be approved by the investigator's research plan, and will decide whether the questions are legitimate.[10] The empirical study of judicial behavior has been going on for 70 years under the banners of legal realism and the Law and Society Association, and often involves statistical analysis that requires that the investigator control for obvious demographic variables like gender, age, or religious affiliation. We have learned much from these studies. Surely the basic realist premise that the personal views of the judge are just as important a factor in decision-making as legal doctrine is no longer open to question. . . .

Professor Frank B. Cross, of the University of Texas Graduate School of Business, observed (on November 3):

I'm a little surprised at the reaction to Dan Pinello's query. And mystified. Rights of privacy are closely related to one's reasonable expectations. I don't think that anyone is out there tapping judge's phone calls to churches. Why do people assume that this affiliation is assiduously being kept secret. If it were, the inquiry presumably would not succeed anyway.

And consider how this has played out in a different context. Evangelical conservatives have run for school boards in order to change policies and introduce creationism into the curriculum. They have sometimes run as "stealth candidates," not disclosing their inclinations. While school board candidates should not be compelled to disclose their religious affiliation, I would expect a good investigative reporter to do some digging.

Professor Wesson persevered (on November 3):

I have no objection at all to Professor Pinello or anyone collecting information from publicly available sources about the religious affiliations of judges who are willing to disclose theirs. I do object to asking members of this list, some of whom no doubt have personal relationships with the judges listed as "affiliation

---

[10] The Institutional Review Board of John Jay College of Criminal Justice of the City University of New York did indeed provide prior approval of the self-administered questionnaire sent to judges.

unknown," to pass on what they know or think they know. It seems clear to me that if these judges wanted the public to know their religious beliefs, it would know by now. I can't agree that the agreement to become a judge carries with it an obligation to make this disclosure.

I've recently heard people passionately defend the proposition that we have a "right to privacy" in the records of our transactions at bookstores and libraries because they would disclose "what we are thinking" – and remember how angry people were at the idea that someone looked for Justice [Clarence] Thomas's video rental records before his confirmation hearings? I'm undecided on the merits of such privacy claims, but surely a more compelling case can be made that nobody (including a judge or a judicial nominee) should have to answer such questions as:

1. Do you believe in God? If so, go to Question 2.
2. What does your God tell you about abortion, capital punishment, and the proper balance of power between state and federal governments? . . .

In response to Professor Wesson's last message, Professor Sanford Levinson, of the University of Texas School of Law, wrote (on November 4):

I disagree strongly, at least under the following circumstances: A person has stated on the public record that his/her belief in God structures everything he/she does (see, e.g., Bill Clinton, George W. Bush, Raoul Gonzalez, a former member of the Texas Supreme Court, and many others who profess to base their actions on "what would Jesus do?"). I certainly want to know what they believe God tells them about abortion, etc., in part because it would be rank idolatry to say, "Well, God says it is wrong, but I realize that my oath to the Constitution takes precedence."

Reacting to the postings of Professors Gunn and Neumann, Professor J. Stephen Clark, of the Albany Law School, argued (on November 3):

Did Hugo Black have a privacy right to conceal his past affiliation with the Ku Klux Klan? Would he have had a privacy right to conceal continuing affiliation with that organization at the time of his appointment to the [Supreme] Court? Does not knowledge of that affiliation raise a serious question about his views on racial equality that would justify further inquiry into his attitudes in order to ascertain what his views are and rebut any presumption raised by his affiliation?

For gay men and lesbians, I submit, affiliation with any number of organized religions raises a quite similar prima facie inference about one's attitudes on sexual-orientation equality – although, admittedly, without some of the more violent connotations of Klan membership.

The reference to the United Methodist Church is interesting in this respect. The official, repeatedly affirmed position of the General Convention of that body is that lesbian and gay relationships are so far inferior to heterosexual relationships as to be affirmatively immoral. The Catholic Church's official position is that they are inherently "disordered," sinful, unnatural, and, obviously, in no sense whatsoever equal to heterosexual relationships. A prospective judge's nominal, official adherence to either of those faiths inevitably raises the question whether the prospective judge views lesbian and gay relationships as inherently immoral, disordered, or inferior. The prospective judge may rebut such an inference, but it is fair to make the inference from the act of voluntary association with the organization that so vehemently expresses the substantive positions I've referenced. And if the prospective judge views gay and lesbian relationships as inherently inferior, is there not a real possibility that such a view will influence the judge's constitutional- or statutory-interpretation decisions involving lesbians and gay men? I think the answer is clearly yes.

... [T]he right to privacy notion just reinforces the prevailing view that people should be permitted to hold and even advocate those views and be regarded by the rest of the world as immune from criticism because it's their "religion." That sets up the nice double standard whereby people may use their religions as a club to beat down lesbians and gay men, but any criticism of those advocates' religious views is somehow anti-religious bigotry. I reject that. If you want to associate with an organization that advocates gay and lesbian inferiority (indeed, total illegitimacy, in some instances) and, especially, if you want to use your religion to establish your views as public policy, your religion is as fair game as membership in the KKK – to which, for many gay men and lesbians, the membership in certain religions is essentially equivalent (again, without perhaps the violence overtones of the Klan).

No. There is no right of public officials to conceal their affiliation with organizations that adopt and promote ideological positions on such issues. If the public official does not agree with the ideology, he or she may disassociate from the group (as Hugo Black did) or may publicly disavow those portions of the ideology with which he or she disagrees. Absent that, the membership supports a rebuttable presumption of agreement with the ideology. And I'm not willing to erect some public-private distinction to shield that ideology from public view and criticism.

Professor Eugene Volokh, of the UCLA School of Law, responded (on November 3):

Professor Clark makes some excellent points – but it seems to me that they cut both ways. On the one hand, the public and the scholarly community do have good reasons to be concerned about the political, ideological, and religious (since religion is highly connected to ideology in many instances) perspectives of its high government officials.

At the same time, imagine that there was a message posted to a similar list [if the internet existed] in, say, the 1950s or 1960s ... stating: "As part of a research project in which I'm involved, I'd like to determine which judges were once members of Communist organizations" – "were once" being a good analogy here, since ... saying that someone "is Catholic", "is Protestant," or "is Jewish" often (though not always) means nothing more than this is the way the person was once raised – "so if you know this about any judges, please pass the information along." Would this be interesting research? Quite probably. Would there be anything illegal about such a query? Not at all; in fact, I'd say that the inquiry would be constitutionally protected.

But would we be thrilled by such an organized attempt to get people to reveal their friends' and acquaintances' affiliations, affiliations that they (again, echoing the current hypo) purposefully omitted from any disclosure sheets that they were asked to fill out? Or what if earlier in this century, someone sent around a query asking for the names of any judges who were actually atheists?

Professor Wesson continued (on November 4):

It seems to me that judges who are "members" of established churches or congregations could not have successfully concealed this information from the investigations that have preceded yours. Those who are left are those whose "affiliations" are a more complicated matter than membership in some organization, or willingness to describe one's own beliefs in a couple of words. Perhaps because I do have friendly relationships with some of the judges you list, I believe that this information shortfall may be a result of these judges having decided they do not wish to be categorized on the basis of their "religious affiliation" or lack thereof.... Our disagreement, or at least my disagreement with some other list members, seems to center around whether this desire is or is not legitimate. I believe it is, and should be respected....

I see that reasonable persons can differ on this question. I must say I particularly disagree with what I take to be the implicit premise of some of the messages [to the discussion list]: that we ought to discover what we can about the privately held religious beliefs of judges so we can consider whether the statistical tendency of persons with similar beliefs to rule for or against interest groups with which we sympathize should lead us to favor or oppose their selection and/or retention in office.

Professor Clark, in private correspondence (April 15, 2001), sums up the issue poignantly:

In my personal view, religious ideology receives a "bye" in the political process – an immunity from scrutiny to which it is not entitled. I don't believe it should be acceptable to criticize someone else's political ideology while it is unacceptable to criticize someone else's religious ideology – particularly if it has the real-world, secular impact on people that Pinello's research suggests it may. It seems to me that once religious conservatives, for example, inject their religious views and, to be blunt, agenda into the public sphere, they open the door to a comprehensive critique of those very religious views. If it's a private matter, it should remain so. If it's going to be determining my secular rights, however, then it is open season for thoroughgoing analysis and critique – both from within the methodology of the particular faith and from without it. Any other course gives a class of people a right to control secular law based on beliefs that they are able to shield from public scrutiny and criticism.

These comments raise serious issues. For example, is it appropriate for scholars to investigate the effects of personal attributes such as religion on judicial decision making? Clearly, political scientists, none of whom questioned the propriety of my research query, think it is. In contrast, some law professors appear to challenge the appropriateness of such investigations, the means by which data are collected for them, or, more fundamentally, the merit of quantitative empirical research in the first place (cf. Cross 1997).[11]

Nonetheless, judges are public officials who make public policies that affect millions of citizens. In fact, informed observers might argue that judges are no less important to policy formation in the United States than legislators and executives. If that is true, then it is appropriate to conduct an empirical investigation of judges' policy formulation. For instance, the personal attribute (political party affiliation) most reliably predicting the policy preferences and actions of chief executives and legislators (Snyder and Groseclose 2000; Ansolabehere, Snyder, and Stewart 2001) in the United States also applies to judges.[12]

More crucially, what should be done with statistical information disclosing a significant correlation between judges' personal attributes and how they discharge the duties of their public office? What if a study performed a comparable statistical analysis of the judicial treatment of abortion rights claims, and similar correlations regarding judges' religious affiliations were discovered (i.e., that Catholic jurists voted against abortion rights significantly more frequently than judges affiliated with other religions)? What about investigations of gender or racial equality claims (cf. Vines 1964)?

Formal litmus tests for public office based on religion or other belief systems manifestly violate American tradition. Yet public knowledge of such correlations may be enough in a democracy. Just as awareness of psychological problems usually is the most important step to therapeutic resolution, the public dissemination of evidence of systematic animus toward lesbians and gay men in American courts revealed here should, by itself, have consequential corrective effects.

---

[11] In this study, 473 (66.5 percent) of 711 state appellate judges who were sent self-administered questionnaires seeking personal attribute information completed and returned the documents. That high response rate indicates that state judges generally thought the inquiry was a legitimate part of scholarly business. Further, the fact that most federal appellate judges revealed their religious affiliations and other personal details to Professors Zuk, Barrow, and Gryski for their *public* database (Zuk et al. 1997) is reinforcing evidence of judicial belief in the propriety of such investigations.

[12] Pinello (1999) (a meta-analysis of 84 judicial behavior studies conducted between 1959 and 1998 revealed that judges' political party affiliations alone explained 48 percent of the ideological variance in federal court decisions and 31 percent in state court cases).

Epilogue

When first identifying lesbian and gay rights cases and sending out questionnaires to judges, I was motivated by parochial concern over how courts treated family. My ambition was modest. *Stare decisis* was a vague, brooding notion from law school, and judicial federalism probably wasn't in my vocabulary. I surely didn't think I was embarking on quantitative appraisals of those topics. Nonetheless, provincial, subject-specific inquiry transformed into investigations of issues vital to the American legal system. The collected information afforded the opportunity for vision far beyond my initial sight. That's the wonder of quantitative empirical research. The paths the data provide hold the promise of unimagined adventures. I urge others to follow their lead.

Appendix 1.1

How Court Decisions Were Identified

I made diligent efforts to identify all appellate rulings touching the rights of lesbians and gay men over the years from 1981 to 2000. Another researcher collecting a global case tally for the same period might produce a different list. Yet I am confident any variation would be inconsequential. Moreover, a difference of a handful of decisions among 400 would not significantly affect the book's statistical findings.

I conducted a *Westlaw* database search for decisions containing the keywords "homosexual," "gay man," "lesbian," "same sex," "sexual orientation," "sexual preference," or their cognates for all federal and state appellate courts during those twenty years. I examined each citation regarding the existence of a lesbian or gay rights claim made to the court. The criteria for inclusion in my case list were (1) the presence of a lesbian or gay litigant (self-identified or alleged) advancing or defending a gay civil right or liberty that was adjudicated on the merits, or (2) an action otherwise directly affecting lesbians and gay men as a class. An example of the latter is *Opinion of the Justices* (NH 1987),[1] rendering an advisory opinion that a proposed bill prohibiting homosexuals from adopting children, being licensed as foster parents, or running day care centers was constitutional. A case unsuitable to the former category is *Sipple v. Chronicle Publishing Co.* (1984), dismissing an invasion-of-privacy action against a newspaper publishing an article disclosing the sexual orientation of a heroic gay man thwarting a presidential-assassination attempt. Sipple

---

[1] Text citations to lesbian and gay rights cases listed in Appendix 1.2 use the format [case name] ([jurisdiction] [year]), while citations to decisions appearing in the book's References section (and not included in an appendix) use just the case name and year.

was gay, but not "advancing or defending a gay civil right or liberty," as commonly understood. More than 95 percent of the *Westlaw* citations were not germane to my study. A large portion of the rejected cases involved assault or homicide prosecutions with "gay panic" themes – defendants claiming provocation or justification defenses (e.g., "I just had to kill him because he propositioned me"). Since the court decisions I searched were appellate, juries there did not embrace gay panic claims. One can only speculate, though, how many times juries *did* welcome them since acquittals are not appealed. Yet what is clear from perusing the database search is that many American gay men are assaulted or killed merely for expressing their sexuality.[2]

The annual case tables compiled by Professor Arthur Leonard and other editors of the *Lesbian/Gay Law Notes*,[3] as well as other sources,[4] augmented the database search. In all, 468 pertinent decisions[5] were found from all federal appellate jurisdictions and forty-seven states. Appendix 1.2 arrays the decisions[6] by jurisdiction, court, and year and marks rulings made in favor of lesbian and gay rights.

---

[2] An interesting research project would compare the numbers of such gay victims with other victims of hate crimes or another appropriate victim subpopulation.

[3] Available at www.qrd.org/qrd/usa/legal/lgln. See Leonard (2000a, 2000b).

[4] Hall (1997), Rubenstein (1997), Markey (1998), and Starr (1998) provided case lists for cross-checking. A *Westlaw* search for *amicus* participation by lesbian and gay legal interest groups (Gay and Lesbian Advocates and Defenders, Lambda Legal Defense and Education Fund, the Lesbian and Gay Rights Project of the American Civil Liberties Union, and the National Center for Lesbian Rights; see Brewer, Kaib, and O'Connor 2000: 383–84; Rimmerman 2002: 55–59) also disclosed pertinent decisions.

[5] The 468 decisions are not from 468 *separate* litigations. Rather, 54 rulings were at both the intermediate appellate court and court-of-last-resort stages in 22 litigations (e.g., see the three California decisions in *Curran v. Mount Diablo Council of the Boy Scouts of America* and the four Virginia *Bottoms v. Bottoms* decisions in Appendix 1.2), 18 rulings were at the intermediate level in eight lawsuits (e.g., *Guardianship of Kowalski* in Minnesota), and 13 decisions were at the court-of-last-resort level in six litigations (*Evans v. Romer* in Colorado, the *Baehr* litigation in Hawaii, *State v. Baxley* in Louisiana, and *Republican Party of Texas v. Dietz* in the Lone Star State).

[6] As noted in Appendix 1.2, only concurring and dissenting opinions in eight decisions (Florida: *Cox v. Florida Department of Health and Rehabilitative Services*; Georgia: *Van Dyck v. Van Dyck*; Louisiana: both decisions in *State v. Baxley*; Maryland: *Neville v. State*; Michigan: *People v. Lino*; North Dakota: *Johnson v. Schlotman*; and West Virginia: *Minshall v. Health Care & Retirement Corp.*) are included in the database. Appendix 1.2 also reveals that case frequency is independent of state population. For example, New York, the second most populous state during the period of interest, has 47 percent more decisions in the study than the largest, California. Indeed, New York has more than twice as many decisions as California per capita. Colorado, by comparison, has *seven* times the per capita decisions of Michigan. Each of sixteen states less populous than Kansas has more

The 468 decisions in the book's database should be at least the population of published federal and state appellate court cases involving lesbian and gay rights claims from 1981 to 2000. Pertinent rulings slipped
through the cracks only if opinions were unpublished or courts never referred to "homosexual," "gay man," "lesbian," "same sex," "sexual orientation," "sexual preference," or their cognates. Although the former
is an intractable problem in judicial behavior research,[7] thirty-one unpublished cases[8] contained in the *Westlaw* database were included here.
Moreover, the odds for courts' never referring to any of the six search
keywords are negligible.[9] Further, the *Lesbian/Gay Law Notes* case tables,
Rubenstein (1997), and five lesbian and gay rights legal interest groups

decisions than the Sunflower State (with none). This incidence disparity is a topic for
future research.

[7] Dubois (1988: 951) (in the late 1980s, only about 15 percent of all California intermediate
appellate court decisions were published); Lee and Lehnhof (2001: 146–47) ("the number
of unpublished decisions in the [U.S.] courts of appeals has risen markedly in recent
years.... By the late 1970s..., nearly half were unpublished, and by 1989 over two-
thirds were unpublished. The latest reports suggest that nearly eighty percent of all federal
appellate opinions are unpublished").

[8] In Appendix 1.2, *Silva v. Sifflard* (1st Cir. 2000), *Mayo v. Kiwest Corp.* (4th Cir. 1996),
Selland v. Perry (4th Cir. 1996), *Scott v. Norfolk Southern Corp.* (4th Cir. 1998), *Thorne v.
U.S. Department of Defense* (4th Cir. 1998), *Gay Inmates of Shelby County Jail v. Barksdale*
(6th Cir. 1987), *Ruth v. Children's Medical Center* (6th Cir. 1991), *Dillon v. Frank* (6th Cir.
1992), *Preston v. Hughes* (6th Cir. 1999), *Peterson v. Bodlovich* (7th Cir. 2000), *Schmidt v.
U.S.* (9th Cir. 1991), *Lewis v. Alcorn* (9th Cir. 1993), *Jackson v. U.S. Department of the Air
Force* (9th Cir. 1997), *Foley v. County of Hennepin* (MN 1998), *McKay v. Johnson* (MN
1996), *Schroeder v. Anfinson* (MN 1998), *Police Officers Federation of Minneapolis v. City of
Minneapolis* (MN 2000), *Delong v. Delong* (MO 1998), *Large v. Large* (OH 1993), *Phillips
v. Phillips* (OH 1995), *Liston v. Pyles* (OH 1997), *State of Ohio Metroparks v. Lasher* (OH
1999), *Cooke v. SGS Tool Company* (OH 2000), *State v. Thompson* (OH 2000), *Collins v.
Collins* (TN 1993), *Price v. Price* (TN 1997), *Eldridge v. Eldridge* (TN 1999), *Thomas v.
Thomas* (VA 1996), *Bottoms v. Bottoms* (VA 1997), *Bottoms v. Bottoms* (VA 1999), and
Webb v. Puget Sound Broadcasting Company (WA 1998).

[9] "Homosexual," "sexual orientation," and "sexual preference" are the more clinical (and
old-fashioned) expressions – more suited to a conservative's pen. "Lesbian," "gay man,"
and "same sex" are more modern, and thus more likely to appear on a liberal's word
processor. Compare, for instance, the repeated references to "homosexual sodomy" by
Justice Byron White (writing for the Court) and Chief Justice Warren Burger (concurring) in *Bowers v. Hardwick* (U.S.Sup.Ct. 1986), with the single usage of "homosexual"
and the multiple mention of "gay" and "lesbian" in the unanimous opinion by Justice
David Souter in *Hurley v. Irish-American Gay, Lesbian and Bisexual Group of Boston* (U.S.
Sup. Ct. 1995). Similarly, in *Romer v. Evans* (U.S. Sup. Ct. 1996), the majority opinion of
Justice Anthony Kennedy refers to "gays and lesbians" almost as frequently as to "homosexuals" and "homosexuality," while Justice Antonin Scalia's dissent uses the latter
exclusively.

served as counterchecks to the database search to assure comprehensive case collection.[10] From those sources, I am aware of only two decisions[11] failing to employ any of the search keywords and of eight unpublished decisions[12] unavailable on *Westlaw* (and therefore, inaccessible to me). Equally important, overlooked cases would occur randomly and thereby not produce any systematic bias in findings.

Of course, concerns about the impact of "the shadow of the law" (e.g., Mnookin and Kornhauser 1979) are ever present. Not only does this study probably miss relevant unpublished decisions, it does not seek cases that were resolved before trial or appellate review, nor those disputes that never were litigated because of the presumed effect of settled law (*stare decisis*). Rather, the approach here is more modest, as outlined above.

[10] I invited the executive or legal directors of Gay and Lesbian Advocates and Defenders, Lambda Legal Defense and Education Fund, the Lesbian and Gay Rights Project of the American Civil Liberties Union, the National Center for Lesbian Rights, and the Servicemembers Legal Defense Network to review my final case list. Based on their comments, I added one decision to the list.

[11] In Appendix 1.2, *Lynda A. H. v. Diane T. O.* (NY 1998) and *Jenkins v. Jenkins* (WV 1994).

[12] *Blain v. Golden State Container* (AZ Ct. App., 05/05/94), *Georgia P. v. Kerry B.* (CA Ct. App., 1st Dist., 02/09/94), *Denton v. Denton* (KY Ct. App., 04/15/94), *Gayheart v. Burns* (KY Ct. App., 1996), *Irish-American Gay, Lesbian, and Bisexual Group of Boston v. South Boston Allied War Veterans Council* (MA App. Ct., 03/01/93), *State v. Harper* (MI Ct. App., 09/09/94), *Mier v. Certified Oil Company* (OH Ct. App., 08/25/97), and *In re Petition of D.L.G. and M.A.H.* (06/27/96).

Appendix 1.2

Federal and State Appellate Cases Adjudicating Lesbian and Gay Rights Claims, 1981–2000

Case names in boldface indicate decisions coded as essential to lesbian and gay rights. Asterisks (*) indicate cases coded as decided in favor of lesbian and gay rights.

United States Supreme Court

1986 *Bowers v. Hardwick*, 478 U.S. 186, 106 S.Ct. 2841, 92 L.Ed.2d 140

1987 *San Francisco Arts & Athletics, Inc. v. U.S. Olympic Committee*, 483 U.S. 522, 107 S.Ct.2971, 97 L.Ed.2d 427

1995 **Hurley v. Irish-American Gay, Lesbian and Bisexual Group of Boston**, 515 U.S. 557, 115 S.Ct. 2338, 132 L.Ed.2d 487

1996 ***Romer v. Evans***, 517 U.S. 620, 116 S.Ct. 1620, 134 L.Ed.2d 855

1998 ***Oncale v. Sundowner Offshore Services, Inc.***, 523 U.S. 75, 118 S.Ct. 998, 140 L.Ed.2d 201

2000 **Boy Scouts of America v. Dale**, 530 U.S. 640, 120 S.Ct. 2446

United States Courts of Appeals

First Circuit

1999 *Higgins v. New Balance Athletic Shoe, Inc.*, 194 F.3d 252

2000 *Rosa v. Park West Bank & Trust Co.*, 214 F.3d 213

Silva v. Sifflard, 215 F.3d 1312, 2000 WL 525573

Second Circuit

1985 *Olivieri v. Ward*, 766 F.2d 690

1998 *Able v. U.S.*, 155 F.3d 628

2000 *Joel A. v. Giuliani*, 218 F.3d 132

Simonton v. Runyon, 232 F.3d 33

Third Circuit
   1986   *U.S. v. City of Philadelphia*, 798 F.2d 81
   1996   **Presbytery of New Jersey v. Whitman*, 99 F.3d 101
   2000   **Sterling v. Borough of Minersville*, 232 F.3d 190
Fourth Circuit
   1981   **Nemetz v. Immigration and Naturalization Service*, 647 F.2d 432
   1990   *Walls v. City of Petersburg*, 895 F.2d 188
   1996   *Hopkins v. Baltimore Gas and Electric Co.*, 77 F.3d 745
              Mayo v. Kiwest Corp., 94 F.3d 641, 1996 WL 460769
              McWilliams v. Fairfax County Board of Supervisors, 72 F.3d 1191
              Selland v. Perry, 100 F.3d 950, 1996 WL 647265
              Thomasson v. Perry, 80 F.3d 915
              Wrightson v. Pizza Hut of America, Inc., 99 F.3d 138
   1998   **Scott v. Norfolk Southern Corp.*, 153 F.3d 722, 1998 WL 387192
              Thorne v. U.S. Department of Defense, 139 F.3d 893, 1998 WL 163632
Fifth Circuit
   1981   **Van Ooteghem v. Gray*, 654 F.2d 304
   1982   *Manale v. City of New Orleans*, 673 F.2d 122
   1983   *Matter of Longstaff*, 716 F.2d 1439
   1984   **Gay Student Services v. Texas A&M University*, 737 F.2d 1317
              Naragon v. Wharton, 737 F.2d 1403
   1985   *Baker v. Wade*, 769 F.2d 289
   1986   *Joachim v. AT&T Information Systems*, 793 F.2d 113
   1994   *Garcia v. Elf Atochem North America*, 28 F.3d 446
   1996   *Oncale v. Sundowner Offshore Services, Inc.*, 83 F.3d 118
   1997   *Plumley v. Landmark Chevrolet, Inc.*, 122 F.3d 308
   1998   **Doe v. Dallas Independent School District*, 153 F.3d 211
Sixth Circuit
   1984   *Brown v. Johnson*, 743 F.2d 408
              Rowland v. Mad River Local School District, 730 F.2d 444
   1987   *Espinoza v. Wilson*, 814 F.2d 1093
              Gay Inmates of Shelby County Jail v. Barksdale, 819 F.2d 289, 1987 WL 37565
   1991   *Ruth v. Children's Medical Center*, 940 F.2d 662, 1991 WL 151158
   1992   *Dillon v. Frank*, 952 F.2d 403, 1992 WL 5436
              Hansard v. Barrett, 980 F.2d 1059
   1995   *Equality Foundation of Greater Cincinnati, Inc. v. City of Cincinnati*, 54 F.3d 261

1990   *High Tech Gays v. Defense Indus. Sec. Clearance Office*, 895 F.2d
        563
1991   *Schmidt v. U.S.*, 930 F.2d 29, 1991 WL 42921
        Schowengerdt v. U.S., 944 F.2d 483
1992   **Beam v. Paskett*, 966 F.2d 1563
        *Pruitt v. Cheney, 963 F.2d 1160
1993   *Lewis v. Alcorn*, 996 F.2d 1225, 1993 WL 206292
1994   **Meinhold v. U.S. Department of Defense*, 34 F.3d 1469
1997   *Holmes v. California Army National Guard*, 124 F.3d 1126
        Jackson v. U.S. Department of the Air Force, 132 F.3d 39, 1997
        WL 759144
        Philips v. Perry, 106 F.3d 1420
1999   **Kelly v. City of Oakland*, 198 F.3d 779
2000   **Hernandez-Montiel v. Immigration and Naturalization Service*,
        225 F.3d 1084
Tenth Circuit
1984   **National Gay Task Force v. Board of Education of the City of
        Oklahoma City*, 729 F.2d 1270
        Rich v. Secretary of the Army, 735 F.2d 1220
1992   *Jantz v. Muci*, 976 F.2d 623
1995   *Walmer v. U.S. Department of Defense*, 52 F.3d 851
Eleventh Circuit
1985   **Hardwick v. Bowers*, 760 F.2d 1202
1995   **Shahar v. Bowers*, 70 F.3d 1218
1997   **Fredette v. BVP Management Associates*, 112 F.3d 1503
        *Gay Lesbian Bisexual Alliance v. Pryor, 110 F.3d 1543
        Shahar v. Bowers, 114 F.3d 1097
        Shahar v. Bowers, 120 F.3d 211
District of Columbia Circuit
1984   *Dronenburg v. Zech*, 741 F.2d 1388
1986   **Doe v. Casey*, 796 F.2d 1508
1987   *Padula v. Webster*, 822 F.2d 97
1988   *Gay Veterans Association, Inc. v. Secretary of Defense*, 850 F.2d
        764
1993   *Doe v. Gates*, 981 F.2d 1316
        *Steffan v. Aspin, 8 F.3d 57
        U.S. Information Agency v. Krc, 989 F.2d 1211
1994   *Steffan v. Perry*, 41 F.3d 677
Federal Circuit
1989   *Woodward v. U.S.*, 871 F.2d 1068

Alabama
Court of Civil Appeals
1985   *Bark v. Bark*, 479 So.2d 42
1993   *H.J.B. v. P.W.*, 628 So.2d 753
1997   **J.B.F. v. J.M.F.*, 730 So.2d 1186
      *R.W. v. D.W.W., 717 So.2d 790
1998   **K.T.W.P. v. D.R.W.*, 721 So.2d 699
      T.K.T. v. F.P.T., 716 So.2d 1235
Supreme Court
1985   *Logan v. Sears, Roebuck & Co.*, 466 So.2d 121
1998   *Ex Parte D.W.W.*, 717 So.2d 793
      Ex Parte J.M.F., 730 So.2d 1190

Alaska
Supreme Court
1985   **S.N.E. v. R.L.B.*, 699 P.2d 875
1997   **University of Alaska v. Tumeo*, 933 P.2d 1147
1999   *Bess v. Ulmer*, 985 P.2d 979

Arizona
Court of Appeals
1986   *Appeal in Pima County Juvenile Action B-10489*, 151 Ariz. 335, 727 P.2d 830

Arkansas
Court of Appeals
1987   *Thigpen v. Carpenter*, 21 Ark.App. 194, 730 S.W.2d 510
1995   *Larson v. Larson*, 50 Ark.App. 158, 902 S.W.2d 254

California
Court of Appeal
1982   **Hubert v. Williams*, 133 Cal.App.3d Supp. 1, 184 Cal.Rptr. 161
1983   **Curran v. Mount Diablo Council of the Boy Scouts of America*, 147 Cal.App.3d 712, 195 Cal.Rptr. 325
1984   **Rolon v. Kulwitzky*, 153 Cal.App.3d 288, 200 Cal.Rptr. 217
1985   *Hinman v. Department of Personnel Administration*, 167 Cal.App.3d 516, 213 Cal.Rptr. 410
1987   *Coon v. Joseph*, 192 Cal.App.3d 1269, 237 Cal.Rptr. 873
      Hart v. National Mortgage & Land Company, 189 Cal.App.3d 1420, 235 Cal.Rptr. 68
1988   **Marriage of Birdsall*, 197 Cal.App.3d 1024, 243 Cal.Rptr. 287
      *Whorton v. Dillingham, 202 Cal.App.3d 447, 248 Cal.Rptr. 405
1990   *Curiale v. Reagan*, 222 Cal.App.3d 1597, 272 Cal.Rptr. 520

Colorado
Court of Appeals
1991 *Hayes v. Smith*, 832 P.2d 1022
1994 *People v. Murphy*, 899 P.2d 294
Rendon v. United Airlines, 881 P.2d 482
Ross v. *Denver Department of Health and Hospitals*, 883 P.2d 516
1995 *Borquez v. Ozer*, 923 P.2d 166
1996 Adoption of *T.K.J. and K.A.K.*, 931 P.2d 488
1998 *Schaefer v. City & County of Denver*, 973 P.2d 717
Supreme Court
1993 *Evans v. Romer*, 854 P.2d 1270
1994 *Evans v. Romer*, 882 P.2d 1335
1996 *People v. Murphy*, 919 P.2d 191

Connecticut
Supreme Court
1996 *Gay and Lesbian Law Students Association v. Board of Trustees*, 236 Conn. 453, 673 A.2d 484
1999 Adoption of *Baby Z*, 247 Conn. 474, 724 A.2d 1035

Delaware
Supreme Court
1993 *Adoption of Swanson*, 623 A.2d 1095

District of Columbia
Court of Appeals
1985 *Gay Rights Coalition v. Georgetown University*, 496 A.2d 567
1987 Gay Rights Coalition v. *Georgetown University*, 536 A.2d 1
1995 Dean v. *District of Columbia*, 653 A.2d 307
In re M.M.D., 662 A.2d 837

Florida
District Court of Appeal
1990 *Boehm v. American Bankers Insurance Group, Inc.*, 557 So.2d 91
1992 *Heilman v. Heilman*, 610 So.2d 60
1993 State v. *Cox*, 627 So.2d 1210
1994 *Matthews v. Weinberg*, 645 So.2d 487
Reeves v. State, 631 So.2d 374
1995 Music v. *Rachford*, 654 So.2d 1234
1996 *Maradie v. Maradie*, 680 So.2d 538
Ward v. *Ward*, 742 So.2d 250

1997   *Packard v. Packard,* 697 So.2d 1292

        Posik v. Layton, 695 So.2d 759

        Rucks v. State, 692 So.2d 976

1999   *Kazmierazak v. Query,* 736 So.2d 106

2000   *Jacoby v. Jacoby,* 763 So.2d 410

        Lowe v. Broward County, 766 So.2d 1199

        Rickard v. McKesson, 774 So.2d 838

Supreme Court

1981   *Florida Board of Bar Examiners Re: N. R. S.,* 403 So.2d 1315

1994   *Code of Judicial Conduct,* 643 So.2d 1037

1995   *Cox v. Florida Department of Health and Rehabilitative Services,* 656 So.2d 902 (Dissent of Anstead and Kogan, JJ. only)

Georgia

Court of Appeals

1985   *Loring v. Bellsouth Advertising & Publishing Corporation,* 177 Ga.App. 307, 339 S.E.2d 372

1996   *Interest of R.E.W.,* 220 Ga.App. 861, 471 S.E.2d 6

Supreme Court

1981   *Owens v. Owens,* 247 Ga. 139, 274 S.E.2d 484

1992   *Crooke v. Gilden,* 262 Ga. 122, 414 S.E.2d 645

1993   *Van Dyck v. Van Dyck,* 262 Ga. 720, 425 S.E.2d 853 (Concurrence of Sears-Collins, J. only)

1995   ½**City of Atlanta v. McKinney,* 265 Ga. 161, 454 S.E.2d 517

1996   *Christensen v. State,* 266 Ga. 474, 468 S.E.2d 188

1997   *City of Atlanta v. Morgan,* 268 Ga. 586, 492 S.E.2d 193

1998   *Powell v. State,* 270 Ga. 327, 510 S.E.2d 18

Hawaii

Supreme Court

1993   *Baehr v. Lewin,* 74 Haw. 530, 852 P.2d 44

1997   *Baehr v. Miike,* 87 Haw. 34, 950 P.2d 1234

Illinois

Appellate Court

1990   *Marriage of Williams,* 205 Ill.App.3d 613, 563 N.E.2d 1195, 151 Ill.Dec. 89

1991   *Marriage of Diehl,* 221 Ill.App.3d 410, 582 N.E.2d 281, 164 Ill.Dec. 73

1993   *Pleasant v. Pleasant,* 256 Ill.App.3d 742, 628 N.E.2d 633, 195 Ill.Dec. 169

1995   *Marriage of Martins,* 269 Ill.App.3d 380, 645 N.E.2d 567, 206 Ill.Dec. 562

Petition of K.M. and D.M., 274 Ill.App.3d 189, 653 N.E.2d 888, 210 Ill.Dec. 693

1996 *Marriage of R.S.*, 286 Ill.App.3d 1046, 677 N.E.2d 1297, 222 Ill.Dec. 498

1999 *Crawford v. City of Chicago*, 304 Ill.App.3d 818, 710 N.E.2d 91, 237 Ill.Dec. 668

Marriage of Weisbruch, 304 Ill.App.3d 99, 710 N.E.2d 439, 237 Ill.Dec. 809

Petition of C.M.A., 306 Ill.App.3d 1061, 715 N.E.2d 674, 239 Ill.Dec. 920

Visitation with C.B.L., 309 Ill.App.3d 888, 723 N.E.2d 316, 243 Ill.Dec. 284

Indiana
Court of Appeals

1981 *D.H. v. J.H.*, 418 N.E.2d 286

1991 *R.E.G. v. L.M.G.*, 571 N.E.2d 298

1992 Pennington v. Pennington, 596 N.E.2d 305

1994 *Teegarden v. Teegarden*, 642 N.E.2d 1007

1998 Knotts v. Knotts, 693 N.E.2d 962

Marlow v. Marlow, 702 N.E.2d 733

1999 *Pryor v. Pryor*, 709 N.E.2d 374

Pryor v. Pryor, 714 N.E.2d 743

Iowa
Court of Appeals

1990 *Hodson v. Moore*, 464 N.W.2d 699

1993 *Hartman v. Stassis*, 504 N.W.2d 129

Marriage of Wiarda, 505 N.W.2d 506

1995 *Marriage of Cupples*, 531 N.W.2d 656

2000 *Marriage of Kraft*, 2000 WL 1289135

Supreme Court

1990 *Marriage of Walsh*, 451 N.W.2d 492

1992 *Marriage of Will*, 489 N.W.2d 394

Kentucky
Court of Appeals

1997 *Ireland v. Davis*, 957 S.W.2d 310

1999 *Brewer v. Hillard*, 15 S.W.3d 1

Supreme Court

1992 *Commonwealth v. Wasson*, 842 S.W.2d 487

Louisiana
Court of Appeal

1984 *Peyton v. Peyton*, 457 So.2d 321

1990   *Lundin v. Lundin*, 563 So.2d 1273
1995   *Scott v. Scott*, 665 So.2d 760
1999   *State v. Smith*, 729 So.2d 648
Supreme Court
1994   *State v. Baxley*, 633 So.2d 142 (Concurrence of Ortique, J. and Dissent of Calogero, J. only)
1995   *State v. Baxley*, 656 So.2d 973 (Dissent of Calogero, J. only)
2000   *State v. Smith*, 766 So.2d 501
Maine
Supreme Judicial Court
1982   *State v. Lovely*, 451 A.2d 900
1998   *Clarke v. Certified Healthcare Corporation*, 714 A.2d 823
Maryland
Court of Special Appeals
1994   *North v. North*, 102 Md.App. 1, 648 A.2d 1025
1997   *Boswell v. Boswell*, 118 Md.App. 1, 701 A.2d 1153
1998   *Broadcast Equities v. Montgomery County*, 123 Md.App 363, 718 A.2d 648
2000   *Gestl v. Frederick*, 133 Md.App. 216, 754 A.2d 1087
       Lapides v. Trabbic, 134 Md.App. 51, 758 A.2d 1114
       S.F. v. M.D., 132 Md.App. 99, 751 A.2d 9
Court of Appeals
1981   *Neville v. State*, 290 Md. 364, 430 A.2d 570 (Dissent of Davidson, J. only)
1998   *Boswell v. Boswell*, 352 Md. 204, 721 A.2d 662
Massachusetts
Appeals Court
1983   *Doe v. Doe*, 16 Mass.App. 499, 452 N.E.2d 293
Supreme Judicial Court
1985   *Madsen v. Erwin*, 395 Mass. 715, 481 N.E.2d 1160
1990   *Collins v. Secretary of the Commonwealth*, 407 Mass. 837, 556 N.E.2d 348
1993   *Adoption of Tammy*, 416 Mass. 205, 619 N.E.2d 315
1994   *Irish-American Gay, Lesbian and Bisexual Group of Boston v. City of Boston*, 418 Mass. 238, 636 N.E.2d 1293
1997   *Adoption of Galen*, 425 Mass. 201, 680 N.E.2d 70
       Melnychenko v. 84 Lumber Company, 424 Mass. 285, 676 N.E.2d 45
1998   *Opinions of the Justices*, 427 Mass. 1211, 696 N.E.2d 502

1999 *Connors v. City of Boston*, 430 Mass. 31, 714 N.E.2d 335

E.N.O. v. L.M.M., 429 Mass. 824, 711 N.E.2d 886

Michigan

Court of Appeals

1993 *Barbour v. Department of Social Services*, 198 Mich.App. 183, 497 N.W.2d 216

1995 *McGuffin v. Overton*, 214 Mich.App. 95, 542 N.W.2d 288

2000 *Mack v. City of Detroit*, 243 Mich.App. 132, 620 N.W.2d 670

Supreme Court

1994 *People v. Lino*, 447 Mich. 567, 527 N.W.2d 434 (Dissent of Levin, J. only)

Minnesota

Court of Appeals

1985 *Blanding v. Sports & Health Club, Inc.*, 373 N.W.2d 784

Potter v. LaSalle Sports & Health Club, 368 N.W.2d 413

1986 *Guardianship of Kowalski*, 382 N.W.2d 861

1987 *Bohdan v. Alltool Mfg., Co.*, 411 N.W.2d 902

1991 *Dignity Twin Cities v. Newman Center and Chapel*, 472 N.W.2d 355

Guardianship of Kowalski, 478 N.W.2d 790

Kulla v. McNulty, 472 N.W.2d 175

1994 *Hanke v. Safari Hair Adventure*, 512 N.W.2d 614

1995 *Lilly v. City of Minneapolis*, 527 N.W.2d 107

1996 *Cummings v. Koehnen*, 556 N.W.2d 586

McKay v. Johnson, 1996 WL 12658

1998 *Foley v. County of Hennepin*, 1998 WL 313546

Schroeder v. Anfinson, 1998 WL 268007

Welfare of G.A.S., 583 N.W.2d 296

2000 *LaChapelle v. Mitten*, 607 N.W.2d 151

Police Officers Federation of Minneapolis v. City of Minneapolis, 2000 WL 719860

Supreme Court

1986 *Potter v. LaSalle Court Sports & Health Club*, 384 N.W.2d 873

1997 *Cummings v. Koehnen*, 568 N.W.2d 418

Mississippi

Supreme Court

1990 *White v. Thompson*, 569 So.2d 1181

1997 *Bowen v. Bowen*, 688 So.2d 1374

1999   *Estate of Reaves v. Owen*, 744 So.2d 799
       Plaxico v. Michael, 735 So.2d 1036
       Weigand v. Houghton, 730 So.2d 581

Missouri

Court of Appeals

1982   *J.L.P.(H.) v. D.J.P.*, 643 S.W.2d 865
       L. v. D., 630 S.W.2d 240
1987   *G.A. v. D.A.*, 745 S.W.2d 726
       S.E.G. v. R.A.G., 735 S.W.2d 164
       Woy v. Woy, 737 S.W.2d 769
1988   *S.L.H. v. D.B.H.*, 745 S.W.2d 848
1989   *J.P. v. P.W.*, 772 S.W.2d 786
       T.C.H. v. K.M.H., 784 S.W.2d 281
1998   *Delong v. Delong*, 1998 WL 15536

Supreme Court

1985   *T.C.H. v. K.M.H.*, 693 S.W.2d 802
1986   *State v. Walsh*, 713 S.W.2d 508
1993   *Nazeri v. Missouri Valley College*, 860 S.W.2d 303
1998   *J.A.D. v. F.J.D.*, 978 S.W.2d 336

Montana

Supreme Court

1997   *Gryczan v. State*, 283 Mont. 433, 942 P.2d 112

Nebraska

Court of Appeals

1997   *Hassenstab v. Hassenstab*, 6 Neb.App. 13, 570 N.W.2d 368

Supreme Court

1998   *State v. Pattno*, 254 Neb. 733, 579 N.W.2d 503

New Hampshire

Supreme Court

1987   *Opinion of the Justices*, 129 N.H. 290, 530 A.2d 21
1991   *Stuart v. State*, 134 N.H. 702, 597 A.2d 1076

New Jersey

Superior Court, Appellate Division

1995   *Adoption of Two Children by H.N.R.*, 285 N.J.Super. 1, 666
       A.2d 535
1997   *Rutgers Council of AAUP Chapters v. Rutgers, The State
       University*, 298 N.J.Super 442, 689 A.2d 828
1998   *Dale v. Boy Scouts of America*, 308 N.J.Super 516, 706 A.2d
       270
1999   *V.C. v. M.J.B.*, 319 N.J.Super. 103, 725 A.2d 13

Supreme Court
  1999 *Dale v. Boy Scouts of America*, 160 N.J. 562, 734 A.2d 1196
  2000 *V.C. v. M.J.B.*, 163 N.J. 200, 748 A.2d 539
New Mexico
Court of Appeals
  1988 *State ex rel. Human Services Department*, 107 N.M. 769, 764
      P.2d 1327
  1992 *A.C. v. C.B.*, 113 N.M. 581, 829 P.2d 660
  1997 *Barnae v. Barnae*, 123 N.M. 583, 943 P.2d 1036
New York
Supreme Court, Appellate Term
  1982 *420 East 80th Company v. Chin*, 115 Misc.2d 195, 455
      N.Y.S.2d 42
  1988 *Koppelman v. O'Keeffe*, 140 Misc.2d 828, 535 N.Y.S.2d 871
Supreme Court, Appellate Division
  1982 *Adult Anonymous II*, 88 A.D.2d 30, 452 N.Y.S.2d 198
  1983 *Adoption of Pavlik*, 97 A.D.2d 991, 469 N.Y.S.2d 833
      420 East 80th Company v. Chin, 97 A.D.2d 390, 468 N.Y.S.2d 9
  1984 *Guinan v. Guinan*, 102 A.D.2d 963, 477 N.Y.S.2d 830
      Matherson v. Marchello, 100 A.D.2d 233, 473 N.Y.S.2d 998
  1985 *Gottlieb v. Gottlieb*, 108 A.D.2d 120, 488 N.Y.S.2d 180
      Under 21 v. City of New York, 108 A.D.2d 250, 488 N.Y.S.2d
      669
  1986 *Anonymous v. Anonymous*, 120 A.D.2d 983, 503 N.Y.S.2d 466
      Dally v. Orange County Publications, 117 A.D.2d 577, 497
      N.Y.S.2d 947
  1987 *Two Associates v. Brown*, 127 A.D.2d 173, 513 N.Y.S.2d 966
  1988 *Braschi v. Stahl Associates Company*, 143 A.D.2d 44, 531
      N.Y.S.2d 562
  1990 *Alison D. v. Virginia M.*, 155 A.D.2d 11, 552 N.Y.S.2d 321
      East 10th Street Associates v. Estate of Goldstein, 154 A.D.2d
      142, 552 N.Y.S.2d 257
      Park Holding Company v. Power, 161 A.D.2d 143, 554
      N.Y.S.2d 861
      Rent Stabilization Association of New York City, Inc. v. Higgins,
      164 A.D.2d 283, 562 N.Y.S.2d 962
  1992 *Gay Teachers Association v. Board of Education*, 183 A.D.2d
      478, 585 N.Y.S.2d 1016
  1993 *Lloyd v. Grella*, 190 A.D.2d 1026, 594 N.Y.S.2d 1007
      Matter of Cooper, 187 A.D.2d 128, 592 N.Y.S.2d 797

Rent Stabilization Association of New York City, Inc. v. Higgins, 189 A.D.2d 594, 592 N.Y.S.2d 255

1994 *Adoption of Anonymous,* 209 A.D.2d 960, 622 N.Y.S.2d 160

Adoption of Jessica N., 202 A.D.2d 320, 609 N.Y.S.2d 209

Paul C. v. Tracy C., 209 A.D.2d 955, 622 N.Y.S.2d 159

Thomas S. v. Robin Y., 209 A.D.2d 298, 618 N.Y.S.2d 356

1995 *Matter of Dana,* 209 A.D.2d 8, 624 N.Y.S.2d 634

1996 *Matter of Christine G.,* 229 A.D.2d 1016, 644 N.Y.S.2d 1016

Yukoweic v. International Business Machines, Inc., 228 A.D.2d 775, 643 N.Y.S.2d 747

1997 *Greenwald v. H & P 29th Street Associates,* 241 A.D.2d 307, 659 N.Y.S.2d 473

Secord v. Fischetti, 236 A.D.2d 206, 653 N.Y.S.2d 551

1998 *Funderburke v. Uniondale Union Free School District No. 15,* 676 N.Y.S.2d 199

Lynda A. H. v. Diane T. O., 243 A.D.2d 24, 673 N.Y.S.2d 989

Raum v. Restaurant Associates, Inc., 675 N.Y.S.2d 343

1999 *Nacinovich v. Tullet & Tokyo Forex, Inc.,* 257 A.D.2d 523, 685 N.Y.S.2d 17

2000 *Acosta v. Loews Corporation,* 276 A.D.2d 214, 717 N.Y.S.2d 47

Levin v. Yeshiva University, 272 A.D.2d 158, 709 N.Y.S.2d 392

Court of Appeals

1983 *People v. Uplinger,* 58 N.Y.2d 936, 447 N.E.2d 62, 460 N.Y.S.2d 514

1984 *Adoption of Robert Paul P.,* 63 N.Y.2d 233, 471 N.E.2d 424, 481 N.Y.S.2d 652

1985 *Under 21 v. City of New York,* 65 N.Y.2d 344, 482 N.E.2d 1, 492 N.Y.S.2d 522

1989 *Braschi v. Stahl Associates Company,* 74 N.Y.2d 201, 543 N.E.2d 49, 544 N.Y.S.2d 784

1991 *Alison D. v. Virginia M.,* 77 N.Y.2d 651, 572 N.E.2d 27, 569 N.Y.S.2d 586

1993 *Rent Stabilization Association of New York City, Inc. v. Higgins,* 83 N.Y.2d 156, 630 N.E.2d 626, 608 N.Y.S.2d 930

1994 *Lloyd v. Grella,* 83 N.Y.2d 537, 634 N.E.2d 171, 611 N.Y.S.2d 799

1995 *Matter of Jacob,* 86 N.Y.2d 651, 660 N.E.2d 397, 636 N.Y.S.2d 716

North Carolina
Court of Appeals
1985   *Warren v. City of Asheville,* 74 N.C.App. 402, 328 S.E.2d 859
1994   *Donovan v. Fiumara,* 114 N.C.App 524, 442 S.E.2d 572
1996   *Pulliam v. Smith,* 124 N.C.App. 144, 476 S.E.2d 446
Supreme Court
1998   *Pulliam v. Smith,* 348 N.C. 616, 501 S.E.2d 898
North Dakota
Supreme Court
1981   *Jacobson v. Jacobson,* 314 N.W.2d 78
1993   *Johnson v. Schlotman,* 502 N.W.2d 831 (Concurrence of Levine, J. only)
Ohio
Court of Appeals
1985   *Roberts v. Roberts,* 22 Ohio App.3d 127, 489 N.E.2d 1067
1986   *Bales v. Hack,* 31 Ohio App.3d 111, 509 N.E.2d 95
1987   *Conkel v. Conkel,* 31 Ohio App.3d 169, 509 N.E.2d 983
1989   *Mohrman v. Mohrman,* 57 Ohio App.3d 33, 565 N.E.2d 1283
1990   *Glover v. Glover,* 66 Ohio App.3d 724, 586 N.E.2d 159
1991   *Gajovski v. Gajovski,* 81 Ohio App.3d 11, 610 N.E.2d 431
     State v. Hadinger, 61 Ohio App.3d 820, 573 N.E.2d 1191
1993   *Large v. Large,* 1993 WL 498127
     Seward v. Mentrup, 87 Ohio App.3d 601, 622 N.E.2d 756
1995   *Greenwood v. Taft, Stettinius & Hollister,* 105 Ohio App.3d 295, 663 N.E.2d 1030
     Phillips v. Phillips, 1995 WL 115426
1996   *Retterer v. Whirlpool Corporation,* 111 Ohio App.3d 847, 677 N.E.2d 417
1997   *Inscoe v. Inscoe,* 121 Ohio App.3d 396, 700 N.E.2d 70
     Liston v. Pyles, 1997 WL 467327
     Schmitz v. Bob Evans Farms, Inc., 120 Ohio App.3d 264, 697 N.E.2d 1037
     State v. Yaden, 118 Ohio App.3d 410, 692 N.E.2d 1097
1998   *Adoption of Doe,* 130 Ohio App.3d 288, 719 N.E.2d 1071
     Tarver v. Calex Corporation, 125 Ohio App.3d 468, 1998 WL 74378
1999   *State of Ohio Metroparks v. Lasher,* 1999 WL 13971
2000   *Cooke v. SGS Tool Company,* 2000 WL 487730
     State v. Thompson, 2000 WL 1876610

Supreme Court

  1990 *Adoption of Charles B.*, 50 Ohio St.3d 88, 552 N.E.2d 884

  2000 *Hampel v. Food Ingredients Specialties, Inc.*, 89 Ohio St.3d 169, 729 N.E.2d 726

Oklahoma

Court of Criminal Appeals

  1994 *Allen v. State*, 871 P.2d 79

  1995 *Sawatzky v. City of Oklahoma City*, 906 P.2d 785

Supreme Court

  1981 *Gay Activists Alliance v. Board of Regents of the University of Oklahoma*, 638 P.2d 1116

  1982 *M.J.P. v. J.G.P.*, 640 P.2d 966

  1995 *Fox v. Fox*, 904 P.2d 66

Oregon

Court of Appeals

  1981 *Ireland v. Flanagan*, 51 Or.App. 837, 627 P.2d 496
        State v. Tusek, 52 Or.App. 997, 630 P.2d 892

  1992 *Merrick v. Board of Higher Education*, 116 Or.App. 258, 841 P.2d 646

  1995 *deParrie v. State*, 133 Or.App. 613, 893 P.2d 541
        deParrie v. City of Portland, 138 Or.App. 105, 906 P.2d 844

  1998 *Tanner v. Oregon Health Sciences University*, 157 Or.App. 502, 971 P.2d 435

  2000 *Harris v. Pameco Corporation*, 170 Or.App. 164, 12 P.3d 524
        Sims v. Besaw's Café, 165 Or.App. 180, 997 P.2d 201

Pennsylvania

Superior Court

  1984 *DeSanto v. Barnsley*, 328 Pa.Super. 181, 476 A.2d 952

  1985 *Constant A. v. Paul C.A.*, 344 Pa.Super. 49, 496 A.2d 1

  1986 *Pascarella v. Pascarella*, 355 Pa.Super. 5, 512 A.2d 715

  1991 *Barron v. Barron*, 406 Pa.Super. 401, 594 A.2d 682

  1992 *Blew v. Verta*, 420 Pa.Super. 528, 617 A.2d 31

  1995 *DeMuth v. Miller*, 438 Pa.Super. 437, 652 A.2d 891

  1996 *J.A.L. v. E.P.H.*, 453 Pa.Super. 78, 682 A.2d 1314

  1999 *D.H. v. B.O.*, 734 A.2d 409
        Mitchell v. Moore, 729 A.2d 1200

  2000 *Adoption of C.C.G. and Z.C.G.*, 762 A.2d 724
        Adoption of R.B.F. and R.C.F., 762 A.2d 739
        T.B. v. L.R.M., 753 A.2d 873

Rhode Island
Supreme Court
  1999   *State v. Mullen*, 740 A.2d 783
  2000   *Rubano v. DiCenzo*, 759 A.2d 959
South Carolina
Court of Appeals
  1987   *Stroman v. Williams*, 291 S.C. 376, 353 S.E.2d 704
  1996   *Doe v. Roe*, 323 S.C. 445, 475 S.E.2d 783
South Dakota
Supreme Court
  1992   *Chicoine v. Chicoine*, 479 N.W.2d 891
  1994   *Van Driel v. Van Driel*, 525 N.W.2d 37
  1998   *Collins v. Faith School District*, 574 N.W.2d 889
Tennessee
Court of Appeals
  1981   *Dailey v. Dailey*, 635 S.W.2d 391
  1993   *Collins v. Collins*, 1993 WL 177159
  1995   *Matter of Parsons*, 914 S.W.2d 889
  1996   *Campbell v. Sundquist*, 926 S.W.2d 250
  1997   *Price v. Price*, 1997 WL 338588
  1999   *Eldridge v. Eldridge*, 1999 WL 994099
           In re Thompson, 11 S.W.3d 913
  2000   *Adoption of M.J.S.*, 44 S.W.3d 41
Texas
Court of Appeals
  1982   *Small v. Harper*, 638 S.W.2d 24
  1992   *State v. Morales*, 826 S.W.2d 201
  1993   *City of Dallas v. England*, 846 S.W.2d 957
  1996   *Evans v. May*, 923 S.W.2d 712
  1997   *Fowler v. Jones*, 949 S.W.2d 442
  1998   *Bailey v. City of Austin*, 972 S.W.2d 180
  1999   *Hotze v. Brown*, 9 S.W.3d 404
Supreme Court
  1994   *State v. Morales*, 869 S.W.2d 941
  1996   *Republican Party of Texas v. Dietz*, 924 S.W.2d 932
  1997   *Republican Party of Texas v. Dietz*, 940 S.W.2d 86
Utah
Court of Appeals
  1994   *Tucker v. Tucker*, 881 P.2d 948

Supreme Court
  1996   *Tucker v. Tucker,* 910 P.2d 1209
Vermont
Supreme Court
  1992   **Nickerson v. Nickerson,* 158 Vt. 85, 605 A.2d 1331
  1993   **Adoptions of B.L.V.B. and E.L.V.B.,* 160 Vt. 368, 628 A.2d 1271
  1997   *Titchenal v. Dexter,* 166 Vt. 373, 693 A.2d 682
  1999   **Baker v. State,* 170 Vt. 194, 744 A.2d 864
Virginia
Court of Appeals
  1994   **Bottoms v. Bottoms,* 18 Va.App. 481, 444 S.E.2d 276
  1996   *Thomas v. Thomas,* 1996 WL 679985
  1997   **Bottoms v. Bottoms,* 1997 WL 421218
         Branche v. Commonwealth, 25 Va.App. 480, 489 S.E.2d 692
  1998   *Piatt v. Piatt,* 27 Va.App. 426, 499 S.E.2d 567
  1999   *Bottoms v. Bottoms,* 1999 WL 1129720
Supreme Court
  1981   **Doe v. Doe,* 222 Va. 736, 284 S.E.2d 799
  1985   *Roe v. Roe,* 228 Va. 722, 324 S.E.2d 691
  1995   *Bottoms v. Bottoms,* 249 Va. 410, 457 S.E.2d 102
  2000   *Arlington County v. White,* 259 Va. 708, 528 S.E.2d 706
Washington
Court of Appeals
  1986   **Marriage of Cabalquinto,* 43 Wash.App. 518, 718 P.2d 7
  1996   **Marriage of Wicklund,* 84 Wash.App. 763, 932 P.2d 652
  1998   *Webb v. Puget Sound Broadcasting Company,* 93 Wash.App.
         1042, 1998 WL 898788
  2000   *Vasquez v. Hawthorne,* 99 Wash.App. 363, 994 P.2d 240
Supreme Court
  1983   **Marriage of Cabalquinto,* 100 Wash.2d 325, 669 P.2d 886
  1997   *Nelson v. McClatchy Newspapers, Inc.,* 131 Wash.2d 523, 936
         P.2d 1123
West Virginia
Supreme Court of Appeals
  1985   **Rowsey v. Rowsey,* 174 W.Va. 692, 329 S.E.2d 57
  1987   **M.S.P. v. P.E.P.,* 178 W.Va. 183, 358 S.E.2d 442
  1994   **Jenkins v. Jenkins,* 191 W.Va. 619, 447 S.E.2d 554
  1998   ** Willis v. Wal-Mart Stores, Inc.,* 504 S.E.2d 648
  2000   *Minshall v. Health Care & Retirement Corp.,* 537 S.E.2d 320
         (Dissent of Starcher, J. only)

Wisconsin
Court of Appeals
1990   *Hatheway v. Gannett Satellite Information Network, Inc.*, 157 Wis.2d 395, 459 N.W.2d 873
       Sporleder v. Hermes, 157 Wis.2d 431, 459 N.W.2d 602
1992   *Phillips v. Wisconsin Personnel Commission*, 167 Wis.2d 205, 482 N.W.2d 121
1993   *Dinges v. Montgomery*, 179 Wis.2d 849, 514 N.W.2d 723, 1993 WL 388288
1995   *State v. Rushing*, 197 Wis.2d 631, 541 N.W.2d 155
1996   *State v. City of Madison*, 205 Wis.2d 110, 555 N.W.2d 409, 1996 WL 544099
Supreme Court
1991   *Interest of Z.J.H.*, 162 Wis.2d 1002, 471 N.W.2d 202
1994   *Angel Lace M. v. Terry M.*, 184 Wis.2d 492, 516 N.W.2d 678
1995   *Custody of H.S.H.-K.*, 193 Wis.2d 649, 533 N.W.2d 419
Wyoming
Supreme Court
1995   *Hertzler v. Hertzler*, 908 P.2d 946

Appendix 2.1

Cases Adjudicating Lesbian and Gay Family Issues,
1981–2000

Case names in boldface indicate decisions coded as essential to lesbian and gay rights. Asterisks (*) indicate cases coded as decided in favor of lesbian and gay rights. Happy faces (☺) indicate child custody, visitation, adoption, and foster-care rulings. Citations may be found in Appendix 1.2.

United States Courts of Appeals
Seventh Circuit
    2000   *Scott v. Commissioner of Internal Revenue*
Ninth Circuit
    1982   *Adams v. Howerton*
    1985   *Sullivan v. Immigration and Naturalization Service*
Eleventh Circuit
    1995   * *Shahar v. Bowers*
Alabama
Court of Civil Appeals
    1985   ☺*Bark v. Bark*
    1993   ☺*H.J.B. v. P.W.*
    1997   ☺**J.B.F. v. J.M.F.*
            ☺**R.W. v. D.W.W.*
    1998   ☺**K.T.W.P. v. D.R.W.*
            ☺*T.K.T. v. F.P.T.*
Supreme Court
    1998   ☺*Ex Parte D.W.W.*
          ☺*Ex Parte J.M.F.*
Alaska
Supreme Court

1985 ☺*S.N.E. v. R.L.B.*
1997 *University of Alaska v. Tumeo*
1999 Bess v. Ulmer

Arizona
Court of Appeals
1986 ☺*Appeal in Pima County Juvenile Action B-10489*

Arkansas
Court of Appeals
1987 ☺*Thigpen v. Carpenter*
1995 ☺*Larson v. Larson*

California
Court of Appeal
1985 Hinman v. Department of Personnel Administration
1987 Coon v. Joseph
1988 ☺*Marriage of Birdsall*
 Whorton v. Dillingham
1990 ☺*Curiale v. Reagan*
1991 ☺*Brian R. v. Santa Clara County Department of Family and Children's Services*
 ☺*Nancy S. v. Michele G.*
1992 Beaty v. Truck Insurance Exchange
 Engel v. Worthington
1997 ☺*West v. Superior Court*
1999 ☺*Guardianship of Z.C.W.*
2000 ☺*Guardianship of Olivia J.*

Colorado
Court of Appeals
1994 Ross v. Denver Department of Health and Hospitals
1996 ☺*Adoption of T.K.J. and K.A.K.*
1998 *Schaefer v. City & County of Denver*

Connecticut
Supreme Court
1999 ☺*Adoption of Baby Z*

Delaware
Supreme Court
1993 *Adoption of Swanson*

District of Columbia
Court of Appeals
1995 Dean v. District of Columbia
 ☺*In re M.M.D.*

Florida
District Court of Appeal
  1992   **Heilman v. Heilman*
  1993   ☺*State v. Cox*
  1994   ☺**Matthews v. Weinberg*
  1995   ☺*Music v. Rachford*
  1996   ☺**Maradie v. Maradie*
          ☺*Ward v. Ward*
  1997   ☺**Packard v. Packard*
          *Posik v. Layton
  1999   ☺*Kazmierazak v. Query*
  2000   ☺**Jacoby v. Jacoby*
          *Lowe v. Broward County
          Rickard v. McKesson
Supreme Court
  1995   ☺*Cox v. Florida Department of Health and Rehabilitative Services* (Dissent of Anstead and Kogan, JJ. only)

Georgia
Court of Appeals
  1996 ☺**Interest of R.E.W.*
Supreme Court
  1981   **Owens v. Owens*
  1992   **Crooke v. Gilden*
  1993   *Van Dyck v. Van Dyck* (Concurrence of Sears-Collins, J. only)
  1995 $\frac{1}{2}$**City of Atlanta v. McKinney*
  1997   **City of Atlanta v. Morgan*

Hawaii
Supreme Court
  1993   **Baehr v. Lewin*
  1997   **Baehr v. Miike*

Illinois
Appellate Court
  1990   ☺*Marriage of Williams*
  1991   ☺*Marriage of Diehl*
  1993   ☺**Pleasant v. Pleasant*
  1995   ☺*Marriage of Martins*
          ☺**Petition of K.M. and D.M.*
  1996   ☺**Marriage of R.S.*
  1999   **Crawford v. City of Chicago*
          *Marriage of Weisbruch

       ☺**Petition of C.M.A.*
       ☺*Visitation with C.B.L.*

Indiana
Court of Appeals
  1981   ☺**D.H. v. J.H.*
  1992   ☺*Pennington v. Pennington*
  1994   ☺**Teegarden v. Teegarden*
  1998   ☺*Knotts v. Knotts*
         ☺*Marlow v. Marlow*
  1999   ☺**Pryor v. Pryor*
         ☺**Pryor v. Pryor*

Iowa
Court of Appeals
  1990   ☺**Hodson v. Moore*
  1993   ☺**Marriage of Wiarda*
  1995   ☺**Marriage of Cupples*
  2000   ☺**Marriage of Kraft*
Supreme Court
  1990   ☺**Marriage of Walsh*
  1992   ☺*Marriage of Will

Kentucky
Court of Appeals
  1997   **Ireland v. Davis*

Louisiana
Court of Appeal
  1984   ☺**Peyton v. Peyton*
  1990   ☺*Lundin v. Lundin*
  1995   ☺*Scott v. Scott*

Maryland
Court of Special Appeals
  1994   ☺**North v. North*
  1997   ☺**Boswell v. Boswell*
  2000   ☺**Gestl v. Frederick*
         **Lapides v. Trabbic*
         ☺**S.F. v. M.D.*
Court of Appeals
  1998   ☺**Boswell v. Boswell*

Massachusetts
Appeals Court
  1983   ☺**Doe v. Doe*

Supreme Judicial Court
- 1993 ☺*Adoption of Tammy*
- 1997 ☺*Adoption of Galen*
- 1998 *Opinions of the Justices*
- 1999 *Connors v. City of Boston*
  - ☺*E.N.O. v. L.M.M.*

Michigan
Court of Appeals
- 1995 ☺*McGuffin v. Overton*

Minnesota
Court of Appeals
- 1986 *Guardianship of Kowalski*
- 1991 *Guardianship of Kowalski*
  - ☺*Kulla v. McNulty*
- 1995 *Lilly v. City of Minneapolis*
- 1996 ☺*McKay v. Johnson*
- 1998 ☺*Schroeder v. Anfinson*
  - ☺*Welfare of G.A.S.*
- 2000 ☺*LaChapelle v. Mitten*

Mississippi
Supreme Court
- 1990 ☺*White v. Thompson*
- 1997 ☺*Bowen v. Bowen*
- 1999 *Estate of Reaves v. Owen*
  - *Plaxico v. Michael*
  - ☺*Weigand v. Houghton*

Missouri
Court of Appeals
- 1982 ☺*J.L.P.(H.) v. D.J.P.*
  - ☺*L. v. D.*
- 1987 ☺*G.A. v. D.A.*
  - ☺*S.E.G. v. R.A.G.*
- 1988 ☺*S.L.H. v. D.B.H.*
- 1989 ☺*J.P. v. P.W.*
  - ☺*T.C.H. v. K.M.H.*
- 1998 ☺*Delong v. Delong*
Supreme Court
- 1985 ☺*T.C.H. v. K.M.H.*
- 1998 ☺*J.A.D. v. F.J.D.*

Nebraska
Court of Appeals
 1997 ☺**Hassenstab v. Hassenstab*
New Hampshire
Supreme Court
 1987 ☺*Opinion of the Justices*
 1991 ☺*Stuart v. State*
New Jersey
Superior Court, Appellate Division
 1995 ☺**Adoption of Two Children by H.N.R.*
 1997 *Rutgers Council of AAUP Chapters v. Rutgers, The State University*
 1999 ☺**V.C. v. M.J.B.*
Supreme Court
 2000 ☺**V.C. v. M.J.B.*
New Mexico
Court of Appeals
 1988 ☺**State ex rel. Human Services Department*
 1992 ☺**A.C. v. C.B.*
 1997 ☺**Barnae v. Barnae*
New York
Supreme Court, Appellate Term
 1982 **420 East 80th Company v. Chin*
 1988 *Koppelman v. O'Keeffe*
Supreme Court, Appellate Division
 1982 **Adult Anonymous II*
 1983 *Adoption of Pavlik*
      **420 East 80th Company v. Chin*
 1984 ☺**Guinan v. Guinan*
 1985 ☺*Gottlieb v. Gottlieb*
 1986 ☺**Anonymous v. Anonymous*
 1987 *Two Associates v. Brown*
 1988 *Braschi v. Stahl Associates Company*
 1990 ☺*Alison D. v. Virginia M.*
      **East 10th Street Associates v. Estate of Goldstein*
      **Park Holding Company v. Power*
      **Rent Stabilization Association of New York City, Inc. v. Higgins*
 1992 **Gay Teachers Association v. Board of Education*

1993   *Matter of Cooper*
         *Rent Stabilization Association of New York City, Inc. v. Higgins
1994   ☺**Adoption of Anonymous*
         ☺**Adoption of Jessica N.*
         ☺**Paul C. v. Tracy C.*
         ☺*Thomas S. v. Robin Y.*
1995   ☺*Matter of Dana*
1996   ☺**Matter of Christine G.*
1997   *Greenwald v. H & P 29th Street Associates*
         Secord v. Fischetti
1998   *Funderburke v. Uniondale Union Free School District No. 15*
         ☺*Lynda A. H. v. Diane T. O.*
         Raum v. Restaurant Associates, Inc.
2000   *Levin v. Yeshiva University*
Court of Appeals
1984   *Adoption of Robert Paul P.*
1989   **Braschi v. Stahl Associates Company*
1991   ☺*Alison D. v. Virginia M.*
1993   **Rent Stabilization Association of New York City, Inc. v. Higgins*
1995   ☺**Matter of Jacob*
North Carolina
Court of Appeals
1996   ☺**Pulliam v. Smith*
Supreme Court
1998   ☺*Pulliam v. Smith*
North Dakota
Supreme Court
1981   ☺*Jacobson v. Jacobson*
1993   ☺*Johnson v. Schlotman* (Concurrence of Levine, J. only)
Ohio
Court of Appeals
1985   ☺*Roberts v. Roberts*
1987   ☺**Conkel v. Conkel*
1989   ☺*Mohrman v. Mohrman*
1990   ☺*Glover v. Glover*
1991   *Gajovski v. Gajovski*
         *State v. Hadinger
1993   ☺**Large v. Large*
         Seward v. Mentrup
1995   ☺*Phillips v. Phillips*

1997 ☺**Inscoe v. Inscoe*
     ☺*Liston v. Pyles*
     **State v. Yaden*
1998 ☺*Adoption of Doe*
Supreme Court
1990 ☺**Adoption of Charles B.*

Oklahoma

Court of Criminal Appeals
1994   *Allen v. State*
Supreme Court
1982 ☺*M.J.P. v. J.G.P.*
1995 ☺**Fox v. Fox*

Oregon

Court of Appeals
1981   **Ireland v. Flanagan*
1998   **Tanner v. Oregon Health Sciences University*

Pennsylvania

Superior Court
1984   *DeSanto v. Barnsley*
1985 ☺*Constant A. v. Paul C.A.*
1986 ☺*Pascarella v. Pascarella*
1991 ☺**Barron v. Barron*
1992 ☺**Blew v. Verta*
1996 ☺**J.A.L. v. E.P.H.*
1999   **D.H. v. B.O.*
     **Mitchell v. Moore*
2000 ☺*Adoption of C.C.G. and Z.C.G.*
     ☺*Adoption of R.B.F. and R.C.F.*
     ☺**T.B. v. L.R.M.*

Rhode Island

Supreme Court
2000 ☺**Rubano v. DiCenzo*

South Carolina

Court of Appeals
1987 ☺**Stroman v. Williams*
1996   **Doe v. Roe*

South Dakota

Supreme Court
1992   ☺*Chicoine v. Chicoine*
1994 ☺**Van Driel v. Van Driel*

Tennessee
Court of Appeals
  1981   ☺*Dailey v. Dailey*
  1993   ☺*Collins v. Collins*
  1995   ☺**Matter of Parsons*
  1997   ☺*Price v. Price*
  1999   ☺*Eldridge v. Eldridge*
         ☺*In re Thompson*
  2000   ☺**Adoption of M.J.S.*
Texas
Court of Appeals
  1982   **Small v. Harper*
  1996   **Evans v. May*
  1997   ☺**Fowler v. Jones*
  1998   *Bailey v. City of Austin*
Utah
Court of Appeals
  1994   ☺**Tucker v. Tucker*
Supreme Court
  1996   ☺*Tucker v. Tucker*
Vermont
Supreme Court
  1992   ☺**Nickerson v. Nickerson*
  1993   ☺**Adoptions of B.L.V.B. and E.L.V.B.*
  1997   ☺*Titchenal v. Dexter*
  1999   **Baker v. State*
Virginia
Court of Appeals
  1994   ☺**Bottoms v. Bottoms*
  1997   ☺**Bottoms v. Bottoms*
  1998   ☺*Piatt v. Piatt*
  1999   ☺*Bottoms v. Bottoms*
Supreme Court
  1981   ☺**Doe v. Doe*
  1985   ☺*Roe v. Roe*
  1995   ☺*Bottoms v. Bottoms*
  2000   *Arlington County v. White*
Washington
Court of Appeals
  1986   ☺**Marriage of Cabalquinto*

1996   ☺**Marriage of Wicklund*
2000   *Vasquez v. Hawthorne*
Supreme Court
1983   ☺**Marriage of Cabalquinto*
West Virginia
Supreme Court of Appeals
1985   ☺**Rowsey v. Rowsey*
1987   ☺**M.S.P. v. P.E.P.*
1994   ☺**Jenkins v. Jenkins*
Wisconsin
Court of Appeals
1990   ☺*Sporleder v. Hermes*
1992   *Phillips v. Wisconsin Personnel Commission*
1993   ☺**Dinges v. Montgomery*
Supreme Court
1991   ☺*Interest of Z.J.H.*
1994   ☺*Angel Lace M. v. Terry M.*
1995   ☺**Custody of H.S.H.-K.*
Wyoming
Supreme Court
1995   ☺*Hertzler v. Hertzler*

Appendix 2.2

Cases Adjudicating Sexual Orientation Discrimination Claims Not Related to Lesbian and Gay Family Issues, 1981–2000

Asterisks (*) indicate cases coded as decided in favor of lesbian and gay rights. Citations may be found in Appendix 1.2.

United States Supreme Court
  1995　*Hurley v. Irish-American Gay, Lesbian and Bisexual Group of Boston*
  1996　**Romer v. Evans*
  2000　*Boy Scouts of America v. Dale*
United States Courts of Appeals
First Circuit
  1999　*Higgins v. New Balance Athletic Shoe, Inc.*
  2000　*Rosa v. Park West Bank & Trust Co.*
　　　　Silva v. Sifflard
Second Circuit
  2000　*Joel A. v. Giuliani*
　　　　Simonton v. Runyon
Third Circuit
  1996　**Presbytery of New Jersey v. Whitman*
Fifth Circuit
  1984　*Naragon v. Wharton*
  1986　*Joachim v. AT&T Information Systems*
Sixth Circuit
  1984　*Brown v. Johnson*
　　　　Rowland v. Mad River Local School District
  1987　*Espinoza v. Wilson*
　　　　Gay Inmates of Shelby County Jail v. Barksdale

1991   *Ruth v. Children's Medical Center*
1992   *Dillon v. Frank*
        Hansard v. Barrett
1995   *Equality Foundation of Greater Cincinnati, Inc. v. City of Cincinnati*
1997   *Equality Foundation of Greater Cincinnati, Inc. v. City of Cincinnati*
        *Stemler v. City of Florence
1999   *Preston v. Hughes*
2000   *Hall v. Baptist Memorial Health Care Corporation*
Seventh Circuit
1996   **Nabozny v. Podlesny*
2000   *Hamner v. St. Vincent Hospital and Health Care Center, Inc.*
        Peterson v. Bodlovich
        Spearman v. Ford Motor Company
Eighth Circuit
1989   *Williamson v. A.G. Edwards and Sons, Inc.*
Ninth Circuit
1990   *High Tech Gays v. Defense Indus. Sec. Clearance Office*
1993   *Lewis v. Alcorn*
Tenth Circuit
1992   *Jantz v. Muci*
Eleventh Circuit
1997   *Shahar v. Bowers*
        Shahar v. Bowers
District of Columbia Circuit
1986   **Doe v. Casey*
1987   *Padula v. Webster*
1993   *Doe v. Gates*
        U.S. Information Agency v. Krc

California
Court of Appeal
1982   **Hubert v. Williams*
1983   **Curran v. Mount Diablo Council of the Boy Scouts of America*
1984   **Rolon v. Kulwitzky*
1991   **Soroka v. Dayton Hudson Corporation*
1993   **Delaney v. Superior Fast Freight*
1994   *Curran v. Mount Diablo Council of the Boy Scouts of America*
1995   **Leibert v. Transworld Systems, Inc.*

1998   *Kovatch v. California Casualty Management Company*
2000   *Murray v. Oceanside Unified School District*
Supreme Court
1998   Curran v. Mount Diablo Council of the Boy Scouts of America

Colorado
Court of Appeals
1995   *Borquez v. Ozer*
Supreme Court
1993   *Evans v. Romer*
1994   *Evans v. Romer*

District of Columbia
Court of Appeals
1985   *Gay Rights Coalition v. Georgetown University*
1987   Gay Rights Coalition v. Georgetown University

Florida
District Court of Appeal
1997   *Rucks v. State*
Supreme Court
1981   *Florida Board of Bar Examiners Re: N. R. S.*

Georgia
Court of Appeals
1985   Loring v. Bellsouth Advertising & Publishing Corporation

Maine
Supreme Judicial Court
1998   Clarke v. Certified Healthcare Corporation

Massachusetts
Supreme Judicial Court
1985   Madsen v. Erwin
1990   *Collins v. Secretary of the Commonwealth*
1994   *Irish-American Gay, Lesbian and Bisexual Group of Boston v. City of Boston*

Michigan
Court of Appeals
1993   Barbour v. Department of Social Services
2000   *Mack v. City of Detroit*

Minnesota
Court of Appeals
1985   *Blanding v. Sports & Health Club, Inc.*
       Potter v. LaSalle Sports & Health Club

1991   *Dignity Twin Cities v. Newman Center and Chapel*
1994   **Hanke v. Safari Hair Adventure*
Supreme Court
  1986   **Potter v. LaSalle Court Sports & Health Club*
New Jersey
Superior Court, Appellate Division
  1998   **Dale v. Boy Scouts of America*
Supreme Court
  1999   **Dale v. Boy Scouts of America*
New York
Supreme Court, Appellate Division
  2000   **Acosta v. Loews Corporation*
North Carolina
Court of Appeals
  1985   **Warren v. City of Asheville*
Ohio
Court of Appeals
  1995   *Greenwood v. Taft, Stettinius & Hollister*
  1996   *Retterer v. Whirlpool Corporation*
  2000   *Cooke v. SGS Tool Company*
Oregon
Court of Appeals
  2000   **Sims v. Besaw's Café*
Pennsylvania
Superior Court
  1995   *DeMuth v. Miller*
Texas
Court of Appeals
  1993   **City of Dallas v. England*
Washington
Court of Appeals
  1998   *Webb v. Puget Sound Broadcasting Company*
West Virginia
Supreme Court of Appeals
  2000   *Minshall v. Health Care & Retirement Corp.* (Dissent of Starcher, J. only)
Wisconsin
Court of Appeals
  1990   *Hatheway v. Gannett Satellite Information Network, Inc.*
  1996   **State v. City of Madison*

Appendix 2.3

Cases of Gays in the Military, 1981–2000

Asterisks (*) indicate cases coded as decided in favor of lesbian and gay rights. Citations may be found in Appendix 1.2.

United States Courts of Appeals
Second Circuit
  1998   *Able v. U.S.*
Third Circuit
  1986   *U.S. v. City of Philadelphia*
Fourth Circuit
  1996   *Selland v. Perry*
          Thomasson v. Perry
  1998   *Thorne v. U.S. Department of Defense*
Seventh Circuit
  1989   *Ben-Shalom v. Marsh*
Eighth Circuit
  1995   *Richenberg v. Perry*
  1996   *Richenberg v. Perry*
Ninth Circuit
  1981   *Hatheway v. Secretary of the Army*
  1983   *Watkins v. U.S. Army*
  1988   **Watkins v. U.S. Army*
  1989   **Watkins v. U.S. Army*
  1991   *Schmidt v. U.S.*
          Schowengerdt v. U.S.
  1992   **Pruitt v. Cheney*

1994   *Meinhold v. U.S. Department of Defense*
1997   *Holmes v. California Army National Guard*
        Jackson v. U.S. Department of the Air Force
        Philips v. Perry
Tenth Circuit
1984   *Rich v. Secretary of the Army*
1995   *Walmer v. U.S. Department of Defense*
District of Columbia Circuit
1984   *Dronenburg v. Zech*
1988   *Gay Veterans Association, Inc. v. Secretary of Defense*
1993   **Steffan v. Aspin*
1994   *Steffan v. Perry*
Federal Circuit
1989   *Woodward v. U.S.*
Connecticut
Supreme Court
1996   **Gay and Lesbian Law Students Association v. Board of Trustees*
New York
Supreme Court, Appellate Division
1993   *Lloyd v. Grella*
Court of Appeals
1994   **Lloyd v. Grella*

Appendix 2.4

Cases Adjudicating the Constitutionality of Consensual Sodomy and Related Solicitation Statutes and Their Enforcement Against Gay People, 1981–2000

Asterisks (*) indicate cases coded as decided in favor of lesbian and gay rights. Citations may be found in Appendix 1.2.

United States Supreme Court
1986   *Bowers v. Hardwick*
United States Courts of Appeals
Fifth Circuit
1985   *Baker v. Wade*
Eighth Circuit
1983   *U.S. v. Lemons*
Eleventh Circuit
1985   *Hardwick v. Bowers*
California
Court of Appeal
1995   *Baluyut v. Superior Court*
Georgia
1996   *Christensen v. State*
1998   *Powell v. State*
Kentucky
Supreme Court
1992   *Commonwealth v. Wasson*
Louisiana
Court of Appeal
1999   *State v. Smith*
Supreme Court
1994   *State v. Baxley* (Concurrence of Ortique, J. and Dissent of Calogero, J. only)

1995   *State v. Baxley* (Dissent of Calogero, J. only)
2000   *State v. Smith*
Maryland
Court of Appeals
1981   *Neville v. State* (Dissent of Davidson, J. only)
Michigan
Supreme Court
1994   *People v. Lino* (Dissent of Levin, J. only)
Missouri
Supreme Court
1986   *State v. Walsh*
Montana
Supreme Court
1997   **Gryczan v. State*
New York
Court of Appeals
1983   **People v. Uplinger*
Ohio
Court of Appeals
1999   **State of Ohio Metroparks v. Lasher*
2000   *State v. Thompson*
Oklahoma
Court of Criminal Appeals
1995   *Sawatzky v. City of Oklahoma City*
Oregon
Court of Appeals
1981   **State v. Tusek*
Rhode Island
Supreme Court
1999   **State v. Mullen*
Tennessee
Court of Appeals
1996   **Campbell v. Sundquist*
Texas
Court of Appeals
1992   **State v. Morales*
Supreme Court
1994   *State v. Morales*
Virginia
Court of Appeals
1997   *Branche v. Commonwealth*

Appendix 2.5

Cases Adjudicating the Free Speech and Free Association Rights of Lesbians and Gay Men, 1981–2000

Asterisks (*) indicate cases coded as decided in favor of lesbian and gay rights. Citations may be found in Appendix 1.2.

United States Courts of Appeals
Second Circuit
   1985   *Olivieri v. Ward*
Fifth Circuit
   1981   *Van Ooteghem v. Gray*
   1984   *Gay Student Services v. Texas A&M University*
Eighth Circuit
   1987   *Sinn v. The Daily Nebraskan*
   1988   *Gay and Lesbian Students Association v. Gohn*
Tenth Circuit
   1984   *National Gay Task Force v. Board of Education of the City of Oklahoma City*
Eleventh Circuit
   1997   *Gay Lesbian Bisexual Alliance v. Pryor*
Oklahoma
Supreme Court
   1981   *Gay Activists Alliance v. Board of Regents of the University of Oklahoma*
Oregon
Court of Appeals
   1992   *Merrick v. Board of Higher Education*

Texas
Supreme Court
   1996   *Republican Party of Texas v. Dietz*
   1997   *Republican Party of Texas v. Dietz*
Washington
Supreme Court
   1997   *Nelson v. McClatchy Newspapers, Inc.*

Appendix 2.6

Miscellaneous Cases Essential to Lesbian and Gay Rights, 1981–2000

Asterisks (*) indicate cases coded as decided in favor of lesbian and gay rights. Citations may be found in Appendix 1.2.

United States Courts of Appeals
Third Circuit
    2000   *Sterling v. Borough of Minersville*
Fourth Circuit
    1981   *Nemetz v. Immigration and Naturalization Service*
    1990   *Walls v. City of Petersburg*
Fifth Circuit
    1983   *Matter of Longstaff*
Ninth Circuit
    1983   *Hill v. U.S. Immigration and Naturalization Service*
    1987   *Schowengerdt v. General Dynamics Corp.*
    1992   *Beam v. Paskett*
    2000   *Hernandez-Montiel v. Immigration and Naturalization Service*
California
Court of Appeal
    1993   *In re Joshua H.*
            People v. M.S.
    2000   *People v. Garcia*
Colorado
Court of Appeals
    1994   *Rendon v. United Airlines*

Florida
District Court of Appeal
  1994 **Reeves v. State*
Indiana
Court of Appeals
  1991 **R.E.G. v. L.M.G.*
Maine
Supreme Judicial Court
  1982 **State v. Lovely*
Nebraska
  Supreme Court
  1998 **State v. Pattno*
Oregon
Court of Appeals
  1995 **deParrie v. City of Portland*
South Dakota
Supreme Court
  1998 **Collins v. Faith School District*
Virginia
Court of Appeals
  1996   *Thomas v. Thomas*

Appendix 2.7

Cases Adjudicating Same-Sex Sexual Harassment Claims, 1981–2000

Asterisks (*) indicate cases coded as decided in favor of lesbian and gay rights. Citations may be found in Appendix 1.2.

United States Supreme Court
1998 *Oncale v. Sundowner Offshore Services, Inc.*

United States Courts of Appeals
Fourth Circuit
1996 Hopkins v. Baltimore Gas and Electric Co.
      Mayo v. Kiwest Corp.
      McWilliams v. Fairfax County Board of Supervisors
      Wrightson v. Pizza Hut of America, Inc.
1998 *Scott v. Norfolk Southern Corp.*

Fifth Circuit
1994 Garcia v. Elf Atochem North America
1996 Oncale v. Sundowner Offshore Services, Inc.
1998 *Doe v. Dallas Independent School District*

Sixth Circuit
1997 *Yeary v. Goodwill Industries-Knoxville, Inc.*

Seventh Circuit
1997 *Doe v. City of Belleville*
      Johnson v. Hondo, Inc.
1999 *Shepherd v. Slater Steels Corporation*

Eighth Circuit
1996 *Quick v. Donaldson Co., Inc.*
1999 *Bailey v. Runyon*
      Schmedding v. Tnemec Company, Inc.

Ninth Circuit
  1999   *Kelly v. City of Oakland.*
Eleventh Circuit
  1997   *Fredette v. BVP Management Associates*
California
Court of Appeal
  1987   Hart v. National Mortgage & Land Company
  1993   *Mogilefsky v. Superior Court*
Kentucky
Court of Appeals
  1999   *Brewer v. Hillard*
Massachusetts
Supreme Judicial Court
  1997   *Melnychenko v. 84 Lumber Company*
Minnesota
Court of Appeals
  1996   *Cummings v. Koehnen*
  2000   *Police Officers Federation of Minneapolis v. City of Minneapolis*
Supreme Court
  1997   *Cummings v. Koehnen*
New York
Supreme Court, Appellate Division
  1996   Yukoweic v. International Business Machines, Inc.
Ohio
Court of Appeals
  1997   *Schmitz v. Bob Evans Farms, Inc.*
  1998   *Tarver v. Calex Corporation*
Supreme Court
  2000   *Hampel v. Food Ingredients Specialties, Inc.*
Oregon
Court of Appeals
  2000   *Harris v. Pameco Corporation*
West Virginia
Supreme Court of Appeals
  1998   *Willis v. Wal-Mart Stores, Inc.*

Appendix 2.8

Defamation Cases Involving Issues of Homosexuality,
1981–2000

Asterisks (*) indicate cases coded as decided in favor of lesbian and gay rights. Citations may be found in Appendix 1.2.

United States Courts of Appeals
Fifth Circuit
  1982   *Manale v. City of New Orleans*
  1997   *Plumley v. Landmark Chevrolet, Inc.*
Alabama
Supreme Court
  1985   *Logan v. Sears, Roebuck & Co.*
Colorado
Court of Appeals
  1991   **Hayes v. Smith*
Florida
District Court of Appeal
  1990   **Boehm v. American Bankers Insurance Group, Inc.*
Minnesota
Court of Appeals
  1987   *Bohdan v. Alltool Mfg., Co.*
  1998   **Foley v. County of Hennepin*
Missouri
Supreme Court
  1993   *Nazeri v. Missouri Valley College*
New York
Supreme Court, Appellate Division
  1984   *Matherson v. Marchello*

Appendix 2.9

Miscellaneous Cases Not Essential to Lesbian and Gay Rights, 1981–2000

Asterisks (*) indicate cases coded as decided in favor of lesbian and gay rights. Citations may be found in Appendix 1.2.

United States Supreme Court
1987   *San Francisco Arts & Athletics, Inc. v. U.S. Olympic Committee*
United States Courts of Appeals
Ninth Circuit
1986   *International Olympic Committee v. San Francisco Arts & Athletics*
Alaska
Supreme Court
1999   *Bess v. Ulmer*
California
Court of Appeal
1991   **Citizens for Responsible Behavior v. Superior Court*
1993   **Long Beach Lesbian and Gay Pride, Inc. v. City of Long Beach*
Colorado
Court of Appeals
1994   **People v. Murphy*
1998   **Schaefer v. City & County of Denver*
Supreme Court
1996   **People v. Murphy*
Florida
District Court of Appeal
2000   *Rickard v. McKesson*
Supreme Court
1994   **Code of Judicial Conduct*

Georgia
Supreme Court
  1981   *Owens v. Owens*
Iowa
Court of Appeals
  1993   *Hartman v. Stassis*
Maryland
Court of Special Appeals
  1998   *Broadcast Equities v. Montgomery County*
Missouri
Court of Appeals
  1987   *Woy v. Woy*
New York
Supreme Court, Appellate Division
  1985   *Under 21 v. City of New York*
Court of Appeals
  1985   *Under 21 v. City of New York*
Oregon
Court of Appeals
  1995   *deParrie v. State*
Texas
Court of Appeals
  1999   *Hotze v. Brown*
Wisconsin
Court of Appeals
  1995   *State v. Rushing*

Appendix 3.1

Further Data Collection, Independent Variables, and Statistical Technique

The unit of analysis in Chapter 3 and following is each judge's vote (Giles and Zorn 2000) in each case essential to lesbian and gay rights. Nonessential decisions play no further part in the book's empirical analysis. Collectively, 201 federal and 809 state judges decided the essential 393 rulings.[1] Individualized cover letters and questionnaires seeking personal attribute information were mailed to the 709 state jurists still[2] active on the courts of interest, with follow-ups sent a month later to nonresponding jurists.[3] Some 474 completed questionnaires (66.9 percent) were received.[4] In addition, *The American Bench*, *Who's Who in American Law*, the *Westlaw* database, state web pages,[5] obituaries, and subscribers to LAWCOURTS (the Internet discussion list sponsored by the American Political Science Association's Law and Courts Section) furnished complete data on 192 additional state judges and supplemented information on returned, but incompletely answered, questionnaires. In all, complete information on the personal attributes of 666 state judges (82.3 percent of that population) was secured. Data on federal judges were obtained principally from Zuk, Barrow, and Gryski (1997). Subscribers to LAWPROF (an Internet discussion list principally among professors at law schools) supplemented this information. Complete data were acquired

---

[1] A handful of people (e.g., David Souter) participated both as federal and state judges.
[2] Data collection for this research began in 1994 and was completed in 2001.
[3] Samples of the cover letter and questionnaire appear as Appendices 3.2 and 3.3.
[4] Babbie (1995: 262) classifies a 70 percent response rate for self-administered questionnaires as "very good."
[5] Listed at www.ncsconline.org.

on 183 federal judges (91.0 percent of the population). Thus, the book analyzes the behavior of a total of 849 judges (84.1 percent).[6]

The total number of judicial votes for which complete data are available is 1,439 (86.4 percent) of 1,665 cast in the 400 decisions and opinions. As Appendix 3.12 demonstrates, no systematic bias results from these incomplete data since only randomly occurring catalysts (such as uncooperativeness, resignation, retirement, and death) prevented comprehensive collection.

Since the dependent variable here is dichotomous, logistic regression supplies beta coefficients assessing the effect of independent variables, applied using SPSS for Windows, Version 7.5.[7]

Empirical study seeks, inter alia, to maximize two competing objectives: the comprehensiveness of an investigation and the accuracy of its data. For example, logistic regression – the quantitative technique providing the statistics about the judicial behavior data I collect – requires complete information on each vote in a data set. Incomplete cases are rejected from the analysis. For instance, if I know five of a judge's attitudinal attributes (age, gender, political party affiliation, race, and service in prior nonjudicial elective office), but lack the sixth (religion), then I cannot use that judge in my study. It's all or nothing for each vote. In short, missing data work directly against an investigation's comprehensiveness. A study analyzing 85 percent of votes is far more persuasive than one with 60 percent.

Yet data accuracy is important, too. Consider the ethnicity of surnames. Suppose the hypothetical judge in the last paragraph were named

---

[6] The replication standard suggests I should list the names of the 849 judges (King 1995; Heise 1999: 814 and 818–819; Epstein and King 2002: 38). Research in the natural and social sciences is based on observation, and this book reports my empirical investigation. In the process, I should make every effort to describe my observational and quantitative methods as thoroughly as possible. Owing to a detailed explanation about how I collected and analyzed the data, anyone should be free to duplicate my efforts and compare the results without having to contact me for additional information.

Unfortunately, I am not at liberty to provide an index of judges' names. In cover letters (Appendix 3.2) accompanying the questionnaires (Appendix 3.3) sent to appellate judges obtaining personal attribute data, I made a pledge to respect respondents' privacy.

[7] Logistic regression transforms the dependent variable by means of a logistic distribution and minimizes the sum of squared errors. In contrast, logit and probit, two other statistical techniques commonly employed for binary dependent variables, maximize the likelihood function. Nonetheless, the three estimators render comparable results in terms of interpretation and are superior to ordinary-least-squares regression when the dependent variable is dichotomous.

Murphy. Most likely, she would be Roman Catholic because her last name is Irish. However, my experience in sending out questionnaires in this study counsels caution. A judge with the surname O'Brien (another Irish Catholic, right?) returned a questionnaire indicating Jewish affiliation. A Manhattan judge named Cohen (a likely Jewish candidate) sent back a questionnaire identifying himself as a Hispanic Catholic. (To protect privacy – which I promised judges in cover letters accompanying the questionnaires[8] – these names are not the actual ones, but are similar enough to make the point.) If, because of her surname alone, I were to identify Judge Murphy as Catholic in my data set (and thereby get one vote closer to comprehensiveness), I might diminish its accuracy. I erred on the side of accuracy.

Variable Overview

Described in Chapter 1, the dependent variable is **outcome**. The major categories of independent variables follow. Descriptions of all variables and their coding rules appear in Appendix 3.4.[9]

Legal Variables
Stare decisis and case characteristics are the indices most frequently used to test the legal model (Segal 1984, 1986; Segal and Spaeth 1993: 44–49; Knight and Epstein 1996).

Precedents bind later cases if the same[10] or higher court earlier decided comparable facts authoritatively. Combining all precedents in just one

---

[8] See note 6 supra. As a result, the names of appellate judges (other than Supreme Court justices whose personal attribute information is in the public domain) do not appear in the book.

[9] Intercoder reliability is not an issue because I did all of the coding.

[10] Precedents from one district of a multidistrict intermediate appellate court generally are not binding precedent on intermediate appellate judges in other districts of the state (California: *Estate of Cleveland* 1993, *Hines v. Superior Court* 1994, and *Wolfe v. Dublin Unified School District* 1997; Florida: *Estate of Schwartz* 1996, *Mancino v. State* 1997, and *Ocasio v. McGlothin* 1998; Illinois: *State Farm Fire and Casualty Company v. Yapejian* 1992; Louisiana: *Graves v. Businelle Towing Corp.* 1996, *New Orleans Rosenbush Claims Service, Inc., v. City of New Orleans* 1994, and *Palmer v. Blue Water Marine Catering, Inc.* 1995; New York: *Mountain View Coach Lines, Inc. v. Storms* 1984 and *People v. Brisotti* 1996; Ohio: *McNeal v. Cofield* 1992 and *Zanetti v. Lieberman* 1994; Tennessee: *Daniel v. Daniel* 1998). Just one state (Indiana) relevant to the study's data has a contrary rule (*Diesel Construction Company, Inc. v. Cotten* 1994 and *Lincoln Utilities, Inc., v. Office of Utility Consumer Counselor* 1996). Accordingly, only precedents from Indiana intermediate appellate courts are coded as controlling intermediate appellate courts in other districts of Indiana.

variable would result in those denying rights pulling judges in one direction while those granting claims tug in the opposite, potentially canceling each other out and thereby hindering detection of otherwise important *stare decisis* forces. Thus, precedents were identified and classified into two groups, **negative precedent** and **positive precedent**.

With regard to fact-based variables, **gay male litigant** tracks whether judges treat gay men differently than other litigants since gay men experience higher levels of antihomosexual prejudice than do lesbians.[11]

As Chapter 1 indicates, court decisions essential to lesbian and gay rights cover several major subject categories. Each serves as a fact-based variable here: **free speech and association, gay family issue, gays in the military, sexual orientation discrimination,** and **sodomy constitutionality.** Essential miscellaneous cases serve as the comparison group.

Attitudinal Variables

Measuring judges' attitudes has been perplexing because of the circularity inherent in predicting future votes by means of past ones. To circumvent this dilemma, Segal and Cover (1989) developed a mechanism for gauging Supreme Court justices' attitudes through content analysis of preconfirmation elite-newspaper editorials. However, this technique is not available for all state and lower federal courts.[12] Instead, sociological background characteristics have received the greatest scholarly attention as proxies for attitudes and values to explain judicial voting behavior.[13]

---

[11] Lewis and Rogers (1999: 126) ("[i]n two meta-analyses of studies that examine gender differences Kite (1984) and Kite and Whitley (1996) demonstrate that men have more negative attitudes than women toward both homosexual behavior and homosexuals themselves. The gender differences increased over time and were widest in attitudes toward gay men. (Men and women had similar views about lesbians)"). These meta-analytic findings may help predict the judicial behavior analyzed here because 84.8 percent of votes in the study were cast by male judges.

[12] But see Emmert and Traut (1994).

[13] E.g., Vines (1964) (examining how judges' party affiliation, religion, service in prior public office, place of birth, location of law school, and location of law practice affected dispositions of 291 race relations cases in the federal district courts of the eleven Southern states from 1954 to 1962); Bowen (1965) (studying the impacts of party ID, religion, status, age, and tenure in criminal cases, civil liberties cases, labor management cases, business regulatory cases, creditor-debtor cases, and landlord-tenant cases for 373 judges on state supreme courts and federal courts of appeals during 1960); and Wold (1974) (using interviews of judges on the highest courts of Delaware, Maryland, New York, and Virginia to investigate the effects of judges' political orientation, class, party affiliation, religion, education, career experience, and age on their role perceptions of "law interpreters" or "lawmakers").

Age. Political views generally become more conservative with age (Jennings and Niemi 1981), and scholars have opined that judges become more conservative as they mature.[14] Further, Gibson (1987) suggested that older people are less tolerant of lesbians and gay men than younger individuals; Haeberle (1999) found elderly respondents to the 1992 and 1996 National Election Studies less supportive of lesbian and gay rights than younger ones; Klawitter and Hammer (1999) discovered that populations with high proportions of young adults were positively correlated with the adoption of antidiscrimination policies for sexual orientation, while older adults were negatively associated with policy adoption; and Lewis and Rogers (1999) reported that data from Gallup and CBS/*New York Times* polls revealed that young people are more gay-supportive than older citizens.

Catholic. Seven studies[15] linked religion to judicial behavior. Additionally, Batson and Burris (1994) found that religion fosters prejudice, and such is the circumstance regarding lesbians and gay men.[16] The legal

---

[14] Bowen (1965) (younger judges voted in favor of criminal defendants, civil liberties plaintiffs, governmental regulatory agencies, labor unions, debtors, and tenants more consistently than older counterparts); Goldman (1966) (judges under 60 voted more favorably for unions in labor cases than judges over 70, when party affiliation was held constant); Ulmer (1973) (age at time of appointment reduced the unexplained variance in justices' support of defendants in criminal cases before the Supreme Court between 1947 and 1956 by 77 percent); and Goldman (1975) (among 2,115 nonunanimous federal appeals decisions between 1965 and 1971, judges' age was significantly correlated to voting behavior in criminal procedure cases, civil liberties cases, labor relations cases, tort litigation, political liberalism, economic liberalism, and judicial activism). Cf. Segal (1986) (no evidence found in search-and-seizure cases that Justices Powell, Stevens, Stewart, and White became more conservative with age).

[15] Vines (1964) (Catholic judges were more integrationist in race relations cases than Protestant judges); Bowen (1965) (Roman Catholic and Jewish judges demonstrated significantly greater support for criminal defendants, regulatory agencies, debtors, and tenants than did Protestant judges); Ulmer (1973) (non-Protestant justices were more liberal in criminal cases than Protestant justices); Nagel (1974) and Goldman (1975) (both found Catholic judges to be more liberal than Protestant judges); Wold (1974) (Catholic and Jewish state supreme court justices self-identified more frequently as "lawmakers," while Protestant justices self-identified much more frequently as "law interpreters"); and Songer and Tabrizi (1999) (evangelical justices on state supreme courts were significantly more conservative than mainline Protestant, Catholic, and Jewish justices in death penalty, gender discrimination, and obscenity cases between 1970 and 1993).

[16] See, e.g., Fisher et al. (1994) (concluding that religious practice and beliefs play a consequential role in creating and maintaining negative attitudes towards gay men and

disputes in Boston[17] and New York[18] over Irish lesbian and gay groups carrying banners in St. Patrick's Day parades offer examples: Opponents of the placards quoted Roman Catholic Church dogma condemning homosexual practices as a major reason for the ban. Catholic judges deciding civil rights cases, then, may have acted on their church's antipathy (Niebuhr 1999) to lesbians and gays[19] – and thus this variable.

Jewish is the second religion variable and first factor measuring the responsiveness of a historically oppressed group to the rights of another.[20] Very high levels of political tolerance and a commitment to permissive social and sexual codes have been found among Jews.[21]

lesbians); and Herman (1997) (a comprehensive study of the antihomosexual policies of conservative Christian groups in the United States).

[17] *Hurley v. Irish-American Gay, Lesbian and Bisexual Group of Boston* (U.S. Sup. Ct. 1995).

[18] *New York County Board of Ancient Hibernians v. Dinkins* (1993).

[19] Danelski (1964: 189–90) ("[t]hose who expected [Justice Pierce] Butler's religion [Roman Catholicism] to have some bearing on his judicial behavior were probably correct." For example, in *Hensen v. Haff* (1934), "an unmarried alien woman left the United States in the company of a married man with whom she had been having sexual relations for some years." Dissenting by himself from the majority's readmission of the woman into the United States, Butler noted "she had entered the country for an immoral purpose, and it made no difference whether the purpose was dominant or subordinate. Thus it appears that morality was Butler's primary value underlying his decision of the case"); Welch et al. (1993) (American Catholics take high levels of conservative cues from clergy on sexual behavior issues such as homosexual rights); and Fabrizio (1999) ("[by 1996, Catholic] bishops had completed their evolution as an interest group, from being hesitant to criticize government officials even in the face of state-sanctioned discrimination [against African Americans] to telling Catholics how they should be organized so they can change the Constitution. They journeyed from a collection of religious leaders with only joint spiritual concerns through a classic economic interest group into a fully engaged morality politics participant").

[20] See Pharr (1988) for a discussion of the "unity of oppression" concept.

[21] Rand National Defense Research Institute (1993: 439) (29 percent of Jews among 5,907 National Opinion Research Center General Social Survey [GSS] respondents between 1988 and 1991 characterized homosexuality as "always wrong," compared with 73 percent of Catholics and 82 percent of Protestants); Cohen and Liebman (1997) (among 32,380 GSS respondents between 1972 and 1994, Jews were significantly more permissive than other Americans with regard to social codes, particularly issues relating to sex); Lewis and Rogers (1999) (in Gallup polling data between 1977 and 1992, Jews were substantially more supportive of employment rights for lesbians and gay men than were Catholics and Protestants); and Schroedel (1999) (9.1 percent of Jews in a 1994–95 national survey of 220 state and local elected officials responded that homosexual relationships were "morally wrong," compared with 40.4 percent of Catholic officials and 51.3 percent of Protestant officials).

Protestants, with 803 votes (55.8 percent), form the bulk[22] of the comparison base for **Catholic** and **Jewish.**[23]

Female is the second variable tracking whether one historically powerless group empathizes with another. Davis, Haire, and Songer (1993), who ascertained that women judges on federal courts of appeals supported claimants in employment discrimination cases and criminal defendants in search-and-seizure cases more than their male counterparts, asserted that women bring a different perspective to the bench – favoring "relationships and inclusion" over "personal autonomy and individual rights." Martin (1993) found that women on state courts ruled with "a female perspective." Moreover, women have more favorable attitudes toward gays and lesbians than do men[24] and are more supportive of homosexual rights.[25]

Minority is the third variable testing the notion that historically powerless groups sympathize with the plight of other minorities. Haeberle (1999) found that African American respondents to the National Election Study were more supportive of lesbian and gay rights than whites, and Dorris (1999) documented that the higher the proportion of African American and Hispanic residents, the more likely the adoption of municipal public employment protection for lesbians and gay men.

---

[22] Protestant judges cast 92.9 percent of the comparison votes. Judges having faiths other than Christian or Jewish voted 19 (2.2 percent) times. Some 42 (4.9 percent) votes were by judges having no religious affiliation.

[23] I considered disaggregating Protestants between fundamentalist groups (as classified by Smith 1987), on the one hand, and moderate and liberal ones, on the other. Yet a data collection problem arose with this idea. Both on the self-administered questionnaires sent out to judges and in judicial biographies, religious affiliation sometimes was indicated merely as "Protestant." Thus, of the 803 votes by Protestant judges in my data set, 138 (17.2 percent) have no greater specification. Since logistic regression rejects entries with missing data, I did not pursue disaggregating Protestant votes in the models.

[24] Herek (1993: 123) ("heterosexual males tend to manifest higher levels of [antihomosexual] prejudice than do heterosexual females, especially toward gay men"); and Kite and Whitley (1996) (meta-analytic review of 97 psychological studies revealed that "[m]en were more negative than women toward homosexual persons").

[25] Haeberle (1999) (among more than 3,500 NES respondents, women supported laws protecting homosexuals from job discrimination 11 percent more than men in 1992, and by 8.7 percent more in 1996; women favored allowing homosexuals to serve in the armed forces by 20.6 percent more than men in 1992, and by 14.6 percent more in 1996); and Schroedel (1999: 110) (among 220 state and local elected officials, "women were somewhat more likely than men to support the general principle of equal employment opportunity applying to homosexuals," although female officials thought lesbians and gay men should be able to serve in the military 25 percent more than male officials).

Prior nonjudicial office. Goldman (1975)[26] and Tate (1981)[27] related that judges who sought or held nonjudicial elective office before taking the bench behaved differently than those who never sought or held prior nonjudicial office.

Democrat. Democratic judges are more liberal than Republican counterparts,[28] and conservatives and Republicans, compared with liberals and Democrats, consistently oppose lesbian and gay rights.[29]

A final attitudinal variable of interest here is the sexual orientation of the judges themselves. However, there is no effective way to collect that data.[30] No judicial biographies or other public references used to compile a significant portion of the personal attribute information on judges in the study lists their sexual orientation. A sexual orientation inquiry might have been included on the questionnaires I sent to judges, but I doubt the question would have been answered. Indeed, a substantial share of returned questionnaires left unanswered the requests about political party affiliation and religion, occasionally with notations that the information was too personal. Moreover, I did not send questionnaires to the vast majority of federal judges because the Zuk et al. (1997) database otherwise comprehensively supplied attribute information. Even if I had sent

---

[26] Federal appeals judges between 1965 and 1971 who had been candidates for elective office tended to support the government in tax, eminent domain, and other fiscal cases less than those who had not sought elective office.

[27] Supreme Court justices between 1946 and 1978 appointed from elective office were more liberal in economic liberalism cases than those who were not appointed from elective office.

[28] Pinello (1999) (meta-analysis of 84 judicial behavior studies conducted between 1959 and 1998 disclosed that judges' party affiliations explained 31 percent of the ideological variance in state courts and 48 percent in federal courts).

[29] Haeberle (1999: 152–53) (among National Election Study respondents in 1992 and 1996, "[a]ll groups of Democrats ... maintain[ed] high levels of support [over 65 percent] both for a law to ban job discrimination and to allow gays and lesbians in the military," while "strong Republican support for employment rights and military service rights [fell] to between 30 and 40 percent in both election-year analyses," and "differences in opinion across ideological categories were greater than the partisan differences"); and Schroedel (1999) (between 13.3 and 18.8 percent of state and local officials self-described as conservative supported applying civil rights laws to homosexuals, while more than 80 percent of liberals did; 69.6 percent of Republican officials believed in equal employment opportunity for lesbians and gay men, while 89.4 percent of Democrats backed it).

[30] Riggle and Tadlock (1999a: 6) ("[t]he most difficult part of research directly investigating gays and lesbians is identifying lesbians and gays. The gay and lesbian population is 'invisible.' Whether a researcher meets someone face to face, makes phone contact, or gives out anonymous confidential questionnaires, that researcher remains at the mercy of the participant to self-identify as lesbian or gay").

questionnaires to all jurists, I suspect the inclusion of a sexual orientation query would have significantly depressed the response rate (Riggle and Tadlock 1999a: 7). In any event, only a handful of lesbian and gay judges are out of the closet publicly,[31] and most of those who are out serve on trial courts. Accordingly, I am unable to include a sexual orientation variable in the models here.

Institutional Factors

Discussing judicial handling of child custody and visitation disputes, Chapter 2 notes that Alabama judges, popularly elected to six-year terms of office, may have been particularly sensitive to conservative public opinion when they voted against the rights of lesbian and gay parents. The institutional variables in this section test that theory.

Pinello (1995) discovered that judicial selection method significantly influenced policy of state supreme courts in criminal procedure appeals and business law. Testing of selection method's power continues in this study by inclusion of three selection variables, with popular election as the comparison base (representing 584 votes, or 40.6 percent).

Appointed is the first component. Votes by federal judges and by state jurists serving in gubernatorial-appointment systems and not subject to popular check through retention elections – the most insulated from negative public opinion about lesbians and gay men[32] – should be more receptive to those claims.

---

[31] Herrick and Thomas (1999: 171–72) ("[o]f the roughly 500,000 elected officials in the United States, approximately 120 are openly gay or lesbian").

[32] Rand National Defense Research Institute (1993: 193) ("[t]he proportion responding 'always wrong' to the GSS question ["What about sexual relations between two adults of the same sex – do you think it is always wrong, almost always wrong, wrong only sometimes, or not wrong at all?"] has shown little variation over the past fifteen years [as of 1993], generally ranging from 70 to 75 percent. A similar stability is seen in the proportion who believe that homosexuality 'should be considered an acceptable alternative lifestyle' in surveys over the past ten years [with between 32 and 38 percent of respondents agreeing with the statement]"); Sherrill (1993) (in 1988, some 35 percent of National Election Study respondents gave lesbians and gay men a "feeling thermometer" score of zero – the most negative score available – and the total percentage of respondents holding negative feelings toward homosexuals was far greater than that of 13 other social groups, including antiabortionists, evangelicals, and people on welfare); Sherrill (1996: 470) (concluding from 1984–94 NES data that "[n]o other group of Americans is the object of such sustained, extreme, and intense distaste [as lesbians and gay men]" and that "[n]ot only is the lack of affection [toward lesbians and gay men] intense, it also is widespread"); Gamble (1997) (among 38 states and localities voting on anti-gay initiatives or referenda between 1977 and 1993, voters approved 79 percent of the proposed limitations on gay rights legislation); and Lewis and Edelson (2000: 194–95)

Legis is the second judicial selection method variable, for votes from South Carolina and Virginia, two of the three states with legislatively selected judiciaries during the period of interest.[33]

Merit is the final selection method variable, involving judges chosen in Missouri Plan or "merit selection" systems characterized by (1) gubernatorial selection constrained to candidates picked by blue-ribbon committees designated by executive, legislative, judicial, and legal elites, and (2) retention elections.

Term. Songer (1995) and Brace and Hall (1997) found that term length is an important institutional variable. There, Democratic judges generally opposed the death penalty but tended to support it when their terms of office were short since American public opinion very much favors capital punishment. Yet Wenzel et al. (1997: 376) offer a different understanding, finding evidence that institutional factors (such as long terms of office) that isolate state courts from political pressures decrease judicial activism: "Systemic features that tie judges closer to the electorate apparently lead to the selection of judges [who] are more willing to consider political as opposed to legal factors in the decision-making process."

Environmental Forces

Chapters 1 and 2 observe that regional analysis of court decisions is inadequate because the judicial treatment of lesbian and gay rights within regions sometimes was very inconsistent. In the South, for example, Florida's appellate courts handled gay people quite favorably, while tribunals in Alabama and Mississippi did not. Likewise in the Midwest, Missouri had the worst record of fostering gay rights, while Minnesota's was one of the best. Accordingly, more discrete and nuanced measures of environmental forces are incorporated here.

Environmental ideology. Berry et al. (1998) constructed dynamic measures of state government ideology, which are employed here. I constructed population-weighted ideology measures for federal appellate judges from the Berry et al. government scores (see Appendix 3.4). **Environmental ideology**'s values ranged from 8.13 for New Hampshire judges' votes in 1987 to 97.10 for a federal district judge sitting by

---

("[g]ay men and lesbians are an unpopular minority [citing numerous public opinion surveys from the 1960s through the 1990s]").

33 The third state, Rhode Island, changed the selection method for its supreme court to a modified Missouri Plan in 1994. Since the two Ocean State decisions in the book's database date from 1999 and 2000, they are not included in this variable.

designation on a court of appeals who was appointed from California in 1962.[34] The larger the score, the more liberal the jurisdiction.

Consensual sodomy law. Chapter 2 notes that state sodomy laws have been used by courts to justify denying civil rights and liberties to lesbians and gay men. Indeed, lesbian and gay rights activists long have claimed that state laws criminalizing consensual sodomy, although unenforced, still encumber lesbian and gay civil rights.[35] This variable tests that hypothesis.

Gay civil rights law. Chapter 2 also points out that Jamie Nabozny was fortunate to live in one of the handful of states with gay civil rights statutes. In holding school officials liable for failing to protect Nabozny from physical and verbal abuse, the federal appellate court specifically relied on the Wisconsin law. Thus, jurisdictions with statewide acts prohibiting discrimination on the basis of sexual orientation may have fostered expansion of lesbian and gay rights.

Temporal Variable

Post-1990. Yang (1998) documented that American public opinion on lesbian and gay issues has improved noticeably since the early 1980s. A dummy variable disaggregates the study's twenty years into two period controls (1981–90 and 1991–2000) to investigate whether time was

---

[34] See the coding rules for **environmental ideology** in Appendix 3.4.
[35] Urvashi Vaid, former executive director of the National Gay and Lesbian Task Force, wrote:

> Even though direct criminal prosecutions under sodomy laws ... are rare, collateral uses of the sodomy laws are frequent.... [State sodomy laws] have been invoked to deny visitation to a lesbian mother in Missouri; to defend the refusal to hire gay police officers by the Dallas Police Department; to prevent two lesbians from establishing a lesbian-feminist retreat center in Mississippi; to oppose the grant of guardianship to Karen Thompson, the lover of Sharon Kowalski, who fought for seven years before winning, in Minnesota; and to deny gay school teachers the right to work in Oklahoma. (1995: 14)

> See also Wald (2000: 9–10) ("[t]he criminalization of sexual activity between consenting adults of the same gender sends a powerful message about the marginal legal status of gays and lesbians"), Rimmerman (2002: 57) ("lesbian and gay activists recognized that sodomy laws themselves needed to be attacked at their core if discrimination was to be ameliorated"), and Hannon (1999: 509):

> [T]he Supreme Court, through its decision in *Bowers v. Hardwick*, has established a framework within which lower courts can infer illegal sexual conduct from homosexual status and thus perpetuate the denial of constitutional rights to homosexuals. This framework is constructed as if the law made being homosexual a criminal offense and has created an environment in which silence about self-identity is encouraged.

important to the evolution of lesbian and gay rights, with the first period as the comparison base.

Interest Group Influence

Gay interest group. The literature on interest group participation as *amici curiae* is substantial (e.g., Songer and Kuersten 1995; Hausegger 1998; Tauber 1998) and suggests inclusion of an interest group variable here.[36]

Control Variables

Court of last resort differentiates votes between intermediate appellate courts and courts of last resort. Likewise, **federal court** separates votes between federal and state tribunals.

Finally, sundry first-order and second-order interaction terms also are used in the analysis to test the full import of independent variables.[37] For example, Brace and Hall (1997) found that judges affiliated with the Democratic party were more likely to oppose the death penalty when they served in states with longer terms of office than in states with shorter terms. Songer (1995) confirmed the same effect in environmental protection cases.

---

[36] Brewer et al. (2000: 383–85) and Rimmerman (2002: 55–59) provide overviews of lesbian and gay legal interest groups. Further, Salokar (2001: 266) notes:

> In 1986, it was former Supreme Court Justice William Brennan who observed, "Rediscovery by state supreme courts of the broader protections afforded to their own citizens by their state constitutions ... is probably the most important development in constitutional jurisprudence of our times" [citation omitted]. And it is this "rediscovery" that has formed the crux of most LGBT [lesbian, gay, bisexual, and transgender] litigation in the 1990s. Under the direction of the Lambda Legal Defense and Education Fund and through the Lesbian and Gay Rights Project of the American Civil Liberties Union (ACLU), litigation at the state level is being undertaken with the sole purpose of establishing a state-based judicial declaration of human rights.

[37] Friedrich (1982) ("it is better analytic strategy to include a multiplicative term than to exclude one"); Hall and Brace (1996: 250) ("[o]verall, ... interactive model[s are] a better representation of the politics of judicial choice [than merely additive models without interactive terms]"); and Traut and Emmert (1998: 1177) ("explanatory variables do not simply have additive effects. Rather, the effects of legal issues, case facts, and electoral processes are conditioned by the effects of [other variables such as] judicial ideology").

Appendix 3.2

Sample Cover Letter Accompanying Self-Administered Questionnaire

Dear Judge _____:

I am collecting data for scholarly research involving one or more decisions by your court. I write for biographical information about yourself, as indicated in the enclosed questionnaire. For reference, my scholarship includes a book, *The Impact of Judicial-Selection-Method on State-Supreme-Court Policy: Innovation, Reaction, and Atrophy* (Greenwood Press 1995), and an article, "Linking Party to Judicial Ideology in American Courts: A Meta-Analysis," *Justice System Journal* 20: 219–54 (1999).

Please be kind enough to take the few minutes necessary to complete the questionnaire and to sign and date the consent form (both of which are on separate sides of the same sheet of paper) and return them to me in the enclosed self-addressed, stamped envelope. My research design requires biographical data for all participating members of the Court. Without complete information, my study will be inconclusive. Accordingly, your anticipated assistance is greatly appreciated.

I shall respect your privacy. The book I am writing divulges data about judges only in aggregate form. For instance, I might say there are X number of Democrats and Y number of Republicans on such-and-such bench, without revealing who is in each group. Hence, your name will not appear in the volume, and I will not otherwise disclose the information about you.

Please feel free to contact me.... Alternatively, you may call ... the Chair of the Institutional Review Board of John Jay College.... Thank you for the anticipated courtesy and cooperation.

Appendix 3.3

Self-Administered Questionnaire Sent to Judges

Front of Form:

Biographical Questionnaire

Judge _____

Court of Appeal of _____

1. In what year were you born?
2. What is your race?
3. What is your religious affiliation (e.g., Roman Catholic, Jewish, Baptist, etc.)?
4. What is your political party affiliation (i.e., Democrat, Republican, or Independent)?
5. From which school did you receive your law degree?
6. Were you ever a criminal prosecutor?
7. Did you hold any other public office prior to becoming a judge? If so, what office(s)?
8. By what means were you *first* selected as a judge to this court (e.g., popular election, gubernatorial appointment, etc.)?

Thank you for your assistance! Please return the completed questionnaire and Consent Form (on the reverse side of this page) to Professor Daniel R. Pinello, Department of Government, John Jay College of Criminal Justice. . . .

Back of Form:

<u>Consent Form</u>

You are being asked to take part in a research study on judicial behavior in state appellate courts in the United States. The Researcher wants to know biographical information about judges deciding cases relevant to particular legal policies addressed by these courts. The study results will facilitate understanding about how American courts function.

All judges solicited to provide biographical information are asked to fill out this form. Neither you nor anyone will be named in the study. **Taking part is entirely voluntary.**

If you have questions about the biographical questionnaire, please contact Daniel R. Pinello at John Jay College of Criminal Justice. . . .

If you have questions about your rights as a volunteer, please contact . . . [the] Institutional Review Board, John Jay College. . . .

Consent Statement: I have read and understood the information above and consent to take part in the study.

Signature: ⎯⎯⎯⎯⎯⎯⎯⎯⎯⎯⎯⎯⎯⎯ Date: ⎯⎯⎯⎯⎯⎯⎯⎯⎯⎯

Appendix 3.4

Variable Coding

<u>Dependent variable</u>

Outcome   1 if vote cast in favor of lesbian/gay claim asserted or defended

     0 if against

<u>Independent variables</u>

Legal variables

Negative precedent   1 if a controlling precedent was against a lesbian and gay rights claim

     0 otherwise

Positive precedent   1 if a controlling precedent was in favor of a lesbian and gay rights claim

     0 otherwise

Gay male litigant   1 if at least one party to a lawsuit was a gay man

     0 otherwise

Gay family issue   1 if case involved child custody, visitation, adoption, or foster care by lesbian/gay parents or their domestic partners, health insurance or other benefits for domestic partners, or same-sex marriage or its approximation

     0 otherwise

Free speech and association   1 if case involved First Amendment claims of free speech or free association rights

     0 otherwise

Gays in the military	1 if case involved service in the U.S. military 0 otherwise
Sexual orientation discrimination	1 if case involved sexual orientation discrimination in the workplace, public accommodations, or housing 0 otherwise
Sodomy constitutionality	1 if case involved the constitutionality of consensual sodomy or related solicitation statutes or their enforcement 0 otherwise

Attitudinal variables

Age	1 if judge's age is between 33 and 49 at time of court decision 2 if judge's age is between 50 and 59 at time of court decision 3 if judge's age is between 60 and 90 at time of court decision
Catholic	1 if judge is Roman Catholic 0 otherwise
Jewish	1 if judge is Jewish 0 otherwise
Female	1 if judge is a woman 0 if judge is a man
Minority	1 if judge is African American, Latino, or Latina 0 otherwise
Prior nonjudicial office	1 if judge held prior nonjudicial elective public office 0 otherwise
Democrat	1 if judge is affiliated with, or ascribed to, the Democratic party 0 otherwise

Institutional variables

Appointed	1 if federal judge or gubernatorially appointed state judge not subject to retention elections 0 otherwise
Legis	1 if legislatively selected state judge 0 otherwise
Merit	1 if Missouri Plan or "merit-selected" state judge 0 otherwise

Term   1 if judicial term of office is less than 8 years
2 if judicial term of office is 8 or 9 years
3 if judicial term of office is 10 or 11 years
4 if judicial term of office is 12 or more enumerated years
5 if judicial term of office is lifetime

Environmental variables

Environmental ideology   Berry et al. state citizen ideology score for year of court decision if state judge selected by popular election or subject to retention election
Berry et al. state government ideology score for year of court decision if state judge subject to reappointment by governor or legislature
Berry et al. state government score for year of initial appointment if judge life tenured (weighted circuit-wide or nation-wide by state population if federal appellate judge; state score if federal district judge sitting by designation)

Consensual sodomy law   1 if enforceable state consensual sodomy law at time of court decision (weighted circuit-wide or nation-wide by state population if federal judge)
0 otherwise

Gay civil rights Law   1 if statewide lesbian and gay civil rights law at time of court decision (weighted circuit-wide or nation-wide by state population if federal judge)
0 otherwise

Temporal variable

Post-1990   1 if the court decision occurred between 1991 and 2000, inclusive
0 otherwise

Interest group variable

Gay interest group   1 if the Gay and Lesbian Advocates and Defenders, Lambda Legal Defense and Education Fund, the Lesbian and Gay Rights Project of the American Civil Liberties Union, the National Center for Lesbian Rights, or the

Servicemembers Legal Defense Network participated as *amicus curiae* or otherwise as counsel
0 otherwise

Control variables

Court of last resort   1 if a vote is cast in a court of last resort
                             0 if in an intermediate appellate court

Federal court   1 if vote cast in a federal court case
                             0 if a state court case

Appendix 3.5

Logistic Regression Statistics for Votes in All Essential Decisions

Independent variable	N	Beta	Impact[a]
Negative precedent (standard error)	280	−0.386* (0.174)	−.096
Positive precedent	154	1.564*** (0.242)	+.340
Gay male litigant	737	0.261 (0.144)	
Gay family issue	846	−1.662*** (0.403)	−.390
Free speech and association	67	−0.351 (0.487)	
Gays in the military	102	−1.728*** (0.456)	−.367
Sexual orientation discrimination	261	−1.785*** (0.406)	−.395
Sodomy constitutionality	111	−1.066* (0.452)	−.250
Age	1,439	−0.182 (0.093)	
Catholic	375	−0.419** (0.152)	−.104
Jewish	200	0.632** (0.212)	+.154
Female	219	0.498** (0.181)	+.123
Minority	101	0.846*** (0.251)	+.201

(*continued*)

(*continued*)

Independent variable	N	Beta	Impact[a]
Prior nonjudicial office	312	−0.346*	−.086
		(0.153)	
Democrat	838	−0.103	
		(0.956)	
Democrat★environmental ideology	838	0.002	
		(0.020)	
Democrat★term	838	0.366	
		(0.263)	
Democrat★environmental ideology★term	838	−0.003	
		(0.005)	
Appointed	498	−4.943	
		(3.246)	
Appointed★environmental ideology	498	0.033	
		(0.044)	
Appointed★term	498	0.081	
		(0.793)	
Appointed★environmental ideology★term	498	0.012	
		(0.011)	
Legis	40	−0.967	
		(4.894)	
Legis★environmental ideology	40	0.164	
		(0.162)	
Legis★term	40	0.269	
		(1.401)	
Legis★environmental ideology★term	40	−0.085	
		(0.050)	
Merit	317	3.043	
		(1.622)	
Merit★environmental ideology	317	−0.029	
		(0.037)	
Merit★term	317	−2.243**	
		(0.709)	
Merit★environmental ideology★term	317	0.033*	
		(0.014)	
Term	1,439	1.780***	
		(0.510)	
Environmental ideology	1,439	0.072**	
		(0.027)	
Environmental ideology★term	1,439	−0.036***	
		(0.009)	
Consensual sodomy law	644	−0.340*	−.085
		(0.162)	

Independent variable	N	Beta	Impact[a]
Gay civil rights law	196	0.545* (0.215)	+.134
Post-1990	999	0.151 (0.147)	
Gay interest group	816	0.312* (0.133)	+.078
Court of last resort	543	−0.087 (0.160)	
Federal court	324	−1.468*** (0.378)	−.341
Intercept		−1.861 (1.427)	

Note: Model N = 1,439; model chi-square = 358.906; df = 39; model p <.0001; −2 log likelihood = 1,635.604; Cox & Snell pseudo-R^2 = .221; Nagelkerke pseudo-R^2 = .221; classified correctly = 71.30%; proportional reduction in error = 41.67%.

[a] Impact of an increase from 0 to 1.

* p < .05; ** p < .01; *** p < .001.

Appendix 3.6

Logistic Regression Statistics for Votes in Courts of Last Resort

Independent variable	N	Beta	Impact[a]
Negative precedent (standard error)	79	0.810* (0.370)	+.182
Positive precedent	36	1.878** (0.666)	+.338
Gay male litigant	242	1.143*** (0.321)	+.268
Gay family issue	344	−7.118 (8.707)	
Free speech and association	23	−8.011 (8.721)	
Gays in the military	11	−5.126 (8.751)	
Sexual orientation discrimination	76	−7.136 (8.711)	
Sodomy constitutionality	74	−6.707 (8.713)	
Age	543	0.076 (0.176)	
Catholic	132	−0.479 (0.281)	
Jewish	64	0.991* (0.458)	+.216
Female	89	0.980** (0.330)	+.217
Minority	36	1.005* (0.458)	+.215

Independent variable	N	Beta	Impact[a]
Prior nonjudicial office	138	−0.289	
		(0.257)	
Democrat	313	−0.994	
		(1.361)	
Democrat⋆environmental ideology	313	0.030	
		(0.026)	
Democrat⋆term	313	0.777	
		(0.505)	
Democrat⋆environmental ideology⋆term	313	−0.012	
		(0.008)	
Appointed	202	−16.526**	
		(5.052)	
Appointed⋆environmental ideology	202	0.188*	
		(0.078)	
Appointed⋆term	202	5.232**	
		(1.610)	
Appointed⋆environmental ideology⋆term	202	−0.073*	
		(0.029)	
Legis	19	11.907***	
		(3.486)	
Legis⋆environmental ideology	19	−0.388***	
		(0.092)	
Merit	131	−5.114	
		(3.055)	
Merit⋆environmental ideology	131	0.224**	
		(0.078)	
Merit⋆term	131	3.250*	
		(1.465)	
Merit⋆environmental ideology⋆term	131	−0.104**	
		(0.033)	
Term	543	−2.201	
		(1.316)	
Environmental ideology	543	−0.015	
		(0.060)	
Environmental ideology⋆term	543	0.038	
		(0.027)	
Consensual sodomy law	263	−0.713*	−.172
		(0.355)	
Gay civil rights law	125	0.834*	+.191
		(0.381)	
Post-1990	407	−0.369	
		(0.302)	

(*continued*)

(*continued*)

Independent variable	N	Beta	Impact[a]
Gay interest group	352	0.632*	+.155
		(0.317)	
Federal court	35	−1.606*	−.371
		(0.643)	
Intercept		7.337	
		(9.154)	

Note: Model N = 543; model chi-square = 213.033; df = 36; model p < .0001; −2 log likelihood = 537.467; Cox & Snell pseudo-R^2 = .325; Nagelkerke pseudo-R^2 = .433; classified correctly = 75.87%; proportional reduction in error = 48.42%.

[a] Impact of an increase from 0 to 1.

* p < .05; ** p < .01; *** p < .001.

Appendix 3.7

Logistic Regression Statistics for Votes in Intermediate Appellate Courts

Independent variable	N	Beta	Impact
Negative precedent (standard error)	201	−0.422 (0.241)	
Positive precedent	118	1.716*** (0.280)	+.374[a]
Gay male litigant	495	−0.169 (0.184)	
Gay family issue	502	−2.199*** (0.511)	−.499[a]
Free speech and association	44	1.589* (0.678)	+.341[a]
Gays in the military	91	−1.585** (0.519)	−.344[a]
Sexual orientation discrimination	185	−2.124*** (0.492)	−.449[a]
Sodomy constitutionality	37	−0.349 (0.621)	
Age	896	−0.409** (0.129)	−.101[b]
Catholic	243	−0.437* (0.208)	−.109[a]
Jewish	136	0.777** (0.270)	+.189[a]
Female	130	0.274 (0.244)	

(*continued*)

(continued)

Independent variable	N	Beta	Impact
Minority	65	1.183***	+.272[a]
		(0.352)	
Prior nonjudicial office	174	−0.320	
		(0.221)	
Democrat	525	−3.096	
		(2.137)	
Democrat★environmental ideology	525	0.055	
		(0.045)	
Democrat★term	525	0.912	
		(0.517)	
Democrat★environmental ideology★term	525	−0.012	
		(0.011)	
Appointed	296	−10.071***	
		(2.514)	
Appointed★environmental ideology	296	0.159***	
		(0.036)	
Legis	21	20.043	
		(66.196)	
Legis★environmental ideology	21	−0.152	
		(1.887)	
Legis★term	21	−14.106	
		(33.790)	
Legis★environmental ideology★term	21	0.164	
		(0.970)	
Merit	186	3.602	
		(3.867)	
Merit★environmental ideology	186	−0.045	
		(0.084)	
Merit★term	186	−4.654**	
		(1.522)	
Merit★environmental ideology★term	186	0.076*	
		(0.031)	
Term	896	2.221**	
		(0.751)	
Environmental ideology	896	0.002	
		(0.044)	
Environmental ideology★term	896	−0.036**	
		(0.014)	
Consensual sodomy law	381	−0.019	
		(0.226)	
Gay civil rights law	71	0.998**	+.236[a]
		(0.327)	

Independent variable	N	Beta	Impact
Post-1990	592	0.573** (0.197)	+.142[a]
Gay interest group	464	0.121 (0.174)	
Federal court	289	−1.500 (0.971)	
Intercept		1.880 (2.305)	

Note: Model N = 896; model chi-square = 321.073; df = 36; model p < .0001; −2 log likelihood = 920.886; Cox & Snell pseudo-R^2 = .301; Nagelkerke pseudo-R^2 = .402; classified correctly = 75.22%; proportional reduction in error = 49.77%.

[a] Impact of an increase from 0 to 1.

[b] Impact of a one-unit increase from the mean of the independent variable.

* p < .05; ** p < .01; *** p < .001.

Appendix 3.8

Logistic Regression Statistics for Votes in Family Cases

Independent variable	N	Beta	Impact
Negative precedent (standard error)	145	−0.467 (0.244)	
Positive precedent	124	1.744*** (0.291)	+.358[a]
Gay male litigant	273	0.219 (0.188)	
Child CVAF issue	595	−0.264 (0.200)	
Age	846	−0.315* (0.123)	−.079[b]
Catholic	215	−0.220 (0.202)	
Jewish	124	1.032*** (0.291)	+.235[a]
Female	124	0.691** (0.251)	+.163[a]
Minority	59	0.995** (0.332)	+.223[a]
Prior nonjudicial office	215	−0.224 (0.189)	
Democrat	541	−1.147 (1.259)	
Democrat⋆environmental ideology	541	0.018 (0.025)	
Democrat⋆term	541	0.737 (0.427)	

Independent variable	N	Beta	Impact
Democrat*environmental ideology*term	541	−0.009 (0.008)	
Appointed	128	−8.462 (5.326)	
Appointed*environmental ideology	128	0.065 (0.069)	
Appointed*term	128	0.614 (1.261)	
Appointed*environmental ideology*term	128	0.009 (0.018)	
Legis	34	−10.316 (13.134)	
Legis*environmental ideology	34	0.579 (0.489)	
Legis*term	34	2.539 (3.386)	
Legis*environmental ideology*term	34	−0.181 (0.128)	
Merit	242	4.191 (2.223)	
Merit*environmental ideology	242	−0.068 (0.049)	
Merit*term	242	−2.885** (0.902)	
Merit*environmental ideology*term	242	0.051** (0.018)	
Term	846	1.576* (0.725)	
Environmental ideology	846	0.068 (0.040)	
Environmental ideology*term	846	−0.035** (0.013)	
Consensual sodomy law	355	−0.586* (0.229)	−.145[a]
Gay civil rights law	126	0.188 (0.289)	
Post-1990	611	0.445* (0.201)	+.111[a]
Gay interest group	471	0.003 (0.176)	

(*continued*)

(*continued*)

Independent variable	N	Beta	Impact
Court of last resort	344	0.160	
		(0.197)	
Federal court	11	−1.294	
		(0.870)	
Intercept		−2.449	
		(1.980)	

Note: Model N = 846; model chi-square = 198.077; df = 35; model p < .0001; −2 log likelihood = 971.279; Cox & Snell pseudo-R^2 = .209; Nagelkerke pseudo-R^2 = .279; classified correctly = 71.28%; proportional reduction in error = 38.65%.
[a] Impact of an increase from 0 to 1.
[b] Impact of a one-unit increase from the mean of the independent variable.
* p < .05; ** p < .01; *** p < .001.

Appendix 3.9

Logistic Regression Statistics for Votes in Nonfamily Cases

Independent variable	N	Beta	Impact[a]
Negative precedent (standard error)	135	−0.433 (0.314)	
Positive precedent	30	1.362* (0.534)	+.311
Gay male litigant	464	0.414 (0.288)	
Free speech and association	67	−0.252 (0.609)	
Gays in the military	102	−2.223*** (0.565)	−.442
Sexual orientation discriminstion	261	−2.065*** (0.521)	−.469
Sodomy constitutionality	111	−0.902 (0.614)	
Age	593	−0.026 (0.161)	
Catholic	160	−0.578* (0.264)	−.141
Jewish	76	0.479 (0.363)	
Female	95	0.256 (0.292)	
Minority	42	0.865* (0.421)	+.210

(continued)

(*continued*)

Independent variable	N	Beta	Impact[a]
Prior nonjudicial office	97	−0.647* (0.309)	−.156
Democrat	297	1.014 (1.965)	
Democrat★environmental ideology	297	−0.001 (0.041)	
Democrat★term	297	0.069 (0.460)	
Democrat★environmental ideology★term	297	−0.000 (0.009)	
Appointed	370	−4.309 (4.938)	
Appointed★environmental ideology	370	0.049 (0.074)	
Appointed★term	370	0.605 (1.301)	
Appointed★environmental ideology★term	370	−0.005 (0.021)	
Legis	6	−15.150 (107.440)	
Legis★environmental ideology	6	0.249 (3.535)	
Merit	75	−6.432 (3.954)	
Merit★environmental ideology	75	0.301* (0.127)	
Merit★term	75	2.730 (2.193)	
Merit★environmental ideology★term	75	−0.104* (0.045)	
Term	593	1.405 (0.991)	
Environmental ideology	593	0.066 (0.047)	
Environmental ideology★term	593	−0.022 (0.018)	
Consensual sodomy law	289	−0.140 (0.292)	
Gay civil rights law	70	1.251** (0.424)	+.294
Post-1990	388	0.186 (0.265)	

Independent variable	N	Beta	Impact[a]
Gay interest group	345	0.716** (0.260)	+.176
Court of last resort	199	−0.619 (0.350)	
Federal court	313	−2.030** (0.695)	−.468
Intercept		−2.935 (2.429)	

Note: Model N = 593; model chi-square = 238.392; df = 36; model p < .0001; −2 log likelihood = 582.059; Cox & Snell pseudo-R² = .331; Nagelkerke pseudo-R² = .442; classified correctly = 76.39%; proportional reduction in error = 50.18%.

[a] Impact of an increase from 0 to 1.

* p < .05; ** p < .01; *** p < .001.

Appendix 3.10

Logistic Regression Statistics for Votes in Custody, Visitation, Adoption, and Foster Care Cases

Independent variable	N	Beta	Impact
Negative precedent	125	−0.401	
(standard error)		(0.301)	
Positive precedent	88	1.044[**]	+.236[a]
		(0.330)	
Gay male litigant	144	0.410	
		(0.267)	
Age	595	−0.421[**]	−.105[b]
		(0.148)	
Catholic	157	−0.537[*]	−.133[a]
		(0.243)	
Jewish	65	0.810[*]	+.187[a]
		(0.390)	
Female	88	1.213[***]	+.268[a]
		(0.325)	
Minority	34	1.003[*]	+.222[a]
		(0.454)	
Prior nonjudicial office	161	−0.079	
		(0.229)	
Democrat	361	−0.470	
		(1.543)	
Democrat★environmental	361	0.006	
ideology		(0.030)	
Democrat★term	361	0.478	
		(0.545)	
Democrat★environmental	361	−0.004	
ideology★term		(0.009)	
Appointed	77	−7.637	
		(6.084)	

Independent variable	N	Beta	Impact
Appointed*environmental ideology	77	0.048 (0.082)	
Appointed*term	77	0.965 (1.523)	
Appointed*environmental ideology*term	77	0.002 (0.022)	
Legis	27	−57.554 (32.213)	
Legis*environmental ideology	27	2.161 (1.145)	
Legis*term	27	15.109 (8.109)	
Legis*environmental ideology*term	27	−0.578* (0.288)	
Merit	199	6.683* (2.786)	
Merit*environmental ideology	199	−0.114 (0.060)	
Merit*term	199	−3.664** (1.179)	
Merit*environmental ideology*term	199	0.066** (0.023)	
Term	595	1.018 (0.948)	
Environmental ideology	595	0.070 (0.052)	
Environmental ideology*term	595	−0.023 (0.018)	
Consensual sodomy law	271	−1.013*** (0.280)	−.246[a]
Gay civil rights law	92	0.606 (0.344)	
Post-1990	427	0.585* (0.263)	+.145[a]
Gay interest group	319	−0.205 (0.227)	
Court of last resort	257	0.010 (0.233)	
Intercept		−2.616 (2.587)	

Note: Model N = 595; model chi-square = 169.219; df = 33; model p < .0001; −2 log likelihood = 655.019; Cox & Snell pseudo-R^2 = .248; Nagelkerke pseudo-R^2 = .330; classified correctly = 70.76%; proportional reduction in error = 39.59%.
[a] Impact of an increase from 0 to 1.
[b] Impact of a one-unit increase from the mean of the independent variable.
* p < .05; ** p < .01; *** p < .001.

Appendix 3.11

Logistic Regression Statistics for Votes of Opinion Writers

Independent variable	N	Beta	Impact[a]
Negative precedent	97	−0.557	
(standard error)		(0.305)	
Positive precedent	34	0.627	
		(0.436)	
Gay male litigant	245	0.094	
		(0.257)	
Gay family issue	260	−1.245	
		(0.654)	
Free speech and association	15	−0.517	
		(0.851)	
Gays in the military	36	−1.474*	−.322
		(0.735)	
Sexual orientation discrimination	89	−1.321*	−.305
		(0.653)	
Sodomy constitutionality	45	−0.797	
		(0.723)	
Age	462	0.046	
		(0.166)	
Catholic	117	−0.566*	−.140
		(0.276)	
Jewish	73	1.009**	+.241
		(0.375)	
Female	66	0.392	
		(0.348)	
Minority	19	2.065*	+.404
		(0.809)	

Independent variable	N	Beta	Impact[a]
Prior nonjudicial office	99	−0.745** (0.287)	−.181
Democrat	265	0.362 (1.613)	
Democrat*environmental ideology	265	0.000 (0.032)	
Democrat*term	265	−0.001 (0.469)	
Democrat*environmental ideology*term	265	0.002 (0.009)	
Appointed	163	−0.776 (4.358)	
Appointed*environmental ideology	163	−0.006 (0.063)	
Appointed*term	163	−0.487 (1.226)	
Appointed*environmental ideology*term	163	0.012 (0.020)	
Legis	12	6.802 (33.942)	
Legis*environmental ideology	12	0.186 (0.961)	
Legis*term	12	−2.984 (15.006)	
Legis*environmental ideology*term	12	−0.132 (0.466)	
Merit	115	2.604 (2.971)	
Merit*environmental ideology	115	−0.041 (0.067)	
Merit*term	115	−1.465 (1.311)	
Merit*environmental ideology*term	115	0.024 (0.027)	
Term	462	1.427 (0.965)	
Environmental ideology	462	0.057 (0.048)	
Environmental ideology*term	462	−0.028 (0.018)	
Consensual sodomy law	200	0.131 (0.269)	

(*continued*)

(*continued*)

Independent variable	N	Beta	Impact[a]
Gay civil rights law	82	0.253	
		(0.348)	
Post-1990	324	0.601*	+.148
		(0.269)	
Gay interest group	284	0.149	
		(0.250)	
Court of last resort	170	0.014	
		(0.285)	
Federal court	104	−0.601	
		(0.688)	
Intercept		−2.406	
		(2.558)	

Note: Model N = 462; model chi-square = 114.210; df = 39; model p < .0001; −2 log likelihood = 526.180; Cox & Snell pseudo-R^2 = .219; Nagelkerke pseudo-R^2 = .292; classified correctly = 69.26%; proportional reduction in error = 37.71%.
[a] Impact of an increase from 0 to 1.
* p < .05; ** p < .01.

Appendix 3.12

Bias Arising from Incomplete Data

An examination of whether a less than complete data set introduces bias is available here regarding one conspicuous personal judicial attribute: gender. Appendix 3.13 displays a model, with the attitudinal variables limited only to judges' gender, for the 1,439 votes in my partial database. Because I was able to identify the gender of all the judges deciding the cases essential to lesbian and gay rights, Appendix 3.14 exhibits the same model using all 1,665 votes from those decisions. Comparing variable significance and impact between the two reduced models permits investigation of whether consequential differences in findings occur from the smaller database.

Female is positively signed, and its p value is .0000 in both reduced models, while its impact statistic varies between +.189 in Appendix 3.13 and +.176 in 3.14. Clearly, no consequential bias between the partial and complete data sets appears regarding this attribute.

Comparing all variables in Appendices 3.13 and 3.14 for which impact statistics are reported reveals the largest variation occurs for **gay male litigant,** which loses statistical significance in the second model (from a p value of .046 to .198). Its impact changes from +.069 to +.041 (not reported in Appendix 3.14), a difference of 68.3 percent (based on the smaller value). However, the next largest variation is just 14.1 percent (for −.105 and −.092 of **negative precedent**). Furthermore, the mean variation for the ten variables with reported impact statistics in Appendix 3.13 is 12.4 percent, while the median is 7.9 percent. Thus, nine of these ten variables have tolerable magnitudes of change between the reduced models.

Indeed, of the fifteen significant variables and interaction terms in Appendix 3.13, only two (**gay male litigant** and **legis∗environmental**

ideology∗term) lose their significance in Appendix 3.14. Both were barely beyond the threshold of significance (p = .046 and .047, respectively) to begin with, and the interaction term involves just 3.1 percent of votes in the complete data set.

As a result, I am confident to conclude that my database of 86.4 percent of the vote population does not create any systematic bias in the book's findings.

Appendix 3.13

Logistic Regression Statistics for a Reduced Model of the Book's Subset of All Votes in All Essential Decisions

Independent variable	N	Beta	Impact[a]
Negative precedent	280	−0.422*	−.105
(standard error)		(0.167)	
Positive precedent	154	1.453***	+.321
		(0.234)	
Gay male litigant	737	0.275*	+.069
		(0.138)	
Gay family issue	846	−1.719***	−.402
		(0.392)	
Free speech and association	67	−0.398	
		(0.469)	
Gays in the military	102	−1.906***	−.393
		(0.440)	
Sexual orientation discrimination	261	−1.837***	−.404
		(0.393)	
Sodomy constitutionality	111	−1.236**	−.284
		(0.438)	
Female	219	0.782***	+.189
		(0.168)	
Appointed	498	−2.508	
		(3.003)	
Appointed∗environmental ideology	498	0.016	
		(0.041)	
Appointed∗term	498	−0.204	
		(0.738)	

(continued)

(*continued*)

Independent variable	N	Beta	Impact[a]
Appointed★environmental ideology★term	498	0.010 (0.011)	
Legis	40	−2.739 (4.910)	
Legis★environmental ideology	40	0.214 (0.165)	
Legis★term	40	0.933 (1.390)	
Legis★environmental ideology★term	40	−0.100* (0.050)	
Merit	317	1.913 (1.569)	
Merit★environmental ideology	317	−0.006 (0.036)	
Merit★term	317	−1.697* (0.680)	
Merit★environmental ideology★term	317	0.022 (0.014)	
Term	1,439	1.542*** (0.443)	
Environmental ideology	1,439	0.055* (0.022)	
Environmental ideology★term	1,439	−0.028*** (0.008)	
Consensual sodomy law	644	−0.141 (0.148)	
Gay civil rights law	196	0.330 (0.205)	
Post-1990	999	0.077 (0.138)	
Gay interest group	816	0.385** (0.128)	+.096
Court of last resort	543	−0.152 (0.153)	
Federal court	324	−1.404*** (0.356)	−.328
Intercept		−1.553 (1.167)	

Note: Model N = 1,439; model chi-square = 261.526; df = 30; model p < .0001; −2 log likelihood = 1,732.983; Cox & Snell pseudo-R^2 = .166; Nagelkerke pseudo-R^2 = .166; classified correctly = 67.20%; proportional reduction in error = 33.33%.
[a] Impact of an increase from 0 to 1.
* p < .05; ** p < .01; *** p < .001.

Appendix 3.14

Logistic Regression Statistics for a Reduced Model of All Votes in All Essential Decisions

Independent variable	N	Beta	Impact[a]
Negative precedent (standard error)	325	-0.371^{*} (0.155)	$-.092$
Positive precedent	171	1.339^{***} (0.219)	$+.296$
Gay male litigant	850	0.164 (0.127)	
Gay family issue	977	-1.924^{***} (0.364)	$-.441$
Free speech and association	69	-0.374 (0.446)	
Gays in the military	116	-1.857^{***} (0.407)	$-.392$
Sexual orientation discrimination	313	-1.887^{***} (0.363)	$-.418$
Sodomy constitutionality	124	-1.384^{***} (0.407)	$-.315$
Female	258	0.732^{***} (0.155)	$+.176$
Appointed	546	-2.844 (2.673)	
Appointed★environmental ideology	546	0.017 (0.037)	
Appointed★term	546	-0.155 (0.667)	
Appointed★environmental ideology★term	546	0.010 (0.010)	

(continued)

(*continued*)

Independent variable	N	Beta	Impact[a]
Legis	52	−4.103	
		(5.148)	
Legis*environmental ideology	52	0.235	
		(0.173)	
Legis*term	52	1.045	
		(1.389)	
Legis*environmental ideology*term	52	−0.086	
		(0.047)	
Merit	401	1.603	
		(1.461)	
Merit*environmental ideology	401	−0.009	
		(0.033)	
Merit*term	401	−1.384*	
		(0.628)	
Merit*environmental ideology*term	401	0.019	
		(0.013)	
Term	1,665	1.426***	
		(0.419)	
Environmental ideology	1,665	0.053**	
		(0.020)	
Environmental ideology*term	1,665	−0.026***	
		(0.007)	
Consensual sodomy law	719	−0.221	
		(0.137)	
Gay civil rights law	239	0.301	
		(0.189)	
Post-1990	1,161	−0.007	
		(0.129)	
Gay interest group	947	0.390***	+.097
		(0.118)	
Court of last resort	598	−0.173	
		(0.140)	
Federal court	353	−1.385***	−.326
		(0.325)	
Intercept		−1.014	
		(1.087)	

Note: Model N = 1,665; model chi-square = 278.828; df = 30; model $p < .0001$; −2 log likelihood = 2,027.261; Cox & Snell pseudo-R^2 = .154; Nagelkerke pseudo-R^2 = .154; classified correctly = 66.31%; proportional reduction in error = 30.15%.
[a] Impact of an increase from 0 to 1.
* $p < .05$; ** $p < .01$; *** $p < .001$.

Summary Statistics for the Variables in Appendix 3.5

Variable	Mean	Standard deviation	Minimum	Maximum
Outcome	.5080	.5001	0	1
Negative precedent	.1946	.3960	0	1
Positive precedent	.1070	.3092	0	1
Gay male litigant	.5122	.5000	0	1
Gay family issue	.5879	.4924	0	1
Free speech and association	.04656	.2108	0	1
Gays in the military	.07088	.2567	0	1
Sexual orientation discrimination	.1814	.3855	0	1
Sodomy constitutionality	.07714	.2669	0	1
Age	2.3787	.7108	1	3
Catholic	.2606	.4391	0	1
Jewish	.1390	.3461	0	1
Female	.1522	.3593	0	1
Minority	.07019	.2556	0	1
Prior nonjudicial office	.2168	.4122	0	1
Democrat	.5820	.4930	0	1
Democrat*environmental ideology	29.5089	28.3717	0	97.10
Democrat*term	1.7172	1.8606	0	5
Democrat*environmental ideology*term	92.1174	114.8797	0	485.50
Appointed	.3461	.4759	0	1
Appointed*environmental ideology	19.7623	29.5175	0	97.10
Appointed*term	1.6018	2.2802	0	5
Appointed*environmental ideology*term	88.8608	135.1517	0	485.50
Legis	.0278	.1644	0	1
Legis*environmental ideology	.8236	5.1336	0	43.20
Legis*term	.07783	.5012	0	4
Legis*environmental ideology*term	2.2576	15.5231	0	171.00
Merit	.2203	.4146	0	1
Merit*environmental ideology	10.2544	20.3786	0	95.75
Merit*term	.5552	1.1833	0	4
Merit*environmental ideology*term	27.5208	62.7762	0	287.25
Term	3.1418	1.5834	1	5
Environmental ideology	51.2225	16.5846	8.13	97.10
Environmental ideology*term	168.2205	110.7866	17.68	485.50
Consensual sodomy law	.4475	.4974	0	1
Gay civil rights law	.1362	.3431	0	1
Post-1990	.6942	.4609	0	1
Gay interest group	.5671	.4957	0	1
Court of last resort	.3773	.4849	0	1
Federal court	.2252	.4178	0	1

Summary Statistics for the Variables in Appendix 3.6

Variable	Mean	Standard deviation	Minimum	Maximum
Outcome	.5322	.4994	0	1
Negative precedent	.1455	.3529	0	1
Positive precedent	.0663	.2490	0	1
Gay male litigant	.4457	.4975	0	1
Gay family issue	.6335	.4823	0	1
Free speech and association	.04236	.2016	0	1
Gays in the military	.02026	.1410	0	1
Sexual orientation discrimination	.1400	.3473	0	1
Sodomy constitutionality	.1363	.3434	0	1
Age	2.3646	.7082	1	3
Catholic	.2431	.4293	0	1
Jewish	.1179	.3227	0	1
Female	.1639	.3705	0	1
Minority	.0663	.2490	0	1
Prior nonjudicial office	.2541	.4358	0	1
Democrat	.5760	.4950	0	1
Democrat*environmental ideology	29.5108	30.0276	0	95.75
Democrat*term	1.5470	1.7259	0	5
Democrat*environmental ideology*term	87.4899	120.5166	0	446.25
Appointed	.3720	.4838	0	1
Appointed*environmental ideology	25.3859	34.9500	0	94.22
Appointed*term	1.5193	2.1544	0	5
Appointed*environmental ideology*term	100.5596	149.2005	0	446.25
Legis	.03499	.1839	0	1
Legis*environmental ideology	.9951	5.7360	0	42.75
Merit	.2413	.4282	0	1
Merit*environmental ideology	10.4106	20.6171	0	95.75
Merit*term	.5562	1.1201	0	4
Merit*environmental ideology*term	26.5874	60.9433	0	287.25
Term	2.8821	1.5358	1	5
Environmental ideology	51.9083	20.4763	8.13	95.75
Environmental ideology*term	160.9444	123.2068	17.68	446.25
Consensual sodomy law	.4843	.5002	0	1
Gay civil rights law	.2302	.4214	0	1
Post-1990	.7495	.4337	0	1
Gay interest group	.6483	.4780	0	1
Federal court	.06446	.2458	0	1

Summary Statistics for the Variables in Appendix 3.7

Variable	Mean	Standard deviation	Minimum	Maximum
Outcome	.4933	.5002	0	1
Negative precedent	.2243	.4174	0	1
Positive precedent	.1317	.3383	0	1
Gay male litigant	.5525	.4975	0	1
Gay family issue	.5603	.4966	0	1
Free speech and association	.04911	.2162	0	1
Gays in the military	.1016	.3022	0	1
Sexual orientation discrimination	.2065	.4050	0	1
Sodomy constitutionality	.04129	.1991	0	1
Age	2.3873	.7127	1	3
Catholic	.2712	.4448	0	1
Jewish	.1518	.3590	0	1
Female	.1451	.3524	0	1
Minority	.07254	.2595	0	1
Prior nonjudicial office	.1942	.3958	0	1
Democrat	.5860	.4930	0	1
Democrat★environmental ideology	29.5078	27.3366	0	97.10
Democrat★term	1.8203	1.9312	0	5
Democrat★environmental ideology★term	94.9218	111.2999	0	485.50
Appointed	.3304	.4706	0	1
Appointed★environmental ideology	16.3542	25.0869	0	97.10
Legis	.02344	.1514	0	1
Legis★environmental ideology	.7197	4.7318	0	43.20
Legis★term	.04018	.2686	0	2
Legis★environmental ideology★term	1.2135	8.0916	0	65.72
Merit	.2076	.4058	0	1
Merit★environmental ideology	10.1597	20.2436	0	70.69
Merit★term	.5547	1.2206	0	4
Merit★environmental ideology★term	28.0865	63.8885	0	227.84
Term	3.2991	1.5918	1	5
Environmental ideology	50.8069	13.6952	11.41	97.10
Environmental ideology★term	172.6301	102.3513	24.26	485.50
Consensual sodomy law	.4252	.4947	0	1
Gay civil rights law	.07924	.2703	0	1
Post-1990	.6607	.4737	0	1
Gay interest group	.5179	.5000	0	1
Federal court	.3225	.4677	0	1

Summary Statistics for the Variables in Appendix 3.8

Variable	Mean	Standard deviation	Minimum	Maximum
Outcome	.5319	.4993	0	1
Negative precedent	.1714	.3771	0	1
Positive precedent	.1466	.3539	0	1
Gay male litigant	.3227	.4678	0	1
Child CVAF issue	.7033	.4571	0	1
Age	2.3582	.7138	1	3
Catholic	.2541	.4356	0	1
Jewish	.1466	.3539	0	1
Female	.1466	.3539	0	1
Minority	.06974	.2549	0	1
Prior nonjudicial office	.2541	.4356	0	1
Democrat	.6390	.4800	0	1
Democrat*environmental ideology	33.6634	28.8426	0	95.75
Democrat*term	1.7577	1.6893	0	5
Democrat*environmental ideology*term	99.1225	111.9537	0	446.25
Appointed	.1513	.3586	0	1
Appointed*environmental ideology	10.4999	26.2332	0	94.22
Appointed*term	.6111	1.5496	0	5
Appointed*environmental ideology*term	40.7644	108.3280	0	446.25
Legis	.04019	.1965	0	1
Legis*environmental ideology	1.1858	6.1658	0	43.20
Legis*term	.1182	.6289	0	4
Legis*environmental ideology*term	3.4098	19.5139	0	171.00
Merit	.2861	.4522	0	1
Merit*environmental ideology	13.7252	23.0719	0	95.75
Merit*term	.7199	1.2939	0	4
Merit*environmental ideology*term	36.4395	70.3640	0	287.25
Term	2.7400	1.3634	1	5
Environmental ideology	52.5335	16.9313	8.13	95.75
Environmental ideology*term	153.2702	106.2448	17.68	446.25
Consensual sodomy law	.4196	.4938	0	1
Gay civil rights law	.1489	.3562	0	1
Post-1990	.7222	.4482	0	1
Gay interest group	.5567	.4971	0	1
Court of last resort	.4066	.4915	0	1
Federal court	.0130	.1134	0	1

Summary Statistics for the Variables in Appendix 3.9

Variable	Mean	Standard deviation	Minimum	Maximum
Outcome	.4739	.4997	0	1
Negative precedent	.2277	.4197	0	1
Positive precedent	.05059	.2193	0	1
Gay male litigant	.7825	.4129	0	1
Free speech and association	.1130	.3168	0	1
Gays in the military	.1720	.3777	0	1
Sexual orientation discrimination	.4401	.4968	0	1
Sodomy constitutionality	.1872	.3904	0	1
Age	2.4081	.7062	1	3
Catholic	.2698	.4442	0	1
Jewish	.1282	.3346	0	1
Female	.1602	.3671	0	1
Minority	.07083	.2568	0	1
Prior nonjudicial office	.1636	.3702	0	1
Democrat	.5010	.5000	0	1
Democrat*environmental ideology	23.5820	26.6083	0	97.10
Democrat*term	1.6594	2.0808	0	5
Democrat*environmental ideology*term	82.1236	118.3081	0	485.50
Appointed	.6239	.4848	0	1
Appointed*environmental ideology	32.9764	28.9240	0	97.10
Appointed*term	3.0152	2.4081	0	5
Appointed*environmental ideology*term	157.4774	139.9893	0	485.50
Legis	.01012	.1002	0	1
Legis*environmental ideology	.3069	3.0491	0	32.86
Merit	.1265	.3327	0	1
Merit*environmental ideology	5.3028	14.3934	0	56.96
Merit*term	.3204	.9578	0	4
Merit*environmental ideology*term	14.7970	47.2197	0	227.84
Term	3.7150	1.6960	1	5
Environmental ideology	49.3537	15.9098	15.85	97.10
Environmental ideology*term	189.5493	113.6937	17.68	485.50
Consensual sodomy law	.4874	.5003	0	1
Gay civil rights law	.1180	.3229	0	1
Post-1990	.6543	.4760	0	1
Gay interest group	.5818	.4937	0	1
Court of last resort	.3356	.4726	0	1
Federal court	.5278	.4996	0	1

Summary Statistics for the Variables in Appendix 3.10

Variable	Mean	Standard deviation	Minimum	Maximum
Outcome	.5160	.5002	0	1
Negative precedent	.2101	.4077	0	1
Positive precedent	.1479	.3553	0	1
Gay male litigant	.2420	.4287	0	1
Age	2.3210	.7336	1	3
Catholic	.2639	.4411	0	1
Jewish	.1092	.3122	0	1
Female	.1479	.3553	0	1
Minority	.05714	.2323	0	1
Prior nonjudicial office	.2706	.4446	0	1
Democrat	.6070	.4890	0	1
Democrat*environmental ideology	30.0120	27.1712	0	94.22
Democrat*term	1.5882	1.6165	0	5
Democrat*environmental ideology*term	83.2577	99.7548	0	446.25
Appointed	.1294	.3359	0	1
Appointed*environmental ideology	8.6935	24.1216	0	94.22
Appointed*term	.5025	1.4241	0	5
Appointed*environmental ideology*term	31.9855	96.7012	0	446.25
Legis	.04538	.2083	0	1
Legis*environmental ideology	1.3758	6.7790	0	43.20
Legis*term	.1361	.6717	0	4
Legis*environmental ideology*term	3.9743	21.3377	0	171.00
Merit	.3345	.4722	0	1
Merit*environmental ideology	15.5695	22.9749	0	70.69
Merit*term	.8336	1.3525	0	4
Merit*environmental ideology*term	40.7063	69.9938	0	227.84
Term	2.6202	1.3258	1	5
Environmental ideology	49.9356	15.4915	8.13	94.22
Environmental ideology*term	137.0785	96.1873	17.68	446.25
Consensual sodomy law	.4555	.4984	0	1
Gay civil rights law	.1546	.3618	0	1
Post-1990	.7176	.4505	0	1
Gay interest group	.5361	.4991	0	1
Court of last resort	.4319	.4958	0	1

Summary Statistics for the Variables in Appendix 3.11

Variable	Mean	Standard deviation	Minimum	Maximum
Outcome	.5065	.5005	0	1
Negative precedent	.2100	.4077	0	1
Positive precedent	.07359	.2614	0	1
Gay male litigant	.5303	.4996	0	1
Gay family issue	.5628	.4966	0	1
Free speech and association	.03247	.1774	0	1
Gays in the military	.07792	.2683	0	1
Sexual orientation discrimination	.1926	.3948	0	1
Sodomy constitutionality	.09740	.2968	0	1
Age	2.3550	.7060	1	3
Catholic	.2532	.4353	0	1
Jewish	.1580	.3651	0	1
Female	.1429	.3503	0	1
Minority	.04113	.1988	0	1
Prior nonjudicial office	.2143	.4108	0	1
Democrat	.5740	.4950	0	1
Democrat*environmental ideology	28.8967	28.0765	0	95.75
Democrat*term	1.5974	1.7985	0	5
Democrat*environmental ideology*term	84.3257	108.8276	0	424.30
Appointed	.3528	.4784	0	1
Appointed*environmental ideology	20.4869	29.9494	0	94.22
Appointed*term	1.5996	2.2707	0	5
Appointed*environmental ideology*term	89.9802	135.0419	0	424.30
Legis	.02597	.1592	0	1
Legis*environmental ideology	.7989	5.1070	0	43.20
Legis*term	.06494	.4370	0	4
Legis*environmental ideology*term	1.8924	13.1966	0	171.00
Merit	.2489	.4329	0	1
Merit*environmental ideology	11.8007	21.5890	0	95.75
Merit*term	.6558	1.2774	0	4
Merit*environmental ideology*term	32.9104	68.2352	0	287.25
Term	3.0368	1.5893	1	5
Environmental ideology	50.8631	15.7703	8.13	95.75
Environmental ideology*term	160.6699	107.9376	17.68	424.30
Consensual sodomy law	.4329	.4960	0	1
Gay civil rights law	.1775	.3825	0	1
Post-1990	.7013	.4582	0	1
Gay interest group	.6147	.4872	0	1
Court of last resort	.3680	.4828	0	1
Federal court	.2251	.4181	0	1

Summary Statistics for the Variables in Appendix 3.14

Variable	Mean	Standard deviation	Minimum	Maximum
Outcome	.5177	.4998	0	1
Negative precedent	.1952	.3965	0	1
Positive precedent	.1027	.3037	0	1
Gay male litigant	.5105	.5000	0	1
Gay family issue	.5868	.4926	0	1
Free speech and association	.04144	.1994	0	1
Gays in the military	.06967	.2547	0	1
Sexual orientation discrimination	.1880	.3908	0	1
Sodomy constitutionality	.07447	.2626	0	1
Female	.1550	.3620	0	1
Appointed	.3279	.4696	0	1
Appointed*environmental ideology	18.6703	28.9998	0	97.10
Appointed*term	1.5093	2.2431	0	5
Appointed*environmental ideology*term	83.3776	132.2881	0	485.50
Legis	.03123	.1740	0	1
Legis*environmental ideology	.9103	5.3457	0	43.20
Legis*term	.09249	.5546	0	4
Legis*environmental ideology*term	2.6348	16.7904	0	171.00
Merit	.2408	.4277	0	1
Merit*environmental ideology	11.2351	21.0079	0	95.75
Merit*term	.6240	1.2550	0	4
Merit*environmental ideology*term	30.9098	66.2962	0	287.25
Term	3.0961	1.5801	1	5
Environmental ideology	50.9805	16.2613	8.13	97.10
Environmental ideology*term	164.3981	109.0563	17.68	485.50
Consensual sodomy law	.4318	.4955	0	1
Gay civil rights law	.1435	.3507	0	1
Post-1990	.6973	.4596	0	1
Gay interest group	.5688	.4954	0	1
Court of last resort	.3592	.4799	0	1
Federal court	.2120	.4089	0	1

Appendix 4.1

Judicial Federalism Variable Coding

Federal constitutional issue	1 if a federal or state case adjudicated a claim based on the federal Constitution 0 otherwise
State constitutional issue	1 if a state case adjudicated a claim based on a state constitution but none based on the federal Constitution 0 otherwise
Privacy clause	1 if a state case from Alaska, Arizona, California, Florida, Hawaii, Illinois, Louisiana, Montana, South Carolina, or Washington 0 otherwise

Appendix 4.2

Appellate Cases Adjudicating Constitutional Issues

Citations may be found in Appendix 1.2.

Federal and State Appellate Cases Adjudicating Federal Constitutional Issues

United States Supreme Court

1986   *Bowers v. Hardwick*

1995   *Hurley v. Irish-American Gay, Lesbian and Bisexual Group of Boston*

1996   *Romer v. Evans*

2000   *Boy Scouts of America v. Dale*

United States Courts of Appeals

Second Circuit

1985   *Olivieri v. Ward*

1998   *Able v. U.S.*

Third Circuit

1996   *Presbytery of New Jersey v. Whitman*

2000   *Sterling v. Borough of Minersville*

Fourth Circuit

1981   *Nemetz v. Immigration and Naturalization Service*

1990   *Walls v. City of Petersburg*

1996   *Selland v. Perry*

        Thomasson v. Perry

1998   *Thorne v. U.S. Department of Defense*

Tenth Circuit
  1984   *National Gay Task Force v. Board of Education of the City of Oklahoma City*
           Rich v. Secretary of the Army
  1992   *Jantz v. Muci*
  1995   *Walmer v. U.S. Department of Defense*
Eleventh Circuit
  1985   *Hardwick v. Bowers*
  1995   *Shahar v. Bowers*
  1997   *Gay Lesbian Bisexual Alliance v. Pryor*
           Shahar v. Bowers [114 F.3d 1097]
District of Columbia Circuit
  1984   *Dronenburg v. Zech*
  1986   *Doe v. Casey*
  1987   *Padula v. Webster*
  1993   *Doe v. Gates*
           Steffan v. Aspin
           U.S. Information Agency v. Krc
  1994   *Steffan v. Perry*
Federal Circuit
  1989   *Woodward v. U.S.*
Arkansas
Court of Appeals
  1987   *Thigpen v. Carpenter*
California
Court of Appeal
  1993   *Engel v. Worthington*
           In re Joshua H.
           People v. M.S.
  1994   *Curran v. Mount Diablo Council of the Boy Scouts of America*
  1995   *Baluyut v. Superior Court*
Colorado
Court of Appeals
  1994   *Ross v. Denver Department of Health and Hospitals*
  1996   *Adoption of T.K.J. and K.A.K.*
Supreme Court
  1993   *Evans v. Romer*
  1994   *Evans v. Romer*
Florida
District Court of Appeal

1993   *State v. Cox*
1994   *Reeves v. State*
Supreme Court
   1995   *Cox v. Florida Department of Health and Rehabilitative Services*
Indiana
Court of Appeals
   1998   *Marlow v. Marlow*
Maine
Supreme Judicial Court
   1982   *State v. Lovely*
Massachusetts
Supreme Judicial Court
   1985   *Madsen v. Erwin*
   1994   *Irish-American Gay, Lesbian and Bisexual Group of Boston v. City*
       of Boston
   1999   *E.N.O. v. L.M.M.*
Michigan
Supreme Court
   1994   *People v. Lino*
Minnesota
Court of Appeals
   1985   *Blanding v. Sports & Health Club, Inc.*
   1991   *Dignity Twin Cities v. Newman Center and Chapel*
   2000   *LaChapelle v. Mitten*
Missouri
Court of Appeals
   1982   *J.L.P.(H.) v. D.J.P.*
       L. v. D.
Supreme Court
   1986   *State v. Walsh*
Nebraska
Supreme Court
   1998   *State v. Pattno*
New Hampshire
Supreme Court
   1987   *Opinion of the Justices*
New Jersey
Superior Court, Appellate Division
   1998   *Dale v. Boy Scouts of America*

Supreme Court
    1999   *Dale v. Boy Scouts of America*

New York
Supreme Court, Appellate Term
    1988   *Koppelman v. O'Keeffe*
Supreme Court, Appellate Division
    1987   *Two Associates v. Brown*
    1990   *Rent Stabilization Association of New York City, Inc. v. Higgins*
    1993   *Matter of Cooper*
              Rent Stabilization Association of New York City, Inc. v. Higgins
    1998   *Raum v. Restaurant Associates, Inc.*
Court of Appeals
    1983   *People v. Uplinger*
    1993   *Rent Stabilization Association of New York City, Inc. v. Higgins*

Ohio
Court of Appeals
    1987   *Conkel v. Conkel*
    1997   *Inscoe v. Inscoe*
              Liston v. Pyles
    2000   *State v. Thompson*

Oklahoma
Court of Criminal Appeals
    1995   *Sawatzky v. City of Oklahoma City*
Supreme Court
    1981   *Gay Activists Alliance v. Board of Regents of the University of Oklahoma*

Oregon
Court of Appeals
    1981   *State v. Tusek*

Pennsylvania
Superior Court
    1985   *Constant A. v. Paul C.A.*
    1995   *DeMuth v. Miller*

Tennessee
Court of Appeals
    2000   *Adoption of M.J.S.*

Texas
Supreme Court
    1996   *Republican Party of Texas v. Dietz*
    1997   *Republican Party of Texas v. Dietz*

Virginia
Court of Appeals
 1997 *Branche v. Commonwealth*
Washington
Court of Appeals
 1998 *Webb v. Puget Sound Broadcasting Company*
Supreme Court
 1997 *Nelson v. McClatchy Newspapers, Inc.*
Wisconsin
Supreme Court
 1991 *Interest of Z.J.H.*
 1994 *Angel Lace M. v. Terry M.*
 1995 *Custody of H.S.H.-K.*

State Appellate Cases Adjudicating State Constitutional Issues

California
Court of Appeal
 1985 *Hinman v. Department of Personnel Administration*
 1991 *Soroka v. Dayton Hudson Corporation*
 2000 *People v. Garcia*
Florida
District Court of Appeal
 1999 *Kazmierazak v. Query*
 2000 *Lowe v. Broward County*
Georgia
Supreme Court
 1995 *City of Atlanta v. McKinney*
 1996 *Christensen v. State*
 1997 *City of Atlanta v. Morgan*
 1998 *Powell v. State*
Hawaii
Supreme Court
 1993 *Baehr v. Lewin*
 1997 *Baehr v. Miike*
Kentucky
Supreme Court
 1992 *Commonwealth v. Wasson*
Louisiana
Court of Appeal
 1999 *State v. Smith*

Supreme Court
  1994   *State v. Baxley*
  1995   *State v. Baxley*
  2000   *State v. Smith*
Massachusetts
Supreme Judicial Court
  1990   *Collins v. Secretary of the Commonwealth*
  1998   *Opinions of the Justices*
  1999   *Connors v. City of Boston*
Montana
Supreme Court
  1997   *Gryczan v. State*
New Jersey
Superior Court, Appellate Division
  1997   *Rutgers Council of AAUP Chapters v. Rutgers, The State University*
Oregon
Court of Appeals
  1992   *Merrick v. Board of Higher Education*
  1998   *Tanner v. Oregon Health Sciences University*
Tennessee
Court of Appeals
  1996   *Campbell v. Sundquist*
Texas
Court of Appeals
  1992   *State v. Morales*
  1993   *City of Dallas v. England*
  1998   *Bailey v. City of Austin*
Supreme Court
  1994   *State v. Morales*
Vermont
Supreme Court
  1999   *Baker v. State*
Wisconsin
Court of Appeals
  1992   *Phillips v. Wisconsin Personnel Commission*

Appendix 4.3

Logistic Regression Statistics for All Votes (with Judicial Federalism Variables)

Independent variable	N	Beta	Impact
Federal court (standard error)	324	-1.298^{***} (0.385)	$-.307^{a}$
Federal constitutional issue	454	-0.771^{***} (0.181)	$-.190^{a}$
State constitutional issue	122	-0.312 (0.282)	
Privacy clause	184	-0.303 (0.218)	
Negative precedent	280	-0.404^{*} (0.175)	$-.101^{a}$
Positive precedent	154	1.689^{***} (0.248)	$+.360^{a}$
Gay male litigant	737	0.316^{*} (0.146)	$+.079^{a}$
Gay family issue	846	-1.920^{***} (0.419)	$-.442^{a}$
Free speech and association	67	-0.045 (0.496)	
Gays in the military	102	-1.750^{***} (0.465)	$-.371^{a}$
Sexual orientation discrimination	261	-1.889^{***} (0.416)	$-.413^{a}$
Sodomy constitutionality	111	-0.994^{*} (0.467)	$-.235^{a}$

(continued)

(*continued*)

Independent variable	N	Beta	Impact
Age	1,439	−0.204* (0.094)	−.051[b]
Catholic	375	−0.452** (0.154)	−.112[a]
Jewish	200	0.648** (0.213)	+.158[a]
Female	219	0.497** (0.182)	+.122[a]
Minority	101	0.821** (0.254)	+.195[a]
Prior nonjudicial office	312	−0.352* (0.154)	−.088[a]
Democrat	838	−0.015 (0.962)	
Democrat★environmental ideology	838	0.001 (0.020)	
Democrat★term	838	0.342 (0.266)	
Democrat★environmental ideology★term	838	−0.002 (0.005)	
Appointed	498	−5.950 (3.291)	
Appointed★environmental ideology	498	0.040 (0.044)	
Appointed★term	498	0.166 (0.813)	
Appointed★environmental ideology★term	498	0.012 (0.012)	
Legis	40	−0.591 (4.927)	
Legis★environmental ideology	40	0.171 (0.164)	
Legis★term	40	0.058 (1.414)	
Legis★environmental ideology★term	40	−0.086 (0.051)	
Merit	317	3.396* (1.658)	
Merit★environmental ideology	317	−0.030 (0.037)	
Merit★term	317	−2.366** (0.727)	

Independent variable	N	Beta	Impact
Merit★environmental ideology★term	317	0.033* (0.015)	
Term	1,439	2.077*** (0.536)	
Environmental ideology	1,439	0.084** (0.028)	
Environmental ideology★term	1,439	−0.041*** (0.010)	
Consensual sodomy law	644	−0.332* (0.165)	−.083[a]
Gay civil rights law	196	0.675** (0.218)	+.164[a]
Post-1990	999	0.162 (0.148)	
Gay interest group	816	0.424** (0.139)	+.106[a]
Court of last resort	543	−0.041 (0.164)	
Intercept		−2.265 (1.460)	

Note: Model N = 1,439; model chi-square = 378.943; df = 42; model p < .0001; −2 log likelihood = 1,615.567; Cox & Snell pseudo-R^2 = .232; Nagelkerke pseudo-R^2 = .232; classified correctly = 71.09%; reduction in error = 41.24%.
[a] Impact of an increase from 0 to 1.
[b] Impact of a one-unit increase from the mean of the independent variable.
* p < .05; ** p < .01; *** p < .001.

Appendix 4.4

Logistic Regression Statistics for Votes in Federal Constitutional Decisions

Independent variable	N	Beta	Impact[a]
Federal court	253	−0.506	
(standard error)		(0.874)	
Privacy clause	30	−2.498**	−.421
		(0.768)	
Negative precedent	106	−0.841*	−.199
		(0.427)	
Positive precedent	44	2.216***	+.458
		(0.600)	
Gay male litigant	331	0.328	
		(0.363)	
Gay family issue	105	−3.165***	−.566
		(0.875)	
Free speech and	64	0.184	
association		(0.849)	
Gays in the military	75	−3.188***	−.531
		(0.829)	
Sexual orientation	130	−2.806***	−.550
discrimination		(0.780)	
Sodomy constitutionality	52	−1.544	
		(0.902)	
Age	454	−0.328	
		(0.211)	
Catholic	114	−0.798*	−.190
		(0.336)	
Jewish	69	1.039*	+.252
		(0.436)	

Independent variable	N	Beta	Impact[a]
Female	68	0.467 (0.370)	
Minority	22	0.774 (0.601)	
Prior nonjudicial office	80	−0.619 (0.361)	
Democrat	223	5.945 (4.656)	
Democrat★environmental ideology	223	−0.121 (0.099)	
Democrat★term	223	−0.567 (0.975)	
Democrat★environmental ideology★term	223	0.018 (0.021)	
Appointed	299	−378.962 (836.219)	
Appointed★environmental ideology	299	4.903 (11.150)	
Appointed★term	299	76.185 (167.243)	
Appointed★environmental ideology★term	299	−0.979 (2.230)	
Legis	3	−5.290 (56.744)	
Merit	63	13.339 (7.768)	
Merit★environmental ideology	63	−0.193 (0.164)	
Merit★term	63	−3.117 (3.390)	
Merit★environmental ideology★term	63	0.050 (0.068)	
Term	454	4.091 (2.235)	
Environmental ideology	454	0.427** (0.143)	
Environmental ideology★term	454	−0.091* (0.040)	
Consensual sodomy law	203	−0.244 (0.357)	
Gay civil rights law	60	2.566*** (0.595)	+.513

(*continued*)

(*continued*)

Independent variable	N	Beta	Impact[a]
Post-1990	278	0.630	
		(0.410)	
Gay interest group	294	0.653	
		(0.410)	
Court of last resort	149	0.353	
		(0.445)	
Intercept		−20.126**	
		(7.189)	

Note: Model N = 454; model chi-square = 232.269; df = 37; model p < .0001; −2 log likelihood = 389.156; Cox & Snell pseudo-R^2 = .400; Nagelkerke pseudo-R^2 = .537; classified correctly = 80.40%; proportional reduction in error = 54.83%.

[a] Impact of an increase from 0 to 1.

* p < .05; ** p < .01; *** p < .001.

Appendix 4.5

Logistic Regression Statistics for Votes in Federal and State Constitutional Decisions

Independent variable	N	Beta	Impact[a]
Federal court	253	−0.642	
(standard error)		(0.721)	
State constitutional issue	122	0.678	
		(0.396)	
Privacy clause	67	−0.714	
		(0.506)	
Negative precedent	127	−0.042	
		(0.305)	
Positive precedent	50	2.324***	+.363
		(0.559)	
Gay male litigant	394	0.058	
		(0.295)	
Gay family issue	158	−3.293***	−.670
		(0.736)	
Free speech and association	67	−0.183	
		(0.730)	
Gays in the military	75	−3.123***	−.611
		(0.732)	
Sexual orientation discrimination	143	−2.353***	−.527
		(0.675)	
Sodomy constitutionality	104	−1.686*	−.398
		(0.747)	
Age	576	−0.172	
		(0.172)	

(continued)

(*continued*)

Independent variable	N	Beta	Impact[a]
Catholic	140	−0.716* (0.282)	−.174
Jewish	83	0.920* (0.365)	+.195
Female	91	0.631* (0.310)	+.140
Minority	36	0.487 (0.450)	
Prior nonjudicial office	99	−0.567 (0.297)	
Democrat	308	2.366 (2.089)	
Democrat⋆environmental ideology	308	−0.029 (0.046)	
Democrat⋆term	308	0.075 (0.489)	
Democrat⋆environmental ideology⋆term	308	−0.000 (0.011)	
Appointed	325	−372.098 (683.961)	
Appointed⋆environmental ideology	325	4.957 (9.118)	
Appointed⋆term	325	74.218 (136.797)	
Appointed⋆environmental ideology⋆term	325	−0.986 (1.824)	
Legis	3	−10.042 (93.971)	
Merit	84	0.554 (3.331)	
Merit⋆environmental ideology	84	0.024 (0.081)	
Merit⋆term	84	−1.048 (1.445)	
Merit⋆environmental ideology⋆term	84	0.011 (0.031)	
Term	576	0.657 (1.011)	
Environmental ideology	576	0.005 (0.053)	
Environmental ideology⋆term	576	−0.010 (0.018)	

Independent variable	N	Beta	Impact[a]
Consensual sodomy law	297	−0.155 (0.306)	
Gay civil rights law	99	1.597*** (0.443)	+.308
Post-1990	391	0.338 (0.325)	
Gay interest group	396	0.951** (0.328)	+.229
Court of last resort	238	0.017 (0.345)	
Intercept		−0.322 (2.795)	

Note: Model N = 576; model chi-square = 239.877; df = 38; model p < .0001; −2 log likelihood = 557.267; Cox & Snell pseudo-R^2 = .341; Nagelkerke pseudo-R^2 = .455; classified correctly = 75.69%; proportional reduction in error = 48.90%.

[a] Impact of an increase from 0 to 1.

* p < .05; ** p < .01; *** p < .001.

Appendix 4.6

Logistic Regression Statistics for Votes in Courts of Last Resort (with Judicial Federalism Variables)

Independent variable	N	Beta	Impact[a]
Federal court	35	−1.290	
(standard error)		(0.678)	
Federal constitutional issue	149	−0.149	
		(0.411)	
State constitutional issue	89	0.264	
		(0.463)	
Privacy clause	58	1.413*	+.284
		(0.590)	
Negative precedent	79	0.933*	+.206
		(0.376)	
Positive precedent	36	1.923**	+.340
		(0.691)	
Gay male litigant	242	1.357***	+.314
		(0.348)	
Gay family issue	344	−7.146	
		(8.796)	
Free speech and association	23	−8.453	
		(8.805)	
Gays in the military	11	−5.129	
		(8.839)	
Sexual orientation discrimination	76	−7.359	
		(8.794)	
Sodomy constitutionality	74	−7.197	
		(8.798)	
Age	543	0.167	
		(0.183)	

Independent variable	N	Beta	Impact[a]
Catholic	132	−0.451 (0.282)	
Jewish	64	1.030* (0.459)	+.222
Female	89	1.070** (0.335)	+.233
Minority	36	1.059* (0.464)	+.223
Prior nonjudicial office	138	−0.212 (0.260)	
Democrat	313	−1.059 (1.375)	
Democrat*environmental ideology	313	0.031 (0.026)	
Democrat*term	313	0.782 (0.510)	
Democrat*environmental ideology*term	313	−0.012 (0.008)	
Appointed	202	−18.570*** (5.279)	
Appointed*environmental ideology	202	0.239** (0.085)	
Appointed*term	202	7.136*** (1.906)	
Appointed*environmental ideology*term	202	−0.113** (0.036)	
Legis	19	17.064*** (4.359)	
Legis*environmental ideology	19	−0.497*** (0.108)	
Merit	131	−7.791* (3.669)	
Merit*environmental ideology	131	0.294** (0.095)	
Merit*term	131	5.400** (1.874)	
Merit*environmental ideology*term	131	−0.155*** (0.044)	
Term	543	−4.046* (1.645)	
Environmental ideology	543	−0.065 (0.068)	

(*continued*)

(*continued*)

Independent variable	N	Beta	Impact[a]
Environmental ideology★term	543	0.077* (0.034)	
Consensual sodomy law	263	−0.413 (0.409)	
Gay civil rights law	125	0.839* (0.388)	+.191
Post-1990	407	−0.342 (0.310)	
Gay interest group	352	0.448 (0.348)	
Intercept		9.081 (9.315)	

Note: Model N = 543; model chi-square = 223.221; df = 39; model p < .0001; −2 log likelihood = 527.279; Cox & Snell pseudo-R^2 = .337; Nagelkerke pseudo-R^2 = .450; classified correctly = 76.61%; proportional reduction in error = 50.00%.

[a] Impact of an increase from 0 to 1.

* p < .05; ** p < .01; *** p < .001.

Appendix 4.7

Logistic Regression Statistics for Votes in Intermediate Appellate Courts (with Judicial Federalism Variables)

Independent variable	N	Beta	Impact
Federal court	289	−1.454	
(standard error)		(1.000)	
Federal constitutional issue	305	−0.749**	−.184[a]
		(0.247)	
State constitutional issue	33	−0.854	
		(0.485)	
Privacy clause	126	−0.737*	−.179[a]
		(0.301)	
Negative precedent	201	−0.510*	−.126[a]
		(0.243)	
Positive precedent	118	1.867***	+.397[a]
		(0.292)	
Gay male litigant	495	−0.109	
		(0.188)	
Gay family issue	502	−2.285***	−.515[a]
		(0.519)	
Free speech and association	44	1.865**	+.379[a]
		(0.687)	
Gays in the military	91	−1.409**	−.315[a]
		(0.526)	
Sexual orientation discrimination	185	−2.161***	−.456[a]
		(0.498)	
Sodomy constitutionality	37	−0.017	
		(0.635)	

(continued)

(*continued*)

Independent variable	N	Beta	Impact
Age	896	−0.447***	−.110[b]
		(0.131)	
Catholic	243	−0.482*	−.119[a]
		(0.211)	
Jewish	136	0.797**	+.193[a]
		(0.273)	
Female	130	0.271	
		(0.247)	
Minority	65	1.206***	+.276[a]
		(0.359)	
Prior nonjudicial office	174	−0.324	
		(0.224)	
Democrat	525	−2.559	
		(2.180)	
Democrat★environmental ideology	525	0.046	
		(0.046)	
Democrat★term	525	0.787	
		(0.525)	
Democrat★environmental ideology★term	525	−0.009	
		(0.011)	
Appointed	296	−11.189***	
		(2.638)	
Appointed★environmental ideology	296	0.179***	
		(0.038)	
Legis	21	23.292	
		(66.158)	
Legis★environmental ideology	21	−0.206	
		(1.886)	
Legis★term	21	−16.452	
		(33.797)	
Legis★environmental ideology★term	21	0.213	
		(0.970)	
Merit	186	4.766	
		(3.972)	
Merit★environmental ideology	186	−0.058	
		(0.085)	
Merit★term	186	−5.135**	
		(1.604)	
Merit★environmental ideology★term	186	0.083**	
		(0.032)	
Term	896	2.792***	
		(0.782)	

Independent variable	N	Beta	Impact
Environmental ideology	896	0.027	
		(0.045)	
Environmental ideology*term	896	−0.046**	
		(0.014)	
Consensual sodomy law	381	0.031	
		(0.231)	
Gay civil rights law	71	1.131***	+.262^a
		(0.328)	
Post-1990	592	0.618**	+.153^a
		(0.200)	
Gay interest group	464	0.212	
		(0.178)	
Intercept		0.735	
		(2.342)	

Note: Model N = 896; Model chi-square = 339.333; df = 39; model p < .0001; −2 log likelihood = 902.626; Cox & Snell pseudo-R^2 = .315; Nagelkerke pseudo-R^2 = .420; classified correctly = 76.23%; proportional reduction in error = 51.81%.
^{a} Impact of an increase from 0 to 1.
^{b} Impact of a one-unit increase from the mean of the independent variable.
* p < .05; ** p < .01; *** p < .001.

Appendix 4.8

Logistic Regression Statistics for Votes in Federal Court Decisions (with Judicial Federalism Variables)

Independent variable	N	Beta	Impact[a]
Federal constitutional issue	253	0.630	
(standard error)		(0.497)	
Negative precedent	119	−0.177	
		(0.455)	
Positive precedent	6	1.176	
		(1.076)	
Gay male litigant	261	−0.391	
		(0.497)	
Gay family issue	11	−0.729	
		(1.132)	
Free speech and association	41	2.569**	+.566
		(0.940)	
Gays in the military	87	−2.357***	−.344
		(0.688)	
Sexual orientation discrimination	137	−2.331**	−.405
		(0.711)	
Sodomy constitutionality	28	−0.722	
		(0.833)	
Age	324	−0.305	
		(0.273)	
Catholic	83	−0.851*	−.149
		(0.414)	
Jewish	46	0.254	
		(0.503)	
Female	46	−0.233	
		(0.456)	

Independent variable	N	Beta	Impact[a]
Minority	23	0.565 (0.650)	
Prior nonjudicial office	42	−0.816 (0.528)	
Democrat	126	1.985*** (0.412)	+.405
Environmental ideology	324	−0.012 (0.013)	
Consensual sodomy law	147	−0.751 (0.514)	
Gay civil rights law	16	1.300 (0.794)	
Post-1990	182	0.653 (0.477)	
Gay interest group	202	1.879*** (0.501)	+.322
Court of last resort	35	0.416 (0.667)	
Intercept		−0.222 (1.399)	

Note: Model N = 324; model chi-square = 154.042; df = 22; model p < .0001; −2 log likelihood = 263.743; Cox & Snell pseudo-R^2 = .378; Nagelkerke pseudo-R^2 = .522; classified correctly = 81.79%; proportional reduction in error = 47.32%.

[a] Impact of an increase from 0 to 1.

* p < .05; ** p < .01; *** p < .001.

Appendix 4.9

Logistic Regression Statistics for Votes in State Court Decisions (with Judicial Federalism Variables)

Independent variable	N	Beta	Impact
Federal constitutional issue	201	-1.095^{***}	$-.267^{a}$
(standard error)		(0.221)	
State constitutional issue	122	-0.244	
		(0.300)	
Privacy clause	184	-0.202	
		(0.221)	
Negative precedent	161	-0.081	
		(0.214)	
Positive precedent	148	1.778^{***}	$+.347^{a}$
		(0.264)	
Gay male litigant	476	0.383^{*}	$+.093^{a}$
		(0.163)	
Gay family issue	835	-2.621^{***}	$-.495^{a}$
		(0.703)	
Free speech and association	26	-2.237^{**}	$-.455^{a}$
		(0.821)	
Gays in the military	15	-2.168^{*}	$-.444^{a}$
		(0.963)	
Sexual orientation discrimination	124	-2.160^{**}	$-.467^{a}$
		(0.717)	
Sodomy constitutionality	83	-1.894^{*}	$-.419^{a}$
		(0.748)	
Age	1,115	-0.254^{*}	$-.063^{b}$
		(0.106)	
Catholic	292	-0.408^{*}	$-.101^{a}$
		(0.175)	

Independent variable	N	Beta	Impact
Jewish	154	0.903***	+.203[a]
		(0.258)	
Female	173	0.595**	+.139[a]
		(0.214)	
Minority	78	0.950**	+.208[a]
		(0.292)	
Prior nonjudicial office	270	−0.281	
		(0.167)	
Democrat	712	−0.153	
		(1.058)	
Democrat⋆environmental ideology	712	0.009	
		(0.021)	
Democrat⋆term	712	0.270	
		(0.396)	
Democrat⋆environmental ideology⋆term	712	−0.003	
		(0.007)	
Appointed	174	−5.974	
		(3.616)	
Appointed⋆environmental ideology	174	0.031	
		(0.048)	
Appointed⋆term	174	−0.148	
		(0.911)	
Appointed⋆environmental ideology⋆term	174	0.019	
		(0.013)	
Legis	40	−1.324	
		(5.262)	
Legis⋆environmental ideology	40	0.190	
		(0.178)	
Legis⋆term	40	0.248	
		(1.488)	
Legis⋆environmental ideology⋆term	40	−0.089	
		(0.054)	
Merit	317	4.167*	
		(1.666)	
Merit⋆environmental ideology	317	−0.044	
		(0.038)	
Merit⋆term	317	−2.652***	
		(0.732)	
Merit⋆environmental ideology⋆term	317	0.038**	
		(0.015)	
Term	1,115	2.127***	
		(0.577)	

(*continued*)

(*continued*)

Independent variable	N	Beta	Impact
Environmental ideology	1,115	0.084**	
		(0.028)	
Environmental ideology*term	1,115	−0.041***	
		(0.010)	
Consensual sodomy law	497	−0.635**	−.155[a]
		(0.200)	
Gay civil rights law	180	0.558*	+.131[a]
		(0.242)	
Post-1990	817	0.253	
		(0.173)	
Gay interest group	614	0.086	
		(0.158)	
Court of last resort	508	0.090	
		(0.179)	
Intercept		−1.362	
		(1.606)	

Note: Model N = 1,115; model chi-square = 268.605; df = 41; model p < .0001; −2log likelihood = 1,263.517; Cox & Snell pseudo-R^2 = .214; Nagelkerke pseudo-R^2 = .214; classified correctly = 72.02%; proportional reduction in error = 37.10%.
[a] Impact of an increase from 0 to 1.
[b] Impact of a one-unit increase from the mean of the independent variable.
* p < .05; ** p < .01; *** p < .001.

Summary Statistics for the Supplemental Variables in Appendix 4.3

Variable	Mean	Standard deviation	Minimum	Maximum
Federal constitutional issue	.3155	.4649	0	1
State constitutional issue	.08478	.2787	0	1
Privacy clause	.1279	.3341	0	1

Summary Statistics for the Variables in Appendix 4.4

Variable	Mean	Standard deviation	Minimum	Maximum
Outcome	.4339	.4962	0	1
Federal court	.5573	.4973	0	1
Privacy clause	.06608	.2487	0	1
Negative precedent	.2335	.4235	0	1
Positive precedent	.09692	.2962	0	1
Gay male litigant	.7291	.4449	0	1
Gay family issue	.2313	.4221	0	1
Free speech and association	.1410	.3484	0	1
Gays in the military	.1652	.3718	0	1
Sexual orientation discrimination	.2863	.4526	0	1
Sodomy constitutionality	.1145	.3188	0	1
Age	2.4670	.6953	1	3
Catholic	.2511	.4341	0	1
Jewish	.1520	.3594	0	1
Female	.1498	.3572	0	1
Minority	.04846	.2150	0	1
Prior nonjudicial office	.1762	.3814	0	1
Democrat	.4910	.5000	0	1
Democrat*environmental ideology	24.5039	27.9019	0	97.10
Democrat*term	1.8568	2.1774	0	5
Democrat*environmental ideology*term	94.1936	123.4354	0	485.50
Appointed	.6586	.4747	0	1
Appointed*environmental ideology	33.7999	28.2330	0	97.10
Appointed*term	3.2203	2.3632	0	5
Appointed*environmental ideology*term	163.2385	136.2781	0	485.50
Legis	.006608	.08111	0	1

(continued)

(*continued*)

Variable	Mean	Standard deviation	Minimum	Maximum
Legis★environmental ideology	.2171	2.6653	0	32.86
Legis★term	.01322	.1622	0	2
Legis★environmental ideology★term	.4343	5.3305	0	65.72
Merit	.1388	.3461	0	1
Merit★environmental ideology	5.6911	14.5855	0	53.25
Merit★term	.3150	.9230	0	4
Merit★environmental ideology★term	13.8535	42.8713	0	213.00
Term	4.0264	1.4781	1	5
Environmental ideology	50.5950	15.9851	8.13	97.10
Environmental ideology★term	205.9404	103.5278	17.68	485.50
Consensual sodomy law	.4471	.4977	0	1
Gay civil rights law	.1322	.3390	0	1
Post-1990	.6123	.4878	0	1
Gay interest group	.6476	.4783	0	1
Court of last resort	.3282	.4701	0	1

Summary Statistics for the Variables in Appendix 4.5

Variable	Mean	Standard deviation	Minimum	Maximum
Outcome	.4757	.4998	0	1
Federal court	.4392	.4967	0	1
State constitutional issue	.2118	.4089	0	1
Privacy clause	.1163	.3209	0	1
Negative precedent	.2205	.4149	0	1
Positive precedent	.08681	.2818	0	1
Gay male litigant	.6840	.4653	0	1
Gay family issue	.2743	.4466	0	1
Free speech and association	.1163	.3209	0	1
Gays in the military	.1302	.3368	0	1
Sexual orientation discrimination	.2483	.4324	0	1
Sodomy constitutionality	.1806	.3850	0	1
Age	2.4219	.7009	1	3

Variable	Mean	Standard deviation	Minimum	Maximum
Catholic	.2431	.4293	0	1
Jewish	.1441	.3515	0	1
Female	.1580	.3650	0	1
Minority	.0625	.2423	0	1
Prior nonjudicial office	.1719	.3776	0	1
Democrat	.5350	.4990	0	1
Democrat★environmental ideology	26.9358	28.6228	0	97.10
Democrat★term	1.7639	2.0599	0	5
Democrat★environmental ideology★term	92.1329	122.2944	0	485.50
Appointed	.5642	.4963	0	1
Appointed★environmental ideology	30.2764	30.1307	0	97.10
Appointed★term	2.7361	2.4601	0	5
Appointed★environmental ideology★term	144.2829	144.2342	0	485.50
Legis	.005208	.07204	0	1
Legis★environmental ideology	.1711	2.3673	0	32.86
Legis★term	.01042	.1441	0	2
Legis★environmental ideology★term	.3423	4.7347	0	65.72
Merit	.1458	.3532	0	1
Merit★environmental ideology	6.9398	18.1648	0	95.75
Merit★term	.3507	.9773	0	4
Merit★environmental ideology★term	18.0303	54.6455	0	287.25
Term	3.6667	1.6440	1	5
Environmental ideology	51.1418	17.3626	8.13	97.10
Environmental ideology★term	192.4724	114.1724	17.68	485.50
Consensual sodomy law	.5156	.5002	0	1
Gay civil rights law	.1719	.3776	0	1
Post-1990	.6788	.4673	0	1
Gay interest Group	.6875	.4639	0	1
Court of last resort	.4132	.4928	0	1

Summary Statistics for the Supplemental Variables in Appendix 4.6

Variable	Mean	Standard deviation	Minimum	Maximum
Federal constitutional issue	.2744	.4466	0	1
State constitutional issue	.1639	.3705	0	1
Privacy clause	.1068	.3092	0	1

Summary Statistics for the Supplemental Variables in Appendix 4.7

Variable	Mean	Standard deviation	Minimum	Maximum
Federal constitutional issue	.3404	.4741	0	1
State constitutional issue	.03683	.1885	0	1
Privacy clause	.1406	.3478	0	1

Summary Statistics for the Variables in Appendix 4.8

Variable	Mean	Standard deviation	Minimum	Maximum
Outcome	.3457	.4763	0	1
Federal constitutional issue	.7809	.4143	0	1
Negative precedent	.3673	.4828	0	1
Positive precedent	.01852	.1350	0	1
Gay male litigant	.8056	.3964	0	1
Gay family issue	.03395	.1814	0	1
Free speech and association	.1265	.3330	0	1
Gays in the military	.2685	.4439	0	1
Sexual orientation discrimination	.4228	.4948	0	1
Sodomy constitutionality	.08642	.2814	0	1
Age	2.5247	.6555	1	3
Catholic	.2562	.4372	0	1
Jewish	.1420	.3496	0	1
Female	.1420	.3496	0	1
Minority	.07099	.2572	0	1
Prior nonjudicial office	.1296	.3364	0	1
Democrat	.3890	.4880	0	1
Environmental ideology	49.2834	15.1816	11.41	97.10
Consensual sodomy law	.4537	.4986	0	1
Gay civil rights law	.04938	.2170	0	1
Post-1990	.5617	.4969	0	1
Gay interest group	.6235	.4853	0	1
Court of last resort	.1080	.3109	0	1

Summary Statistics for the Variables in Appendix 4.9

Variable	Mean	Standard deviation	Minimum	Maximum
Outcome	.5552	.4972	0	1
Federal constitutional issue	.1803	.3846	0	1
State constitutional issue	.1094	.3123	0	1
Privacy clause	.1650	.3714	0	1
Negative precedent	.1444	.3516	0	1
Positive precedent	.1327	.3394	0	1
Gay male litigant	.4269	.4949	0	1
Gay family issue	.7489	.4339	0	1
Free speech and association	.02332	.1510	0	1
Gays in the military	.01345	.1153	0	1
Sexual orientation discrimination	.1112	.3145	0	1
Sodomy constitutionality	.07444	.2626	0	1
Age	2.3363	.7209	1	3
Catholic	.2619	.4399	0	1
Jewish	.1381	.3452	0	1
Female	.1552	.3622	0	1
Minority	.06996	.2552	0	1
Prior nonjudicial office	.2422	.4286	0	1
Democrat	.6390	.4810	0	1
Democrat*environmental ideology	32.9699	28.4425	0	95.75
Democrat*term	1.6511	1.6496	0	5
Democrat*environmental ideology*term	93.3159	112.2859	0	446.25
Appointed	.1561	.3631	0	1
Appointed*environmental ideology	11.1848	27.0349	0	94.22
Appointed*term	.6143	1.5418	0	5
Appointed*environmental ideology*term	43.0819	112.2216	0	446.25
Legis	.03587	.1861	0	1
Legis*environmental ideology	1.0630	5.8107	0	43.20
Legis*term	.1004	.5675	0	4
Legis*environmental ideology*term	2.9137	17.5823	0	171.00
Merit	.2843	.4513	0	1
Merit*environmental ideology	13.2342	22.2845	0	95.75
Merit*term	.7166	1.3006	0	4

(*continued*)

(*continued*)

Variable	Mean	Standard deviation	Minimum	Maximum
Merit★environmental ideology★term	35.5179	69.3018	0	287.25
Term	2.6018	1.3929	1	5
Environmental ideology	51.7868	16.9377	8.13	95.75
Environmental ideology★term	145.5022	108.9971	17.68	446.25
Consensual sodomy law	.4457	.4973	0	1
Gay civil rights law	.1614	.3681	0	1
Post-1990	.7327	.4427	0	1
Gay interest group	.5507	.4976	0	1
Court of last resort	.4556	.4982	0	1

Appendix 5.1

Precedential Variable Coding for Intermediate Appellate Courts

Negative precedent, same court	1 if a controlling precedent was against a lesbian and gay rights claim and came from the same district or circuit as the intermediate appellate court deciding the case 0 otherwise
Positive precedent, same court	1 if a controlling precedent was in favor of a lesbian and gay rights claim and came from the same district or circuit as the intermediate appellate court deciding the case 0 otherwise
Negative precedent, higher court	1 if a controlling precedent was against a lesbian and gay rights claim and came from a higher appellate court of the same state (if a state case) or the U.S. Supreme Court (if a federal case) 0 otherwise
Positive precedent, higher court	1 if a controlling precedent was in favor of a lesbian and gay rights claim and came from a higher appellate court of the same state (if a state case) or the U.S. Supreme Court (if a federal case) 0 otherwise

Negative precedent, other district   1 if a precedent was against a lesbian and gay rights claim and came
from a district within the state different from the intermediate appellate court deciding the case (if a state
case) or from another circuit (if a
federal case)
0 otherwise

Positive precedent, other district   1 if a precedent was in favor of
a lesbian and gay rights claim and
came from a district within the state
different from the intermediate appellate court deciding the case (if a
state case) or from another circuit (if
a federal case)
0 otherwise

Appendix 5.2

Cases Decided Under the Influence of Controlling Precedent*

Unless otherwise indicated, case citations appear in Appendix 1.2.

Case	Controlling precedent
United States Courts of Appeals	
First Circuit	
Rosa v. Park West Bank & Trust Co.	*Higgins v. New Balance Athletic Shoe, Inc.*
Silva v. Sifflard	*Higgins v. New Balance Athletic Shoe, Inc.*
Fourth Circuit	
Walls v. City of Petersburg	*Bowers v. Hardwick*
Selland v. Perry	*Thomasson v. Perry*
Thorne v. U.S. Department of Defense	*Thomasson v. Perry*
Fifth Circuit	
Matter of Longstaff	*Boutilier v. I.N.S.*, 387 U.S. 118 (1967)
Baker v. Wade	*Doe v. Commonwealth's Attorney*, 425 U.S. 901 (1976)
Sixth Circuit	
Gay Inmates of Shelby County Jail v. Barksdale	*Bowers v. Hardwick*

* If intermediate appellate court cases were decided under the influence of both higher court and same court precedents, only the former is listed here.

Dillon v. Frank

Equality Foundation of Greater Cincinnati, Inc. v. City of Cincinnati

Stemler v. City of Florence
Seventh Circuit
Hamner v. St. Vincent Hospital and Health Care Center, Inc.
Peterson v. Bodlovich
Spearman v. Ford Motor Company
Eighth Circuit
U.S. v. Lemons
Ninth Circuit
Hatheway v. Secretary of the Army

Hill v. U.S. Immigration and Naturalization Service
Watkins v. U.S. Army (1983)
Schowengerdt v. General Dynamics Corp.

Watkins v. U.S. Army (1988)
Watkins v. U.S. Army (1989)
High Tech Gays v. Defense Indus. Sec. Clearance Office
Schmidt v. U.S.
Schowengerdt v. U.S.
Pruitt v. Cheney
Lewis v. Alcorn

Meinhold v. U.S. Department of Defense
Holmes v. California Army National Guard
Jackson v. U.S. Department of the Air Force
Philips v. Perry
Tenth Circuit
Jantz v. Muci

Ruth v. Children's Medical Center
Romer v. Evans

Romer v. Evans

Ulane v. Eastern Airlines, Inc., 742 F.2d 1081 (1984)
Nabozny v. Podlesny
Ulane v. Eastern Airlines, Inc.

Doe v. Commonwealth's Attorney

Beller v. Middendorf, 632 F.2d 788 (1980)
Boutilier v. I.N.S.

Beller v. Middendorf
DeSantis v. Pacific Telephone & Telegraph Co., 608 F.2d 327 (1979)
Bowers v. Hardwick
Bowers v. Hardwick
Bowers v. Hardwick

Bowers v. Hardwick
Bowers v. Hardwick
Bowers v. Hardwick
DeSantis v. Pacific Telephone & Telegraph Co.
Bowers v. Hardwick

Bowers v. Hardwick

Bowers v. Hardwick

Bowers v. Hardwick

Bowers v. Hardwick

Curran v. Mount Diablo Council of the Boy Scouts of America (1994)	*Curran v. Mount Diablo Council of the Boy Scouts of America* (1983)
West v. Superior Court	*Curiale v. Reagan*
Guardianship of Z.C.W.	*Nancy S. v. Michele G.*
Guardianship of Olivia J.	*Nancy S. v. Michele G.*

Florida
District Court of Appeal

Reeves v. State	*State v. Stalder*, 630 So.2d 1072 (1994)
Ward v. Ward	*Maradie v. Maradie*
Packard v. Packard	*Maradie v. Maradie*

Georgia
Supreme Court

City of Atlanta v. Morgan	*City of Atlanta v. McKinney*
Powell v. State	*Christensen v. State*

Illinois
Appellate Court

Petition of K.M. and D.M.	*Marriage of Pleasant*

Indiana
Court of Appeals

Pennington v. Pennington	*D.H. v. J.H.*
Teegarden v. Teegarden	*D.H. v. J.H.*
Knotts v. Knotts	*D.H. v. J.H.*
Marlow v. Marlow	*Pennington v. Pennington*

Iowa
Court of Appeals

Marriage of Wiarda	*Marriage of Walsh*
Marriage of Cupples	*Marriage of Walsh*

Louisiana
Court of Appeal

Scott v. Scott	*Lundin v. Lundin*

Maryland
Court of Special Appeals

Boswell v. Boswell	*North v. North*

Massachusetts
Appeals Court
  Doe v. Doe   *Bezio v. Patenaude*, 381 Mass. 563,
                           410 N.E.2d 1207 (1980)
Supreme Judicial Court
  Adoption of Galen   *Adoption of Tammy*

Minnesota
Court of Appeals
  Blanding v. Sports & Health   *Potter v. LaSalle Sports & Health*
    Club, Inc.   *Club*
  Guardianship of Kowalski (1991)   *Guardianship of Kowalski*
                         (1986)
  Foley v. County of Hennepin   *Bohdan v. Alltool Mfg. Co.*

Mississippi
Supreme Court
  Bowen v. Bowen   *White v. Thompson*
  Weigand v. Houghton   *White v. Thompson*

Missouri
Court of Appeals
  J.L.P.(H.) v. D.J.P.   *N.K.M. v. L.E.M.*, 606 S.W.2d 179
                         (1980)
  G.A. v. D.A.   *N.K.M. v. L.E.M.*
  S.E.G. v. R.A.G.   *T.C.H. v. K.M.H.*
  S.L.H. v. D.B.H.   *T.C.H. v. K.M.H.*
  J.P. v. P.W.   *T.C.H. v. K.M.H.*
  T.C.H. v. K.M.H.   *T.C.H. v. K.M.H.*
  Delong v. Delong   *T.C.H. v. K.M.H.*
Supreme Court
  J.A.D. v. F.J.D.   *T.C.H. v. K.M.H.*

Montana
Supreme Court
  Gryczan v. State   *State v. Ballew*, 166 Mont. 270, 532
                         P.2d 407 (1975)

New Hampshire
Supreme Court
  Stuart v. State   *Opinion of the Justices*

New York
Supreme Court, Appellate Term
  420 East 80ᵗʰ Company v. Chin

  Koppelman v. O'Keeffe

Supreme Court, Appellate Division
  Anonymous v. Anonymous

  *Dally v. Orange County
  Publications*
  *Braschi v. Stahl Associates
  Company (1988)*
  Alison D. v. Virginia M.

  *East 10ᵗʰ Street Associates v.
  Estate of Goldstein*
  Park Holding Company v. Power

  *Rent Stabilization Association of
  New York City, Inc. v. Higgins*
  (1990)
  *Gay Teachers Association v.
  Board of Education*
  *Rent Stabilization Association of
  New York City, Inc. v. Higgins*
  (1993)
  Adoption of Anonymous
  Paul C. v. Tracy C.
  Matter of Christine G.
  Lynda A. H. v. Diane T. O.
  *Raum v. Restaurant Associates,
  Inc.*
Court of Appeals
  People v. Uplinger

  *Rent Stabilization Association of
  New York City, Inc. v. Higgins*

Hudson View Properties v. Weiss, 86
A.D.2d 803, 448 N.Y.S.2d 649
(1982)
Braschi v. Stahl Associates Company
(1988)

DiStefano v. DiStefano, 60 A.D.2d
976, 401 N.Y.S.2d 636 (1978)
Matherson v. Marchello

Two Associates v. Brown

Braschi v. Stahl Associates Company
(1989)
Braschi v. Stahl Associates Company
(1989)
Braschi v. Stahl Associates Company
(1989)
Braschi v. Stahl Associates Company
(1989)

Braschi v. Stahl Associates Company
(1989)
Braschi v. Stahl Associates Company
(1989)

DiStefano v. DiStefano
DiStefano v. DiStefano
Matter of Jacob
Alison D. v. Virginia M. (1991)
Braschi v. Stahl Associates Company
(1989)

People v. Onofre, 51 N.Y.2d 476,
434 N.Y.S.2d 947, 415 N.E.2d
936 (1980)
Braschi v. Stahl Associates Company
(1989)

North Dakota
Supreme Court
 Johnson v. Schlotman   *Jacobson v. Jacobson*

Ohio
Court of Appeals
 Inscoe v. Inscoe   *Conkel v. Conkel*
 State v. Thompson   *State v. Faulk*, Ohio Supreme Court,
              Case No. 78-1443 (June 16,
              1979, unreported)

Oklahoma
Supreme Court
 Fox v. Fox   *M.J.P. v. J.G.P.*

Pennsylvania
Superior Court
 Pascarella v. Pascarella   *Constant A. v. Paul C.A.*
 Barron v. Barron   *Constant A. v. Paul C.A.*
 T.B. v. L.R.M.   *J.A.L. v. E.P.H.*

South Dakota
Supreme Court
 Van Driel v. Van Driel   *Chicoine v. Chicoine*

Tennessee
Court of Appeals
 Price v. Price   *Matter of Parsons*
 Eldridge v. Eldridge   *Dailey v. Dailey*

Texas
Court of Appeals
 City of Dallas v. England   *State v. Morales* (1992)

Utah
Court of Appeals
 Tucker v. Tucker   *Kallas v. Kallas*, 614 P.2d 641
              (1980)

Virginia
Court of Appeals
 Bottoms v. Bottoms (1994) *Roe v. Roe*
 Bottoms v. Bottoms (1997) *Bottoms v. Bottoms* (1995)
 Piatt v. Piatt   *Bottoms v. Bottoms* (1995)

Bottoms v. Bottoms (1999)   *Bottoms v. Bottoms* (1995)
Supreme Court
Bottoms v. Bottoms   *Roe v. Roe*

Washington
Court of Appeals
Marriage of Cabalquinto (1986)   *Marriage of Cabalquinto* (1983)
Marriage of Wicklund   *Marriage of Cabalquinto* (1983)

West Virginia
Supreme Court of Appeals
M.S.P. v. P.E.P.   *Rowsey v. Rowsey*
Jenkins v. Jenkins   *Rowsey v. Rowsey*

Wisconsin
Supreme Court
Custody of H.S.H.-K.   *Interest of Z.J.H.*

Appendix 5.3

Logistic Regression Statistics for Votes in Intermediate Appellate Courts (with Expanded Stare Decisis *Variables)*

Independent variable	N	Beta	Impact
Negative precedent, same court (standard error)	136	−0.749* (0.300)	−.182[a]
Positive precedent, same court	64	0.682 (0.350)	
Negative precedent, higher court	121	0.893** (0.319)	+.215[a]
Positive precedent, higher court	63	2.742*** (0.432)	+.479[a]
Negative precedent, other district	189	−1.056*** (0.291)	−.252[a]
Positive precedent, other district	96	0.111 (0.342)	
Gay male litigant	495	−0.185 (0.189)	
Gay family issue	502	−2.058*** (0.530)	−.472[a]
Free speech and association	44	2.226** (0.702)	+.422[a]
Gays in the military	91	−0.639 (0.603)	
Sexual orientation discrimination	185	−1.945*** (0.506)	−.421[a]
Sodomy constitutionality	37	−0.839 (0.640)	

(continued)

(*continued*)

Independent variable	N	Beta	Impact
Age	896	−0.399** (0.132)	−.098[b]
Catholic	243	−0.381 (0.211)	
Jewish	136	0.755** (0.276)	+.184[a]
Female	130	0.262 (0.248)	
Minority	65	1.206*** (0.360)	+.277[a]
Prior nonjudicial office	174	−0.367 (0.230)	
Democrat	525	−3.479 (2.161)	
Democrat⋆environmental ideology	525	0.065 (0.046)	
Democrat⋆term	525	1.020 (0.529)	
Democrat⋆environmental ideology⋆term	525	−0.014 (0.011)	
Appointed	296	−13.126*** (2.720)	
Appointed⋆environmental ideology	296	0.204*** (0.039)	
Legis	21	24.288 (66.155)	
Legis⋆environmental ideology	21	−0.270 (1.885)	
Legis⋆term	21	−18.698 (33.761)	
Legis⋆environmental ideology⋆term	21	0.291 (0.969)	
Merit	186	3.832 (3.908)	
Merit⋆environmental ideology	186	−0.048 (0.085)	
Merit⋆term	186	−4.822** (1.535)	
Merit⋆environmental ideology⋆term	186	0.080** (0.031)	
Term	896	2.767*** (0.788)	

Independent variable	N	Beta	Impact
Environmental ideology	896	0.006	
		(0.045)	
Environmental ideology*term	896	−0.045**	
		(0.014)	
Consensual sodomy law	381	−0.006	
		(0.234)	
Gay civil rights law	71	1.045**	+.245[a]
		(0.339)	
Post-1990	592	0.787***	+.193[a]
		(0.206)	
Gay interest group	464	−0.030	
		(0.181)	
Federal court	289	−1.259	
		(0.992)	
Intercept		1.349	
		(2.348)	

Note: Model N = 896; model chi-square = 354.219; df = 40; model p < .0001; −2 log likelihood = 887.740; Cox & Snell pseudo-R^2 = .327; Nagelkerke pseudo-R^2 = .435; classified correctly = 75.89%; reduction in error = 51.13%.
[a] Impact of an increase from 0 to 1.
[b] Impact of a one-unit increase from the mean of the independent variable.
* p < .05; ** p < .01; *** p < .001.

Summary Statistics for the Supplemental Variables in Appendix 5.3

Variable	Mean	Standard deviation	Minimum	Maximum
Negative precedent, same court	.1518	.3590	0	1
Positive precedent, same court	.07143	.2577	0	1
Negative precedent, higher court	.1350	.3420	0	1
Positive precedent, higher court	.07031	.2558	0	1
Negative precedent, other district	.2109	.4082	0	1
Positive precedent, other district	.1071	.3095	0	1

References

Aden, Steven H. 2000. "A Tale of Two Cities in the Gay Rights Kulturkampf: Are the Federal Courts Presiding over the Cultural Balkanization of America?" *Wake Forest Law Review* 35: 295.

"After California, What's Next for Judicial Elections?" 1987. *Judicature* 70: 356.

Alexander, Larry. 1989. "Constrained by Precedent." 63 *Southern California Law Review* 63: 1.

Amar, Akhil Reed. 1985. "A Neo-Federalist View of Article III: Separating the Two Tiers of Federal Jurisdiction." *Boston University Law Review* 65: 205.

1991. "Parity as a Constitutional Question." *Boston University Law Review* 71: 645.

Ansolabehere, Stephen, James M. Snyder, Jr., and Charles Stewart III. 2001. "The Effects of Party and Preferences on Congressional Roll Call Voting." *Legislative Studies Quarterly* 26: 533.

Ashenfelter, Orley, Theodore Eisenberg, and Stewart J. Schwab. 1995. "Politics and the Judiciary: The Influence of Judicial Background on Case Outcomes." *Journal of Legal Studies* 24: 257.

Atkins, Burton M., and Justin J. Green. 1976. "Consensus on the United States Courts of Appeals: Illusion or Reality?" *American Journal of Political Science* 20: 735.

Babbie, Earl. 1995. *The Practice of Social Research*. Belmont, Calif.: Wadsworth.

Bachrach, Peter, and Morton S. Baratz. 1962. "The Two Faces of Power." *American Political Science Review* 56: 947.

1970. *Power and Poverty: Theory and Practice*. New York: Oxford University Press.

Badgett, M. V. Lee. 2001. *Money, Myths, and Change: The Economic Lives of Lesbians and Gay Men*. Chicago: University of Chicago Press.

Bailey, Robert W. 1999. *Gay Politics, Urban Politics: Identity and Economics in the Urban Setting*. New York: Columbia University Press.

Banks, Christopher P. 1992. "The Supreme Court and Precedent: An Analysis of Natural Courts and Reversal Trends." *Judicature* 75: 262.

1999. "Reversals of Precedent and Judicial Policy-Making: How Judicial Conceptions of *Stare Decisis* in the U.S. Supreme Court Influence Social Change." *Akron Law Review* 32: 233.

Barnes, David W. 2001. "Too Many Probabilities: Statistical Evidence of Tort Causation." *Law and Contemporary Problems* 64: 191.

Bator, Paul M. 1963. "Finality in Criminal Law and Federal Habeas Corpus for State Prisoners." *Harvard Law Review* 76: 441.

1981. "The State Courts and Federal Constitutional Litigation." *William and Mary Law Review* 22: 605.

Batson, C. Daniel, and Christopher T. Burris. 1994. "Personal Religion: Depressant or Stimulant of Prejudice and Discrimination?" In Mark P. Zanna and James M. Olson (eds.), *The Psychology of Prejudice: The Ontario Symposium.* Mahwah, N.J.: Lawrence Erlbaum Associates.

Baum, Lawrence. 1993. "Making Judicial Policies in the Political Arena." In Carl E. Van Horn (ed.), *The State of the States*, 2nd ed. Washington, D.C.: CQ Press.

1994. "Remarks." *Law and Courts* 4: 3.

1997. *The Puzzle of Judicial Behavior.* Ann Arbor: University of Michigan Press.

1998. *American Courts*, 4th ed. Boston: Houghton Mifflin.

Beiner, Theresa M. 1999. "What Will Diversity on the Bench Mean for Justice?" *Michigan Journal of Gender and Law* 6: 113.

Bergman, Jed I. 1996. "Putting Precedent in Its Place: *Stare Decisis* and Federal Predictions of State Law." *Columbia Law Review* 96: 969.

Berry, William D., Evan J. Ringquist, Richard C. Fording, and Russell L. Hanson. 1998. "Measuring Citizen and Government Ideology in the American States, 1960–93." *American Journal of Political Science* 42: 327.

Blasius, Mark (ed.). 2000. *Sexual Identities, Queer Politics.* Princeton, N.J.: Princeton University Press.

Blaustein, Albert P., and Roy M. Mersky. 1978. *The First One Hundred Justices: Statistical Studies on the Supreme Court of the United States.* Hamden, Conn.: Archon Books.

Blendon, Robert J., John M. Benson, Mollyann Brodie, Drew E. Altman, Richard Morin, Claudia Deane, and Nina Kjellson. 2000. "America's Changing Political and Moral Values." In E. J. Dionne, Jr., and John J. DiIulio, Jr. (eds.), *What's God Got to Do with the American Experiment?* Washington, D.C.: Brookings Institution Press.

Bork, Robert H. 1990. *The Tempting of America: The Political Seduction of the Law.* New York: Simon and Schuster.

Bowen, Don Ramsey. 1965. "The Explanation of Judicial Voting Behavior from Sociological Characteristics of Judges." Ph.D. dissertation, Yale University.

Brace, Paul, and Melinda Gann Hall. 1990. "Neo-Institutionalism and Dissent in State Supreme Courts." *Journal of Politics* 52: 54.

1993. "Integrated Models of Judicial Dissent." *Journal of Politics* 55: 914.

1995. "Studying Courts Comparatively: The View from the American States." *Political Research Quarterly* 48: 5.

1997. "The Interplay of Preferences, Case Facts, Context, and Rules in the Politics of Judicial Choice." *Journal of Politics* 59: 1206.

Brenner, Saul, Timothy M. Hagle, and Harold Spaeth. 1990. "Increasing the Size of Minimum Winning Original Coalitions on the Warren Court." *Polity* 23: 309.

Brenner, Saul, and Harold J. Spaeth. 1995. *Stare Indecisis: The Alteration of Precedent on the Supreme Court, 1946–1992*. New York: Cambridge University Press.

Brenner, Saul, and Marc Stier. 1996. "Retesting Segal and Spaeth's *Stare Decisis* Model." *American Journal of Political Science* 40: 1036.

Brent, James C. 1999. "An Agent and Two Principals: U.S. Court of Appeals Responses to *Employment Division, Department of Human Resources v. Smith* and the Religious Freedom Restoration Act." *American Politics Quarterly* 27: 236.

Brewer, Sarah E., David Kaib, and Karen O'Connor. 2000. "Sex and the Supreme Court: Gays, Lesbians, and Justice." In Craig A. Rimmerman, Kenneth D. Wald, and Clyde Wilcox (eds.), *The Politics of Gay Rights*. Chicago: University of Chicago Press.

Brisbin, Richard A., Jr. 1996. "Slaying the Dragon: Segal, Spaeth and the Function of Law in Supreme Court Decision Making." *American Journal of Political Science* 40: 1004.

Brown, Jennifer Gerarda. 2000. "Sweeping Reform from Small Rules? Anti-Bias Canons as a Substitute for Heightened Scrutiny." *Minnesota Law Review* 85: 363.

Busch, Beverly G. 1999. " 'Seek the Welfare of the City': Theological Orientations and Political Participation in the United States." Paper presented at the Annual Meeting of the Midwest Political Science Association, Chicago, April 15–17.

Bush v. Gore. 2000. 531 U.S. 98.

Button, James W., Barbara A. Rienzo, and Kenneth D. Wald. 1997. *Private Lives, Public Conflicts: Battles over Gay Rights in American Communities*. Washington, D.C.: CQ Press.

Cain, Patricia A. 1993. "Litigating for Lesbian and Gay Rights: A Legal History." *Virginia Law Review* 79: 1551.

2000. *Rainbow Rights: The Role of Lawyers and Courts in the Lesbian and Gay Civil Rights Movement*. Boulder, Colo.: Westview Press.

Caldeira, Gregory A. 1994. "Review of *The Supreme Court and the Attitudinal Model*." *American Political Science Review* 88: 485.

Caldeira, Gregory A., and John R. Wright. 1988. "Organized Interests and Agenda Setting in the U.S. Supreme Court." *American Political Science Review* 82: 1109.

1990. "*Amici Curiae* Before the Supreme Court: Who Participates, When, and How Much?" *Journal of Politics* 52: 782.

Caminker, Evan H. 1994. "Why Must Inferior Courts Obey Superior Court Precedents?" *Stanford Law Review* 46: 817.

Camp, Bryan T. 1997. "Bound by the BAP: The *Stare Decisis* Effects of BAP Decisions." *San Diego Law Review* 34: 1643.

Canon, Bradley C. 1993. "Review of *The Supreme Court and the Attitudinal Model*." *Law and Politics Book Review* 3: 98.

Carp, Robert A., and Ronald Stidham. 2001. *Judicial Process in America*, 5th ed. Washington, D.C.: CQ Press.

Carrington, Paul D., Daniel R. Meador, and Maurice Rosenberg. 1976. *Justice on Appeal*. St. Paul, Minn.: West.

Cauthen, James N. G. 2000a. "Expanding Rights Under State Constitutions: A Quantitative Appraisal." *Albany Law Review* 63: 1183.

2000b. "Judicial Innovation Under State Constitutions: An Internal Determinants Investigation." *American Review of Politics* 21: 19.

Chambers v. Florida. 1940. 309 U.S. 227.

Chemerinsky, Erwin. 1988. "Parity Reconsidered: Defining a Role for the Federal Judiciary." *UCLA Law Review* 36: 233.

1991. "Ending the Parity Debate." *Boston University Law Review* 71: 593.

Chevron U.S.A., Inc. v. Natural Resources Defense Council, Inc. 1984. 467 U.S. 837.

Cohen, Linda R., and Matthew L. Spitzer. 1994. "Solving the *Chevron* Puzzle." *Law and Contemporary Problems* 57: 65.

Cohen, Mark A. 1991. "Explaining Judicial Behavior or What's 'Unconstitutional' About the Sentencing Commission?" *Journal of Law, Economics and Organization* 7: 183.

1992. "The Motives of Judges: Empirical Evidence from Antitrust Sentencing." *International Review of Law and Economics* 12: 13.

Cohen, Steven M., and Charles S. Liebman. 1997. "American Jewish Liberalism: Unraveling the Strands." *Public Opinion Quarterly* 61: 405.

Crenson, Matthew A. 1971. *The Un-Politics of Air Pollution: A Study of Non-Decisionmaking in the Cities*. Baltimore, Md.: Johns Hopkins Press.

Cross, Frank B. 1997. "Political Science and the New Legal Realism: A Case of Unfortunate Interdisciplinary Ignorance." *Northwestern University Law Review* 92: 251.

Cross, Frank B., and Emerson H. Tiller. 1998. "Judicial Partisanship and Obedience to Legal Doctrine: Whistleblowing on the Federal Courts of Appeals." *Yale Law Journal* 107: 2155.

Cross, Frank B., Michael Heise, and Gregory C. Sisk. 2002. "Above the Rules: A Response to Epstein and King." *University of Chicago Law Review* 69: 135.

Danelski, David J. 1964. *A Supreme Court Justice Is Appointed*. New York: Random House.

1986. "Causes and Consequences of Conflict and Its Resolution in the Supreme Court." In Sheldon Goldman and Charles M. Lamb (eds.), *Judicial Conflict and Consensus*. Lexington: University Press of Kentucky.

Daniel v. Daniel. 1998. 1998 WL 55000.

Davis, Sue, Susan Haire, and Donald R. Songer. 1993. "Voting Behavior and Gender on the U.S. Courts of Appeals." *Judicature* 77: 129.

D'Emilio, John. 1983. *Sexual Politics, Sexual Communities: The Making of a Homosexual Minority in the United States, 1940–1970*. Chicago: University of Chicago Press.

2000. "Cycles of Change, Questions of Strategy: The Gay and Lesbian Movement after Fifty Years." In Craig A. Rimmerman, Kenneth D. Wald, and Clyde Wilcox (eds.), *The Politics of Gay Rights*. Chicago: University of Chicago Press.

Diesel Construction Company, Inc. v. Cotten. 1994. 634 N.E.2d 1351.

Donovan, Todd, Jim Wenzel, and Shaun Bowler. 2000. "Direct Democracy and Gay Rights Initiatives after *Romer.*" In Craig A. Rimmerman, Kenneth D. Wald, and Clyde Wilcox (eds.), *The Politics of Gay Rights.* Chicago: University of Chicago Press.

Dorris, John B. 1999. "Antidiscrimination Laws in Local Government: A Public Policy Analysis of Municipal Lesbian and Gay Public Employment Protection." In Ellen D. B. Riggle and Barry L. Tadlock (eds.), *Gays and Lesbians in the Democratic Process: Public Policy, Public Opinion, and Political Representation.* New York: Columbia University Press.

Duberman, Martin. 1993. *Stonewall.* New York: Dutton.

Dubois, Philip L. 1988. "The Illusion of Judicial Consensus Revisited: Partisan Conflict on an Intermediate State Court of Appeals." *American Journal of Political Science* 32: 946.

Eckstein, Harry H. 1975. "Case Study and Theory in Political Science." In Fred I. Greenstein and Nelson W. Polsby (eds.), *Handbook of Political Science* 1: 79. Reading, Mass.: Addison-Wesley.

Eisenberg, Theodore, and Sheri Lynn Johnson. 1991. "The Effects of Intent: Do We Know How Legal Standards Work?" *Cornell Law Review* 76: 1151.

Eisenhower, James J., III. 1988. "Four Theories of Precedent and Its Role in Judicial Decisions." *Temple Law Review* 61: 871.

Ellison, Christopher G., and Marc A. Musick. 1993. "Southern Intolerance: A Fundamentalist Effect?" *Social Forces* 72: 379.

Emmert, Craig F. 1992. "An Integrated Case-Related Model of Judicial Decision Making: Explaining State Supreme Court Decisions in Judicial Review Cases." *Journal of Politics* 54: 543.

Emmert, Craig F., and Carol Ann Traut. 1994. "The California Supreme Court and the Death Penalty." *American Politics Quarterly* 22: 41.

Epstein, Lee, and Gary King. 2002. "The Rules of Inference." *University of Chicago Law Review* 69: 1.

Epstein, Lee, Jeffrey A. Segal, Harold J. Spaeth, and Thomas G. Walker. 1994. *The Supreme Court Compendium: Data, Decisions, and Developments.* Washington, D.C.: Congressional Quarterly.

Eskridge, William N., Jr. 1994. "Gaylegal Narratives." *Stanford Law Review* 46: 607.

———. 1999. *Gaylaw: Challenging the Apartheid of the Closet.* Cambridge, Mass.: Harvard University Press.

Estate of Cleveland. 1993. 17 Cal.App.4th 1700, 22 Cal.Rptr.2d 590.

Estate of Schwartz. 1996. 673 So.2d 116.

Estin, Ann Laquer. 1997. "When *Baehr* Meets *Romer*: Family Law Issues After Amendment 2." *University of Colorado Law Review* 68: 349.

Evans v. Evans. 1960. 185 Cal.App.2d 566, 8 Cal.Rptr. 412.

Ex Parte H.H. 2002. 830 So.2d 21.

Fabrizio, Paul. 1999. "Evolving into Morality Politics: U.S. Catholic Bishops' Statements on American Politics from 1792 to the Present." Paper presented at the Annual Meeting of the Midwest Political Science Association, Chicago, April 15–17.

Fisher, Marc, and Paul Farhi. 1997. "Baptists Vote to Boycott Disney Fare; 'Ellen,' Gay Policies Ignite Church Protest." *Washington Post*, June 19, p. A1.

Fisher, Randy D., Donna Derison, Chester F. Polley III, Jennifer Cadman, and Dana Johnston. 1994. "Religiousness, Religious Orientation, and Attitudes Towards Gays and Lesbians." *Journal of Applied Social Psychology* 24: 614.

Flemming, Gregory N., David B. Holian, and Susan Gluck Mezey. 1998. "An Integrated Model of Privacy Decision Making in State Supreme Courts." *American Politics Quarterly* 26: 35.

Friedman, Lawrence M. 1986. "The Law and Society Movement." *Stanford Law Review* 38: 763.

Friedrich, Robert J. 1982. "In Defense of Multiplicative Terms in Multiple Regression Equations." *American Journal of Political Science* 26: 797.

Gamble, Barbara S. 1997. "Putting Civil Rights to a Popular Vote." *American Journal of Political Science* 41: 245.

Garland, James Allon. 2001. "The Low Road to Violence: Governmental Discrimination as a Catalyst for Pandemic Hate Crime." *Law and Sexuality* 10: 1.

Gay Lib v. University of Missouri. 1977. 558 F.2d 848 (8th Cir.).

George, Tracey E. 1998. "Developing a Positive Theory of Decisionmaking on U.S. Courts of Appeals." *Ohio State Law Journal* 58: 1635.

George, Tracey E., and Lee Epstein. 1992. "On the Nature of Supreme Court Decision Making." *American Political Science Review* 86: 323.

Gerber, Scott D., and Keeok Park. 1997. "The Quixotic Search for Consensus on the U.S. Supreme Court: A Cross-Judicial Empirical Analysis of the Rehnquist Court Justices." *American Political Science Review* 91: 390.

Gerhardt, Michael J. 1991. "The Role of Precedent in Constitutional Decision-making and Theory." *George Washington Law Review* 60: 68.

Gerry, Brett Christopher. 1999. "Parity Revisited: An Empirical Comparison of State and Lower Federal Court Interpretation of *Nollan v. California Coastal Commission*." *Harvard Journal of Law and Public Policy* 23: 233.

Gerstmann, Evan. 1999. *The Constitutional Underclass: Gays, Lesbians, and the Failure of Class-Based Equal Protection.* Chicago: University of Chicago Press.

Gibson, James L. 1987. "Homosexuals and the Ku Klux Klan: A Contextual Analysis of Political Tolerance." *Western Political Quarterly* 40: 427.

Giles, Michael W., and Christopher Zorn. 2000. "Gibson versus Case-Based Approaches." *Law and Courts* 10: 10.

Gill, Jeff. 2001. "Interpreting Interactions and Interaction Hierarchies in Generalized Linear Models: Issues and Applications." Paper presented at the Annual Meeting of the American Political Science Association, San Francisco, August 30–September 2.

Gillman, Howard. 2001. "What's Law Got to Do with It? Judicial Behavioralists Test the 'Legal Model' of Judicial Decision Making." *Law and Social Inquiry* 26: 465.

Goldman, Sheldon. 1966. "Voting Behavior on the United States Courts of Appeals, 1961–1964." *American Political Science Review* 60: 374.

1975. "Voting Behavior on the United States Courts of Appeals Revisited." *American Political Science Review* 69: 491.

1997. *Picking Federal Judges: Lower Court Selection from Roosevelt Through Reagan*. New Haven: Yale University Press.

Graber, Mark A. 2002. "Constitutional Politics and Constitutional Theory: A Misunderstood and Neglected Relationship." *Law and Social Inquiry* 27: 309.

Graves v. Businelle Towing Corp. 1996. 673 So.2d 311.

Green, John C. 2000. "Antigay: Varieties of Opposition to Gay Rights." In Craig A. Rimmerman, Kenneth D. Wald, and Clyde Wilcox (eds.), *The Politics of Gay Rights*. Chicago: University of Chicago Press.

Griswold v. Connecticut. 1965. 381 U.S. 479, 85 S.Ct. 1678.

Grodin, Joseph R. 1989. *In Pursuit of Justice: Reflections of a State Supreme Court Justice*. Berkeley: University of California Press.

Groot, Roger D. 1971. "The Effects of an Intermediate Appellate Court on the Supreme Court Work Product." *Wake Forest Law Review* 7: 548.

Grossman, Joel B. 1966. "Social Backgrounds and Judicial Decision-Making." *Harvard Law Review* 79: 1551.

Gruhl, John. 1980. "The Supreme Court's Impact on the Law of Libel: Compliance by Lower Federal Courts." *Western Political Quarterly* 33: 502.

Haeberle, Steven H. 1996. "Gay Men and Lesbians at City Hall." *Social Science Quarterly* 77: 190.

1999. "Gay and Lesbian Rights: Emerging Trends in Public Opinion and Voting Behavior." In Ellen D. B. Riggle and Barry L. Tadlock (eds.), *Gays and Lesbians in the Democratic Process: Public Policy, Public Opinion, and Political Representation*. New York: Columbia University Press.

Haider-Markel, Donald P. 2000. "Lesbian and Gay Politics in the States: Interest Groups, Electoral Politics, and Policy." In Craig A. Rimmerman, Kenneth D. Wald, and Clyde Wilcox (eds.), *The Politics of Gay Rights*. Chicago: University of Chicago Press.

Haider-Markel, Donald P., and Kenneth J. Meier. 1996. "The Politics of Gay and Lesbian Rights: Expanding the Scope of the Conflict." *Journal of Politics* 58: 332.

Hall, Jeffrey L. 1997. "Coming Out in West Virginia: Child Custody and Visitation Disputes Involving Gay or Lesbian Parents." *West Virginia Law Review* 100: 107.

Hall, Melinda Gann, and Paul Brace. 1989. "Order in the Courts: A Neo-Institutional Approach to Judicial Consensus." *Western Political Quarterly* 42: 391.

1992. "Toward an Integrated Model of Judicial Voting Behavior." *American Politics Quarterly* 20: 147.

1996. "Justices' Responses to Case Facts: An Interactive Model." *American Politics Quarterly* 24: 237.

1999. "State Supreme Courts and Their Environments: Avenues to General Theories of Judicial Choice." In Cornell W. Clayton and Howard Gillman (eds.), *Supreme Court Decision-Making: New Institutionalist Approaches*. Chicago: University of Chicago Press.

Halley, Janet E. 1993. "Reasoning About Sodomy: Act and Identity in and After *Bowers v. Hardwick*." *Virginia Law Review* 79: 1721.

1999. *Don't: A Reader's Guide to the Military's Anti-Gay Policy*. Durham, N.C.: Duke University Press.

Hannon, Sherene D. 1999. "License to Oppress: The Aftermath of *Bowers v. Hardwick* Is Still Felt Today: *Shahar v. Bowers.*" *Pace Law Review* 19: 507.

Hart, Robert A., Jr., and David H. Clark. 1999. "Does Size Matter? Exploring the Small Sample Properties of Maximum Likelihood Estimation." Paper presented at the Annual Meeting of the Midwest Political Science Association, Chicago, April 15–17.

Hasen, Richard L. 1997. " 'High Court Wrongly Elected': A Public Choice Model of Judging and Its Implications for the Voting Rights Act." *North Carolina Law Review* 75: 1305.

Hasnas, John. 1995. "The Myth of the Rule of Law." *Wisconsin Law Review* 1995: 199.

Hausegger, Lori. 1998. "The Impact of Interest Groups on Judicial Decision Making: A Comparison of Women's Groups in the U.S. and Canada." Paper presented at the Annual Meeting of the American Political Science Association, Boston, September 3–6.

Heise, Michael. 1999. "The Importance of Being Empirical." *Pepperdine Law Review* 26: 807.

Hensen v. Haff. 1934. 291 U.S. 559.

Herek, Gregory M. 1993. "On Prejudice Toward Gay People and Gays as Security Risks." In Marc Wolinsky and Kenneth Sherrill (eds.), *Gays and the Military: Joseph Steffan versus the United States*. Princeton, N.J.: Princeton University Press.

Herman, Didi. 1997. *The Antigay Agenda: Orthodox Vision and the Christian Right*. Chicago: University of Chicago Press.

Herman, Susan N. 1991. "Why Parity Matters." *Boston University Law Review* 71: 651.

Herrick, Rebekah, and Sue Thomas. 1999. "The Effects of Sexual Orientation on Citizen Perceptions of Candidate Viability." In Ellen D. B. Riggle and Barry L. Tadlock (eds.), *Gays and Lesbians in the Democratic Process: Public Policy, Public Opinion, and Political Representation*. New York: Columbia University Press.

Hines v. Superior Court. 1994. 12 Cal.Rptr.2d 216.

Huang, Chi, and Todd G. Shields. 2000. "Interpretation of Interaction Effects in Logit and Probit Analyses: Reconsidering the Relationship Between Registration Laws, Education, and Voter Turnout." *American Politics Quarterly* 28: 80.

Idleman, Scott C. 2000. "Tort Liability, Religious Entities, and the Decline of Constitutional Protection." *Indiana Law Journal* 75: 219.

Ifill, Sherrilyn A. 2000. "Racial Diversity on the Bench: Beyond Role Models and Public Confidence." *Washington and Lee Law Review* 57: 405.

Jackson, Vicki C. 1998. "*Printz* and *Testa*: The Infrastructure of Federal Supremacy." *Indiana Law Review* 32: 111.

Jennings, M. Kent, and Richard G. Niemi. 1981. *Generations and Politics*. Princeton, N.J.: Princeton University Press.

Johnson, Charles A. 1987. "Law, Politics, and Judicial Decision Making: Lower Federal Court Uses of Supreme Court Decisions." *Law and Society Review* 21: 325.

Keen, Lisa, and Suzanne B. Goldberg. 1998. *Strangers to the Law: Gay People on Trial.* Ann Arbor: University of Michigan Press.

Kerr, Orin S. 1998. "Shedding Light on *Chevron*: An Empirical Study of the *Chevron* Doctrine in the U.S. Courts of Appeals." *Yale Journal on Regulation* 15: 1.

King, Gary. 1995. "Replication, Replication." *PS: Political Science and Politics* 28: 444.

———. 1997. *A Solution to the Ecological Inference Problem: Reconstructing Individual Behavior from Aggregate Data.* Princeton, N.J.: Princeton University Press.

King, Gary, Robert O. Keohane, and Sidney Verba. 1994. *Designing Social Inquiry: Scientific Inference in Qualitative Research.* Princeton, N.J.: Princeton University Press.

Kite, Mary E. 1984. "Sex Differences in Attitudes Toward Homosexuals: A Meta-Analytic Review." In John De Cecco (ed.), *Homophobia: An Overview.* New York: Haworth.

Kite, Mary E., and Bernard E. Whitley, Jr. 1996. "Sex Differences in Attitudes Toward Homosexual Persons, Behaviors, and Civil Rights: A Meta-Analysis." *Personality and Social Psychology Bulletin* 22: 336.

Klawitter, Marieka, and Brian Hammer. 1999. "Spatial and Temporal Diffusion of Local Antidiscrimination Policies for Sexual Orientation." In Ellen D. B. Riggle and Barry L. Tadlock (eds.), *Gays and Lesbians in the Democratic Process: Public Policy, Public Opinion, and Political Representation.* New York: Columbia University Press.

Klein, Benjamin. 1976. "Comment." *Journal of Law and Economics* 19: 309.

Knight, Jack, and Lee Epstein. 1996. "The Norm of *Stare Decisis.*" *American Journal of Political Science* 40: 1018.

Kohut, Andrew, John C. Green, Scott Keeter, and Robert C. Toth. 2000. *The Diminishing Divide: Religion's Changing Role in American Politics.* Washington, D.C.: Brookings Institution Press.

Koppelman, Andrew. 2000. "Why Gay Legal History Matters." *Harvard Law Review* 113: 2035.

———. 2002. *The Gay Rights Question in Contemporary American Law.* Chicago: University of Chicago Press.

Kornhauser, Lewis A., and Lawrence G. Sage. 1993. "The One and the Many: Adjudication in Collegial Courts." *California Law Review* 81: 1.

Kosma, Montgomery N. 1998. "Measuring the Influence of Supreme Court Justices." *Journal of Legal Studies* 27: 333.

Kovacs, Kathryn E. 1999. "Accepting the Relegation of Takings Claims to State Courts: The Federal Courts' Misguided Attempts to Avoid Preclusion Under *Williamson County.*" *Ecology Law Quarterly* 26: 1.

Landes, William M., and Richard A. Posner. 1976. "Legal Precedent: A Theoretical and Empirical Analysis." *Journal of Law and Economics* 19: 249.

Landes, William M., Lawrence Lessig, and Michael E. Solimine. 1998. "Judicial Influence: A Citation Analysis of Federal Courts of Appeals Judges." *Journal of Legal Studies* 27: 271.

LaPiana, William P. 1994. *Logic and Experience: The Origin of Modern American Legal Education.* New York: Oxford University Press.

Latzer, Barry. 1996. "Toward the Decentralization of Criminal Procedure: State Constitutional Law and Selective Disincorporation." *Journal of Criminal Law and Criminology* 87: 63.

Lee, Emery G., III. 2000. "Federal Rights, Federal Forum: Section 1983 Challenges to State Convictions in Federal Court." *Case Western Reserve Law Review* 51: 353.

Lee, Thomas R., and Lance S. Lehnhof. 2001. "The Anastasoff Case and the Judicial Power to 'Unpublish' Opinions." *Notre Dame Law Review* 77: 135.

Leonard, Arthur S. 2000a. "A Retrospective on the *Lesbian/Gay Law Notes*." *New York Law School Journal of Human Rights* 17: 403.

2000b. "Chronicling a Movement: 20 Years of *Lesbian/Gay Law Notes*." *New York Law School Journal of Human Rights* 17: 415.

Lewis, Gregory B. 1997. "Lifting the Ban on Gays in the Civil Service: Federal Policy Toward Gay and Lesbian Employees since the Cold War." *Public Administration Review* 57: 387.

Lewis, Gregory B., and Jonathan L. Edelson. 2000. "DOMA and ENDA: Congress Votes on Gay Rights." In Craig A. Rimmerman, Kenneth D. Wald, and Clyde Wilcox (eds.), *The Politics of Gay Rights*. Chicago: University of Chicago Press.

Lewis, Gregory B., and Marc A. Rogers. 1999. "Does the Public Support Equal Employment Rights for Gays and Lesbians?" In Ellen D. B. Riggle and Barry L. Tadlock (eds.), *Gays and Lesbians in the Democratic Process: Public Policy, Public Opinion, and Political Representation*. New York: Columbia University Press.

Lim, Youngsik. 2000. "An Empirical Analysis of Supreme Court Justices' Decision Making." *Journal of Legal Studies* 29: 721.

Lincoln Utilities, Inc., v. Office of Utility Consumer Counselor. 1996. 661 N.E.2d 562.

Lindquist, Stefanie A., and Kevin Pybas. 1998. "State Supreme Court Decisions to Overrule Precedent, 1965–1996." *Justice System Journal* 20: 17.

Maltz, Earl. 1980. "Some Thoughts on the Death of *Stare Decisis* in Constitutional Law." *Wisconsin Law Review* 1980: 467.

1988. "The Nature of Precedent." *North Carolina Law Review* 66: 367.

Maltzman, Forrest, James F. Spriggs II, and Paul J. Wahlbeck. 2000. *Crafting Law on the Supreme Court: The Collegial Game*. New York: Cambridge University Press.

Mancino v. State. 1997. 689 So.2d 1235.

Marcus, Eric. 1993. *Making History: The Struggle for Gay and Lesbian Equal Rights, 1945–1990*. New York: HarperCollins.

Markey, Karen. 1998. "An Overview of the Legal Challenges Faced by Gay and Lesbian Parents: How Courts Treat the Growing Number of Gay Families." *New York Law School Journal of Human Rights* 14: 721.

Marotta, Toby. 1981. *The Politics of Homosexuality*. Boston: Houghton Mifflin.

Marquis, Christopher. 2001. "Military's Ouster of Gays Rose 17 Percent Last Year." *New York Times*, June 2, p. A9.

2002. "Military Discharges of Gays Rise, and So Do Bias Incidents." *New York Times*, March 14, p. A22.

Martin, Elaine. 1993. "View from the State Bench: Gender Roles." In Lois Lovelace Duke (ed.), *Women in Politics: Insiders or Outsiders*. Englewood Cliffs, N.J.: Prentice Hall.

Marvell, Thomas. 1984. "The Rationales for Federal Question Jurisdiction: An Empirical Examination of Student Rights Litigation." *Wisconsin Law Review* 1984: 1315.

McDonnell, Thomas Michael. 1998. "Playing Beyond the Rules: A Realist and Rhetoric-Based Approach to Researching the Law and Solving Legal Problems." *University of Missouri at Kansas City Law Review* 67: 285.

McNeal v. Cofield. 1992. 78 Ohio App.3d 35, 603 N.E.2d 436.

Merrill, Thomas W. 1992. "Judicial Deference to Executive Precedent." *Yale Law Journal* 101: 969.

Merryman, John Henry. 1954. "The Authority of Authority: What the California Supreme Court Cited in 1950." *Stanford Law Review* 6: 613.

1977. "Toward a Theory of Citations: An Empirical Study of the Citation Practice of the California Supreme Court in 1950, 1960, and 1970." *Southern California Law Review* 50: 381.

Michael H. v. Gerald D. 1989. 491 U.S. 110, 109 S.Ct. 2333.

Miranda v. Arizona. 1966. 384 U.S. 436, 86 S.Ct. 1602.

Mnookin, Robert H., and Lewis Kornhauser. 1979. "Bargaining in the Shadow of the Law: The Case of Divorce." *Yale Law Journal* 88: 950.

Morrison v. State Board of Education. 1969. 1 Cal.3d 214, 461 P.2d 375, 82 Cal.Rptr. 175.

Mountain View Coach Lines, Inc. v. Storms. 1984. 102 A.D.2d 663, 476 N.Y.S.2d 918.

Murdoch, Joyce, and Deb Price. 2001. *Courting Justice: Gay Men and Lesbians v. the Supreme Court*. New York: Basic Books.

Nadler v. Superior Court. 1967. 255 Cal.App.2d 523, 63 Cal.Rptr. 352.

Nagel, Stuart S. 1974. "Multiple Correlation of Judicial Backgrounds and Decisions." *Florida State University Law Review* 2: 258.

Nard, Craig Allen. 1995. "Empirical Legal Scholarship: Reestablishing a Dialogue Between the Academy and Profession." *Wake Forest Law Review* 30: 347.

Neuborne, Burt. 1977. "The Myth of Parity." *Harvard Law Review* 90: 1105.

New Orleans Rosenbush Claims Service, Inc., v. City of New Orleans. 1994. 641 So.2d 545.

New York County Board of Ancient Hibernians v. Dinkins. 1993. 814 F.Supp. 358.

New York Times v. Sullivan. 1964. 376 U.S. 254, 84 S.Ct. 710.

Niebuhr, Gustav. 1999. "Vatican Tells Priest and Nun to End Their Gay Ministry." *New York Times*, July 14, p. A14.

Norton v. Macy. 1969. 417 F.2d 1161.

Ocasio v. McGlothin. 1998. 719 So.2d 918.

One Eleven Wines & Liquors, Inc., v. Division of Alcoholic Beverage Control. 1967. 50 N.J. 329, 235 A.2d 12.

Pacelle, Richard. 1996. "Seeking Another Forum: The Courts and Lesbian and Gay Rights." In Craig A. Rimmerman (ed.), *Gay Rights, Military Wrongs*. New York: Garland.

Pacelle, Richard L., Jr., and Lawrence Baum. 1992. "Supreme Court Authority in the Judiciary: A Study of Remands." *American Politics Quarterly* 20: 169.

Palmer v. Blue Water Marine Catering, Inc. 1995. 663 So.2d 780.

Payne v. Tennessee. 1991. 501 U.S. 808.

People v. Brisotti. 1996. 169 Misc.2d 672, 652 N.Y.S.2d 206.

Peterson, David W., and John M. Conley. 2001. "Of Cherries, Fudge, and Onions: Science and Its Courtroom Perversion." *Law and Contemporary Problems* 64: 213.

Pharr, Suzanne. 1988. *Homophobia: A Weapon of Sexism.* Inverness, Calif.: Chardon Press.

Pinello, Daniel R. 1995. *The Impact of Judicial-Selection Method on State-Supreme-Court Policy: Innovation, Reaction, and Atrophy.* Westport, Conn.: Greenwood Press.

———. 1996. "Review of G. Alan Tarr (ed.), *Constitutional Politics in the States: Contemporary Controversies and Historical Patterns.*" *Law and Politics Book Review* 6: 135.

———. 1999. "Linking Party to Judicial Ideology in American Courts: A Meta-Analysis." *Justice System Journal* 20: 219.

Posner, Richard A. 1992. *Sex and Reason.* Cambridge, Mass.: Harvard University Press.

Pritchett, C. Hermann. 1948. *The Roosevelt Court: A Study in Judicial Politics and Values, 1937–1947.* New York: Macmillan.

Quinn, John R. 1996. " 'Attitudinal' Decision Making in the Federal Courts: A Study of Constitutional Self-Representation Claims." *San Diego Law Review* 33: 701.

Rand National Defense Research Institute. 1993. *Sexual Orientation and U.S. Military Personnel Policy: Options and Assessment.* Santa Monica, Calif.: Rand.

Reed, Douglas S. 1999. "Popular Constitutionalism: Toward a Theory of State Constitutional Meanings." *Rutgers Law Journal* 30: 871.

Revesz, Richard L. 1997. "Environmental Regulation, Ideology, and the D.C. Circuit." *Virginia Law Review* 83: 1717.

———. 2002. "A Defense of Empirical Legal Scholarship." *University of Chicago Law Review* 69: 169.

Richards, David A. J. 1999. *Identity and the Case for Gay Rights: Race, Gender, Religion as Analogies.* Chicago: University of Chicago Press.

Richards, Mark J., and Herbert M. Kritzer. 2002. "Jurisprudential Regimes in Supreme Court Decision Making." *American Political Science Review* 96: 305.

Riggle, Ellen D. B., and Barry L. Tadlock. 1999a. "Gays and Lesbians in the Democratic Process: Past, Present, and Future." In Ellen D. B. Riggle and Barry L. Tadlock (eds.), *Gays and Lesbians in the Democratic Process: Public Policy, Public Opinion, and Political Representation.* New York: Columbia University Press.

Riggle, Ellen D. B., and Barry L. Tadlock (eds.). 1999b. *Gays and Lesbians in the Democratic Process: Public Policy, Public Opinion, and Political Representation.* New York: Columbia University Press.

Rimmerman, Craig A. 2002. *From Identity to Politics: The Lesbian and Gay Movements in the United States.* Philadelphia: Temple University Press.

Rimmerman, Craig A., Kenneth D. Wald, and Clyde Wilcox (eds.). 2000. *The Politics of Gay Rights*. Chicago: University of Chicago Press.

Rivera, Rhonda R. 1979. "Our Straight-Laced Judges: The Legal Position of Homosexual Persons in the United States." *Hastings Law Journal* 30: 799.

——— 1999. "Our Straight-Laced Judges: Twenty Years Later." *Hastings Law Journal* 50: 1179.

Rivers, Douglas. 1998. "Review of Gary King, *A Solution to the Ecological Inference Problem: Reconstructing Individual Behavior from Aggregate Data*." *American Political Science Review* 92: 442.

Robinson, William S. 1950. "Ecological Correlations and the Behavior of Individuals." *American Sociological Review* 15: 351.

Rosenberg, Gerald N. 1994. "Remarks." *Law and Courts* 4: 6.

——— 2000. "Across the Great Divide (Between Law and Political Science)." *Green Bag* 2nd series, 3: 267.

Rubenstein, William B. 1997. *Cases and Materials on Sexual Orientation and the Law*, 2nd ed. St. Paul, Minn.: West.

——— 1999. "The Myth of Superiority." *Constitutional Commentary* 16: 599.

Salokar, Rebecca Mae. 2001. "Beyond Gay Rights Litigation: Using a Systemic Strategy to Effect Political Change in the United States." In Mark Blasius (ed.), *Sexual Identities, Queer Politics*. Princeton, N.J.: Princeton University Press.

Schacter, Jane S. 1997. "*Romer v. Evans* and Democracy's Domain." *Vanderbilt Law Review* 50: 361.

Schauer, Frederick. 1987. "Precedent." *Stanford Law Review* 39: 571.

Schlegel, John Henry. 1995. *American Legal Realism and Empirical Social Science*. Chapel Hill: University of North Carolina Press.

Schlegel v. United States. 1969. 416 F.2d 1372 (Ct.Cl.).

Schmidhauser, John R. 1962. "*Stare Decisis*, Dissent, and the Background of the Justices of the Supreme Court of the United States." *University of Toronto Law Review* 14: 194.

Schroedel, Jean Reith. 1999. "Elite Attitudes Toward Homosexuals." In Ellen D. B. Riggle and Barry L. Tadlock (eds.), *Gays and Lesbians in the Democratic Process: Public Policy, Public Opinion, and Political Representation*. New York: Columbia University Press.

Schuck, Peter H. 1989. "Why Don't Law Professors Do More Empirical Research?" *Journal of Legal Education* 39: 323.

Schuck, Peter H., and E. Donald Elliott. 1991. "To the *Chevron* Station: An Empirical Study of Federal Administrative Law." *Duke Law Journal* 1990: 984.

Schultz, Vicki, and Stephen Petterson. 1992. "Race, Gender, Work, and Choice: An Empirical Study of the Lack of Interest Defense in Title VII Cases Challenging Job Segregation." *University of Chicago Law Review* 59: 1073.

Segal, Jeffrey A. 1984. "Predicting Supreme Court Cases Probabilistically: The Search and Seizure Cases, 1962–1981." *American Political Science Review* 78: 891.

——— 1986. "Supreme Court Justices as Human Decision Makers: An Individual-Level Analysis of the Search and Seizure Cases." *Journal of Politics* 48: 938.

——— 1999. "Supreme Court Deference to Congress: An Examination of the Marksist Model." In Cornell W. Clayton and Howard Gillman (eds.), *Supreme Court*

Decision-Making: New Institutionalist Approaches. Chicago: University of Chicago Press.

Segal, Jeffrey A., and Albert D. Cover. 1989. "Ideological Values and Votes of U.S. Supreme Court Justices." *American Political Science Review* 83: 557.

Segal, Jeffrey A., and Harold J. Spaeth. 1993. *The Supreme Court and the Attitudinal Model.* New York: Cambridge University Press.

    1994. "Preferences vs. Precedent: An Empirical Test of the Legal Model." Paper presented at the Annual Meeting of the American Political Science Association, New York, August 28–31.

    1996. "The Influence of *Stare Decisis* on the Votes of United States Supreme Court Justices." *American Journal of Political Science* 40: 971.

Sherrill, Kenneth. 1993. "On Gay People as a Politically Powerless Group." In Marc Wolinsky and Kenneth Sherrill (eds.), *Gays and the Military: Joseph Steffan versus the United States.* Princeton, N.J.: Princeton University Press.

    1996. "The Political Power of Lesbians, Gays, and Bisexuals." *PS: Political Science and Politics* 29: 469.

Sickels, Robert J. 1965. "The Illusion of Judicial Consensus: Zoning Decisions in the Maryland Court of Appeals." *American Political Science Review* 59: 100.

Sipple v. Chronicle Publishing Co. 1984. 154 Cal.App.3d 1040, 201 Cal.Rptr. 665.

Sisk, Gregory C., Michael Heise, and Andrew P. Morriss. 1998. "Charting the Influences on the Judicial Mind: An Empirical Study of Judicial Reasoning." *New York University Law Review* 73: 1377.

Smith, Rogers M. 1994. "Remarks." *Law and Courts* 4: 8.

Smith, Tom W. 1987. "Classifying Protestant Denominations." General Social Survey Methodological Report No. 43.

Snyder, James M., Jr., and Tim Groseclose. 2000. "Estimating Party Influence in Congressional Roll-Call Voting." *American Journal of Political Science* 44: 193.

Solinine, Michael E. 1991. "Rethinking Exclusive Federal Jurisdiction." *University of Pittsburgh Law Review* 52: 383.

Solimine, Michael E., and James L. Walker. 1983. "Constitutional Litigation in Federal and State Courts: An Empirical Analysis of Judicial Parity." *Hastings Constitutional Law Quarterly* 10: 213.

    1999. *Respecting State Courts: The Inevitability of Judicial Federalism.* Westport, Conn.: Greenwood Press.

Songer, Donald R. 1995. "Integrated Models of State Supreme Court Decision Making." Paper presented at the Annual Meeting of the American Political Science Association, Chicago, August 31–September 3.

Songer, Donald R., and Martha Humphries Ginn. 2002. "Assessing the Impact of Presidential and Home State Influences on Judicial Decisionmaking in the United States Courts of Appeals." *Political Research Quarterly* 55: 299.

Songer, Donald R., and Ashlyn Kuersten. 1995. "The Success of *Amici* in State Supreme Courts." *Political Research Quarterly* 48: 31.

Songer, Donald R., and Stefanie A. Lindquist. 1996. "Not the Whole Story: The Impact of Justices' Values on Supreme Court Decision Making." *American Journal of Political Science* 40: 1049.

Songer, Donald R., and Reginald S. Sheehan. 1990. "Supreme Court Impact on Compliance and Outcomes: *Miranda* and *New York Times* in the United States Courts of Appeals." *Western Political Quarterly* 43: 297.

Songer, Donald R., and Susan J. Tabrizi. 1999. "The Religious Right in Court: The Decision Making of Christian Evangelicals in State Supreme Courts." *Journal of Politics* 61: 507.

Songer, Donald R., Jeffrey A. Segal, and Charles M. Cameron. 1994. "The Hierarchy of Justice: Testing a Principal-Agent Model of Supreme Court–Circuit Court Interactions." *American Journal of Political Science* 38: 673.

Songer, Donald R., Reginald S. Sheehan, and Susan B. Haire. 2000. *Continuity and Change on the United States Courts of Appeals*. Ann Arbor: University of Michigan Press.

Spaeth, Harold J., and Jeffrey A. Segal. 1999. *Majority Rule or Minority Will: Adherence to Precedent on the U.S. Supreme Court*. New York: Cambridge University Press.

Spriggs, James F., II, and Thomas G. Hansford. 2001. "Explaining the Overruling of U.S. Supreme Court Precedent." *Journal of Politics* 63: 1091.

Starr, Karla J. 1998. "Adoption by Homosexuals: A Look at Differing State Court Opinions." *Arizona Law Review* 40: 1497.

State Farm Fire and Casualty Company v. Yapejian. 1992. 152 Ill.2d 533, 605 N.E.2d 539.

Stearns, Maxwell L. 1995. "Standing Back from the Forest: Justiciability and Social Choice." *California Law Review* 83: 1309.

Stevens, Robert. 1983. *Law School: Legal Education in America from the 1850s to the 1980s*. Chapel Hill: University of North Carolina Press.

Stone v. Powell. 1976. 428 U.S. 465.

Strasser, Mark. 1997. *Legally Wed: Same-Sex Marriage and the Constitution*. Ithaca, N.Y.: Cornell University Press.

Swanson, Rick A., and Albert P. Melone. 1995. "The Partisan Factor and Judicial Behavior in the Illinois Supreme Court." *Southern Illinois University Law Journal* 19: 303.

Tarr, G. Alan. 1994. "The Past and Future of the New Judicial Federalism." *Publius* 24: 63.

Tate, C. Neal. 1981. "Personal Attribute Models of the Voting Behavior of U.S. Supreme Court Justices' Liberalism in Civil Liberties and Economic Decisions, 1946–1978." *American Political Science Review* 75: 355.

Tauber, Steven C. 1998. "On Behalf of the Condemned? The Impact of the NAACP Legal Defense Fund on Capital Punishment Decision Making in the U.S. Courts of Appeals." *Political Research Quarterly* 51: 191.

Thomas, Kendall. 1992. "Beyond the Privacy Principle." *Columbia Law Review* 92: 1431.

Traut, Carol Ann, and Craig F. Emmert. 1998. "Expanding the Integrated Model of Judicial Decision Making: The California Justices and Capital Punishment." *Journal of Politics* 60: 1166.

Ulmer, S. Sidney. 1959. "An Empirical Analysis of Selected Aspects of Lawmaking of the United States Supreme Court." *Journal of Pubic Law* 8: 414.

1973. "Social Background as an Indicator to the Votes of Supreme Court Justices in Criminal Cases: 1947–1956." *American Journal of Political Science* 17: 622.

Unah, Isaac. 1997. "Specialized Courts of Appeals' Review of Bureaucratic Actions and the Politics of Protectionism." *Political Research Quarterly* 50: 851.

United States ex rel. Fong Foo v. Shaughnessy. 1955. 234 F.2d 715.

Vaid, Urvashi. 1995. *Virtual Equality: The Mainstreaming of Gay and Lesbian Liberation.* New York: Anchor.

Vines, Kenneth N. 1964. "Federal District Judges and Race Relations Cases in the South." *Journal of Politics* 26: 337.

Vitiello, Michael, and Andrew J. Glendon. 1998. "Article III Judges and the Initiative Process: Are Article III Judges Hopelessly Elitist?" *Loyola of Los Angeles Law Review* 31: 1275.

Wahlbeck, Paul J. 1998. "The Development of a Legal Rule: The Federal Common Law of Public Nuisance." *Law and Society Review* 32: 613.

Wald, Kenneth D. 2000. "The Context of Gay Politics." In Craig A. Rimmerman, Kenneth D. Wald, and Clyde Wilcox (eds.), *The Politics of Gay Rights.* Chicago: University of Chicago Press.

Wald, Kenneth D., James W. Button, and Barbara A. Rienzo. 1996. "The Politics of Gay Rights in American Communities: Explaining Antidiscrimination Ordinances and Policies." *American Journal of Political Science* 40: 1152.

Walker, Thomas G. 1972. "A Note Concerning Partisan Influences on Trial-Judge Decision Making." *Law and Society Review* 6: 645.

Weber, Mark C. 1994. "Complex Litigation and the State Courts: Constitutional and Practical Advantages of the State Forum over the Federal Forum in Mass Tort Cases." *Hastings Constitutional Law Quarterly* 21: 215.

Weinberg, Martin S., and Colin J. Williams. 1974. *Male Homosexuals.* New York: Oxford University Press.

Welch, Michael R., David C. Leege, Kenneth D. Wald, and Lyman A. Kellstedt. 1993. "Are the Sheep Hearing the Shepherds? Cue Perceptions, Congregational Responses, and Political Communication Processes." In David C. Leege and Lyman A. Kellstedt (eds.), *Rediscovering the Religious Factor in American Politics.* Armonk, N.Y.: M. E. Sharpe.

Wenzel, James P., Shaun Bowler, and David J. Lanoue. 1997. "Legislating from the State Bench: A Comparative Analysis of Judicial Activism." *American Politics Quarterly* 25: 363.

Wiehl, Lis. 2000. "Judges and Lawyers Are Not Singing from the Same Hymnal When It Comes to Allowing the Bible in the Courtroom." *American Journal of Trial Advocacy* 24: 273.

Wilcox, Clyde, and Robin Wolpert. 2000. "Gay Rights in the Public Sphere: Public Opinion on Gay and Lesbian Equality." In Craig A. Rimmerman, Kenneth D. Wald, and Clyde Wilcox (eds.), *The Politics of Gay Rights.* Chicago: University of Chicago Press.

Wold, John T. 1974. "Political Orientations, Social Backgrounds, and Role Perceptions of State Supreme Court Judges." *Western Political Quarterly* 27: 239.

Wolfe v. Dublin Unified School District. 1997. 56 Cal.App.4th 126, 65 Cal.Rptr.2d 280.

Wolinsky, Marc, and Kenneth Sherrill (eds.). 1993. *Gays and the Military: Joseph Steffan versus the United States*. Princeton, N.J.: Princeton University Press.

Woodward, Bob, and Scott Armstrong. 1979. *The Brethren: Inside the Supreme Court*. New York: Avon Books.

Yackle, Larry W. 1994. *Reclaiming the Federal Courts*. Cambridge, Mass: Harvard University Press.

Yang, Alan S. 1998. *From Wrongs to Rights: Public Opinion on Gay and Lesbian Americans Moves Toward Equality*. Washington, D.C.: National Gay and Lesbian Task Force.

Zanetti v. Lieberman. 1994. 1994 WL 668037.

Zuk, Gary, Deborah J. Barrow, and Gerard S. Gryski. 1997. "Multi-User Database on the Attributes of United States Appeals Courts Judges, 1801–1994." Study No. 6796, Inter-University Consortium for Political and Social Research (www.icpsr.umich.edu).

Author Index

Case Index

Subject Index

ABC, 152n6
abortion, 131, 146, 161
abuse of discretion, 21
adoption, 73, 76, 96, 145n1;
    see also child custody,
    visitation, adoption, and
    foster care
African Americans: attitudes of,
    toward gay people, 220; cognizance
    of rights of, 75; examples of,
    as judges, 28, 31, 42, 96; impact
    of, as judges, 1, 87, 98, 147–49;
    rights of, compared with those
    of gay people, 130; see also
    minority
age (independent variable), 91, 98,
    218
age, and its effect on attitudes toward
    gay people, 218; examples of, 28,
    40; impact of, on judges, 1, 147–49,
    151
AIDS, 9
Alabama, 12, 13n16, 22, 27, 32, 40,
    54, 69, 72, 98, 110n10, 144, 222,
    223; Court of Civil Appeals, 23–25,
    27, 29; Supreme Court, 25, 26,
    28–30, 33, 69, 98; term of office,
    29, 70
Amendment 2, 72–73, 145n1
American Bench, 155n9, 214

American Civil Liberties Union,
    115n15, 130n14, 150, 164n4,
    166n10, 225n36
American Political Science
    Association, 4n5, 214
American Psychiatric Association, 128
amicus curiae, examples of, 53; see also
    interest groups
appellate judges, compared with trial
    judges, 21–22
appointed (independent variable), 91,
    92, 98, 112–14, 222; see also judicial
    selection method
Arkansas, 12, 144
atheists, 127, 160; see also precedential
    atheists
attitudinal model, 5, 70, 75, 154–55;
    and child custody, visitation,
    adoption, and foster care, 17;
    defined, 4; examples of, 28, 31,
    37–38, 40, 42, 93, 96, 98, 99,
    102n33; findings on, 79–85;
    variables of, 217–22

Baptists, 89n21, 91
Bauer, Gary, 19, 20
best interests of the child, 17, 84, 130,
    144
bias, methodological, arising from
    incomplete data, 215, 253–54